# The Differing Uses of SYMBOLIC AND CLINICAL APPROACHES IN PRACTICE AND THEORY

Proceedings of
The Ninth International Congress
For Analytical Psychology,
Jerusalem, 1983

Luigi Zoja and Robert Hinshaw, Editors



DAIMON
VERLAG
ZÜRICH

*Symbolic and Clinical Approaches in Practice and Theory,* edited by Luigi Zoja and Robert Hinshaw.

Cover by Joel T. Miskin

ISBN 3-85630-504-1

# Contents

# Editors' Preface

The Ninth Congress of the International Association for Analytical Psychology was held at the Jerusalem Hilton Hotel from March 15–22, 1983. The theme, *The Differing Uses of Symbolic and Clinical Approaches in Practice and Theory*, drew twenty-five presentations in the forms of morning papers, workshops, and so-called 'nocturnes', attended by hundreds of Jungian analysts who had made their ways to Jerusalem from around the world.

One of C. G. Jung's most basic tenets was that a therapist must find his or her own individual way of working; each analyst is unique. The different approaches to the Congress theme varied as widely as the origins and personalities of the contributors, providing fertile ground for lively debate far into the Israeli night.

The careful reader of this volume will note inconsistencies not only in approach, but also with regard to spelling (British, U.S.), capitalization, italicization, footnoting and other aspects of style. It is our view that, within certain limits, it is preferable to leave the presentations as much as possible in the original form rather than to force them into one consistent style or another. Individual viewpoints are thus also reflected in the somewhat diverse modes of presentation here, which to us seems appropriate.

Sadly, one contributor, Mario Moreno, died shortly after the Congress. His paper (which had been presented by Luigi Zoja) could not be proofread and the sources of quotations were not available. Under the circumstances, we elected to print the paper as is, without references.

We would like to express our appreciation to those journals which made previously published papers available for this collection. On the opening page of each chapter, reference is made to any previous publication known to us.

The papers making up this volume reveal much self-questioning on the part of contemporary Jungian analysts. Just as the Jerusalem

Congress served to bring each participant to reflect on his or her own approach and biases and to be more aware of relating with the psyche in a particular way, so may it be hoped that this volume will stimulate its readers.

Milan and Willerzell,
December, 1985 Luigi Zoja and Robert Hinshaw

# Opening Address

Hans Dieckmann (Berlin)

C. G. Jung has taught us to live between the opposites. The initiation of an analytical psychologist consists of learning the path of the serpent, avoiding fixation in a scyllian or charybdian position. The conscious point of view and the relation to his own unconscious must be flexible enough to respond appropriately to the needs and the emerging material of the patient. This process takes place inside the so-called *vas hermeticum* created by the analytical structure and by the transference/counter-transference relationship.

My first question is: Symbolic approach on the one hand, clinical approach on the other hand – are they opposites at all?

My second question is: If they are opposites – are these opposites so strong and contrary that they have the tendency to split the Jungian community, which has so far lived in a well-established state of the psychological *materia prima?* Could this even lead to a division some day into symbolists and clinicians?

Im reading most of the papers prepared for this congress, I had the impression that these two approaches are not disturbing the theory of Analytical Psychology. Symbolic, or, as Henderson says, cultural-anthropological approaches, are overlapping with clinical ones. The clinical method of dealing directly with the patient's personal problems goes hand in hand with the search for a symbol. According to alchemical wisdom, this makes the *transitus* easier. Some papers put the emphasis more on symbolism, others more on clinical aspects. But, on the whole, I have a feeling of peace and harmony between the two. It seems to me that Jungian analysts have solved the problem of combining the opposites and have reached the third stage in alchemy by being hermaphroditic analysts.

Is this the whole reality and the truth? I doubt it. If you walk through the Jungian groups in different countries, keeping your ears open, you will hear various remarks. You will hear, for example, that the so-called 'symbolist' is unable to cure really ill patients who want to be cured from their personal suffering and who do not want to undergo a highly symbolic process of individuation. On the other hand, you will hear the symbolists saying that some colleagues are no longer real Jungian analysts, but actually neo-Freudians. The word 'neo-Freudian' has acquired a touch of abusiveness. The analysis of the personal unconscious, including the suffering of every day, is, in the eyes of some symbolists, a minor matter for a minor spirit which is not able to grasp and to understand the pearls of wisdom coming from archetypes and the collective unconscious.

We have chosen the theme of this congress together, and therefore let me state that there are opposites constellated inside and outside of ourselves with which we have to deal. The use of amplification with dreams or fantasy contents to draw up the archetypal structure of the collective unconscious, to find the point, the well, the flower from which all energy and rebirth comes, is different from another method with which we also have to deal: it is the direct dealing with the patients' problems, linking them to the infantile contents of childhood. As Jung said, the journey with father and mother up and down many ladders represents the making conscious of infantile contents that have not been integrated, and he added that he had never seen an analyst, including himself, who did integrate all of these contents. But Jung also said clearly that the point of view of his school is symbolic in contrast to the causal-reductive method of Freud. So I believe we have our problem and we have the split between opposite positions which we simply must accept.

The path between the opposites is hard, difficult, full of struggles, aggressions, fears and anxieties. We all have experienced some of this in our own histories. Leaving the personal problems aside, these opposites have been apparent in the sharp discussions between Zürich and London which have been published in the Journal of Analytical Psychology. We find it again in the split between AIPA and CIPA, between SAP and Alternative Training, as well as in various discussions between certain societies of Northern America, and between Berlin and Stuttgart. Because all contents of our consciousness are linked with the unconscious and the self, sometimes these differences gain religious dimensions. I remember the Zürich Congress where we tried without success to determine who should have the right of calling himself a Jungian analyst – a genuine one – and who should be expelled. I don't want to foster highly controversial positions. They always arise if there is no more dialogue, but rather a power struggle between human beings. Inferiority and superiority are constellated as well as dogmatism, obstinacy, justification, envy, fury, and even fanatacism. We are analysts, and we all should know our shadow personalities, with which we have to live. We all know that these shadows grow in groups. But being analysts, we all should also know that we have to live with our dark brother. We are not able to separate from him, either by discussion, or more consciousness, or splitting. The more conscious we become, the more the darkness in our unconscious grows. This is probably the reason for the many splits, difficulties, and differences that psychoanalysts have experienced in their history and for the many struggles which this particular group of highly individuated Jungians also must bear.

We are here in Jerusalem, the town which is in itself a symbol of wholeness. She is the town in which the three great religions have their holy sites. She is the town in which, more than in any other place, the people of the three religions live together. From the start of her history until to-day, she has never been a peaceful town. I will not repress in this connection that some of our colleagues have been apprehensive about coming to this troublesome place. But what counts for me in the final result is the fact that Jerusalem is also the town in which so many different opinions and religions have coexisted over the centuries. The men in the street of the three religions have worked and lived and loved together, not without tears and suffering, but with an unbroken determination not to leave this place.

Jung did not create a theoretical system of Analytical Psychology and I have always found that extremely wise. He had the opinion that this would be premature. It could and would obstruct or block further development. We know too little about psyche and soul, he said to friends, to implement such a fixed theory. That could destroy the life and liveliness of soul and symbolic development out of the collective unconscious. I have seen a variety of different opinions, thoughts, creative fantasies, and theoretical concepts in our Jungian community, ever since I have become part of it. If we take individuation really seriously, we should not let ourselves be led astray, even if we run into difficulties.

I may add one more personal impression. Coming from internal medicine, I had at first a strong clinical inclination. The more I worked as an analyst, the more I experienced the symbolic approach. Nevertheless, I have never been able to throw one aspect overboard and I will always struggle to combine the two. Sometimes I have felt successful in this combination and sometimes I have hopelessly failed. I do not think that I have solved the problem of becoming what I wanted to be: a symbolic clinician or a clinical symbolist. The wholeness, symbolized by New Jerusalem, is still in heaven in the hand of God. All we can do is to listen to the voice of the others, their opinions, their thoughts, their emotions. We can speak together and can learn from each other. This will probably be more valuable than striving for a harmony we cannot achieve.

In this spirit, I wish the congress a very good start.

# The Father's Anima as a Clinical and as a Symbolic Problem*

John Beebe (San Francisco)

I want to begin with four clinical examples of the psychodynamic problem I have in mind. Like all clinical examples, they are part fiction, part fact.

My first example is of a young man in his late twenties, to whom it wouldn't have occurred to go into analysis. He was a surpassingly beautiful servant in the house of a bisexual Captain of the Egyptian Guard. This master had acquired this Jewish youth initially "for a lewd purpose", but discovering that his comely servant was serious about his Judaism he managed to sublimate his attraction to the young man. He treated him as a son and gave him a favored position in his home. The Captain's wife could not so easily contain her physical longing for the young man. She persistently entreated the servant for sex, which he always refused her, explaining that he could not betray a master who had treated him kindly. Exasperated, the woman finally played a trick: she seized the unsuspecting servant by his shirt as if to draw him near. When, as she expected, he tore himself forcibily from her grasp, she had a bit of his clothing in hand with which to prove to her husband that the young man had made a pass at her. A tribunal was called, and though no one really believed the Captain's wife, the young man was sent to prison on the grounds that he had called his mistress' honor into question.

For the Biblical Joseph, who was the unfortunate servant, this imprisonment turned out to be decisive. His skill at interpreting other prisoners' dreams became known to the Pharoah, who had a 'big' dream

* Reprinted by permission of *The Journal of Analytical Psychology*, where it appeared in revised form in Vol. 29, No. 3 (July 1984).

that none of his usual consultants could interpret. Joseph's refusal of Potiphar's wife led to his rise under a far more powerful master, the Pharoah.

My second example, from the analysis of a contemporary man, is an amplification of the Joseph story. This man, also in his late twenties, found himself making rapid advances in his chosen career. He felt supported in his advancement over his fellows at work by the seemingly endless encouragement of his fatherly Jungian analyst. This analyst managed to provide a wonderfully non-intrusive holding environment that contained the patient utterly in a sense that his every step toward self-advancement would meet with the unconditional positive regard of the analyst. Under the spell of this 'anima fathering', the patient had come to regard his entire life as one of continuous advancement. And then he had the following dream:

> I was in a classroom with other students, possibly a nursery school. I was absorbed in the positive maternal atmosphere of the teacher, humming at her desk. I felt at one with the other students, who were all working quietly at their different desks. I didn't actually see anyone in the room, nor did I need to, so contained was I within the pleasant classroom atmosphere. Suddenly an angry male figure, 'The Father', entered the room, harshly interrupting the comfortable atmosphere with angry words toward the motherly teacher.
>
> "How could you let this happen?" the father demanded. "Look at him!" I was suddenly acutely conscious of myself and my surroundings. Now I could see that all the other students were wearing red tunics and I a coat of many colors.

This dream registers the impact of the analyst's stance upon the patient. For the analyst's anima was in fact the motherly teacher, so skilled at creating a containing environment that she was not allowing the patient to become conscious. And the terrible father was the split-off envious and hostile side of the analyst's attitude toward his patient.

This dream was the analysand's first intimation that in and outside the analytic situation, his obvious capacities might arouse envy and competitive feelings from others, and another anima response than unconditional positive regard from his analyst. Yet this experience of his analyst's unconscious hostility toward him helped to make him aware of the creativity of his own, rather extraverted anima. This anima developed into a very useful political sense that enabled him to survive many difficult situations en route to the realization of his scholarly gifts.

My third example is also drawn from the analytic situation. This analysand was a man is his middle thirties who found himself in the throes of an acute marital crisis. This man became gripped by a passion for someone younger and more physically alluring than his faithful and familiar spouse. Discussions with neither the spouse nor the analyst seemed to transform this all-consuming passion. In the midst of deciding what to do, the man dreamed:

> I'm in the kitchen. I turn on the water, which is badly hooked up to the plumbing in the bathroom in the next room. Water comes out of every pipe in the kitchen. It's good clean water, almost like crystal clear spring water, but the plumbing is in awful shape. My father is there. I say, "Dad, what do I do about this?" He's absent-minded, absorbed in his thoughts. He doesn't acknowledge that I've said anything.

Shortly after, the man terminated both his marriage and his analysis in order to pursue his passion. Despite the aggressive explosiveness of his decision, the patient was able to find his way back into his marriage for another try and into a more focused relationship to his unconscious life than had previously been possible for him. He was ready to fix his own plumbing.

My fourth (and final) example involves a similar decision to live out, rather than refuse, the call to eros, and it provides amplification for the third case. This example is taken from the documented life history of the head of a religious state who prayed to God his father to test him in his faith. This wartime political leader's wish was not long in being granted. Shortly after his prayer, the head of state caught sight of the beautiful wife of one of his most loyal military officers. Unable to contain his passion, the leader summoned the wife and slept with her. She conceived that night, and when her pregnancy became known to him, the head of state decided that he would get rid of the husband by sending him to the front lines. The loyal officer was killed in action, and Bathsheba married King David of Israel.

God was not slow in expressing his displeasure. For the way in which he took the wife of Uriah the Hittite, David was to suffer greatly. The child conceived of their tryst died in infancy, and continuous warfare was to plague David's forty-year reign. He was not allowed to build the Temple, and for a six-month period suffered from leprosy. And he had to endure a long, troublesome rebellion at the hands of his favorite son, Absalom.

But despite all this, David never regretted his choice of Bathsheba, and apparently neither did God, once the shabby beginning of their intimacy had been punished. David atoned for the enormity of his sin and continued his life with her. Bathsheba became pregnant again, and this time her son was Solomon, a personification of the wisdom David had gleaned from his experience.

David was visited at his bedside by Bathsheba a final time when he was dying, and he followed her good advice to make Solomon the next King of Israel.

Solomon turned out to be an excellent King, and was allowed by God to build the Temple.

These are my four examples. It is obvious, I think, that in each, a man has an anima experience which requires a choice.

In the first two examples, the men decide to resist the seductions of the anima figure so as to realize the anima potentiality in themselves. The men in the second two examples decide to go with the pull of the anima into a deepened consciousness of eros, even at the cost of betraying loyal partners and traditional values.

What I want you most to see, however, is that in each case, the anima problem that is being presented to the man is not purely his own but rather one presented to him by a father figure. These father figures are: Potiphar, the all-accepting analyst, the affect-isolating personal father, and God. And Potiphar's wife, the warmly maternal nursery school teacher, the outpouring of the pure water of life from the poor plumbing, and Bathsheba in all her glory represent anima problems these father-figures have left to the sons to solve.

In each of my examples, the task of the son-figure is to relate to his 'father's' anima problem in such a way that its energy becomes his own.

Making the father's anima problem into an inner experience of his own usually requires from the son a refusal to go the way that the father's anima would apparently desire. Joseph realizes his own anima potential by not sleeping with Potiphar's wife. The first analysand stops allowing his analyst to carry the anima function for him and becomes conscious of his own capablities. The married second analysand chooses to live out the libidinal problem his father would rather ignore. And David goes against God's will in making someone God has presented merely as temptation into a legitimate wife who will mother his future heir.

These four situations are examples of a transfer of energy I regard as decisive for the individuation of a man, the way in which the anima becomes his own, free of his father's influence.[1]

I find it helpful to think of the anima as the emotional attitude a man takes toward anything he reflects upon. Perhaps his most consistent anima is the one toward the role he is playing in life; this is certainly the anima that affects his fate. It is his working spontaneous sense of his life, the way he approaches his life and the way he reflects upon it. But when I speak of the father's anima, I am referring to the father's working sense of his son's life, the emotional attitude that the father takes toward his son. This emotional attitude is communicated to the son as his father's felt sense of the younger man's worth.

The father's emotional attitude toward his son is normally ambivalent, and there is usually splitting in any father's experience of that ambivalence.

One father feels primarily loving and protecting, while another is painfully aware of an attitude of rejecting resentment toward his son. Often, the surfacing of another pole in addition to what seems to be the dominant attitude comes as a shock to both father and son. Yet, as I have tried to show in my examples, it is the unsuspected side of the father's anima that provides the greatest opportunities for the son's own anima development.

The stories of Joseph and David define two extremes, two opposite patterns of a father's anima's effects on the later individuation of his son. In the Joseph story, or pattern, the father's anima is in her most approving aspect as idealizing love, directly projected onto the son. In the David story, or pattern, the father's anima is withheld from the son in an attitude of devaluing distancing and paranoid envy. Under conditions of love, Joseph becomes ingratiating; under conditions of abandonment, David becomes resourceful. Yet in later development, Joseph has to learn to protect himself from the tricksterish, envious hostility that is concealed within his father's apparently endless love for him. And David is driven to forcibly seize hold of the affective response that has been withheld, rather than simply endure his emotional isolation with compensatory efforts at poetic and heroic self-validations. Both men have to deal with the parts of the anima their fathers have not revealed to them, and these split-off parts emerge synchronistically in the sons' encounters with actual women. Joseph is forced to

[1] There is of course a parallel process by which a woman frees her feminine energy from her father's sphere of influence. Linda Leonard has published a superb book on this subject with the title, *The Wounded Woman: Healing the Father-Daughter Relationship.* (Ohio: Swallow Press, 1982)

experience the withheld trickster pole of his father's anima through Potiphar's wife. He must learn to withdraw from this kind of woman and survive her treachery if his development is to proceed. David's need for the withheld loving pole of his father's anima drives him to a series of passionate encounters with women – Bathsheba was his 100th wife – until his own identification with the heroic trickster gives way.

If we look more deeply into the stories of Joseph and of David, as found not only in the Bible but in the legends surrounding these collected by Louis Ginzberg, the process of anima differentiation within each pattern becomes more clear. What you should be listening for as I retell these stories is how the father's anima is gradually transferred to the son.

Let me start again with Joseph. Joseph's father was Jacob, a grandson of Abraham, and though Jacob had four wives, Rachel was by far his favorite. But Rachel watched the other wives bear Jacob ten sons. At last God let her bear Joseph. When a second son, Benjamin, was born to her, Rachel died in childbirth. Ginzberg tells us that

> Joseph's beauty of person was equal to that of his mother Rachel, and Jacob had but to look at him to be consoled for the death of his beloved wife. Reason enough for distinguishing him among his children. As a token of his great love for him, Jacob gave Joseph a coat of many colors, so light and delicate that it could be crushed and concealed in the closed palm of one hand.[2]

Thomas Mann, in his own retelling of the story, makes the coat of many colors into Rachel's wedding garment. We can see that the anima role in his father's life had been placed onto Joseph, and the young Joseph behaved accordingly. He "painted his eyes, dressed his hair carefully, and walked with a mincing step". And young Joseph also felt called upon to carry his father's relation to the unconscious. He bore tales about his brothers home to Jacob and reported mediumistic dreams which had portent for the future of their tribe. In effect, he began to pre-empt the function of Jacob's anima in looking out for the family unconscious.

[2] Biblical quotes are taken from the King James Version of the Bible. Quotes from Louis Ginzberg's compilation of legends are taken from the one-volume abridgement of his scholarly classic, *The Legends of the Jews* (which is in several volumes.) The one-volume work is entitled *The Legends of the Bible.* (Philadelphia: The Jewish Publication Society of America, 1975)

In telling one such dream, Joseph said,

> "Behold, I have dreamed a dream more; and behold, the sun and the moon and the eleven stars made obeisance to me."
> And he told it to his father, and to his brethren: and his father rebuked him, and said unto him, "What is this dream that thou hast dreamed? Shall I and thy mother and thy brethren indeed come to bow down ourselves to thee and to the earth?"
> And his brethren envied him; but his father observed the saying.

I want you to notice the splitting in the father's response as reported here. On the one hand, Jacob is leading the brothers on in their envy of Joseph. On the other hand, he "observes the saying", that is, profits from the mediumistic anima function that his son is performing for him. Joseph is trapped by Jacob's idealizing transference to him into a grandiose exhibitionism which arouses Jacob's envy, which Jacob then transfers onto the brothers so that his conscious idealization of Joseph can be maintained.

Yet the envy they carry for Jacob, the shadow side of Jacob's idealization, is actually the force that serves to free Joseph from this dangerously inflating situation and sets him on the road of his own individuation. Jacob sets Joseph up by sending him out to inquire after his brothers; they strip off the coat of many colors and throw Joseph into a pit while they decide whether to kill him or sell him into slavery.

In the father's tricksterish deviousness in sending Joseph to his collapse, we can see that Jacob really wanted to reclaim the anima with which he had invested his son. The coat of many colors is brought back to him stained with the blood of a slaughtered animal, and he is told that Joseph has been torn to pieces by a wild beast, though in fact Joseph has been sold into slavery. Jacob's trick enables him, with the aid of his other sons' treachery, to win back his authority over the unconscious destiny of the tribe.

In Egypt, the two sides of the father's anima are expressed by a single figure, Potiphar's wife, whose behavior fits the pattern of 'seduce, then destroy'. After initial idealization, she too divests Joseph of some of a fine garment Potiphar had given him, and she deprives Joseph of influence and authority by having him sent to prison.

Prison is a chance for Joseph to reflect, as was the pit, and through these depressing experiences one feels him beginning to grasp that there is a side of any father figure which is bound to resent the anima investment he has made in a son. Indeed, unless a young man realizes this, he is in for some rude shocks, particularly in the area of his career.

When a once-encouraging father-figure snatches back his anima, it can feel like a major betrayal.

But with Joseph, each divestiture of the father's anima leads not to irreparable narcissistic injury but rather to the further development of what Donald Kalsched has called 'interiority'. When finally Joseph emerges from prison to take his destined role beside the Pharoah as the steward who will see Egypt and the world through the famine, he is a very different person from the youth who naively paraded his dreams before his father and his brothers.

Having demonstrated that Pharoah's disturbing dream predicts a famine, Joseph advises Pharoah to "look out a man discreet and wise, and set him over the land of Egypt" to oversee the storing up of food against the lean years.

Pharoah said unto his servants, "Can we find such a one as this is, a man in whom the Spirit of God is?" and then to Joseph,

"Forasmuch as God hath shewed thee all this, there is none so discreet and wise as thou art."

And he then makes Joseph second in command, giving him his ring, a gold chain and "vestures of fine linen", and makes him to ride in the second chariot which he had.

As Pharoah puts it to Joseph, "only in the throne will I be greater than thou."

This investiture is a very different process than the one which prevailed in Jacob's house! Here the Pharoah manages his ambivalence about sharing power by retaining his own anima connection to his Royal Self as supreme authority.

Joseph, for his part, never tries to pre-empt that authority, even when called to the intimate task of interpreting the Pharoah's dreams.

It is at this point that Joseph is allowed to marry. The Bible tells us that his bride is a daughter of Potiphera, who is described as a priest. This name is virtually the same as Potiphar, but the change in vocation from military captain to religious priest suggests that the attitude of the father figure has changed toward Joseph from one of defense to one of religious sacrifice in response to Joseph's maturing consciousness. The father figure at this stage is no longer a tribal patriarch using the pattern of seduction and destruction in order to maintain his power; he is an initiatory father who yields the anima to the son as his sacred duty to help the son become a father figure in his own right.

The rest of Joseph's story reveals that he can now deal with the tricksterish side of his original father's anima. When his brothers come to

Egypt during the famine to buy grain, he plays meaningful tricks upon them, demonstrating not only that he can handle them, but also that he is willing to share the guilt of betrayal with them. He really sets them free from having to carry the envious side of Jacob's anima, and makes them glad to yield to him his rightfully superior position over them.

Once Joseph has learned to deal with both the idealizing and the tricksterish pole of his father's anima, Jacob is satisfied and ready to die. Joseph has his own anima, his own interior relation to ideals and to tricks, and his father complex is at an end. He has gracefully solved the problem of achieving anima fertility without acquiring it at his father's expense.

Now when we turn to the David story, we find ourselves in a very different pattern, where anima fertility (represented now by the continuation of the kingship) can *only* be achieved at the father's expense. In this pattern, the son does not suffer from the trickster but is himself the trickster, and ruthlessness, not grace, is what the son must display to survive. David is the type of son who starts his journey through life feeling that his father is somehow ashamed of him. The trickster side of the father's anima has been projected onto him, and so he is always somewhat doubtful in his father's eyes, however remarkable his attributes and achievements.

Of David's father, Ginzberg tells us:

> In spite of his piety, Jesse was not always proof against temptation. One of his slaves caught his fancy, and he would have entered into illicit relations with her had his wife, Nazbat, ... not frustrated the plan. She disguised herself as the slave, and Jesse, deceived by the ruse, met his own wife. The child borne by Nazbat was given out as the son of the freed slave, so that the father might not discover the deception practiced upon him. The child was David.

In our words, the father's anima has projected her trickster pole onto David. David grew up a living reminder of Jesse's "regrettable lapse of piety", tragically cut off from the idealizing side of Jesse's anima. Therefore his early life is a continuous effort to prove his worth to himself and to father figures, and the tragedies of his mature years can be understood as his ultimate attempts to connect with the love and forgiveness that his father had withheld.

It is clear that the discovery of David's true stature comes as a shock to Jesse. This discovery is made by Samuel the anointer, who is told by God, displeased with the rule of Saul, Israel's first King, that a new King is needed, and that this King will be the son of Jesse. Jesse presents seven sons to Samuel, but the oil will not flow from Samuel's horn onto any of their heads. Finally Jesse brings forth David from the fields, the oil flows, and David's mother Nazbat reveals the deception she had practiced. Only then does Jesse recognize David as his legitimate son.

Almost immediately thereafter, David is summoned to Saul's court, to comfort Saul with the musical ability David learned in his lonely years as a shepherd on his father's estate. Once again, David is in a compromised position, a trickster who knows, as he plays to soothe the paranoid Saul, that he will one day be the usurper of Saul's throne. Nevertheless, though his efforts to win over Saul's moody anima are only temporarily successful, David is able during these years to win a bit of the love from the father that he needs. He gets even more from Saul's son, Jonathan. For, just as Joseph's brothers carried the envious side of Jacob's idealizing transference to Joseph, so Jonathan carries the homoereotic loving side of Saul's paranoid transference to David. Upon Jonathan's death, David notes,

> very pleasant hast thou been unto me: thy love to me was wonderful, passing the love of women.

But where Joseph took favoritism for granted, David is much more cautious upon finding appreciation at Saul's court. He asks, for instance, to be Saul's armor-bearer, but he avoids wearing Saul's armor when he goes to slay Goliath – the counterposition to Joseph's naive acceptance of the coat of many colors.

Even so, the slaying of Goliath – David's attempt to win Saul's approval with a grand, heroic gesture – backfires. Saul's ambivalence toward David is resolved in favor of envy, and David is eventually driven from Saul's court to live as a renegade, who hides in caves and gradually gathers supporters for his own cause. Pathetically, he continues to try to prove his loyalty to Saul whenever the two come in contact, and there is one episode when David cuts off just a snippet of Saul's royal garment with his knife when Saul walks into a cave where David is hiding in darkness. This motif is the reverse of the trick Potiphar's wife played in taking a piece of Joseph's shirt, for David's trick is his way of showing his loyalty to the father figure and his right to his love, demonstrating that he means no bodily harm to Saul. But once again, Saul is only temporarily won over and soon reverts to his murderous pursuit of his hated rival.

During this period, David begs bread for his men from a wealthy landowner. Suspicious of this band of renegades, the landowner refuses, but his wife Abigail, meeting David on the road, decides that she wants to help him. When she tells her husband her positive opinion of David and her desire to feed him and his men, her husband has a heart attack and dies. Abigail becomes one of David's wives. Unlike Joseph, David must claim the anima literally over the dead bodies of father figures.

He cannot officially become King of Israel until Saul dies in battle, along with Jonathan. It is in the light of this pattern that we can better understand why the analysand who dreamed that his kitchen was overflowing with poorly-contained libido was forced to seek the solution to his problem outside of his marriage and his analysis. The failure of his analysis to contain him (in contrast to the Joseph-like analysand, who was too contained by his analysis) was directly related in his dream to the failure of his original father to lend support or even acknowledgment to his libidinal dilemmas. Where the original father's anima has been this withholding, it is not unusual for the analysand in crisis to find his male analyst's efforts to contain him within the analytic situation relatively unhelpful. Nor may the spouse's empathy be enough to contain him in his marriage when, as sooner or later they must, the possibilities of life that the father has withheld emerge. Often, the father's faulty container must be broken before genuine containment can occur.

I think this is the real reason David broke God's commandment in sending Uriah to his death: he had to have the connection to Bathsheba on his own terms. For with Bathsheba finally his own, love and not treachery gains the upper hand in David's character. When his son Absalom dies during his later political rebellion, David weeps so loudly and so long that he compromises his power over those who have fought so long and hard against Absalom on his behalf. (This is the counterpole to Joseph's weeping apart from his brothers in order to maintain his political authority over them in Egypt.)

Psalm 51 is said to have been written by David as a prayer for absolution for his guilt over Uriah. In the psalm, one senses that David has begun to reflect upon the pattern of his life. He refers specifically to the tricksterish circumstances of his birth as the genesis of his own longstanding tricksterism:

> Behold, I was shapen in iniquity; and in sin did my mother conceive me.

This self-reflection seems to be based in a genuine interest in the meaning of his own life. His next words to God are:

> Behold, thou desirest truth in the inward parts; and in the hidden part thou shalt make me to know wisdom.

We can therefore understand the sacrifice of the loyal Uriah as a symbolic solution to the problem presented to David by his father's anima. The sacrifice of Uriah represents the end of David's bondage to his original pattern. This pattern had locked him into the role of an eternal soldier of God, forever seeking new hero tests with which to prove himself worthy of God's admiration. His unforgivable sin freed David from such heroic overcompensation and allowed him to become initiated into the experience of God's mercy. In response to David's new attitude of humble supplication, God makes a reciprocal sacrifice of his wrath and allows David to keep Bathsheba.

The change in God which accompanies the change in David parallels the way Potiphar the captain gives way to Potiphera the priest within Joseph's story.

At this point in both stories, heroic devotion to a father who makes use of the anima for his own unfathomable purposes ends, and a truly religious cooperation between son and father begins.

The son experiences the anima for the first time as a more truly caring emotional attitude toward himself. At this stage, the two patterns are really one, the point of both being to effect the father's transfer of the anima to a son conscious enough to make wise use of her protection.

# Desymbolization and the Reorganization of the Symbol in the Psychotherapy of Schizophrenia*

Concetto Gullotta (Rome)

## Introduction

The main purpose of this paper is to put into focus one eminently practical aspect of psychotherapeutic experience with the schizophrenic.

I hope to emphasize how (without taking too much into consideration the various existing theories on this topic) attention must be concentrated essentially on the therapist and on what he is coming up against, in addition to the type of imagination he must have in order to accomplish his task in the best way possible.

I also hope to indicate how the adoption of a particular type of imagination and the therapist's effort, both psychological and ethical, to persevere in it can give unhoped-for and important therapeutic results. The expression of this is the gift which the patient presents to the therapist (as well as to himself) in the form of material of a highly symbolic content (dreams, deliria, drawings), material that aims with its creative eruption to reintegrate autonomously the components of a shattered ego with the help of the therepautic relationship.

The often insurmountable difficulty of translating imagination and experience into conceptual language has led me to use a title for this brief presentation which is certainly hermetic. First of all, then, I shall try to explain what I mean by desymbolization and the reorganization of the symbol.

* Reprinted by permission of the *Rivista di psicologia analitica,* where it appeared in Anno 14°, N. 27, 1983.

As we all know, the schizophrenic patient often shows himself to be too difficult for, or not quite suitable for psychological therapy, but despite these difficulties, over the past few decades various authors have taken up this subject, encouraged mainly by the studies begun by Jung. The studies to which I am here referring are diverse and belong to various schools. They all, however, have in common, besides classical and dynamic psycopathology and the various interpretations given it, a gap regarding the psychological experience which the therapist goes through during therapy with a schizophrenic patient.

I have said "goes through" but it would seem more correct to say "ought to go through" since, as we all know, it is not easy, not even possible to enter into a psychological relationship with a schizophrenic. By desymbolization, then, I mean the climax of a sequence of experiences gone through by the therapist in the first phase of the relationship with the schizophrenic patient.

I consider this phase to be indispensable as a preparatory moment for the relationship itself; I would even hold for the improbability of being able to establish a relationship with a schizophrenic patient if the therapist does not go through this type of experience.

The experience consists of a voluntary detachment from ego consciousness on the part of the therapist and of a silent and docile approach which is attentive at a deeper level where the symbolic forms present themselves in the patient in their strong and primitive compactness, expressing in deliria, drawings and dreams the dawnings of the development of consciousness.

It would be well to specify here that the word "symbol" as contained in the expression "desymbolization" has the general meaning which we find in philosophers, epistomologists and psychoanalysts such as Cassirer, Piaget and Arieti; it indicates the product of that universal function proper to the animal man that allows him to indicate the objects of the external and interior world by means of culturally defined substitutes. Language is the principal, but not the only example of this function. The function itself is that which is commonly called the symbolic function. We might define the schizophrenic as one who has lost the common symbolic function of man and is therefore no longer capable of establishing that interpersonal language which is based exclusively on such a symbolic function.

If we accept the hypothesis of Jung that the ego of the schizophrenic is temporarily, when it is not definitively, immersed in the collective unconscious, we could also say that in him a universe of symbols which we might call primordial or archetypal has taken the place of the normal and common symbolic function.

Returning briefly to our title, by "reorganization of the symbol", I mean a process activated in the psyche by means of the presence of the therapist. It is he who, from the intricate mass of archetypal symbolism, little by little leads the ego of the schizophrenic to the use of language as a means of interpersonal communication and, at the same time, to action as a means of affirming the personality in the surrounding world.

It should therefore be clear that in this presentation, the word symbol will be used in two senses, each of which, distinct from the other, can be traced back to two well-differentiated universes of man. On the one hand, the symbol *is* the normal and universal function of the ego. On the other hand, it *is* the archetypal image which leads back to a sphere of meanings which are completely different and specific.

As far as this presentation is concerned, the schizophrenic is assumed to be one who has lost the common and universal function of man and the therapist is assumed to be he who accepts the risk of going into that dark subterranean world of the archetypal symbol, the only one which is still available within the schizophrenic as a possibility of human understanding which does not isolate him completely.

One might ask at this point: who is the therapist of schizophrenia?

What requisites are necessary, even indispensable for the therapist who would venture into a therapy of this nature? What must his inner attitude be?

From what we have said so far, the therapist appears as the navigator of two seas: on the one hand, the sea of the ego with its secure harbour – this is a sea which is well-known. On the other hand, the open sea, the ocean of the collective unconscious with its unforeseeable aspects and with its sudden and terrible storms. The therapist is an adventurer by destiny. He leaves, we might say here metaphorically, his sea and his harbour to plough the waves of uncertain, hostile and dangerous waters, waters which can, however, lead him to the discovery of new or re-found continents. The adventure which he embarks upon by destiny might be explained in this way: he already knows this ocean; within the folds of his soul, sprites and elves, witches and monsters have already made themselves seen. He knows both the victories and the defeats of the eternal wars of the spirit. Only when he returns to that little Ithaca of consciousness is he recognized, and then only by this scar – this sign impressed on his flesh which shapes and models his personality.

But if these are the images with which the therapist of psychosis presents us, let us also try with our thoughts to understand his spiritual characteristics, the intimate world of his experiences. And therefore we come to yet another question: what constitutes a psychological experience of this type (that is, the setting with the psychotic patient) and what does psychological training, which allows for an approach to the psychotic, imply?

The answer will be valid not only for Jungian, but for every type of psychological therapy. One should also ask, then (but not here and now), what it is that, in this regard, differentiates Jungian psychology from other psychological theories.

Before going any further and giving an answer to the questions which we have thus far posed (who is the therapist of schizophrenia and what is he like?), it should be kept in mind that the psychological experience with the psychotic adds nothing sublime or ineffable to human experience as such, but it establishes the global horizon of this and indicates its foundation.

At this point, the experience with the psychotic suggests to me more than one answer. I should here like to formulate, on the basis of four fundamental components, what, in my opinion, summarizes them all:
– the experience of precariousness or of dependence;
– the experience of our destiny of death;
– the experience of transcendence;
– the experience of foundation.

Let us take them one by one.

*The experience of precariousness or of dependence:* this consists in the discovery of the fact that we become ourselves only in virtue of others, of the things and of the situations in the midst of which we find ourselves living. We 'become' by means of the relationships we establish. We are 'value', or better, we are projections of value. We have a 'name', but better we are a name in composition. And our becoming value and our acquiring an identity is entrusted to others. Our schizophrenic patient has not been able to have this experience because of the vicissitudes of his family history, or perhaps also because of fate. We therapists place ourselves before him with the intention of substituting and suturing this wound which is more than narcissistic. The expressions of descriptive psychology will never help us completely to understand the depth of this wound if at the same time tragic and saving suffering does not once again become acute in us.

This condition of precariousness and of dependence can be expressed in two ways: we are a gift, and we are creatures. When this experience is accepted and lived globally, it becomes an experience leading to psychological growth. Finally, it is an experience of a religious nature (in the non-confessional sense of that term).

*The experience of our destiny of death.* This experience accompanies us all through life. We are born to die, that is, to reach our completion. This means that: every situation is initiated in order to be terminated; every event of our lives brings with it the yearning for completion. And further still, every act of ours, every gift which we receive serves to lead us to the fullness of life, serves to help us die well.

The schizophrenic, with his incomplete life, with his being without meaning, with the death of the common symbolic function, induces in us an experience of death without meaning, of wasted life, of indescribable defeat.

Whereas man in general authenticates his existence only if every decision he makes and every relationship he experiences actually lead to the fulfillment of existence and therefore carry him on to death, the psychotherapist is called, through the psychotic, by a meaningless death, to give meaning to his action by the acceptance of his own death. This crucial dialectic is at the origin of profound depressions in the therapist, vital and existential depression, at times even psychotic, often sustained by the apparition of dream images activated by the process of "symmetrical identification" of which Benedetti speaks.

*The experience of transcendence:* This consists in sensing that the continual tension is growing stronger and stronger and at the same time in discovering that no situation and no person can completely satisfy this need. We are not sufficient unto ourselves nor is any other thing sufficient for us. The recurrent temptation is to imagine a situation or person who in the future might satisfy completely this need we have of goodness, being, happiness and life. But if a situation of this type never really exists, then our imagining it and running after it only leads to an illusory life (and this is the neurotic experience). The schizophrenic, at the ego level, knows no way to transcendence, and we could add that he does not know of, nor have the possibility of even an illusory life. What we, with a topographical vision of things, call the parts of his divided ego will not allow him to approach fiction, nor reality, nor illusion nor essence.

Our relationship with the schizophrenic symmetrically makes us lose the relation with all of those ego images which we have constructed in our personal histories; using analytical language, we can say that we too lose the symbolic function. We can say of ourselves that we 'desymbolize', that we too land in that pre-human field of experience where relations are not of a dialogic but rather of a pre-logical nature.

This phase of desymbolization is, for the therapist, the most dramatic of all and we can't even foresee how long it will last. We do know, however, that it is exactly this which contact with the schizophrenic procures for us. If we wanted to, we could even define it as a self-induced psychosis.

The therapist now, by means of that particular type of imagination which allows him to experience himself as devoid of symbols, or desymbolized, is able to have, by means of what could be called a *via negativa*, a fundamental experience, an experience which can find analogies only in the mystic process. In this phase, he re-lives his personal moment of primary anguish and, identifying with the patient, he historicizes the memory of it. He reacquires, dangerously, material distant from his own consciousness, and what we are saying can find confirmation in his dreams of countertransference.

It should be kept well in mind that in this phase, the danger for the therapist is great, and it would be advisable to undertake this type of experience under supervision.

*The experience of foundation:* This is essential for the origins of dualized psychological life and for the opening to the symbolic dimension.

All of the preceding experiences are prone to lead to desperation (and the patient before us reminds us of that continuously) until they are translated into the experience of foundation. This consists in the discovery that life has meaning; that is, that vital tension has a reason, that love has a goal that in an adequate way calls forth love itself; that the search for one's own truth has a real motivation, namely, the right to existence, and that man's path therefore has a solid foundation. One might even think that man is a creature badly put together, an error of nature, and that his progressive becoming has no real outlet (his name is pronounced in the void). One could in this way say that his reaching fulfilment is a definite end with no continuity (his 'exit' is a losing of himself in the nothing); in the same way, one could argue that his transcendence does not emerge from dependence, but means his fading into the other. When it is trust that calls forth love, it is lived without reservations, and when trust is psychological faith, it guides us along a path which is ever new. Moreover, when this psychological faith becomes trust in life itself, it allows us to bear every situation and come forth renewed. It is then discovered that there is a foundation and that being a man is a project which can be accomplished; strong is the man who can manage to bear himself.

We can say then, to conclude this theoretical presentation on the possible experiences of the therapist (activated by the meeting with the schizophrenic and implying a continual revision of his own life), that, in the loss of the image and therefore in desymbolisation, one can catch a glimpse of the apparition of the prototype symbol as that original possibility man possesses for indicating things by means of a communicable mental process.

If these are more or less the thoughts and reflections of the therapist vis-à-vis psychosis, if the psychotherapeutic preoccupation is that of entering, thanks to his imagination, the depths of the psychotic world not merely to remain on the level of the formal description of the contents, but rather to continue into the analytical deciphering of them, i.e., to the understanding of, and to the psychodynamics of these same contents, then he will have as his result-gift a 'psychotic production of high symbolic level'.

We see, then, that this result-gift derives not only from the elaboration of the fantasy objects of the patient, but also from our availability as therapists to let ourselves be interested, moved, impressed, made enthusiastic by them. In point of fact, without the movements of our psyche, of our body, of us as we are in our entirety, creative therapy would not exist, but rather only the psychological examination of the individual who stands before us.

The therapist abandons the symbolic world of his own ego and in the silence of a relationship which is fundamentally impossible, he meets the other on a distant and remote level. In this way, he becomes the 'living symbol' for the patient. In the process of identification, the therapist substitutes himself for the fragmented ego of the patient, for his lost symbolic function and he becomes the necessary bridge which links and reconciles those archetypal images which have overcome consciousness.

Jung's concept of the autonomy of the psyche in the presence of and within mental illness can't help but emerge at this point and it shows its own validity.

I should now like to illustrate the history of a paradigmatic analytical psychotherapy which took place with a schizophrenic patient by showing a number of his drawings, all of which are high symbolic and also quite artistic.

The patient began therapy at the age of 27; the first psychotic disturbances had manifested themselves at the age of 17. The diagnosis was borderline syndrome and the treatment consisted in the administration of drugs. His relatives and family remember him as being absent-minded, neglectful and distracted. He was not even capable of completing his secondary school studies. At the age of 23, he was hospitalized for two months in a psychiatric clinic with a diagnosis of catatonic schizophrenia. The treatment prescribed was 10+10 cycles of E. S. and the administration of drugs. Between the ages of 17 and 23, he had suffered recurring episodes of anorexia alternating with bulimia.

The intercritical clinical phases (between the ages of 17 and 27) were characterized by total speech-lessness, autism, and minimal delirious moments with the exception of some persecutory outbreaks. For the first 6 months of psychological therapy (3 sessions per week), the patient continued to take drugs and came accompanied by his mother. Later he progressively reduced the use of these drugs and began coming to the sessions alone. For the first year and a half of therapy, he never spoke, except to give some positive or negative indications to questions. The data of his anamnesis which are known to me have come from clinical records. The mother, who was the only member of the family with whom I spoke, added nothing, except for this far from consoling observation: "I just can't understand how he became ill and why."

After a year and a half of this psychological relationship consisting exclusively in silent meetings, or should I say, 'reciprocal contemplation', Andrea, that was the patient's name, brought and showed me spontaneously during one of the sessions, his first drawing.

The titles I give to these drawings are the ones Andrea himself gave to each of the images (see reproductions at the end of this chapter). There are 50 drawings in all and, in my opinion, they represent a typical example of psychotic art. With the idea that psychosis corresponds to an eruption of creativity, several authors maintain that psychopathological art is the art of patients who, for the first time in their lives, develop an artistic activity. Indeed, during psychosis they seek by means of this art to overcome the disorganization and the chaos into which they have been thrown by the psychotic process.

Here one can observe the beginnings of the recovery of the physiognomic formal and symbolic function.

The outline of the drawing and the colour have become more expressive.

In speaking about the drawings with me, Andrea for the first time, related this story: "When I was 11 years old, my father went hunting with a close friend of the family. I found out later that, at night, by accident, he had killed him. Just at that time, I was sent away from home to a boarding school; my classmates told me everything and even showed me the cuttings from the newspapers where everything was reported. My father was in prison for a short time, but was then found innocent. At home we never spoke about this matter, but I always thought that my father had intentionally killed this friend because he was my mother's lover."

This story, related for the first time with its real and fantastic elements, unleashed some moving and dramatic moments. Like an old ballad singer from the High Middle Ages, Andrea told as best he could, within the space of a real relationship, about the adventures and the roots of his own consciousness. At the end of the therapy, which lasted a total of 6 years, he gave me as a gift his drawings, thereby showing his detachment, though humanly difficult, from this content. At the same time, by means of the *per-donum,* he accomplished the highest and most significant feat of the human spirit: that of pardoning his own history (accepting the determining causes of it) and therefore also his own destiny.

Before concluding, I should like to refer to a particular type of work that was done on these same drawings after organizing them according to a criterion that was different from the chronological one that has been used in the sequences presented here so far. The illustrations that we shall now see have been organized on the basis of content.

It should be noted that the patient had undergone twenty E.S. and, as can be seen from his anamnesis, his symptomatology showed memory gaps which are demonstrated in a certain temporal-spatial disorientation. So I tried, perhaps a bit arbitrarily, to help along the process of reintegration by organizing some image sequences according to the historicist norms of the symbolic function of the ego.

Following this criterion, other archetypal contents such as the theme of fire, of the tree, moon, anima, etc. were focused on, interpreted and discussed, but for reasons of space, these cannot be illustrated here.

In conclusion then, we can say that the psychotherapy of psychosis, as a modality of dialogic communication cannot be justified as a work of doctrinal investigation and research if it is not recognized as being founded upon the nature of man himself in its quality of existence; and not in terms of man in general, but of the single man in the concreteness of his existence.

Moreover, the single man is never alone; he is in need of help, and in search of help, and he can both receive and give this help. And so each person in psychotherapy works for himself and for others and makes of the analytical task life and nourishment for his own life, which will in turn be life and nourishment for others.

The process of desymbolization and the reorganisation of the symbol express these alternating situations in the therapist, and they witness in schizophrenia, beyond just the illness, the greater circle which encompasses existence. "Suffering dominates nosography."

---

## Illustrations

1

2

*Illustration 1:* A man hunting by night on the banks of a lake.

*Illustration 2:* Representation of the psychic illness at the beginning and the loss of the physiognomic and formal capabilities along with that of the symbolic function. The outline and infantile use of colour should be noted here.

3

4

*Illustration 3:* A man cannot go along his road as a mountain blocks the path; immersing himself in the sea, he is submerged beneath the waves.

*Illustration 4:* A man is about to drown, but finds a box which contains a strong and living spirit; he is fished out from death. In the top left-hand corner, the woman is under a glass bell-jar.

5

5a

5b

5c

*Illustration 5:* The journey: along a road, by sea, across a river, through the desert.

6   7

*Illustration 6:* The cave man, fire and the good moon.

*Illustration 7:* The tribe and the red moon (notice the warrior with the lance, the woman near the fire with no arms, the elephant, etc.)

8   9

*Illustration 8:* The primitive couple (both figures are armed).

*Illustration 9:* The separated couple (the two figures both have the same arms), the moon and the dragon.

10   11

*Illustration 10:* The man and the woman climb the sacred mountain.

*Illustration 11:* The man is punished by death because he has found the fire of the mountain. The woman helps the man.

12   13

*Illustration 12:* The man is afraid of the woman, of the tree, of the mountain, of the sea, of the moon and of the night.

*Illustration 13:* The man is afraid of the woman; in the shadow, the monsters wait in ambush.

14   15

*Illustration 14:* In order to go with the woman, it is first necessary to cut down the tree; the tree has the head of the woman and lives with the snake.

*Illustration 15:* The men and the squinting moon; I'm afraid of the men (at this point, persecutory fantasies with homosexual content came up).

16   17

*Illustration 16:* The monster and I are tied to two columns of fire; two women come to free me, one with a lamp, the other without.

*Illustration 17:* The witch, who gives birth to the fire, casts a spell; the bad moon looks on.

18   19

*Illustration 18:* The doctors say that I must eat, but I can't; the table is set on the back of a dragon.

*Illustration 19:* The spell of the witch has sent the man to the moon.

20   21

*Illustration 20:* From earth, the wise man looks at the moon.

*Illustration 21:* I leave the moon and the lunatic woman to return to earth.

22   23

*Illustration 22:* On earth, there is fire and there are trees.

23a   24

*Illustration 23:* On earth there are towns and cities.

*Illustration 24:* On earth, there is the woman with her lamp.

25   26

*Illustration 25:* A couple looks at the sea and the approach of a storm.

*Illustration 26:* (This is the next-to-last drawing of the series.) The indolents in the first circle of Dante's hell (we can notice here: Dante, Virgil and the damned, who are chasing a violet flag, all stung by insects). This unusual and isolated theme in the drawings of Andrea led me to ask him if he had ever identified himself with an indolent person. He gave no answer. The answer was to be found, however, in the following drawing (the last of the series).

27   28

*Illustration 27:* A man hunting by night on the banks of a lake.

*Illustration 28:* As can be noted, the style is completely different, and the shadow in the black-and-white drawing is absent. There is also rain, which was absent from the other drawing; the moon is missing, and the whole thing seems to represent a rainy morning twilight.

A

*Illustration A*: Historical development which touches on the following periods: Stone Age, Greek, Roman, Medieval and Modern periods.

B

*Illustration B:* The same work was carried out on other archetypal contents: the house as a symbol of the Self and as the progressive accomplishment of a relational life (from the cave to the house in the city).

C

*Illustration* C: The journey as the image of detachment from the chaotic elements towards more organized and individual contents and vice versa, as the image of the deepening of ego consciousness towards symbolic content of an archetypal nature.

D

*Illustration D:* The Medieval period seen as the recovery and transformation of various archetypes by means of alchemical transformation.

# Bibliography

*S. Arieti:*
Interpretation of Schizophrenia. Basic Books, Inc., Publishers, New York, 1974.
*M. Augè:*
Simbolo, Funzione, Storia. Liguori Editore, 1982.
*G. Benedetti:*
Alienazione e personazione nella psicoterapia della malattia mentale. Giulio Einaudi Editore, 1980.
*B. Callieri:*
Quando vince l'ombra, problemi di psicopatologia clinica. Città Nuova, 1982.
*C. G. Jung:*
Psicogenesi delle malattie mentali. Beringhieri, 1971.
*E. Kris:*
Ricerche psicoanalitiche sull'arte. Giulio Einaudi Editore, 1957.
*G. Maffei:*
Il mestiere di uomo. Ricerca sulla psicosi. Marsilio Editore, Venezia, 1977.
*N. Micklem:*
The Intolerable Image, the Mythic Background of Psychosis. Spring, 1979. Spring Publications, Dallas, Tx.
*N. Micklem:*
On Hysteria: The Mythical Syndrome. Spring, 1974. Spring Publications, Dallas, Tx.
*Rafael López-Pedraza:*
Hermes and his Children (out of print). Spring Publications, Zurich, 1977.
*Rafael López-Pedraza:*
Moon MADNESS! Titanic Love. A meeting of Pathology and poetry in: Images of the untouched. The Pegasus Foundation Series I. – The Dallas Institute of Humanities and Culture. Spring Publications Inc. Dallas, Tx. 1982.
*J. W. Perry:*
The Far Side of Madness. Prentice Hall Inc. 1974.
*M. Trevi:*
Testo, Interpretazione, Simbolo. Rivista di psicologia Analitica. Astrolabio, 26/82.

# Depressed Patients and the *coniunctio**

Judith Hubback (London)

## Introduction and Theme

There are six particular people – patients – whose lives and therapies are at the empirical core of this paper. What they have in common is that each of their mothers was seriously depressed during her son's or daughter's infancy and childhood. The other thing they have in common is that they had their analytical therapy with the particular analyst that I am, and that over the years I have had a growing interest in trying to find our more about what it is that enables someone effectively to emerge from long-term depressions. I would like to isolate one particular factor from those, often explored and discussed, concerning the nature, the manifestations and the treatment of depression. I am thinking of a factor whose absence could be a great disadvantage, but whose presence can enable a patient to become, in the course of therapy and time, less depressed, less frequently so, and less paralysingly; such a factor might also help the person to be less aggressive towards others and facilitate the development of a truly viable sense of self.

Those thoughts have become the theme of this paper: too many and too strong negative archetypal images are absorbed by an infant or young child from a depressed mother, most particularly if she is a bereaved woman who is still caught up in her anger and sadness, so that she cannot direct herself towards the baby and genuinely smile into its eyes. Not enough validation of its loveableness is offered to such an infant at the stage in life when that experience is essential for a healthy

* Reprinted by permission of *The Journal of Analytical Psychology*, where this article appeared in expanded form in Vol. 28, No. 4 (October 1983).

self-belief to develop, which will be based on enough internal feeling that there is more growth than destructiveness both in himself and in his environment. To alter the attitudes stemming from those early inner and outer pathological experiences, an analytical therapist makes herself available for a relationship to grow within which a number of *coniunctiones* can occur: if, at the level of the objective psyche, as manifested in the analyst, there is a well-established *coniunctio* of internal images, and if the patient is able to identify with that inner healer – whose outer scars may still be evident – then what is happening is that both archetypal structuralist concepts and the findings of developmental research are confirmed.

I am not speaking simply about the patient's need to (I quote Jung) "kill the symbolic representative of the unconscious, i. e. his own *participation mystique* with animal nature… the Terrible Mother who devours and destroys, and thus symbolises death itself" (Jung, 1, p. 328). The patient with a depressed mother does need to emerge from an unconscious identification with his mother because of the killing quality of her depression, and needs to cease participating in her anger and sadness. If for the term *participation mystique* we substitute the words and concepts *unconscious identification* then I can go along with the way Jung used Lévy-Bruhl's term. Identifying with those structures in the analyst which have developed as a result of her working on instinctual 'animal nature' in herself, can and does happen within the therapeutic relationship; projections and introjections can be discerned and described. I think they are marvellous, but not mystical.

The patient with a depressed mother is suffering from a serious narcissistic wound. I develop in this paper the theme that such patients benefit greatly – perhaps essentially – from the analyst using to the full a combination of developmental observations and her own internal search for harmony, for *coniunctio*.

Without giving detailed descriptions of the six patients mentioned earlier, I will simply say that the character and quality of their mothers' depressive reactions to the loss of either their husband or an earlier child ran the whole spectrum of possibilities: paranoid, manic, animus-ridden, schizoid, closed, sulky, aggressive, obsessional, and suicidal. Some of these patients made images, or allowed the images to make themselves, easily and early on in their analyses, others with difficulty and much later. They also varied in their ability to fantasise in the transference, and to dream. Each of them suffered from internal impoverishment.

## Self-feeling, Narcissistic Deprivation and Depression

The depressed patient whose mother was *not* subject to depression brings to his analyst pathological material which is principally his own. The one whose mother is known to have been seriously depressed when he was very young will be listened to by an analyst with her ear ready to try to extricate the mother's bad internal self-view from the patient's fantasies about it. There are cross-currents of identifications which can be navigated successfully, if slowly, through transference manifestations and counter-transference self-analysis. It is not just the familiar process of enabling the patient to separate out from his mother and to develop firm but not rigid boundaries between himself and every later representative of that first object, that first partner, but rather it is the task of analysing his fantasies about his mother's inner life. They cannot be assumed to be totally fantastic, or 'merely' subjective. The analyst's familiarity with her own inner life and willingness to use it indirectly in her work, will be a major factor in analysing the patient effectively. She has to be bold, and enough *in* her own residual depression, or depressive phases, and at the same time to have good enough boundaries, to distance herself enough from her depressive tendencies so that the patient can use them in the transference, that is symbolically.

The symbolic attitude and approach to the patient (Hubback 2) whose mother was depressed brings together the understanding of environmental influence, of developmental studies and of archetypal disposition. Jung has written of the *a priori* existence of "organising factors", the archetypes, which are to be understood as inborn modes of functioning that constitute, in their totality, man's nature. The chick does not learn to come out of the egg – it possesses this knowledge *a priori* (Jung 3, p. 328). He also insisted that "the archetype in itself is empty and purely formal ... a possibility of representation ... the representations themselves are not inherited, only the forms, and in that respect they correspond in every way to the instincts, which are also determined in form only" (Jung 3, p. 79). The ethologists' theory of internal release mechanisms is in line with that formulation. In another passage Jung wrote: "*the contents of the child's unconscious fantasies* can be referred to the personal mother only in part, since they often contain clear and unmistakable allusions which could not possibly have reference to human being" (ibid).

We can also observe normal infants when they are in the grip, early on, of desperate hungry anxiety, infants who gradually grow less anxious and angry when there have been repeated experiences of their hungry, demanding, and envious attacks being responded to. Working for many months or even years, may be necessary with patients who despair of ever becoming free from hatefulness. They feel over-full of hate against the apparently ungiving mother-analyst, and over-full of terror that she will hate them for hating her.

The fantasies that such patients have are very extremist. On two separate occasions, with two different patients, I took marginally longer to answer the bell when they arrived. One, a woman, said she had, in those instants, imagined me lying on the floor of my room, dead from a heart attack. The other, a man, fantasied that my husband had been killed in a motor accident and I had been called away. On another occasion, a man patient fantasied dying then and there, while lying on the couch, of heart failure, which would give me, he hoped, the most difficult situation I had ever had to deal with. That was the day after he had voiced both a grossly idealised description of me, and his miserable envy, saying: "you have a really good, balanced, internal self-feeling, you believe in yourself. I don't." I told him I saw the imagined "heart attack" as a suicical fantasy of self-punishment following the envious attack on me of the day before, but that he was also telling me that he was very much alive, to be able to go at me like that, with such attacking hunger. His response was: "YES! I'll attack, and attack, and attack again! I'm very hungry!" The following week, the atmosphere between us changed. The feeling arose in him that there was a "we", and he remembered some of the earlier positive phases of the analysis. He smiled on arrival, ruefully, he grew gentler. And he even managed a joke.

In the therapies with such patients it was never any use to skimp on the long process of working through the experiences of unsatisfied narcissism or the images associated with them. Time and again the transference and counter-transference projections, when elucidated, showed how the lack of outgoing and positive response of the personal mother had contributed in a major way to the patient having not only a consciously poor self view and an unconsciously grandiose and arrogant one, but an actively negative one. It was when that self-attacking view was in the ascendent that the structures in forming the analysis were put to the greatest strain. The patients I am talking about were all either extremely sensitive to even the minutest alteration in externals, my appearance, or the room, or they defended themselves against their sensitivity being apparent. Each of them in his or her own particular way would make use of whatever came to hand to try to demonstrate how inadequately they considered I was treating them and how impossible was any change. Things were as bad as could be, always had been and always would be. There was no time any more, only timeless hell. Their very present despair could only be reached with the help of accumulated experiences in the analysis, from which they gradually discovered that change, time and development do exist. They began to recognise the alternation of hell and heaven. Then, in time, those extremes were modified.

Both patient and analyst have their own personal and actual selves which stem from primal body-experiences of psychosomatic unity. The self is a concept which is the best possible way of referring to the sense of selfhood that each person needs if he is to use, rather than be misled by, what he gets from other people – identifications. He needs to have boundaries, and a sense of those boundaries, before he can identify healthily. If the actual mother fails to grant the infant boundaries, otherness, individuality, and aloneness, as she has not detached herself from the image of another person to whom she was ambivalently over-attached, then she ties the infant in a false closeness based on her unconsciously identifying with her own abandoned self that she has projected into the infant. That infant is then grossly overburdened.

His mother's angry depression is experienced by him in infancy and childhood as though it were his own capacity to attack, to defeat and to be defeated. Each of us in our original undifferentiated libido has the potential to direct it positively or negatively (experiencing the world as giving us nourishing food or destructive poison, love or hate, life or death, etc.); the infant whose mother is depressed over-develops his negative potential. The infant's need to discover the difference between despairing loneliness and positive separateness is not met by a mother who has not achieved it herself. Such a mother offers the infant a model of much more bad than good, as compared with a model (or image) of a person who discovers that the self contains both, and that the loving, constructive, forces can defeat the destructive ones.

## Questions connected with Technique and Counter Transference

The problem of where the most powerful source of pathology lies for any particular patient may, or may not, affect the course of the analysis.

How much does it matter whether the analyst gives great weight (in the reflections she does not communicate directly to the patient) to the presumed influence of the mother's unworked-through mourning, or adopts the other course of paying major attention to the patient's autonomous imagery? How much difference does it make to the healing process, to the development of reconciling and integrating forces, to the patient's potential for continued self-analysis and further improvement of personal relationships after he has separated from the analyst, if there has been concentration on one approach to the problem and neglect of the other? Or, is the wisest course to work with no framework of theory at all, no model associated with any group or school?

Only tentative answers can be offered here. Several of the patients produced images of quite exceptional force. But the transference projections were very powerful, whether there was much or little imagery. The mother's unworked-through mourning seemed to me to be still exerting a pathological influence. I observed that the introjected image of a depressed mother became more amenable to analysis at times when I myself either was, or was believed by the patient to be, depressed. The analysis became more stressful. It was important then that I should try to understand what losses or personal failings I had not yet mourned. It would be defensive idealisation to see myself as fully individuated, or so free from ever being disturbed by personal emotions, that no affect leaked from me to a patient.

Integration of all kinds of shadow material proceeded when I was able to use a combination of intuition, memory and theoretical concepts to come to something I hoped could be dignified with the name understanding. That is where acquaintance with, and reflection on, other schools of analysis and other arts and sciences can be of great help.

Granting full acknowledgement to powerlessness is very necessary if the analyst is to avoid getting enmeshed in the patient's projective identification. The illusion of omnipotence must be dissolved. Being myself a parent, I find that unhappy or anxious affects in relation to one or other of my children can on occasion intrude and cause me to associate (privately) to a patient's perhaps similar experiences. Usefully, however, I find that they tend to see my professional persona as giving them a convenient experience of me being a sort of father to them. None of those I am speaking about had an effective father – he was either physically or psychologically not available to them. With most of these patients, the father transference has been frequent, necessarily negative at first, gradually or intermittently becoming positive and useful in that way. The evidence of dreams and fantasies has, however, accumulated and attacks on the-father-whom-the-mother-had-come-to-hate could be convincingly detected via attacks on me or self-attacks. A male patient's self-attacking actions make me feel angry with myself, as I believe a father does, when he worries about whether he is being a good-enough father to his son.

As a mother in the transference, I find that the counter-transference affect, perhaps more frequently experienced than anger, is that of a nearly despairing kind, with predominance of a defensive splitting of affect. One patient in particular had received a great deal of despair projected from her mother, who seems to have been oblivious of her own pathological attitudes. In the mother and the daughter the negative animus was very powerful. In the counter-transference, I had phases of losing self-confidence, and at times felt that I was not the right analyst for her.

An adequately functioning partnership within the analyst of libido both from the self and from the ego structures is necessary for treating a patient who is defending against ego-development by blanking, which can represent total destruction. I remember the dream of one of my patients: she looked in a mirror, and saw no-one, nothing. Some time later, she was feeling upset and was talking about my approaching holiday: she described how I "vanish into thin air" when she knows I am away from home. If she can not make an image of me being in a particular and familiar place, she is imageless. She can not reconcile terror and hope. The parental imagos are, in her, not so much negative (e. g., hated or feared or despised), but more dangerously, they disappear completely at difficult junctures. I do not know whether they have an existence of their own, so that their disappearance happens *to* her, or whether she has an as-yet not fully known anger against them so that unconsciously it is she who *makes* them disappear.

From the point of view of the day to day work with that patient, my experience is that if I interpret that she is actively blanking and destroying, that feeds her capacity to develop on the ego side and to begin emerging from the dangers attendant upon such imagos. The central criterion I use is to try to speak within the transference in such a way as to foster her potential for experiencing herself as an individual, subject to certain forces but not entirely at their mercy.

When a patient begins to feel sure of being an individual he will credit the other person with individuality. When the healing process is at work and the old imago of *mater dolorosa* is less in power, and the introjection of her is less strangling, then a reconciling symbol appears in a dream, or a fantasy. There is only time for one, abbreviated, example: the dreamer was mixing a drink, at a party, for his sister, his wife and his daughters; the drink was made up of milk and of semen. Also at the party, in a communicating room, were his professional colleagues.

That dream shows, first, a man's use of body imagery, secondly, his desire to reconcile himself with certain closely related females who usually received various anima projections from him, and thirdly the desire that there should be a better internal communication than previously in his feelings about himself as a family man and as a worker.

The purposive nature of instincts, as Jung saw, "their dynamic motivating character" as they "pursue their inherent goals" (Jung 3, p. 43), releases healing and creative symbols since, in the analytical treatment, the patient has been put in touch with his capacity to connect the conscious mind with growth processes from the unconscious.

## Attacks of Envy and Envious Attacks

The flow of reconciling symbols is often held up by renewed envious attacks on the analyst. The stage of hungry envy (Hubback 4), is followed by the second stage of denigratory envy. Sarcasm, scorn and cynicism are the consulting-room versions of the emotions belonging to the stage at which 'the infant in the patient' is trying to emerge from its deep-seated fears of another abandonment.

So it happens that there is a new envious attack in a fantasy or a dream just when it seemed possible that real progress had been achieved. For example: the absence of my car from its usual place in the street outside was said to "mean" that I had gone off to enjoy myself with someone I found more attractive than the patient. Another patient dreamed that he met me on the doorstep of my house as I departed, most elegantly dressed, with a high and mighty Afghan hound which bared its teeth fiercely while I took no notice of him.

The patient who has been enviously attaking the analyst as the present representative of the once-powerful mother gradually comes to recognise such dreams and fantasies, and discovers how to reconcile the warring emotions. Where work with such a patient is concerned, there is an optimistic passage in Jung's paper entitled "Concerning the archetypes and the anima concept": "The projection ceases the moment it becomes conscious, that is to say when it is seen as belonging to the subject" – but a footnote to that runs as follows: "There are, of course, cases where, in spite of the patient's seemingly sufficient insight, the reactive effect of the projection does not cease, and the expected liberation does not take place. I have often observed that in such cases meaningful but unconscious contents are still bound up with the projection carrier. It is these contents that keep up the effect of the projection, although it has apparently been seen through" (Jung 3, para. 121 and footnote 17).

## Mysterium Coniunctionis

The dissociation between spirit and matter, of which Jung wrote a great deal in the last chapter of *Mysterium Coniunctionis*, is comparable – in the world of several of the patients described here – to the dissociation between the imagos of each of the two parents. Others can not make contact with any image of loving parents. Much work has to be done before the depth and extent of the dissociation is well enough appreciated, which lends weight to Jung's statement that 'a *conscious* situation of distress is needed in order to activate the archetype of unity' (Jung 5, p. 540). Then, in the Epilogue, he enquires whether the psychologist can throw out the antagonistic forces, or whether he had not better "admit their existence... bring them into harmony and, out of the multitude of contradictions, produce a unity, which naturally will not come of itself, though it may – *Deo concedente* – with human effort" (Ibid. p. 555).

I have long been struck by just that – the great and total 'human effort' that the patient puts into the therapeutic work at this difficult stage. He or she is often in a renewed state of depression, angry and sore, or again in an ambivalent mood towards me. The affect in dreams and fantasies is either painful, or split off. One patient, for example, who was recovering from a serious schizoid depression, dreamed of the parental pair in a car, under which there was a smouldering fire, perhaps a bomb, and the dreamer/son saved them just before the petrol tank blew up. Presence of mind – ego capacity – was required of him, as well as warmth of feeling. The dreams of a woman patient over many months grew around images of the limitless sea and then other kinds of water, with a gradual diminution of boundlessness, of isolation, of nameless terrors, and a steady growth of pictures in which some focus of safety was perceptible, places or situations where there were square enclosures or encircled areas, a potential coming-together, a possible *coniunctio*.

The *coniunctio* and harmonisation of internal imagos is unlikely to take place if the analyst does not find the right combination within herself of responsiveness and self-boundaries. If she can keep her sense of self she will be able to become the internal representative of the union of the opposing pair.

The search for harmony was the driving force behind many of the thinkers of the fifteenth, sixteenth and seventeenth centuries, men in public life as well as philosophers. The parallel between their yearnings for harmony and the researches of the alchemists of those centuries gives added significance to the internal searches for *coniunctio* of depressed patients.

The reconciling symbols have to be alive ones for each of us. A particular patient may have no inclination whatsoever to make a living connection with the mythologies, or the arts which appeal to his analyst. It is the psychology of conjunction which has to be understood and appreciated.

## REFERENCES

1. Jung, C. G. (1912). *Symbols of Transformation. Coll. wks,* 5.
2. Hubback, J. (1969). 'The Symbolic Attitude in Psychotherapy', J. analyt. Psychol., 14, 1.
3. Jung, C. G. (1936). *The Archetypes and the Collective Unconscious. Coll. wks,* 9, 1.
4. Hubback, J. (1972). 'Envy and the Shadow', *J. analyt. Psychol.,* 17, 2.
5. Jung, C. G. (1956). *Mysterium Coniunctionis. Coll. wrks,* 14.

# Pathology of the Self and Symbolic Approach*

Mario Moreno (Rome)

The recent spate of psychoanalytical studies on narcissism has led several authors, such as Kohut, Kernberg, Grunberger, Sassanelli and others, to contrast, in an increasingly marked and clear-cut way, the pulsional or objective dimension of psychic life, which corresponds to the classical theoretical structures of id, ego and superego, and the narcissistic dimension, which corresponds to a structure designated as the *self*. The development of a sense of identity and self-esteem would seem to be grounded in the narcissistic dimension, in the normal structuring of a cohesive self. As a consequence of this distinction, alongside the neurotic pathology characterized by the classical structural conflict, a pathology of the self has gradually taken form. It is interpreted as a consequence of a failure or an imperfect structuration of the self within the framework of the psychic system formed by the infant and the maternal care.

The limits of this clinical entity cannot be clearly defined, even on the basis of psychoanalytical literature itself. Some authors identify the pathology of the self with narcissistic disorders of the personality, others include schizoid and borderline cases in this pathology, and finally, still others widen these limits to include many behavioural disorders such as anorexia nervosa, bulimia, drug addiction, etc., as well as some serious phobic conditions. The prevailing tendency, however, is to limit this term to a type of pathology which is contiguous but not wholly superimposable to the psychoses, that is, the narcissistic neuroses of classical psychoanalytical nosography.

* Due to the untimely death of the author, this paper was not able to be revised or proofread by him. No record was found of the sources of certain quotes and references and so they appear here without footnoting.

Let us now consider Analytical Psychology: When Jung described – in *The Ego and the Unconscious* – the dialectical situation of the ego between the *persona* and the *anima*, he implicitly opposed a narcissistic dimension to an objectual relationship dimension, albeit with reference to a more complex stage of personality integration. Recently, Fordham has written that an identification with the *persona* occurs in patients who have failed to develop a sense of the self sufficiently adequate for achieving a state of individual unity. Fordham thus likens the concept of identification with the *persona* to Winnicott's concept of the *false self*.

If we are going to talk about a pathology of the self within the framework of Analytical Psychology, then we must bear in mind the different conceptions of the term, the 'self'. Freud and his disciples consider the self as a part of the ego, as a content of the ego: attention is focused on the representation of the self organised into a system and on its articulation with the object representations in the course of the development of the ego.

According to Rosemary Gordon, the majority of psychoanalysts use the term self, first introduced by Hartman in 1950, for what she calls the 'introspective' part of the ego. They believe it powers the capacity to experience oneself with continuity and cohesion through time and space, and to be aware of one's own identity. Some analysts, however, have moved away from this position. Jacobson, for instance, though stating that a realistic self-image reflects only the state and characteristics of the ego, admits the existence of a primitive self as a primary psychosomatic unity, from which representations of the self and of the object, which are at first fused with one another, would gradually become differentiated within the ego.

For Winnicott, the distinction between the *false self* and the *true self* would seem to imply a concept of the self which is not confined to the representation of the self. According to Winnicott, the self is the product of a process of maturation from a state of dependency to a state of autonomy, whereby the child's innate potential finds an adequate environmental support.

Jung, on the other hand, describes the Self as both the goal of the individuation process and the archetypal structuring function of the same process. The Self manifests itself to consciousness with images of unity and totality which convey a need for fusion, for communion and a union of the opposites.

Thus, the Jungian Self is the guiding factor, the stage-manager of a project involving the different archetypal potentials and at the same time, the Self is the goal of this project; it is simultaneously the process and the structure, as rightly pointed out by Trevi, who states that it is just this thinking in the form of correlated opposites which constitutes the distinctive feature of the Jungian methodology.

Certainly, a sharp differentiation between the Freudian self and the Jungian Self seems easy enough. However, as Mario Jacoby recently observed, Kohut himself, though considering the self a psychic structure resulting from the internalisation of an empathically mirroring self-object, and though denying the existence of a primary self, had, in his last works, placed the self at the centre of the psychological universe. He came to admit that the 'nuclear self' is a centre of initiative which contains the project (blueprint) that must be implemented throughout the course of one's life, and, finally, that the self is 'unknown in its essence'. In the self, he described a bipolarity formed by a dynamic pole endowed with ambitious initiative, and a representative pole that elaborates significant goals.

Jacoby compares individuation with the narcissistic libido postulated by Kohut, the maturation of which would produce results such as empathy, creativity, humour and wisdom. Rosemary Gordon, too, stresses the analogy between Kohut's concept of mature narcissism and of the shifting from a "little self" to a self which has expanded to include parts of the world, and the Ego-Self axis in the individuation process.

In commenting on one passage of the apocryphal Acts of John in "The Psychology of Mass", Jung speaks of the Self as a totality, supraordinate to the ego, which comprehends consciousness and unconscious; as of an 'unknowable', paradoxically subject and object simultaneously. Jung compares the Self to a mirror, which, on one hand, reflects the subjective consciousness of the person looking into it, while on the other side, also 'knowing' the *anthropos*, the Christ; it does not merely reflect the empirical man, but it also shows him as a (trascendental) whole. He who looks into this mirror no longer sees himself as an isolated being, but as united with the One. Without the objectification of the Self, which provides an Archimedean point from which the ego can be seen as a phenomenon, the ego itself would remain caught in a hopeless subjectivity. If this Jungian epistemological approach is taken into account, then both the hypertrophy of the ego complex and the compensatory inflationary activation of the collective unconscious, i.e., of the archetypes, would seem to contribute to the pathology of the Self. The Self, a totality supraordinate to the ego and comprehending consciousness and the unconscious, is materialized into powerful archetypal images that threaten to inflate the ego, which seeks autonomy but is fascinated by omnipotence; which seeks separation but is still charmed by fusion; which aims at detachment and self-sufficiency but feels threatened by a loss of enthusiasm and meaning; which strives for a realistic evaluation but indulges in idealising itself and the other.

The pathology of the Self – lack of identity and self-esteem probably attributable to disturbances in the primary relationship – can be interpreted, following Neumann, as an early pathological intensification of the ego complex, i.e., a self-sufficient egocentrism, or as an activation of individual archetypal functions, and it is possible to accept both hypotheses simultaneously by simply changing the point of view. Likewise, in proposing a Jungian reading of the myth of Narcissus, I have pointed out the need to look at the tragedy of Narcissus not only from the viewpoint of the ego, but also from the viewpoint of the Self. In the *Ego perspective,* Narcissus seems to have a desperate need for reflecting himself in order to 'become', to take on identity. His need is never lessened, not even when he realizes that he is in love with his own reflection. He is unable to respond to love, not even the love of Echo, who, with her echolalia, promises some sort of verbal reflection. As Neumann states, the deprived and needy ego is prematurely awakened in narcissism, and soon compelled to become independent and self-sufficient. Narcissus concentrates only on himself and makes no investment in external objects. His death seems the natural outcome of this self-sufficient isolation, this refusal to communicate. From this death is born, as a 'transformed' product, the flower Narcissus, which can be easily connected to the *anima* as a relationship archetype and to feeling as the function which links people to each other.

But Narcissus' death, inasmuch as it is a drowning in the water of the pool in which he mirrors himself, can also be interpreted as a regression to the uroboric phase, as a return to the symbiosis mentioned by Mahler and Jacobson; that is to say, the phase in which maternal care and the mother's face itself act as the mirror in which the ego wishes to constitute itself and take on its own identity.

When we view the question from the angle of the *Self*, however, we must focus our attention on the *image* with which Narcissus falls in love.

Having reviewed the different interpretations of the myth of Narcissus in the history of our culture, Murray Stein concludes that Narcissus lacks the 'psychologizing alternative' of maintaining the projected content at image level and using it to reflect the unconscious holes of our vision. The vision of ourselves that we find in the eyes of our beloved one, says Stein, can become an opportunity for self-reflection and connection with the unconscious anthropos, with the 'greater' man who dwells within us.

Starting from similar imagistic premises, Bianca Garufi sees in the myth of Narcissus the time of love and respect of the ego Narcissus for the image, and she also sees in it the time of indifference toward and refusal of one's body. "There is in Narcissus", Garufi states, "an absolute love of the ego for the image; the ego annihilates itself, it surrenders, in front of the reflected psychic image, that is to say, the psyche itself."

Giuseppe Luigi Aversa states that "Narcissus' love for his reflection is not only... love and identification in one's own reflection, in one's own phantasmal replica, but it can also be an attempt to love oneself as if another, as the need for being another... it can be not only a libidinal stagnation of the ego, but also a demand of the ego to transcend and 'futurify' itself".

Bernard Sartorius, in an attempt to understand the myth of Narcissus in existential terms, sees in it the defeat of introspection, the spell of the image of the Self which is necessary but hopelessly destined to failure. Hence, Narcissus dies out of languor. In this sense, Sartorius adds, the efforts of the psychologists who want to help man to discover himself fall utterly within the framework of the myth of Narcissus: their efforts and their failure are both necessary and unavoidable. All these interpretations are centered on the image, albeit viewed from opposite angles. Garufi and Aversa, on the one hand, envisage the triumph of the image and almost the death of the ego which is assimilated to consciousness; on the other hand, Stein and Sartorius believe that the image fails in its reflecting function: he who looks at his reflection in the water is unable to find anything but his own ego and he dies because he is unable to conceive utopia. Perhaps these are exactly the extremes offered by the perspective of the self.

Whenever our attention turns to the image, it is the archetypal foundation of the myth of Narcissus that unfolds, and with it the archetypal core of narcissism. The few Jungian authors who have taken this standpoint have all made reference to the *puer aeternus.* In an essay on the narcissistic foundation of the puer and puella personality structure, Jeffrey Satinover, for instance, states that those in which the puer archetype is predominant are afflicted with an identity problem because of disturbances in the introverted reflection of their Self. Narcissus – he says – becomes enamoured of his own reflection because he has *no consciousness of himself.* According to this author, the puer psychology is characterized by alternating inflation and depression, states of grandiosity in which the self is constellated, and states of fragmentation.

Fordham, as is known, assumes two forms of the Self: the total Self and the partial selves. Primary unity can no longer be attained once 'deintegration' has occurred in childhood. A tendency to recover what is forever impossible lingers on, something similar to the *Ego ideal,* which remains from the Freudian primary narcissism. Aspects of the self are emphasized by the relationship with society; when social identifications break down, however, one returns to infancy and a relationship with the puer archetype is established. If I have understood Fordham's thought correctly, it is this very archetypal 'deintegration' which would distinguish narcissistic regression.

In an essay written in 1979, Schwartz-Salant states that narcissism corresponds to the spirit archetype with its capacity of providing value, and he has indicated the alchemical Mercurius as the analogous archetype of the narcissistic phenomenology. In a later interesting monograph, this author further states that, in his opinion, a first phase of transformation of the narcissistic character implies the shifting from a negative to a positive puer-senex relationship, which involves a greater capacity for introspective reflection as well as a greater creativity. Thus, the problems of the puer would seem to coincide with this first stage of transformation which, in turn, would correspond to the myth of Narcissus. In the second stage, the transformation would involve the feminine.

Therefore, in the perspective of the Self, of the transcendental totality which, as Jung says, allows the ego not to remain isolated in hopeless subjectivity, the image under whose spell Narcissus falls turns out to be an archetypal image which threatens to inflate the ego, but at the same time, ensures a connection with the Self.

In reductive terms, we can speak of an *ego-ideal,* or perhaps, in more up-to-date terms, of a *grandiose self.* Viewing it archetypally, however, we must speak of the *puer aeternus,* the divine child, an all-powerful figure which promises the reunion with God, the surmounting of limitation and the renewal of values.

The confirmation of this archetypal reading of Narcissus can only come from the field of pathology, where, to the narcissistic imprint, there correspond the different aspects of puer phenomenology. In the *narcissistic personality,* the inflation of the ego by the negative aspects of the puer is clearly apparent in symptomatology: hand in hand with fantasies of grandiosity goes the inability to undergo efforts or make sacrifice, as well as intolerance of criticism (and interpretations). At the level of interpersonal relationships, there is a contrast between the deep-felt need for admiration and love, and the pride of needing no one, between idealising and enviously denying the other, between a mirror-transference, in which the other must only reflect the narcissistic grandiosity, and an idealising transference where the grandiosity is projected onto the other.

In this case, Narcissus can only find his own ego in the water; the image fails its function as a reflection and bestower of meaning. The feeling of emptiness and insignificance is actually akin to envy and rage. The foolishly ambitious and irresponsible character described by Von Franz as 'puer neurosis' seems to correspond rather accurately to the narcissistic character disorder.

In *anorexia nervosa,* the archetypal inflation concerns aspects of the puer which could well be called spiritual, although we have here a spirituality confined essentially to denying the body, and the material. The body-mind dichotomy is exasperated and the spiritual degenerates to mental control of the body.

In this case, Narcissus is really in love with the weightless image of his body, which redeems him from dependence, from ties, from need. As Stroud says, the woman afflicted by anorexia is torn between her desire of being independent and her fear of having to exist without a strong support. The body is lived as something alien; there is an attempt at levitating oneself, to attain a feeling of transcendence. It is an attempt at getting rid of parental bonds through a 'terrifying passion for purity'. *Bulimia,* on the other hand, represents the failure and hypercompensation of this attempt. In *bulimia,* also, the puer archetype predominates, but here everything is more absurdly ambitious, the defeat is continuous, the Great Mother unendingly imposes her rights. The childish gluttony degenerates the puer to a grandiosity never confirmed by facts, and always frustrated when it is projected onto the idealised other.

Within this framework, the impulse to *bulimia* can be compared to drug addiction which, as Kernberg says, is "an attempt to feed the grandiose self".

At least in the more serious *phobic states,* the Ego-Narcissus seems to be continuously oscillating between, on the one hand, the uroboric regression in the pool, the loss of identity because of the return to the symbiosis with the mother, and, on the other hand, a more or less grandiose and all-powerful isolation where the outside world takes on the constraining, suffocating and persecutory features of a negative senex.

But I have no wish to review the entire pathology to finally discover the narcissistic foundation of each case. Just as an example, certainly each *borderline* situation in which the ego, so as not to be split, is compelled to bear a very strong dialectic tension between the polarities just mentioned in speaking of serious phobic states, can be spoken of as a pathology of the Self.

The actual psychotherapeutic accessibility of many cases is linked exactly to a phase of 'trespassing', so to speak, in this area where the ego is no longer totally inflated by an archetype of the collective unconscious. Nor does it seek a fictitious identity by assuming standing values of collective consciousness, that is identifying itself with the *persona.* Under this condition of relative regression and of identity crisis, the Self can emerge as a new project, as a new model, and the Ego-Self axis can be reestablished.

The possibility of favouring this transformation process in the psychotherapeutic relationship amounts to a receiving and accepting of those types of transference which Kohut calls narcissistic, that is the mirror transference and the idealising transference. As far as my experience is concerned, these modes of relationship are always present at the same time, though with different emphasis. We might say, perhaps, that at the very moment when the analyst accepts the patient's control and is prepared to reflect the grandiose self, he presents himself as an empathic positive object-Self suitable for idealisation. The transformative effectiveness of this encounter is based, however, on the mutual patient-analyst involvement, which includes conscious and unconscious aspects. In "The Psychology of the Transference", Jung describes the quaternity, with reference to the alchemical process, as a conscious and unconscious transformative exchange within the framework of the patient-analyst relationship; it is a paradigm of the union of opposites, with the death of the old ego and the rebirth of the Self; it is the dialectic model of every real encounter. It is a mutual game of projections and introjections of negative and positive parts of the Self, and hence an archetypal transference-countertransference through which the grandiose self of the patient reveals, beyond the general exhibitionistic need, its numinosity and it becomes manifest as an image of the *puer aeternus*, emanating from and anticipating the real Self.

The idealised analyst-parent, in his turn, shows himself as the carrier of the split parts of the Self which could not be integrated because of early splitting of the ego. The precocious ego is poor, greedy and envious; it suffers from a feeling of inner emptiness and lack of meaning, and it continously seeks confirmation in attention from the other.

Fordham believes that, in cases in which a nucleus of the Self has never developed, a *transference psychosis* must be undergone in order to unify the split personality. This transference psychosis occurs in the analytical relationship when there is a severe regression. According to Fordham, this is distinguished by the appearance of childish impulses, by difficulty in bearing partings and by alterations in the sense of reality aimed at protecting the good-object analyst from envy and rage. Fordham also states that, in the transference psychosis, interpretation would seem less important than the constant presence of the analyst with his function of control.

However I feel that, whether we speak of narcissistic transference or of transference psychosis, the emergence of the Self, its integration in the personality as an ego ideal and the formation of a new identity all depend on the activation of the transcendental function, that is to say, of the symbolic capacity which conveys the cultural assimilation of unconscious contents. This is why the occurence within the analytical container of an imaginative game of introverted reflection which, as Jung suggested, should be maintained "within the frame of traditional mythology", is an essential therapeutic factor. By protecting the patient from his envy and rage by means of the countertransference, and by encouraging him to face the frustration of his exhibitionistic needs, we do indeed help him overcome the compulsive tendency to inflation. Thus, the archetypal factors can unfold in a positive way in the form of creative imagination.

# On the Role of the Isis/Osiris Myth and of the Egyptian Book of the Dead in the Treatment of a Case of Pathological Mourning

Pierre Solié (Paris)

"Myth", Jung tells us in *Psychology and Education*[1], "is an attempt of the unconscious to save consciousnes from a regression that threatens it. It has a therapeutic value because it gives an adequate expression to the dynamism on which rests the complexity of the individual. In that, it is not the result of a causally explainable personal complex, but on the contrary, an expression of archetypal mechanisms that predate the development of individual consciousness."

The clinical case which I would like to consider is an illustration of the validity of this point of view.

Laure was referred to me by her uncle, who was a colleague and a friend of mine. She was twenty-four years old and was studying psychology while working in a center for young drug addicts. I should say, rather, that she was attempting to work, as it turned out that she was in the process of becoming more and more depressed, "empty", feeling herself pulled down into an abyss peopled by monsters. She felt fragmented; each stimulus, external or internal, was experienced as a part of herself, separate from the others and from the outside world. She remained aware of these phenomena even though she felt confused and deperson-alized when they became more acute.

All these symptoms, though of a psychotic nature, did not constitute a psychosis, but an intermediary state often called "borderline". Her dreams – be they daydreams or those that occurred during her sleep –

[1] C. W. vol. 17.

circled around the phenomenon of death; the death of her mother nine years earlier and for whom she still mourned.

Her mourning took the form of a "loss of soul"; she felt empty, fragmented and depersonalized. But when Laure reconnected to her "soul" in the form of the presence in herself of her resurrected mother, all these symptoms became reversed. She felt herself to be in a state of fullness and exaltation, and had playful fantasies and dreams.

In short, to put a name to this pathological state, one would speak in her case of a manic-depressive borderline syndrome.

The loss of her mother put her in a state of hypo-melancholia; her return, in a hypo-manic state.

During those nine years, and especially during the months that preceded her work with me, Laure struggled desperately to recapture the presence that fulfilled her. Everything was pressed into service toward this end: mementos, photographs, memories, tapes of her mother's voice made two days before her death, places where they had been together, in other words, an imaginary circuit of the realm that lies beyond death itself; this we will consider again, as it is what started me on the path of the Book of the Dead of the ancient Egyptians and of the myth which lies at its root.

Laure had had an absent father. Sick, he spent the best part of his time painting faces of Christ and of clowns. A year after his wife's death, he remarried; his second wife was a friend of the family with whom Laure, then sixteen years old, could not establish a feeling relationship of any depth. What is more, she was unable to forgive her father for what she saw as an adulterous relationship. It was at that time that she began to suffer from acne, and it did not yield to any of the usual treatments, but cleared up rapidly after the start of her therapy with me.

When Laure came to me, she had already consulted several Freudian colleagues toward whom she had developed a massive transference and a wish to merge, which the therapists reflected back to her. She either left them, or was gently asked to leave. After our first session, I was tempted to do the same or, even worse, to suggest a possible hospital stay. My friendship with her uncle deterred me from such an action.

At that time, I was myself dealing with the manifestations in me of the Great Mother Goddess and of her Sons/Lovers. It was undoubtedly the true reason that made me accept Laure's total transference, and accept to live out with her this pathological mourning of her mother. Of her mother, and of mine, who had died when I was eleven.

As early as the third session, Laure's descriptions of her visions caught my attention: the walk toward the tomb and the kingdom beyond; the fight against a gigantic, slimy snake; the enormous and threatening doors, and, between them, strange birds with human heads, crocodiles and snakes; wildly growing, threatening plants; mermaids and princes who, on closer look, turned into fetid and slimy matter. Then, suddenly, the Kingdom of "Mommy"; islands, gardens, woods, trees, canals, rushing water, rest, peace, happiness itself.

"I am Mommy and she is me, totally", she used to say. But very soon, everything became petrified, rigid, and Laure found herself back in her stone walls, her arid rocks, her endless emptiness and the monsters that inhabited it.

Where had I heard this specific theme of the Afterlife? Suddenly a revelation, a flash: the Book of the Dead. But which one? The Bardo-Thodol of Tibet or the much older one of the Egyptians? Both, to be sure.

A fundamental difference between them is that the Bardo requires the soul of the dead person – and therefore requires of us – that it, and we, abandon the archetypal images that present themselves to us and which live within us either positively or negatively – because those images represent the illusion (Maya) – of wishes (Karma) – still tied to this world.

The forty-nine days that the Bardo lasts, the intermediary period between life and total death, are spent fighting against the invasion of the persecuting, seductive imaginary which inflates the ego and depersonalizes it. The fate of the soul of the dead depends on the result of this battle. Either the soul will be completely freed from the imaginary Maya, or it will remain its prisoner and will have to go through another incarnation in the drive-ridden body that it had not been able to forego.

The Egyptian Book of the Dead, on the other hand, assures us that these archetypal images have a totally objective – not illusory – reality. Broadly speaking, these images are the same in the two approaches to the afterlife mentioned here; they include mourning, initiation and freedom from death "now".

But in one of those two, it is necessary to confront and fight them in order to free oneself from them; in the other, what is necessary is to go beyond them through a conscious confrontation with the imaginary "maya-like" illusion, thus opening the way to a new level of illusion which is no longer quite an illusion. Along with Henry Corbin, I call this consciousness "imaginal".

The *imaginary* does not allow any distance to the images; they take over the ego, leading to madness and eventually to death. The *imaginal* places between the images and the ego a conscious "subject" that can hold them at a distance and eventually play with them in what Winnicot called the playing and imaginary space, and the Greeks had called the metaxic space.

I understood then, that the way my Freudian counterparts had chosen for Laure resembled the "dry" way of the Bardo-Thodol, without referring to it, I imagine. What Laure so much needed was the "moist" way of the ancient Egyptians.

It was vital for her to believe in the objective reality of these images of the "intermediary period". Only they would need to be transformed from imaginary drives that lived in her and alienated her, into an imaginal confrontation Spirit/Drive and thus given some distance through the mediation of a third principle: a subject. Otherwise the stage would be left to the depressive, depersonalizing void or to the ego-inflating mania. In order to survive, she needed to recover the image of her dead mother, still caught in the intermediary Bardo-like stage, so that she would be able at the same time to find her own identity, her own ego, now merged with, and absorbed by, her mother. She needed to travel, along with her mother's soul, the way of the dead and, especially, to go through the Doors of the Kingdom of Osiris to reach the room of the weighing of the soul/heart (Ba/Ab) and to undergo there the judgement of Osiris, followed by her eventual liberation and "osirinization", or her possible condemnation, psychosis and death in the fearsome maw of the Devourer of Hell who awaits her victims next to the scale.

I asked Laure what she knew of these two Books of the Dead. She knew nothing of their existence, the Passion of Christ being the only Book of the Dead to which her Christian upbringing had exposed her. But, through her dreams, she showed the resurrection of the dead and mummified body of her mother – a resurrection which, in turn, would resurrect her own soul, masculine animus and feminine Ka-double – taking place in the crucible of the maternal body; in other words, in the image of the mother with which she merges.

Either Laure loses this "womb" and is thrown into hell (emptiness, depression, feeling scattered), or she finds it again and rises into Paradise (fullness, elation, at-oneness). She cannot move out of this

Manichean split between good and bad objects. She cannot join them by relativizing her idealizations, positive (good objects, mania), as well as negative (bad objects, depression). The absence of mother sends her back to the negative side of the mother archetype, to the bad mother who, instead of giving life, destroys it in infernal torments; to the Devourer of the judgement of Osiris. There is no boundary between the lost body of the mother and her won. She remains in a typical universe of primary narcissism, where the existence of the Other is excluded. The acceptance of the Other would separate her from such primary narcissism by giving her autonomy and bringing about the birth of an ego with which to relate to the Self – shattering in her the original Oneness of the universe – even if this Oneness is split between heaven and hell. What is missing is earth to mediate the heaven/hell dichotomy and to reduce the grandiosity of the original split to a human dimension.

Laure leaves the Kingdom of the Dead (depression) only to enter into the Kingdom of the everlastingly living (mania). Between them there is no "spinal cord", no Djed Pillar – spine of Osiris – resurrected from the dead by his soul-sister Isis.

Laure had not known this erect pillar. Her father, who could, or should, have incarnated it, had not taken on that role. So much so, that Laure's fantasies as a child put her in the position of husband to her mother – an inverted Oedipal triangle, except that one cannot properly speak of an Oedipal constellation at such an archaic level. Laure is not the daughter/lover of the father, but she is, through the animus, the son/lover of the mother. She endlessly self-begets herself in her mother's womb much like the sons/lovers of the old mythologies of the Great Mother: Tammuz, Dummuzi, Marduke in Mesopotamia, Adonis in Phoenicia, Attis in Asia Minor and, of course, Osiris in Egypt.

Even though Laure has homosexual tendencies, she is not homosexual, nor is she unfeminine; as she is not really psychotic, so is she not really homosexual. She cannot break the repetition compulsion which ties her to the womb of her first birth – her mother – but what she is searching for is the womb of her second birth; in other words, a mother no longer imaginary (drives), but imaginal (spiritual), who would assume for her the symbolic mediation between a lowered heaven and an elevated hell.

Paradoxically, as she wished herself husband to her mother, so she was asking me – a substitute for her absent father – to play the part of the mother of second birth, the part played in the Egyptian myth by the Goddess Isis – my anima. She herself is in the role of Osiris her animus – dead, scattered and strewn over the surface of the earth of Upper and Lower Egypt.

Once I had understood this, I trusted myself, rightly or wrongly, to share some of these elements with Laure, starting with what Jung called amplification of the pattern of her dreams.

From then on, one might ask which one of us – Laure or myself – did the therapy. I would say that we both did; I was only ahead of her. But she forced me to elaborate, day by day, blow by blow, the practical and theoretical aspects needed in her case and in mine. The archetypes would be our guides instead of the personal complexes already labeled by others. Fortunately, we also had what preceded consciousness; by this, I mean the myths.

If Laure is Osiris and forces me to be for "him" her Isis of second birth, then let us trust the myth to guide us. It sustained Egyptian civilization for more than three thousand years; it spilled over to Greece, to Rome and to the early years of Christianity.

I will not, at this point, retell the myth of Isis and Osiris. I will only emphasize two of its elements:

1) The penis of Osiris was eaten by fishes of the Nile and lost forever; this forced Isis to replace it with a Holy Phallus of rebirth, before which she bowed and which she taught all of Egypt to worship. We will call it, with Jung, her animus.

2) Osiris, reconstituted though castrated, is resurrected by Isis and becomes the God of the Underworld of second birth, in other words, a kind of mother of second birth. This womb of rebirth I will call, with Jung, the anima.

The Egyptian Book of the Dead is somewhat less known than the myth on which it is based. I will only say two things about it:

1) The first night in the Kingdom of the Dead is described as the phase of darkness for the soul of the dead; the soul follows in total unconsciousness the path of Ra – the sun – for whose rebirth at dawn Osiris labors. The soul follows it and is reborn with it to travel the sky of the day in a phase that one could call manic.

2) The second night in the Kingdom of Osiris, named the "going in after the coming forth", forces this same soul to face the perils that Laure described in her depressive phase. The soul is able to face those perils because of the knowledge it has of the prayers and the sayings of the Book of the Dead inspired by the Isis-Osiris myth. It is during those

encounters that the soul undergoes, among other things, the judgement of Osiris, the famous scale on which rest the heart/soul on one side, and the feather of Justice, the goddess Maat, on the other. Through this judgement, the soul is either washed of its faults and enters into the field of the Blessed (or field of reeds), or is condemned to everlasting damnation in the maw of the Egyptian Leviathan, Apep, Seth or the devouring Sekhmet.

To return now to Laure: When she first came to me, Laure was still unconsciously in the first night (depressed state) and the first day (manic state), these phases taking place on a background of schizoparanoid fantasies. She had not started the "going in after the coming forth". She had not started the dialogue with the guardian of the bark of Ra-Osiris during the second night. She had already contacted Hathor-Isis – the mother reborn in herself and her fields of reeds and of peace – but it was only in her manic state. She had not conquered them by consciously facing the last judgement of Osiris/Maat and the twelve hours of the second night of the Dead. This is what she proceeded to do quite rapidly.

The clinical evolution went through three stages.

1) The second collective birth. At my request, Laure began to read and to study the Egyptian Book of the Dead. This was, for me, a unique case in which I barely intervened.

Spontaneously during each session – and we met four and five times a week at first – she stretched out on the sofa and covered herself up with the various pillows that were on it. Like Osiris in his sarcophagus, or in his frozen field, she rejoined her mother in Hell (Duat and Amenta) and with her faced "fire throwing" Apep. Lying there covered, she moved in darkness between the coils of the monster; she protected herself from the human-headed birds (Ba) and the strange goddesses carrying the pupils of Horus in their hands. She viewed the fourteen mounds of the dead gods and turned them into sanctuaries for Osiris. She found the fourteen parts of the "frozen" gods and recreated the castrated god. Then, like Isis, she raised for him a triumphant phallus before which she worshipped, and from which she was able to differentiate herself, without losing its presence in her soul. She endowed it with a "face of glory" which she no longer desperately needed to find in every man – starting with me.

There she also built him a womb of second birth by facing up to his judgement. Her confession took an active, affirmative form; she displayed all her small perversions, exhibitionism and homosexuality among them. I was barely able to contain an exhibitionistic episode quite "out of the pillows". But these small perversions, these partial drives, were lived out more or less symbolically during the sessions and were the promise that her scattered being was being reconstituted.

Absolved of her sins, her Ba-Ab (heart-soul) having finally weighed less than the feather of Maat on the scale of the ultimate tribunal, she was saved from the death mother, the devouring one who awaited her with her jaws open.

Then I – my anima – became the one who, Isis-like, took over the task of being her mother of rebirth in the underworld. "You're becoming Mommy", she said to me. "That allows me to merge and, paradoxically, it allows me a certain distancing, because, by projecting Mommy on you, I free myself from her." I therefore became, like Osiris, her womb of second birth allowing her a second gestation in Amenta-Hell. In the same way, I had become her phallus of second birth, allowing her a second fecundation in Amenta-Heaven. In fact, I had, in turn, played all the parts of the God Osiris and of his sister/lover Isis as they were needed in the course of the various months, days or hours…

She was then able to differentiate herself from this womb of second birth before which she bowed, as she had bowed before the phallus, without losing it in her soul, because she no longer wanted it in the same way.

She gave this womb, too, a "face of glory" which she no longer needed to find in every woman she met, starting with herself, as she had located it now in a different place, an imaginal one.

2) The second phase of the therapy was that of the second birth of lineage and synchronicity. Laure was from the nobility and had two different names: Laure de X de Y. The second of those names had struck me, as it had been the name of the village where I was born until the name was slightly altered in the seventeenth; as, for example, a change from Beaumont to Belmont. Two days before I was to go away for my vacation, Laure, who had now been in therapy with me for about a year, asked me where I was going. I told her, to a small village whose name would most probably mean nothing to her. She insisted and I gave her the name of the village. She jumped to her feet almost screaming: "It's my village! My name is the one it had until the seventeenth century." I feared the explosion of a delusion, but the following day, she brought me her family tree and I had to recognize the truth of her assertions. Her family, ennobled by Louis XIV, had since

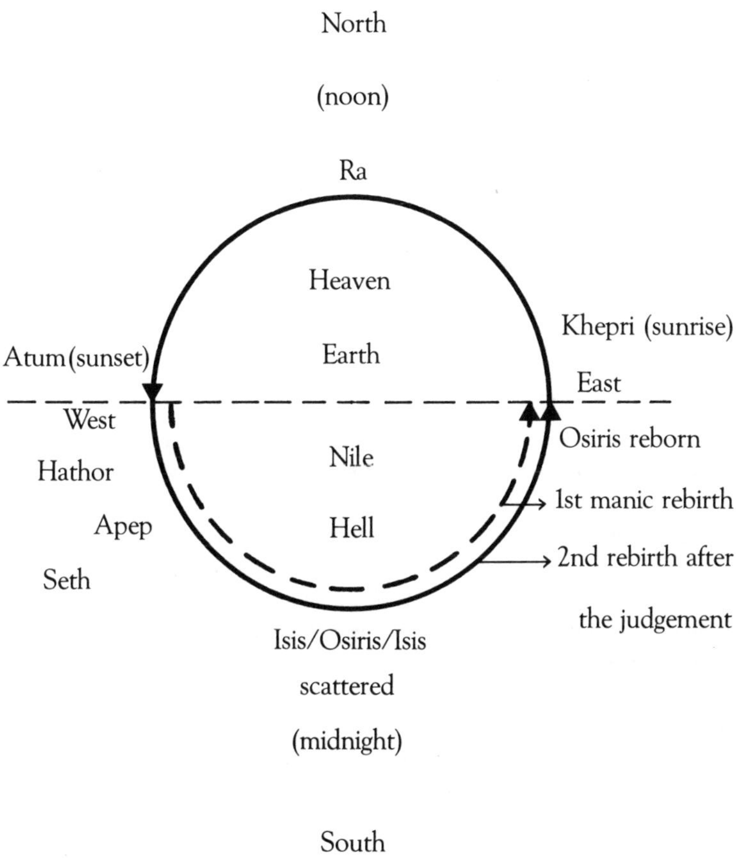
North
(noon)
Ra
Heaven
Earth
Khepri (sunrise)
Atum (sunset)
East
West
Osiris reborn
Hathor
Nile
1st manic rebirth
Apep
Hell
2nd rebirth after
Seth
the judgement
Isis/Osiris/Isis
scattered
(midnight)
South

left the village in the south of France and moved north. Laure had never gone there.

A year later, while I was there on vacation, I allowed her to come and we together undertook the pilgrimage to the source of her family, including the land itself from which she derived her name.

Strange coincidence, stranger even than the one that had brought her to me at a time when, hoping for a glimpse of what Jung called individuation, I was in the process of wrestling with the archetype of the Great Mother of death and rebirth.

Strange coincidence, also, that the apartment in which she had spent her childhood up to the time of her mother's death had been in close proximity to the one I then occupied and which I left at about the same time.

3) The second birth on the individual level. Laure wanted me to go and see that apartment with her and to help her to recreate its nooks and crannies in order to reconstitute the parts of her personality which were scattered and left behind in it, along with her dead mother.

I did not accede to her request.

Then, she recreated the place on paper, and many sessions were occupied with this endeavor. She even brought her older brother with her, asking him to verify before me the accuracy of her reconstitution and to throw light on some obscure or forgotten points.

In the same way, she brought to my office and left with me numerous objects that had belonged to her mother, much like the amulets that were placed in the wrappings of the mummy and in the sarcophagus. We looked at pictures of her mother; we listened several times to the tape of her mother's voice. I read her childhood essays that had to do with her family; I looked at the drawings she had done during that time of her life. Then, as she did not recognize herself in mirrors, I took a mirror and together we studied her image until she began, little by little, to recognize it as seen in my eyes and mirrored back to her.

For over three years now, she has been working part-time in an institution for physically handicapped children, living with one foot in ancient Egypt and one in the contemporary western world. Perhaps she will one day let go of the Egyptian imaginal world, if I let go of it myself – but it is such a strengthening presence in our desiccated civilization! Even if it is only a picture book to us, if we contemplate those pictures with the eye of Horus, we experience their power.

# The Partner Relationship in Individual Analysis: The Symbolic and Concrete Approach*

Hans-Joachim Wilke (Berlin)

The English version of the theme of the Ninth International Congress of the International Association for Analytical Psychology includes the word 'approach'; and to characterise our practical and theoretical work on the human psyche as an approach is most appropriate, as the Latin word from which the English word derives, *appropinquare,* to approach something, suggests that what is approached is not something merely concrete and objective. In the Vulgate, for example, James 4, 8 reads: *Appropinquate deo et appropinquabit vobis,* translated by Luther as *Nahet Euch zu Gott, so nahet Er sich zu Euch* – "Approach God and He will approach you" ("Draw nigh to God and he will draw nigh to you", in the Authorised Version).

The theme of the Congress specifies that there are at least two modalities in our approach: one more clinical, the other more symbolic, the use of which depends on the demands of the symptoms which have been constellated. I take 'clinical approach' in the sense of a concrete and specifically medical attitude towards the suffering of the patient, an attitude evoked by that suffering. A symbolic approach, on the other hand, is primarily psychological, an attempt to understand the sense, meaning and aim, a search for what is hidden below the surface, in order to make the complexities of the patient's neurosis comprehensible.

* Reprinted by permission of *The Journal of Analytical Psychology.* This article originally appeared in Vol. 29, No. 3 (July 1984).

It seems important to me that both these modalities of the therapeutic approach are neither specifically psychoanalytic nor specifically Jungian, but are, and always have been, deeply rooted in medical practice. I do not regard this as our tradition which excludes non-medical colleagues, but rather as one which has included them in both aspects from, it may be said, earliest times.

When dealing with pain and chronic suffering, doctors in the past treated and regarded the sick organ as having a symbolic reference, in that a diseased leg, for example, could appear in the sufferer's dreams; to understand diseased organs as representing factors in the relationship with the therapist seems to me an important means of helping to bring about relief, especially in cases of chronic, incurable suffering, in organic medicine as well as in psychotherapy. The problems in dealing with such suffering were highlighted by C. T. Frey in a paper read at the Rome Congress (Frey 3, p. 132).

That is not to say, however, that good doctors neglected the actual, or concrete, clinical care of the patient. Good therapists likewise will always be able to integrate both these aspects of mental suffering, the symbolic and the clinical, spontaneously and without complicated deliberation. At the same time, we know only too well that even the best of us cannot *always* be good therapists, and that we are only too often bad therapists as, for example, when we do not succeed in bringing about integration.

If we focus our attention on the relationships and partnerships of our patients, we can see that when psychotherapy is accused of being hostile to relationships, such as those of marriage and the family, and as tending to destroy a patient's relationships in order to cure the individual, this could be due, in part, to the fact that the clinical and symbolic aspects have been insufficiently integrated. It is true that some analyses fail because of the patient's own neurotic relationships, much as some married couples separate through one partner going into therapy. Under the title of 'Coupling-uncoupling', Robert Stein of Beverly Hills has emphasised the elementary needs for both binding *and* freedom (Stein 10, p. 432). In terms of such a polarity, it is only to be expected that, with or without the effects of therapy, relationships sometimes break up because of the individual urge for freedom, whereas under different conditions the autonomous development of a person will fail because of his, or her, relationships. The ideal of inner freedom within a relationship is a rare and imperfect achievement.

The interacting dynamics of individual and social factors in the development of life are not only complicated and, therefore, hard to understand, but also often surpass the limits of our therapeutic knowledge. We have to admit that the powers that shape our fate lie not only in the neurosis but also in factors which are beyond our present concepts of personality and disease. When we trace back the failure of a relationship or a marriage to the neurosis of one or both partners, our view can only refer to partial aspects. When Faust invoked the 'Spirit of Earth' and felt he was his equal, the Spirit answered, "You come equal to the spirit you comprehend, not to me". The *daemons* of our patients would answer in a similar manner were we to confront them with our own explanations of the dynamics of the development of life.

## I. The symbolic approach to problems of relationship

In spite of such limitations to our understanding, it is, nonetheless, remarkable how frequently the dynamics of a neurosis develop in marital or other partner relationships in such a way as to destroy those relationships, leading to a failure which goes against all conscious intentions. Dreams and images often reveal clearly that the meanings and goals of inner development are quite different from how consciousness understands them. An inner symbolic process demands maturation, individuation and self-determination and the endurance of separation and solitude; it constellates pain and mourning. It is just these experiences, however, which the ego and consciousness try to avoid, either by contriving ever new relationships, or by clinging to relationships which are now out-dated.

*Case example*

A forty-year-old woman entered group therapy with me hoping to become better adapted to her marriage, which had been in difficulties for over ten years, and to prevent an impending separation. Nevertheless, therapy led to divorce.

This woman had great difficulty in understanding and accepting the fact that she had never really wanted and loved the man she had married. She felt ashamed to admit that she had chosen him rather than another, more loving, man (who was, however, physically less attractive) because he looked so 'impressive'. It was quite apparent to her even before marriage, but she denied it, that her future husband was unreliable, unstable, inconsiderate and showed the beginnings of alcohol dependence.

Her husband had never been the 'handsome man' of her dreams; he only looked the part. For fifteen years, he had fought a losing battle against the demand to conform to the inner ideal his wife had of him, and by way of protest, as well as through inclination, had taken increasingly to alcohol, to an extent which finally led to states of delirium and an inability to work.

The patient's ideal of a marriage partner derived from the animus; she had related to the self-image that her father presented – the distant and severe father which she had adored and idealised in childhood. Only later did it become apparent that many traits she attributed to her father-imago were in distinct contrast to what he was in reality.

Her father was a small, slight man whose outward appearance had given him an inferiority complex for which he tried to compensate with obsessional severity, orderliness, pedantry and erect posture. He not only loved his daughter – his only child – but dominated her by inadequate and often sadistic acts of intimidation, acts which had led to the patient's anxiety neurosis. There was the same discrepancy, even to the point of caricature, between the patient's imagos of them and the reality, of both father and husband. This very capable woman, who was solely responsible for managing the practical needs of her family, could only drive her car safely and without anxiety when she was accompanied by her husband. To fulfil this protective function, it was sufficient for her 'handsome husband' to be lying unkempt and blind drunk in the car. In the view of the group, a puppet could have rendered the same service for the patient and would have been less of a burden.

The group's phantasy image of a husband as a puppet brings up, rightly perhaps, a central symbol of the self, already amplified with almost Jungian understanding by Heinrich von Kleist in his story, *Über das Marionettentheater* (Kleist 8); while Hans Dieckmann has contributed an interesting case description in his book, *Träume als Sprache der Seele,* referring to the dream of a young man (Dieckmann 2). There is, however, no space here to develop the relation between this amplificatory material and the dynamics of the group, and to show how aspects of the self can become effective in group therapy.

In spite of his unconscious symbolic function, it was quite apparent that the patient's husband was of no significance, either as a real person, or in any real capacity. He was reduced to being a carrier of projections of patriarchal values and norms, and these enabled the patient to preserve, on the conscious level, a rather childlike, girlish and submissive attitude to him despite her own competence and independence.

What the group and I found so difficult to understand was how factors such as the final separation from the patriarch (long depotentiated), the renunciation of childlike attitudes and dependence (only seemingly existent), the acceptance of responsibility and the endurance of solitude – factors, all of which had been in existence for a long period of time, together with other implications of separation and divorce, should weigh so heavily on the patient, and be charged with so much guilt feeling and so much anxiety about punishment. Again and again she seemed to flee, as it were, to an island of anxious, girlish childlikeness.

It seems to me that often we do not take seriously enough the grief and pain of separation from those neurotic and illusionary islands of childhood, defended with so much strength and energy against the storms of life. Thus we demand too much of our patients, for the reintegration of a delegated mental function always remains a difficult, laborious and painful process. In this case, the incongruous delegation was perfectly apparent and contradictory to the husband's nature, since he was not only expected to live and to incarnate the patient's own weakness, but, at the same time, be the great and handsome man.

After considerable effort, the patient succeeded in making some decisive steps towards individuation. Changes that for fifteen years she had demanded only from her partner, she finally accomplished for herself. Today, in retrospect, almost ten years after her therapy, she realises that the break-up of her marriage was a decisive turning-point in her life.

If we consider this relationship and its chronic failure on the symbolic level, we can speak of it, *inter alia,* as a failure of the process of symbolisation relative to the relationship. Speech is probably the most general and also the most differentiated field in which symbolic processes are projected, a subject examined, for example, by S. Kreitler in an interesting experimental psychological study (Kreitler 9). The poetic use of language, provided we listen carefully and absorb ourselves in the poetic images, enables us, by comparison, to elucidate the failure of relationships on the level of linguistic symbolisation.

Togetherness and steadfastness in love are expressed very simply and naïvely in an old German folksong:

| | |
|---|---|
| *Du bist mîn, ich bin dî,* | Thout art mine, I am thine, |
| *des solt du gewis sîn.* | Of that must thou be sure. |
| *Du bist beslozzen* | Thou art locked |
| *in mînem herzen;* | In my heart; |
| *verlorn is das sluzzelîn* | Lost is the little key |
| *du muost immer drinne sîn* | Within must thou always be |

Very similar is the well-known Beethoven setting of a text about the mutuality of love:

| | |
|---|---|
| *Ich liebe Dich, so wie Du mich* | I love you as you love me |
| *Am Abend und am Morgen.* | In evening and in morning. |
| *Noch war kein Tag, wo Du und ich,* | Nor was there day, nor can there be, |
| *Nicht teilten unsere Sorgen…* | When we shared not our caring… |
| *Gott schütze Dich, erhalt Dich mir,* | God protect you, keep you mine, |
| *Schütz und erhalt uns beide.* | Protect and keep us both. |

And in his twenty-second sonnet, Shakespeare describes the solicitude of love:

Bearing thy heart, which I will keep so chary
As tender nurse her babe from faring ill.

The inner turbulence and sensitive openness of love is expressed in Klabund's version of "Die Verlassene" (The Abandoned), from *Poems of a hundred beautiful women* by Lao Tse:

I am so full of love and moved
By the wind like a tree, full of blossom.

In analyses, too, we come across well-formulated and clear expressions of relatedness. Towards the end of a long analysis dealing with severe problems of symbiotic relationship, a patient said: "Now I can be completely at home with myself – and, at the same time, be completely at home with you", thus signifying a state of inner relatedness and an openness to inner self and outer world which seems to be perfectly in accord with what Judith Hubback meant when she spoke of the need "to need and to relate to him as another person" (translated into German as *Begegnung als ganzer Person,* i.e., as a whole person) (Hubback 4).

Poetry also exemplifies, for the most part in its linguistic images, how and why failures in relationship and love come about in life. Effi Briest, a female literary figure in the writings of Theodor Fontane, says of her husband on her deathbed: "He was so good and honourable, as only a human being without love can be."

The words which my patient used were, likewise, strikingly apt. The deficiency in the entire relationship is documented in terms of her ideal of the 'handsome man' who does not represent love and togetherness, but status, prestige, persona, desire for admiration and similar features, none of which can be considered as a sound basis for marriage. They are the very features that had previously distorted and destroyed her relationship with her parents.

The failure of the relationship – the symbolic process represented its actuality on the one hand, and its meaning and fulfilment on the other – resided not so much in its false and neurotic contents as in the fact that these contents continued to remain unconscious. The dialectical interaction between conscious and unconscious did not take place. Had the patient been able to realise consciously before her marriage that she was attracted only by the 'handsome man' – a rather hollow persona – she might, even at that stage, have been able to renounce her chosen partner.

## II. Conjoint Couple Interviews *(Konfliktpartner-Setting)*: A clinical method for use during crises in relationships and in individual analysis.

The analytical process serves quite another purpose when applied to situations that develop on a more concrete and extraverted level of life, and there is a lack of those inner conditions without which relations cannot be realised. The problem for many people then resides primarily in concrete external circumstances. To add a symbolic meaning, to understand it as the effect of inner processes, does not help the patients at all because the distress caused by the reality situation does not allow them to adopt an introverted attitude. We then have to consider the neurosis in terms of inner and outer conditions and to take the partners seriously as real human beings and as carriers of the conflicts we have to work on.

Such a profound concern with personal and social relationships is implicit in Jung's basic attitude. Jung's most important concept, individuation, is intimately related not only to the human individual but also to society. The individuation process is:

> an internal and subjective process of integration and… it is an equally indispensable process of objective relationship (Jung 6, para. 448). For without the conscious acknowledgement and acceptance of our fellowship with those around us there can be no synthesis of personality (Jung 6, para. 444).

With regard to this aspect of relationship, I have learned after many years of experience, often threatening, to adapt my methods in order to deal with these difficult and critical conflictual situations. When individual analysis brings up dangerous crises in relationships, I introduce a method that I call the 'Conjoint Couple Interview' *(Konfliktpartner-Setting)* (Wilke 11).

Provided we work exclusively or predominantly within the setting of personal analysis, the alchemical metaphor of the *vas hermeticum* can be taken as an acceptable image for the protective sphere of the analytical situation in which disturbances and outside influences are safely excluded.

Situations arise, however, when I have to integrate relatives or partners into this *vas hermeticum* if a failure in the analysis is to be prevented or its potentiality considerably reduced.

In addition, changes in the relationship between the patient and his partner can be constellated which are decisive for the inner development of both, not only in the transference. In terms of the *vas hermeticum*, I have learned not only to take the *bene clausum*, the 'sealing off', aspect into consideration, but also the 'openness', indispensable if additional ingredients or catalysts are to be introduced into the analysis.

Medical ethics play an important rôle here; they are deeply rooted in medico-legal systems enshrined in the Hippocratic oath (Kleeberg 7). It is difficult to reconcile this with the other extreme, which is part of the analytical code of practice and which demands honesty and openness. It is only when our silence and discretion is based on fundamental human integrity that we can hope that the shadow will not be dragged out of talkative gossip.

I am, therefore, if necessary, always prepared to concentrate entirely on the relationship and its conflicts and, should the situation require it, to give a seat in the consulting room to the partner most involved in those conflicts.

I will now briefly summarise the conditions and requirements for such a situation:

1. Any long-standing relationship of a problematic nature contains a pathogenic complex; for example, a projective mechanism, the basis of the patient's conflict, which binds him, or her, through neurotic symptoms to a partner and which is the source of further material producing conflict. Sometimes the conflict escalates to the point of murderous, or suicidal tendencies. In these instances, the psychopathology is charac-

terised for the most part by unusually fixed or static projections or by a dissociation of contents, which are frequently the consequences of early object dissociations or object losses.

2. During an introductory phase of at least three months, the fruitfulness of this approach should already be evident. Not until I have in phantasy, and perhaps also in dreams, made myself familiar with the situation as it affects the three people concerned (analyst, analysand and partner) do I inform the patient of my approach, so that he can give it adequate thought. If the patient can accept the approach, and after he has worked through the characteristic hopes, anxieties and dangers (for example, the danger of collusion), he may then submit it to the partner, who can begin to work on it in the same way. New impulses may flow into the imaginative processes of both partners which enables them, even at this early stage, to look at their differences in a more constructive light so that they can initiate the 'Setting' of their own accord, or even dispense with it.

I will deal with only a few aspects of how such therapy is carried out.

1. First the partner of the patient is given the opportunity to present his views of the problem. It is not long before the patient intervenes, correcting the partner and defending his own views which, hitherto, had been the only ones presented. As often as not, it takes only a few words before both partners engage in a quarrel such as they never dared risk at home, giving vent to outbursts of violence seldom encountered during the working through of such projections in their individual and group therapy. In this situation, the therapist seems to act as guarantor that the destructive impulses will not be acted out and result in physical violence.

The quarreling partners force upon the therapist, often with much vehemence, the rôle of referee, a rôle which could endanger the setting since, in this situation, neither judgement nor condemnation are demanded. The function required is that of a mediator, one who takes a neutral stance, an interpreter who can throw a bridge over the abyss of misunderstanding.

2. Temporal limitations and thematic centralisation make analytical work of this kind similar to focal therapy. It is often evident that both partners are participating in the same pathogenic complex, taking up complementary rôles which, once accessible, they can then work through jointly. A depressive phase, for example, gives rise in both partners to deep-rooted and regressive longings for security and depen-

dence. Each expects of the other a maternal abundance, and in the reliving of early genetic experiences, the image of the withholding, retaining bad breast is mutually revived. Both partners display reactions of disappointment, rage and biting remarks, no possible understanding of which can be achieved without the help of the therapist.

3. As regards the organising of sessions, I offer in most cases a double session every week or every second week. Five to ten, or twenty or twenty-five such sessions over a period of six to eighteen months are sufficient to bring the relationship out of its stagnant phase and to stimulate a development which will lead either to a reconciliation or to a separation. After the termination of partner therapy, it is often difficult for the patient to readjust to exclusively individual analysis, which is carried on at the same time as the partner therapy, though with a reduced number of weekly sessions.

When the third person – the partner – joins the therapy and later leaves, I find this rocks the boat for a time. But it also becomes clear that the more direct dealings in the intermediate phases of the Conjoint Couple Interview sessions can be extremely profitable.

4. The violence and destructiveness of the partner's confrontations have often aroused in me extreme apprehension and anxiety, and this made it clear that I was neither so strong, nor so conflict-prone as I had thought myself to be. But it also taught me that the human psyche can develop a greater capacity for forgiveness and for making good, even after quite seriously destructive and harmful quarrels, than I had previously believed possible. In my opinion, these aspects of analytical psychology are all too rarely discussed, though much depends on them in our work. It was, therefore, a valuable personal experience to have had to expose myself to the pressures of destructive and, on occasion, even murderous conflicts.

To complete the picture, we also have to understand the symbolic meaning of the clinical setting. With careful preparation, we invite the partners to an *opus* both risky and dangerous. If all goes well, a small part of Christian Rosencreutz's 'Chemical Marriage' can be realised and the partners transformed into the 'Royal Couple', understanding that process in our modern terms of transformation and relationship. The rôle of the therapist would then be, to express it in the terminology of an ancient text, that of the virgin who invites the other to become her partner, to participate in the mystery (Andreae 1).

## III. Combining or separating the clinical and symbolic approaches

I began with, and have tried to follow, both the clinical and symbolic approaches, and I believe that both aspects are represented in and among us to a greater or lesser degree. If, on the one hand, there is the so-called clinician, slightly inclined, perhaps, towards positivism and more strongly extraverted, who cultivates the technical side of our work, there is also, on the other hand, the analyst, probably more introverted and more strongly interested in symbolic meanings, for whom even good clinical results would never be wholly satisfactory unless he had gained a sufficient understanding of the effective forces and symbols involved. In this paper I have presented, first, my attempts to deal with a relationship in which the potential symbolic functioning was pathological through being reduced to a merely allegorical level. Second, and as regards the clinical aspect, I presented my Conjoint Couple Interview, which I have developed by experiment, refinement, experience and critical judgement. And this, too, is a part of our craft.

Unlike the medical practice, we do not differentiate between clinicians and 'symbolists' but between clinicians and theorists; but in this sense, our symbolic approach is not only theoretical but also clinical. My Conjoint Couple Interview cannot be purely a clinical procedure, for it is only through an understanding of the symbolic meaning of what is taking place in relationships that any positive result can be obtained. We have thus reached the point where differentiation between these two aspects no longer seems feasible. That is to say, effective therapy can only be both clinical and symbolic – it must integrate both aspects. If these aspects are split too widely apart, if they are too one-sidedly divided up between different therapeutic personalities, the scope of our work will be impaired.

These two approaches, the clinical and the symbolic, also represent the relation of the general and abstract to the individual and concrete; and I surmise that, while the clinician within and among us has a better relationship to the concrete and the individual, the 'symbolist' can obtain a better understanding of the general. Jung exemplified this when he wrote:

> There are, as we all know, no universal elephants, only individual elephants. But if a generality, constant plurality, of elephants did not exist, a single individual elephant would be exceedingly improbable (Jung 5, para. 1).

We cannot experience the symbolic dimension and its actual content without a sufficient understanding of the concrete and the individual, and, vice-versa, the concrete gains its meaning only through symbolic understanding. There is a dialectical and interdependent relationship between them.

Thus, as regards my case examples and methodology, I could equally well have used them the other way round. I could have used the example of the woman patient and made a clinical methodology the object of the discussion within the procedure of a group, just as much as I could have used the Conjoint Couple Interview to demonstrate the symbolic dimension of marital strife.

Where human relationships are concerned, the concrete realisation in external reality is as important as symbolic meaning and significance. Both aspects are effective and real, and in successful relationships cannot be separated nor sometimes even distinguished from one another. Moreover, unless we enter into relationship with serious intent, our understanding can only be theoretical, so that we can easily remain in the realm of abstraction and even of narcissism.

Both analytical psychology and Jung himself, from the earliest beginnings, strongly emphasised the therapeutic importance of the relationship as opposed to the more technical and methodological approaches of other schools. This applies also to our training, for without the personal relationship of analyst and supervisor, analytical psychology cannot be taught or learned. Were this thread of personal tradition severed, the living content of analytical psychology and psychoanalysis would have to be recovered from our libraries, and this seems hardly possible. In the guise of modern science, as in other little known disciplines, something of that early personal tradition, predominant up to the Middle Ages, still survives.

To distinguish between the two aspects – the clinical and the symbolic – can be meaningful only if they are thereby brought together, and that integration gives a really fair chance to relationships in therapy and in personal life.

## Summary

In the first part, a short case example is given to show how the neurotic symbolic function of one partner leads to a failure in relationship and marriage. The first steps to individuation become possible after freedom from neurotic symbolisation has been achieved. In the second part, the Conjoint Couple Interview *(Konfliktpartner-Setting)*, a clinical method for use when crises of relationship arise during a personal analysis, is described. Finally, it is clearly shown that, while a distinction can be made between the clinical and symbolic approaches, they are ultimately inseparably linked in all fruitful therapeutic work.

## References


1. Andreae, J.V. (1616). *Die Chymische Hochzeit.* Munich, O.W.Barth-Verlag, 1957.
2. Dieckmann, H. (1972). *Träume als Sprache der Seele.* Stuttgart. Bonz.
3. Frey-Wehrlin, C.T. (1978). 'Behandlung chronischer Psychosen.' *Analytische Psychologie,* 9, 2, p.132.
4. Hubback, J. (1983). 'Depressed patients and the *coniunctio.*' *J. analyt. Psychol.,* 28, 4. See also this volume, pp.37ff.
5. Jung, C.G. (1935). 'Principles of practical psychotherapy.' *Coll. Wks,* 16.
6. – (1946). 'The psychology of the transference.' *Coll. Wks,* 16.
7. Kleeberg, J. (1979). *Eide und Bekenntnisse in der Medizin.* Basel. Karger.
8. Kleist, H. von (1810). *Über das Marionettentheater.* Gesammelte Werke, Vol I. Leipzig. Insel Verlag.
9. Kreitler, S. (1965). *Symbolschöpfung und Symbolerfassung.* Munich/ Basel. Reinhardt-Verlag.
10. Stein, R.M. (1980). 'Coupling-Uncoupling', in J. Beebe (Ed.), *The Proceedings of the 8th Annual Congress for Analytical Psychology.* Fellbach-Oeffingen. Bonz.
11. Wilke, H-J. (1981). 'Die Beziehungskrise in der Einzelanalyse.' *Analytische Psychologie,* 12, 3.

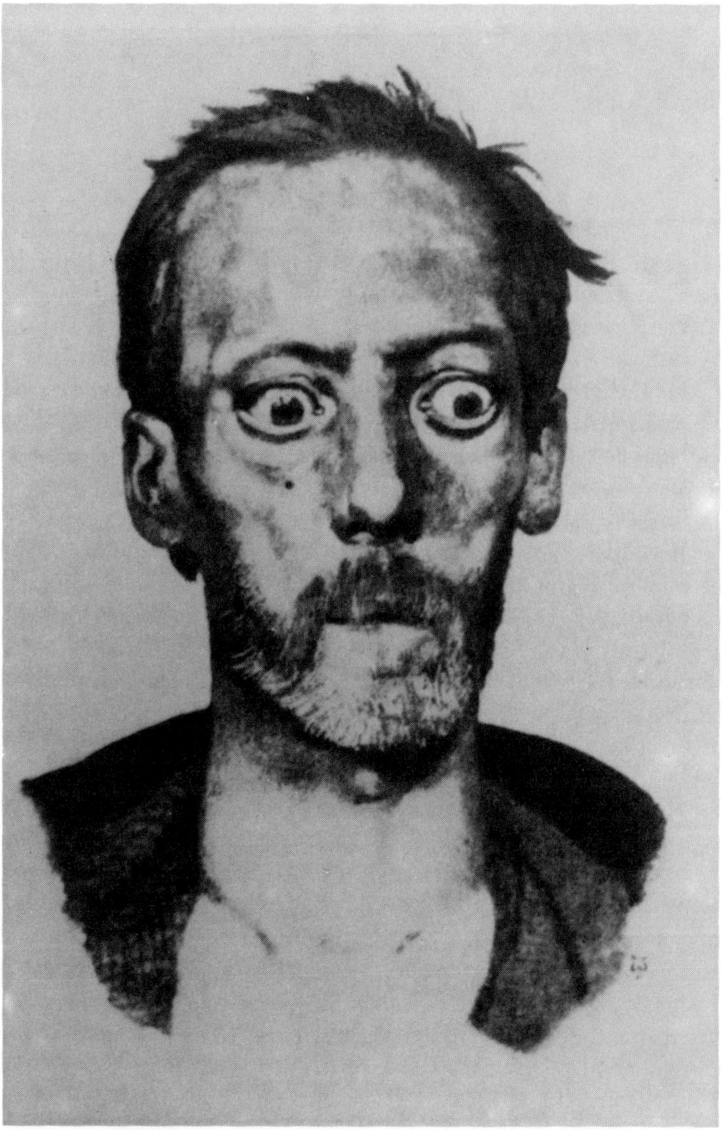

*Basedow'sche Krankheit* from: E. Bramwell, 1891, published in: Das Bild der Kranken, H. Vogt, Bergmann Verlag, München, 1980.

# *Horroris Morbus*
# Unit of Disease and Image of Ailing*

Alfred J. Ziegler (Zürich)

It was not a foregone conclusion that the Western World would be as scientifically minded as it turned out to be. Used in the broadest sense of the term, *the spirit of craftsmanship,* the manual arts, which for our purpose may be equated with scientific method, might not have evolved beyond its harmless inceptions. After the event, it looks as though we were caught up in some kind of collective madness, embued with the same superbity and delusionary certainty which we are accustomed to find in all types of delusions. At this stage, it is as if this madness had no valid competitor on the wide-open hunting grounds of presentday culture; justified, as it were by so-called objective necessity, it seems to stalk our lives persistently – following the image of progress. Inherent in the scientific method is the fact that its products are also characterized by haughtiness and must per force "ride on high". Irrespective of whether they are small or large, simple or sophisticated, they are always mere constructs – to be developed and improved upon at will. Mathematics is *a priori* part and parcel of such products, inasmuch as the mental movement involved in mathematics is also highly "stilted": no matter how much it may have developed, it still reckons on and with the fingers. It continues to digitalize. Moreover, to justify itself and its constructs, the scientific mind uses another method, germane to the spirit inherent in it: statistics. The word is derived from the Latin word *stare,* meaning "to stand", "to remain standing", "to per-sist", and other things along the same lines. Immaculately conceived by the scientific method, statistics would then be the craft which figures out to what extent a construct may be able to "sub-sist", or to "stand up".

* Translation Ruth E. Horine

Inspired by the same high-mindedness, the scientific method also managed to turn medicine into something that "stands up", a structure; and what used to be undefined forms of ailing became *statistical units of disease.* They became constructs, composed of an ever increasing number of building elements. It is striking that they never form a whole but remain statistically correlated sums of these very elements – to be enlarged upon *ad libidum.*

Although it was often assumed that, with the inclusion of the so-called mental element, the units of disease had been substantially enriched by something that was qualitatively different, they remained unchanged in nature. For, all the psychic elements which were added to the existing constructs simply got their own slots in the scientific system. No material (physical), or psychic element can be determinant for the unit of disease; only the scientific spirit within us could conceive of such a notion.

Moreover, what has been said so far applies not only to diagnostics, but also to etiology: the units of disease preserve the cumulative nature of an artful construct, even if a so-called cause, such as a bacterium, or a pathogenic mother, can be held responsible. And ultimately, the units of disease preserve the nature of a construct, despite the fact that we may know how to "handle", or treat them, as, for example, with drugs, or by psychological means. Both as regards etiology and treatment they remain proud constructs of our scientific mind, the products of craftsmanship in the broadest sense of the word.

In order to make the vision of the mad catholicity of medical scientism more meaningful, I should like to recall how the *morbus Basedow* was discovered. Often this is quite a spectacular disease of the thyroid which is caused by an over-production of thyroxin, the hormone of the thyroid gland. In 1840 Karl Adolf von Basedow described the structure of the disease for the first time in the "Wochenschrift für die gesamte Heilkunde". According to his findings, it consisted of three pathological elements, namely, bulging eyes, rapid pulse and a soft, diffuse goiter. A little later, this triad was complemented by Basedow's addition of nearly all the major symptoms of the illness named after him: tremor of the hands, perspiration, diarrhoea, loss of weight, febrility, loss of hair and shortness of breath.

At first, Basedow's published work was ignored; but as of 1860, a flood of complementary material began to appear. For one thing, the mortal danger of the disease was discovered along with a wide range of psychic symptoms and mental causes: general agitation accompanied by insomnia, a bizarre aversion to heat, and finally, phenomena that are reminiscent of schizophrenia, such as paranoid thinking and hallucinations. The disease was observed to occur after a shock, and also in connection with excessive dependence on the parents, after loss of relationship, or in cases of inadequate sexual adaptation.

Be that as it may, in the 140 years that have elapsed since then, medical efforts attached themselves almost exclusively to the scientific approach, i.e., the *logos of craftmanship:* they contributed to the accumulation of a remarkable body of knowledge about a statistical unit of disease, and no doubt we would look upon the creative accomplishments of our forebears and contemporaries with great pride were it not for the sneaking suspicion that perhaps the descendants of Tantalus also attended the act of creation.

For, owing to the fact that scientific-mindedness managed to hold Western man in its spell to an extent which can hardly be assessed, the meaning of its constructs has been watered down correspondingly. The miracles of science – including those of medical science – have become commonplace. Just as flying, which was nothing but a dream once upon a time, has become an everyday activity, so the miracles of the Bible have become trivialities of daily life. Notwithstanding its successful diligence, medicine is suffering increasingly from a kind of chlorosis, which it shares with all thc other branches of science. This anemia is a late variation of occidental nihilism, which began with the Enlightenment, i.e., a period of especially great progress.

For example, at the outset, the etiological, diagnostic and therapeutic research into Basedow's disease was endowed with an elitist sense of honor, whereas in this day and age, it is likely that only those who think along the lines of Nietsche's eternal yesteryears can keep alive the spirit of the founding fathers. Today we know of no fewer than 50 thyroid diseases, each of which is liable to call for hundreds of examinations: clinical tests of the metabolism, the blood circulation, the central nervous system and the muscular system; endocrinological laboratory tests, calorimetric and psychopathological examinations, immunological and histological investigations, etc., etc....

All things considered, this should lead to increased admiration of modern medical science, were it not for a dim feeling that, unwittingly, *medicine is entering a kind of no-man's-land;* that it had in fact resided there before and owed its successes to the very barrenness of the land. At the same time, it is also as if we had reached a point where we would be quite prepared to forego these successes, fraught with promises but leading strictly nowhere, in order to look for life in our very illnesses.

Ladies and Gentlemen, *illnesses come to life on the yonder side of the scientific stance, in imaginative reflection,* unwitting awe, or even in diffident delight, to use – frivolously to be sure – Kant's phraseology describing the enjoyment of art; here illness is no longer an open-ended construct but a closed Gestalt, a mythologem incarnate.

It is as if in a *diagnosis by image,* something of the original meaning of the word "image" caught hold of us: the imitation (from the Latin imitare) of a figure (by sorcerers) to cast a spell, i.e., a magic force. Whereas the diseases appear out of reach, as if hidden behind an invisible veil, surrendering, as it were, meekly to our machinations when looked upon from the scientific stance, they reveal themselves with suddenness when we gaze at them non-intentionally. Their nature unfolds and what has previously been inaccessible becomes palpable. This applies to the patient as well as the person who is prepared to offer help. And both become permeable to each other in the Platonic eros relationship to the primordial image.

In today's official medicine, which behaves in a thoroughly Aristotelian manner, we are far from anything like this – to wit, the nomenclature for diseases, in which we find no trace of the magic that is implicit in the image. Units of disease require rational, or functional designations, or at least names referring to the person who fabricated the disease as a construct. Hence we refer, for example, to the *morbus Basedow.* As a matter of fact, not even the name given to "his" sickness by Basedow himself, viz. "bulging eye consumption", managed to survive – not because it was too long, but for its magic imagery, which automatically evokes the appropriate archetypal associations. In today's world, it is not permissible to call diseases by their names!

If we were to make things quite plain and included the proper feeling content in the name for the morbus, we would have to speak of the "*horror sickness*", as the Latin word covers just about every shade of meaning, ranging from shuddering with fever to holy terror. Horror can also be associated with the bulging eyes and goiter, since these symptoms occur when someone is about to be strangled as well. It also encompasses physiological changes, such as racing and tripping of the heart, superficial, halting breathing, trembling, perspiring, diarrhoea, and even loss of hair and a devouring appetite with nothing to show for it.

The amplifications *morbus Basedow* inspires when we think of it as "bulging eye consumption" are numerous but they are few compared to those which come to mind when it is described as the "horror sickness". Metaphors can probably be found in nearly all mythologies and religions. We merely need to recall Rembrandt's picture of Belshazzar's feast, with the latter staring at the ghostly writing on the wall, "mene tekel u-pharsim", which spelled his own and his empire's doom. In Greek mythology, we find a parallel in the Gorgons, and in Buddhism we have the terrifying guardians of the temple, whose task it is to watch over devotional activities.

Whenever we come up against such a fundamental discrepancy between the image of an ailment and the unit of disease, causal thinking will not manage to "get it together". We have to look for other ways and means to "get *at*" its genesis. Looking for mental causes will not do either, because they, too, are mere *causae.* Following our theme, this means that the question about pathogenesis cannot be put in terms of psychogenesis or somatogenesis as alternatives, but in terms of whether it is understood from the scientific stance, or whether we experience our insights with the kind of awe inspired by the sight of an image.

For this reason, the only alternative to causality, i.e., pathogenesis due to causal factors, is to look at images – in particular images of disease – with an eye to their propensity for *transformation into something analogous.* From this stance, it becomes relatively easy to recognize in these images the figures, which, transformed, hold us in the grip of their cruel power (cf. Goethe's *Faust I*). We rediscover in them what we are accustomed to see as a human trait of character, experiencing them as its somatized form, its materialization.

This does not by any means apply only to psychosomatic, or functional disturbances but also to genuine physical illnesses. The imaginal experience makes no fundamental distinction, the difference is merely one of degree. Only the varying depths of somatization are acknowledged. Turning once again to the example of Basedow's disease, we discern nothing but a fairly familiar state of alarm behind the odd picture of horror presented by the disease. Horror is a variant of stress. It does not belong exclusively to the realm of pathology, but characterizes human life, indeed living nature as a whole. It is characteristic of civilization perceived as a jungle of existence.

Basedow's disease would then be its most far-reaching *metamorphosis into matter.* Far more than in vegetative distonia, which is often associated with similar symptoms, the Basedow patient gives the impression of being truly possessed by horror as an alien power. He is much more driven by it than the distonia patient. The disease is experienced as something very alien to the patient's personality, and it seems as if the horror affects his body in a manner that is all the more spectacular, the more extensively he has banned it from his consciousness.

The greater the need for a kind of *belle indifférence,* or a world that is hale and whole, the deeper the materialization of the horror, it would appear. No doubt this is the reason for which the *mene tekel* of Belshazzar appears in the midst of unsuspecting festive pleasures, that the Gorgons hover over seas as smooth as a mirror and that the eye-rolling guardians of the temple are connected with Buddhist quietism. Finally, we find that in psychosomatic literature great emphasis is placed on the Basedow patient's tendency to dissimulate and to put up contraphobic mechanisms.

Just as the way in which the image of an ailment originates is not equivalent to how it is "brought on", so the relevant therapy cannot consist of mere treatment, or "handling" of the pathological phenomenon. All the scientific hustle and bustle would be out of place. There are no injections, no families are restored to psychological health, or jobs organized. Reflecting on the image of the ailment without intent occurs in complete stillness, as it were, in the dead silence of a timeless instant.

This is how the *primordial image is revealed to us through the image of the ailment. It also engenders movement, something shifts.* We are no longer the same as before; it seems as if something changed in the metabolism of the ferments, affecting the substance of the disease. Thus, "diffident delight" in the image of the ailment does not purport to correct the construct of the pathology, but brings about a transformation in the state of the illness. Whatever has turned into concrete, material illness is expected to be re-sorbed into life lived. Whatever carries on an odd autonomous existence should resurface as a mode of existence. What has been held spellbound in matter has to be re-deemed, or ab-solved as it were.

Such redemption bears, however, only a remote resemblance to the kind of resplendent health aimed at by scientific medicine. For, the substance redeemed from matter and taken up by life is and remains dark in quality; to relieve it of its somatic quality, we form an alliance with the sickness considered taboo.

And what is redeemed by life from *morbus Basedow* is nothing but horror, with the redeemed substance holding to its sinister mode of existence. What happens here is nothing other than what certain primitive populations have been practising as a cult all along at their annual horror festivities, namely, the integration of terror. For, it is no good to have ever-lasting peace and quiet.

Ladies and gentlemen, to sum up: there is a *fundamental inconsistency between units of disease and images of ailing.* They differ in regard to diagnosis, etiology and therapy. The discrepancy is so great because of the difference in the approach to the understanding of illness. They are objects of typologically *different modes of perception and bear witness to the different worlds we live in.*

In other words: units of disease and images of ailing are so far apart because one is *a manifestation of our scientific mind* and the other *an expression of our artistic nature.* The difference is fundamental because science and art are mutually exclusive. One is the other's feeble-mindedness as well as its complement.

No doubt many misunderstandings in psychosomatic medicine are due to typologically different modes of understanding diseases and the fact that we are not sufficiently aware of the peculiarity and the far-reaching consequences of these different approaches. Most of the controversies that arise in medicine whenever "psyche", so-called, comes up for discussion are probably the result of epistemological naïveté. What other reason could there be for the fact that the statistical estimates of the ratio of psychosomatic illness in the population fluctuates between 10 and 90%? We can only assume that no doubt different yardsticks are being used for the assessment of this ratio.

On the basis of the aforegoing, there would be justification for approaching every type of illness, diagnostically as well as therapeutically, both as a unit of disease and as an image of ailment. Yet, experience shows that a huge distinction is made in actual practice and official attitudes. Ever since science has come to consider the field of healing as falling within its exclusive and jealously guarded purview, medicine, practised as the art it originally was, has remained a leisure-time occupation. We look on it as a luxury, or possibly as a good topic for the theater season. It would seem that an approach to medicine through the image must of necessity be considered opium for the people. As a result, we disregard the benefits of tremendous and vital possibilities for diagnosis, as well as etiological understanding and therapy.

*And what of the future?* In spite of it all, it does seem to me as though an increasing number of people are able to evaluate both the successes and the anemic results of heroic medicine more realistically and that they are yearning for the return of the art, the images, which are the sole harbingers of life.

# The Use of Symbols in the Context of Psychotherapy of Psychosis

Viktor Zielen (Frankfurt a. M.)

The somewhat vague title of my paper reflects the initial general and impersonal relationship during therapy of patients suffering from psychosis or patients threatened by psychosis. This paper covers how a patient can be guided away from an undefinable distance and a mythical strangeness and thus discover his personality once again.

During our first interview, the 52-year-old patient, Gudrun, surprised herself and also me with the mythical aspects of her fate. After she had made a few introductory remarks about her life, she immediately brought up the subject of the birth of twin boys on a Whit Sunday. Since her husband proved to be impotent, she let herself become illegimately pregnant by a healthy man in order to become a mother. To this, she remarked: "I prayed and received twins from a well-built man." The husband accepted the sons but at a later date he took the initiative in forming a relationship with a younger woman.

Gundrun's own birth also shows peculiarities. She was born on a Good Friday. The grandmother, who was present at the birth, predicted: "A difficult life lies ahead for this child." Whereupon the mother, who was deeply disappointed at the birth of a daughter (she should have produced a son as a matter of prestige), bit her mother-in-law in the earlobe. The patient experienced her mother as cold and rejecting. Consideration of others and fulfillment of duty were inculcated into her by her mother with tough persistency. The mother became ill with cancer at the end of the Second World War and the daughter, who was 20 years old at the time, was saved from having to enter military service by nursing her. In the sense of the family mythos, the patient formulates this fact as follows: "Nursing my mother was like being given birth to a second time." Shortly after the mother's death, the father, who had had a liaison with another woman for a long time, remarried. He also died of cancer two years later.

Gudrun, who in the meantime had become engaged, married during the same year as her father's death. The marriage situation was a complete disappointment for this academically-educated woman – she a psychologist and her husband a pharmaceutical chemist. Gudrun was already disappointed during the wedding night and had the feeling that she had sold herself to a man she didn't love; even today she can visualize herself in the sparsely furnished apartment just after the war. She was a housewife and employed as a chemist's assistant, whereby, as she says, she took on the mother role towards the man. The husband, who is about the same age, immediately began to make provisions for 'old age' by building houses. Gudrun deceived her husband with the architect and in the following period formed various friendships with men.

This life account sounds like a fateful accusation and apology. Burning questions occur in Gudrun's consciousness, behind which the central theme is guilt. The therapeutic talks soon quite clearly show that, according to the daughter's experiences, the role patterns of mother and father exclude one another and a type of double-bind situation emerges. Following the guidelines of her mother, Gudrun had several years of a 'Cinderella' existence behind her before, according to her father's example, she began to lead a double life. Her relationships with men seem not only to be steered by sensual demands but also by unconscious mythical fantasies. The incestual fantasies lodged here were fulfilled in a relationship with a cousin, who was nine years older and who took over the role of father for her. Behind this incestual behaviour, there exists for Gudrun, in the sense of her mythical apprehension, a search for something greater, perhaps the calling to a heavenly wedding, a *Hieros gamos*. Could anything else, other than communication with God, reconcile and forgive the guilty feelings creeping into the depths of her soul? The peculiar circumstances of her birth on a Good Friday, as well as that of her twin sons on a Whit Sunday, are incontestable indications from above not to be overlooked. Clearly, a greater godly power directly determines Gudrun's life and that of her sons. This hidden life immediately becomes the subject of therapy and everything points to the fact that Gudrun is going to act it out in the therapy.

During the next interview, the atmosphere between us is already erotically-laden to the extreme. Gudrun sits silently before me, beaming at me intensively with her steel-grey eyes. Then she says: "You remind me of an uncle in Rome." She explains that the uncle from Rome is a cousin of her mother's who, as a Jesuit priest, read the mass at her conversion about 25 years ago. With the nine-year-older cousin from Bonn, who also belonged to her mother's side of the family, she lived for several years on something like an eternal journey. They had the desire to grow old together, but the cousin didn't get a divorce because of his family. When she put him under pressure, he answered, "Then go and find yourself someone younger." Consequently, she separated from the cousin and took up with a younger colleague she had met at a congress. Now, in the therapy, she has landed herself with a 'Jungian'.

The key word, 'younger man' which, at the same time, turned into 'Jungian', clearly emphasizes the compact offer of communication, which was immediately thrust at me at the beginning of the second interview. Gudrun more or less takes over the leading role in the therapy. She searches for a 'mutual' experience which, as I carefully comment, must not be destroyed by interpretation, i. e., by making aware of the backgrounds. Gudrun, who is really aiming at a training analysis, admits that it is difficult, talking rationally, to find herself in the situation of a patient. On her way out, she even assures herself whether the experiences will remain within the walls. Rather abruptly and with the intention of a double entendre, I answer, "The doors here in this room are quite tight."

My answer represents a hidden counter-reaction to the affective, overdone, intensive courting behaviour of the patient. I feel Gudrun's closeness to psychosis.

Now, as we know, the patient who enters into a psychosis in the yonder area of the psyche not only acts by order of the unconscious psyche – mythologically speaking, by order of a chthonic god – but in the death pole of the psyche, he becomes himself an incarnation of a chthonic numinose power.

Therefore, N. Micklem very subtly differentiates between the fixation of the soul as an archetypal fixation and the accompanying apperception or the disturbed apperception brought about by this, whereby he means the incapacity to establish a reflecting relationship with the symbolic pictures.

In a primary disturbance, the pictures flowing from the unconscious not only affect the conciousness of the patient but also the conciousness of the therapist. Because of their fascination, they distract us from their content and, at the same time, they tempt us with their mysteries. The therapist who is engaged in the treatment of psychosis finds himself, like his patient, within the dimension of the mythical.

This creates an especially archaic type of relationship in which the patient and the therapist are not only consciously but, at the same time, also unconsciously bound to each other. The analyst's unconscious mind therefore becomes an organic part of the treatment, i.e. a type of therapeutic instrument, which takes care of the affective relief in the therapeutic field. Simultaneously, it becomes the 'magical bag' which collects the archaic reactions and pictures flowing from the patient and locks them away so that the therapeutical dialogue does not have to be interrupted. On the other hand, the patient himself discovers a protection which allows him to expose his consciousness to the consuming and hypnotical experiences without succumbing to them. He may even, like his mythical forefathers Odysseus or Perseus, return to the light of the conscious world as the servant of life bearing the death-bringing secret.

In the third interview, Gudrun brings with her an intense dream which points to the oncoming psychosis:

She finds herself sitting on a bench with a gardener in an early spring garden. She sees lovely brown earth, the greater part of which has been dug over. She takes over the arrangement of the flowerbeds, decides where to plant the flowers, and she is astonished about the certainty of her own judgement. On her right, she sees a river with a strong current in which horses and boys are swimming. The boys, aged between 8 and 10 years, are playing spitefully with the horses, who are submitting to this. A few horses are swimming as if they are dead, looking white under the water. One horse becomes enraged. It rises from the water, its head becoming bigger all the time, its mouth becoming crocodile-like, and a boy disappears into it like Jonas in the stomach of the fish. The horse gallops on, and they are all afraid of it. Finally, it also runs after Gudrun. She now finds herself in an apartment, opens the door to a bedroom, and runs into the bathroom, the horse at her heels; then she risks the jump out of the window into the garden, and awakes.

The partly archaic nature of the dream is just as alarming as Gudrun's highly charged behaviour during the interview. This situation demands extreme reserve. I make myself react to my patient's fantasies with the same reserve and composure as I did to her acting-out, provoking and seductive behaviour.

As an analyst with unlimited interest in the occurrences originating in the psychic process, this means for me to refrain from all interventions which may increase the inner activities of my patient and thus weaken her readiness for reflection. This particularly refers to dreams touching traumatic moments in Gudrun's life. On the therapeutic side, it is of utmost importance for me to find points of entry which allow the patient a personally valid relationship with her dreams and her behaviour in therapy, so as to protect her from the danger of inflation of her consciousness.

Now, we must not forget that Gudrun includes the therapist in her dream. According to her associations, he is the gardener, who advises her about the planting of the spring garden into which she escapes from the dangerous horse. Thus the prognosis appears to be positive. Furthermore the therapist has been employed by Gudrun on an objective level. Yet the archetypal nature of certain dream contents and, in particular, the behaviour of the patient during therapy is in striking conflict with the otherwise somewhat favourable prognostic aspects. It would, therefore, be too dangerous and disturbing for the therapy to endeavour a direct analysis of the transference aspects. The relationship thriving in a climate of erotic heat aims at a transpersonal reality not to be clearly defined, in which neither the patient nor the therapist appears to be personally touchable. Another point is that Gudrun's behaviour also releases in unconscious fantasies her analyst, which ties him directly to the mythical fantasies of his patient. This may be considered an advantage because he can then avail himself of intuitive possibilities in the sense of a uroboric transference relationship, which is extremely important for the course of the therapy. Or to express it differently: the archaic relationship between patient and analyst is the prerequisite for therapeutic interventions to reach the patient.

Should a formulation be at all possible, then, in retrospect, Gudrun's fantasies intuitively picked up by the analyst could have read: "Measure the depths of my love so that I can render myself a true heavenly lover" or, as fantasy close to consciousness: "I need you, your protection, but I'm sure that you, as a mortal man, are not enough – your reserve angers me, so my nature must search on."

The analyst's fantasies and, as Gudrun's dream indicates, the constellated archetypal pictures, lie within the range of the *Magna Mater* and the hero. The near-psychosis character of the dream belongs to the elementary process of transformation, as well as to the numinose negative death pole of the soul. So the patient appears not only as a flowing river, as earth ready for planting but also as a raging death demon in the form of the crashing, devouring horse which drives the dreamer into confusion. Thus Gudrun, with her weakened 'ego' finds herself in, as it appears, an inexplicable conflict with the oppressive basic powers of her soul. In this situation, I follow every one of the patient's remarks with reserve and with extreme attentiveness. I lock away the fantasies in my unconscious, in my 'magical bag', at the same time silently putting them into a category of a not yet definable sense as I try to create a milder affective atmosphere. I interprete the alarming illusions as a warning against impulsive actions. To help control reality, so urgently required in Gudrun's case, I make it clear at the same time, that an acting-out of her fantasies would not only stand in the way of her innermost search of the mind's sources, but would also lead the therapy into a *cul-de-sac* and thus, in the end, bring it to a close.

As a result of the events described, during the next three months the patient gives the impression of beginning to be able to see her conflicts on a more personal level, in order to treat them in a reflective manner in her relationship to the analyst. Moreover, it appears that the danger of a psychosis developing has been successfully dampened.

A few weeks later, during the agreed holiday, events hastily follow each other. Without discussing the matter with her analyst, Gudrun takes part in a therapy group. The theme in the group was, 'myself, as a raw egg'. When the egg broke, Gudrun fell into a long period of psychosis. The egg introduced into the group becomes the world egg, and its breakage brings about the end of the Age of Pisces.

Aquarius empties his bucket. The patient becomes a Goddess of the Stars, who has been called upon to convert herself and to convert mankind. At home, she lets a bucket of water overrun to clean the house from attic to cellar.

In her role, she entirely represents a feminine Star Goddess; she opens her window during the night so that her soul's lover, the moon man, can come to her. She hears the moon growling next to her. Then she repeatedly unites herself with the moon in an estatic transport of love and consummates the heavenly marriage. During the next day, she shaves off her pubic hair like a nun and considers all human males as inferior beings. She has the claim of a woman who is loved by the God of Fertility, The God over all women; she is loved by the moon man himself.

The condition of psychosis lasts six to eight weeks, without the analyst learning about it. The insulted husband consults a psychiatrist, who prescribes a neuroleptic medicine. The patient herself stops taking the medicine after 10 days; she is able to outwardly keep control to a certain extent.

Gudrun experiences her re-emerging from the archaic mental condition with great relief. For her, it is a type of rebirth which is accompanied by favourable aspects. A dream-like picture before sleeping characterizes the new development:

She sees in the twilight a beautiful horse peacefully grazing in a pasture. Upon waking up, she writes: "Pleased that I may live on" and "life's instincts endeavour to collect themselves despite aging". About a month later, Gudrun informs the analyst about the events experienced and aks him to continue the therapy. She talks about the past experiences with a naivety, rather like a child telling a fairy story. The erotic tension in the therapeutic relationship has vanished entirely.

Gudrun is resolute and is able to perceive the normality not only in her environment but also inside herself. Her dreams are almost completely free of any archaic ingredients. Paradoxically, however, in context they are still going to be filled with symbolic knowledge acquired by reading, for a long period of time, particularly with word and number symbols. The relearning programme is not disturbed by this. The patient has dreams of small children, princess dreams, learning dreams. The experiences within the therapy, her being accepted in the sense of an archaic relatedness, guide Gudrun during the course of a year and help her to differentiate and to understand not only the intuitive-fantasyful strength, but also the logical-classifying strength as a constitutional part of her personality. In an attitude of meditative learning which, at the same time, has been inspired by her dreams, Gudrun handles her problems based on the newly achieved self-identification with greater emphasis and more responsibility. The example of changing relationships with men, which in many ways is very meaningful for the patient, is taken up again and newly worked on. Gudrun admits her lack of consideration when satisfying her own sexual instincts. She becomes frightened in retrospect about the possibility of the implicated derailing into psychosis. Thoughts of morality take over and activate her consciousness. From a general great feeling of guilt towards life, a personal guilt complex is uncovered. She feels moved in her soul as regards the relationships with several men and, at the same time, is filled with an immense grief. Her sorrow and shock increase as she discovers that her relations with many hindered a deeper relationship with one, above all with her father. Thus, she recalls that she was never really close to her father. Gudrun begins to search for the figure of her father behind the varying aspects of all the men she believed herself to have loved.

With increasing participation, she collects remembrance on remembrance of her father and, in retrospect, mourns for him.

At this point, Gudrun finds herself at an initial termination point of therapy, which simultaneously is expressed in great symbolic pictures. These figures are also to conclude this paper, whereby I must refrain from describing in more detail intermediate stages which would be quite important for the understanding of the process.

On her wedding anniversary, Gudrun introduces the following dreams into our interview. The first is as follows:

> I walk along the right-hand side of a forest path. Coming towards me with serene composed steps is a noble lady. I notice that the face belongs to the body of an animal, a very proud brown mare. The exchange of glances between this noble face and myself is fulfilling, almost painful. Suddenly, I have the feeling that I, as I now am, approach old age. I, myself, and this face nod lightly to each other, as if we are exchanging goodbyes. Then I pass the centaurlike creature, taking the path from whence it came, whereas the centaurlike woman takes the path from whence I came. We both muse about the path meant for each one of us.

The dream suddenly infers Gudrun's mythos.

The centaurlike creature, the beautifully formed mare with the noble woman's face expresses the entire vitality, the passionate desires, the life and love-lust of a strong woman. The numinosity belonging to a centaurlike nature explains, in retrospect, the achievement and also the existence of an archaic mental unity during psychosis. When analysing the dream material, the sense inferred to the mythical figure creates at the same time the possibility of an inner reconciliation with age, which, as the dream also indicates, clears the path into the future.

The next two dreams confirm this development:

> Gudrun is in her place of birth. With her firstborn son clinging to her hand, she visits her parents. In front of the gate of the grandparent's house, her father's brother, in the role of the family patriach, receives her firstborn son with great joy. She is very happy about this, especially because of the guilty feelings she has towards her children.

Gudrun dreams further:

> She is looking for her mother, who is working in the garden. She reaches a wall which frightens her. Suddenly she realizes that the sea lies behind the

> walls and she wants to see it. She climbs onto the wall and sees a bay which opens into the open sea. Her father is standing up to his chest in water in the middle of the bay. He is standing there like a great rock of an earlier dream, which towers up out of the sea. As she looks at her father, he sinks slowly under the water.

The patient's father complex disperses, thus I say quite spontaneously to Gudrun: "Father's spell is broken, the soul has accepted him."

The constituting conditions on the side of the therapist are alert frankness, reserve, assiduity and courage to accept and endure the emerging figures and the reactions of the soul. The analyst thus creates in his consciousness the prerequisites for his patient to tolerate overpowering, frightening or otherwise negative visions. From the inner resonance of person-related behaviour, security and understanding can be achieved step-by-step within the patient and thus may then develop into the capability of self-reflection. It is part of the process itself that the course of the search for the personality in the sense of a primary attitude is hardly, or not at all, known to the patient. It would be disturbing or even detrimental if the analyst were consciously to direct the patient towards this or even make it clear.

A decisive important step in therapeutic processes would be to emphasize the merging of functions, in the sense of C. G. Jung – in the case of our patient, the merging of her intuition and thinking functions. The changes thus occurring in the 'ego'-attitude and, therefore, the 'ego'-identity prepares for the reflexive, therapeutic, effective dispute with the inner visions and emotions. A further decisive step is the simultaneously related awakening of a moral responsibility against oneself as a whole person. This allows the patient to come to terms with his fate in a fruitful manner. The living through of the often painful torturing circumstances of life proves to be a fire which leads to differences, effecting decisions.

Thus the patient learns hesitantly and step-by-step to recognize whether, and to what extent, his actions express his person as a whole, or whether they are the result of partial instinct-controlled impulses, or perhaps also the reaction of the complexes occupying his consciousness, or, what is the same thing, the machinations of his part-personalities.

Such disturbances cannot be adjusted or overcome without the guiding help of therapy. This is possible, however, if the therapist recognizes the processes of the soul as an instinctive archetypally-controlled procedure which is mutually acknowledged by him and the patient. Not only the conscious, but also the unconscious nature of the mutual relationship form the foundations for the largely discreet, as well as sympathetic, tender reflection of the soul's courses over a longer period. The mirroring relationship gradually changes within the course of the development into an initial mutual reflection, which is then replaced step-by-step by the self-reflection of the patient and taken over by the patient. The occurrences, together with the parallel energetic unloading of the crucial complex, lead to the building up of a whole personality.

Turning briefly back to the case of Gudrun, one might say that, within a therapy lasting three to four years, Gudrun has made a development which shows a differentiating of her personality, insofar as she is on the way to individuality. In any case, as I have endeavoured to illustrate, she is able to recognize and translate the sense of her dreams to a great extent without the aid of her analyst. Within herself, she takes tender leave from the centaurlike woman, who returns along the path of the unconscious from whence Gudrun came and, sorrowfully, prepares herself for old age. She understands and takes responsibility for her life's guilt as a mother and accepts with pleasure the reconciliation offered to her by the family patriach as representative of her enforced moral instance. Finally, she lets the supernaturally false picture of her father, her complex, sink back into the depths of her soul, after she has acknowledged him personally as her father. In any event, this is what the final dreams say, as the patient herself interpretes them.

## Bibliography

1. Micklem, N.: Das unerträgliche Bild. Gorgo, Z. archetypische Psychol. bildhaftes Denken, Heft 3 (1980).
2. Neumann, E.: Zur Psychologie des Weiblichen (Rascher, Zürich 1953).

# Is there still a Place for the Medical Model?

Louis Zinkin (London)

Although the question of models for psychoanalysis raises enormous problems, this paper must be brief and so I will limit myself to only one point: we should not abandon the medical model. I say this because we have increasingly found reasons to reject this model, to view it with distaste, and to seek to replace it with another, the individuation model.

Indeed, the theme of this congress – Clinical and Symbolic Approaches – suggests that we have some sort of choice. If we really did, which of us would not choose the symbolic? I am going to suggest that this choice is not ours in any absolute sense. We are all doctors, whether or not we call ourselves that, whether or not we have received a medical training. We cannot manage without the medical model. Once we accept this fact, we become open to two possibilities: first, it need not be the only model; second, if it is used correctly and not abused, it can actually be a good model.

Jung himself never abandoned it, but he had the rare gift of tolerating opposites in himself throughout his life. I was fascinated to discover, on reading *Memories, Dreams, Reflections,*[1] that Jung thought he might have become a surgeon if he had had the money. There must have been something attractive to him in the figure of the doctor who works miracles on the unconscious patient, the expert who combines detailed knowledge of the human body with consummate technical mastery. What a far cry this idea seems from the Jung who developed the idea of individuation. We know, of course, from the same book that Jung had two personalities, that Jung the doctor, the eminent psychiatrist, was

[1] C. G. Jung, *Memories, Dreams, Reflections,* (recorded and edited by Aniela Jaffé; London, Routledge, and Kegan Paul, 1963).

only one side of him. It is easy, however, to draw false conclusions from the split in Jung if one side is valued at the expense of the other. It would be wrong to regard his Number One personality as a false self and the Number Two as a true self, just as it would be wrong to regard the Number One as sane and Number Two as mad. What is essential is to see Jung as a whole person, to value each side only in relation to the other and to attempt to integrate the two. This was Jung's life-work, both for himself and for us. One can find quite as many examples of his using the medical model as one can of his attacking it. Though not so often quoted, this is one of numerous examples of paradox in his work.

Paradox can be stimulating or profoundly moving, but it can also be exasperating. Jung was, as I have said, tolerant of contradiction and this can be understood in two ways: one is that he had to live with his two personalities and had to keep them both alive. The other is that his whole psychological theory was of opposites which could not be resolved except at a higher level. Nevertheless, Jung, in his published writings, the Collected Works, was not writing poetry but was trying to evolve a scientific theory of the psyche, and no theory, to be credible, can contradict itself.

It seems to me that, in a theoretical paper at congresses such as this, it is important that we do not confuse theory *about* the psyche with the psyche itself. In describing the psyche, it may be illuminating to speak of an Apollonian and Dionysian principle of lightness and clarity, and darkness and profundity, but in our theories we must try to be clear. Some may say that the human psyche cannot be the object of a scientific theory, but this was not Jung's position. Although he was well aware of the *limits* of theories, of books compared with the living experience of people, he saw himself, nevertheless, as a psychologist, and wrote many books.

It can be argued, of course, that analytical psychology is not a scientific theory at all, that the soul cannot live if subjected to the constraints of a scientific theory. This would seem to be the position of James Hillman, for example. Others would argue that advances in science, particularly in physics, have helped us to present Jung's work as a scientific discipline. Marie-Louise von Franz is a notable exponent of this view. Both views could be amply supported by quotations from Jung. I think both are right. But I do think that there is a distinction between a model and a theory, which is crucial in this kind of controversy. Although there is a good deal of overlap in the use of these two words, I would regard a theory (at least in its modern sense) to imply a co-ordinated set of hypotheses *about* something. They seek to explain things in a satisfactory way and if they fail to do this, the theory must be changed or may even be discarded. A theory is therefore highly abstract and represents an achievement of consciousness. It may have deeply unconscious archetypal roots, but these are irrelevant to the *application* of theory. Theory can be sharply distinguished from practice in the sense that practice concerns the application of theory, or, more colloquially, what we do in practice may not exactly conform to our theories. A model, on the other hand, can give rise to both theory and practice, e.g., a model of psychotherapy may indicate a technique, a way of handling the material, as well as referring to a theory of the human mind.

While theories are consciously evolved, models may be totally unconscious and may be arrived at only by examining assumptions. (Many people, for example, would see an epileptic fit as possession by a bad spirit. This would not be a theory as to the 'cause of epilepsy' but simply the expression of a model.) In other words, we can manage, to a large extent very well, without theories, but not without models, because models are really ways of experiencing and acting. A scientific theory, which can be shown to be true or false, requires also a scientific model, the scientific way of looking at the world. This, the model, is neither true nor false. It may be regarded as useful or not, but opinions vary. Some analysts say they are not 'strong on theory'. They try to learn theory when training, but sometimes apologetically, sometimes proudly, they work without it. The word 'intuitive' is often used to describe them. But they cannot possibly work without models. These models are often 'unconscious' in the sense that Jung usually used the word. Human beings seem different from animals in becoming aware of their models, which means becoming self-conscious, but these are always 'as if' constructions requiring analogies. The awareness is never complete, a fact which the word 'archetypal' recognises. Models are much more understood as archetypal than are theories, because we know they can never be disproved, never 'falsified'.

As well as using the term 'medical model' in this paper, which will, perhaps, be generally accepted, I am also using the term 'individuation-model', which may be less easy to accept. By using the words 'individuation-model', I wish to make it clear that I am not speaking about individuation, but referring to a model in which the idea of individuation has a place. It is thus analagous to the medical model and, like it, can give rise to both a theory and a practice. In other words, individuation is both a process to be understood and a goal or task of therapy requiring a proper attitude or technique in the therapist.

Because models, as opposed to theories, can very often be a set of unconscious assumptions, models often come into conflict, e. g., with a medical model: one may wish to relieve a patient of depression, but with the individuation model, one may consider that the patient 'needs' his depression. It can easily be seen that this involves not two different theories, but two different models employing value-systems. A well-equipped analyst, in my view, should be able to use *both* approaches – not to treat the models like competing theories. In practice, he may switch between the two. He may, at times, be helping his patient to *be* depressed, but he also sees depression as an adversary to be overcome.

In dealing with this conflict, it is helpful to imagine a 'supramodel': the opposites can be reconciled at a higher level. In practice, it is sufficient simply to know that there must be such a supramodel without actually knowing what it is. This enables the analyst to tolerate his own apparent inconsistency as he switches from one model to the other. Neither the medical model (wanting the patient to get better) nor the individuation-model (wanting the person to know more of and be more of himself) is 'better' than the other.

I should like to take up here an interesting suggestion made by James Hillman.[2] He has expressed his belief that every model must have within it the grounds for its misuse or abuse; that we should not, for example, blame Jungians for their paranoia and exonerate Jung, since their paranoia is partly to be found in his Self model. We should not blame Paul for his Christian asceticism, or the Church, but look to Jesus, the Original model. In other words, the shadow of a model is already in it. It is tempting to reply to this that a model is simply a tool and that the user of a tool must take responsibility for its correct use, but I can see that this begs the very question that Hillman raises, because the designer of the tool must bear responsibility for the possibility of its misuse. A hammer can be used for murder as well as for carpentry. My reply would be rather that a shadow is cast by an object; it is not properly regarded as part of an object. Every model must have a line drawn round it. This delineates what it *excludes*, as well as what it includes. It is this very exclusion which necessitates other models. There are better tools than a hammer for killing a man if this is what we wish to do.

[2] James Hillman, Private communication.

Perhaps it might be objected that I am taking the shadow metaphor too literally here; nevertheless, the shadow does stand for 'what is rejected', so if every model has to have a boundary to be identifiable, the construction of the boundary 'rejects' what lies outside.

In nature there are no distinctions. Lines which divide are operations of the human mind (a dominant hemisphere function). The very act of making models is thus an attack on nature, a Promethean act, a stealing from the Gods, as James Hersh[3] has aptly put it. It is precisely because any one model excludes other possible ones that I advocate a multi-model approach, a set of tools, rather than one. Hersh's idea that we need a model of model-making exactly corresponds to my idea of a supramodel using systems theory: the Promethean myth is also, of course, a subsystem.

Let us now look at the construction which we call the medical model. It is a highly abstract one and difficult in practice to abstract from our concrete knowledge of doctors and nurses, clinics and hospitals and smells of disinfectants. So, although I have so far been talking about the medical model as though we all know what it is, I expect that each of us would define it differently, perhaps very influenced by personal experience.

One way out is to say that it is, of course, an archetype, and that archetypes can only be approached through symbols, and perhaps point to an engraving of Asclepius holding his caduceus and say: "*That is the medical model.*"

I think, at this juncture, that it might be more useful (not more true) to view it as a model of a relationship involving at least two people. It is thus a social fact. A patient is etymologically one who 'bears suffering'. In this sense, we all have our patients even though there may be a few of us who so dislike the medical model that we call them 'clients'. But whether patient or client, what is being described is a social role which makes sense only in relation to another. One can only be a patient or client *of* someone. The patient and the doctor form a dyad which is essential to the medical model. What is involved in this relationship? The bare bones of it are contained in the following situation:

Somebody (called a patient) goes to somebody else (called a doctor) because he feels something to be wrong with his health. He expects the doctor to have special knowledge, to be an expert in such matters or at least sufficiently expert to be able to ascertain whether there *is* anything

[3] James Hersh, *Model-making and the Promethean Ego* (Spring Publications, 1982).

wrong, *what* is wrong (diagnosis), how serious it is (prognosis) and what, if anything, can be done about it (treatment). He expects to pay the doctor in exchange. I am sure there will be objections to this formulation, but let me hasten to explain that the doctor need not be called a doctor, nor the patient a patient. We don't need to argue about what constitutes health, only agree that there is such a thing. The doctor doesn't really have to be an expert though he does have to be thought to be one. The treatment may be free (but perhaps there must still be a fee which is *not* paid). The doctor and the patient could even be the same person and the whole thing may not happen at all; it can just be an idea. I have deliberately phrased it, in fact, as a set of expectations or assumptions and the model does not assume that any of these assumptions should be conscious. The patient may be a baby or an animal or a man lying unconscious in the street. We are speaking, therefore, of a set of expectations or assumptions which may or may not be 'in the mind' of any one individual. The pattern is deeply embedded in our society, but is also to be found in the most primitive and distant culture, though in this case it will merge into other forms, such as the god, the priest, the shaman and the magician. In the deepest levels of the psyche, the archetypes merge into each other.

So my very reduced highly intellectual concept of a medical model – a pure abstraction – is *also* an archetypal idea. Essentially, my model is of a social relationship and intellectually we can account for this in two different ways. Either we can say: the archetype pre-exists in the collective unconscious and therefore finds its expression in society, and the figures of the doctor and the patient are *projections* onto people of these collective elements, or else we can say that individuals are born into a society where these *relationships* pre-exist and the individual *introjects* these relationships so that (without being aware of it) they determine his expectations and his unspoken assumptions. I don't think either of these formulations is more true than the other. It is the beauty of Jung's model of the psyche that it allows of both formulations. Unlike Freud's model, Jung's is not based on causality. When it was discovered that the earth went round the sun, this did not displace the idea that the sun went round the earth. Instead, we have two different ways of viewing the same thing. The new way did prove a useful way, continue profitably to think of the sun rising and setting.

So it seems to me, and this is the main point of my argument, that the medical model, grounded as it is on an archetype proving to be difficult to discard, should not by any means be abandoned. The analyst should, on the contrary, have it in his repertoire of models which he can apply in his understanding of his patient's communications, as well as know something about its limitations, its traps and the hideous distortions which it can bring about.

Before taking up the reasons commonly given amongst analysts for rejecting the medical model, I should like first to consider some objections to the individuation model, because this is the one Jungians prefer. While I value the idea of individuation and have called it the supreme goal of any psychotherapy, it makes no sense whatever if isolated from other models – even less sense than the medical model. Jung's thought, as expressed in his model of the psyche, was hierarchical, which can be clearly seen in the diagrams of the psyche he used in his seminars. He arranged those diagrams in levels in a particular order, each level containing and including the contents of the lower levels. The supreme archetype was the self – but it *included* the persona, the shadow, the anima, the father and mother, the child, the trickster, the old wise man, the saviour and the conjunction, etc. He was inclined to think of individuation as a progression through stages, each of which had to be gone through and integrated before proceeding to the next. We rarely see an individual patient going through this orderly sequence, but it provides a model. The word 'transcendent', which Jung used in his 'transcendent' function is often misused to suggest a kind of leap into another world without keeping our feet on this one. The richness as well as the weakness of the individuation model is that it is a holistic one. The whole is not simply the individual as a whole – it includes everything in every individual, every nation, every culture, every mythology. It has no limits, no time and no space. It is a kind of suprasystem. Now the notion of a suprasystem is a useful one if it contains subsystems and if even the suprasystem is seen to be a subsystem of some other system, and this is, in fact, how Jung regarded his model – even though he did not have the benefit of General Systems theory.

Individuation, the pursuit of 'wholeness', has, in itself, no meaning, because a whole needs to have parts, both internal divisions and limits as well as external boundaries, before it can be conceived of as a whole. The whole individual is, moreover, one who is both suprasystem and subsystem. He knows what belongs to him and to what he belongs. I regard individuation as the endless process of acquiring both these kinds of knowledge. Logically it has no beginning and no end, and therefore the idea of progress cannot be applied.

The medical model might be regarded by some as a subsystem of the individuation model, but I would be equally happy to regard it the other way round. We could regard dementia, for example, as an incurable obstacle to individuation – incurable, that is, in our present state of knowledge – but a fever would be a curable one. On the other hand, we could, as Jung was inclined to do, consider which of our patients might be suitable to undergo an individuation process and which might be more suitable for other methods, e. g., hypnotic suggestion, a Freudian reductive analysis, drugs, ECT, behavioral therapy, or no treatment at all. Even to enter into such a discussion is to use the medical model, and individuation could be just one available treatment.

Let us now consider the attacks on the medical model. Jung was one of the first to attack it, but nowadays the attacks come from many other directions. A brief list of these objections (not exhaustive) would be:

1. It is impersonal – the patient is seen not as a person but in terms of his disease.

2. It aims at relieving symptoms, at best concerning itself with the cause rather than the meaning of symptoms for the patient and may be content to relieve symptoms at considerable cost to the integrity of the patient.

3. It sets the doctor up as an expert or, to use Lacan's happy phrase, "the subject who is supposed to know",[4] which he is not.

4. It is based on a naive optimistic view of health which denies the realities of death and decay.

5. It reduces the patient to an object. This means he is *passive*, plays no part in his own case, is *mystified* and *alienated*.

6. The whole process becomes over-institutionalised and may be used politically – to serve an ideology and to manipulate others.

My point is really to accept all these objections but to see them as dangers resulting from misuse of the model, which are particularly great if we use it as our only model, rather than one amongst many.

Let me now try briefly to reply to such objections in the case of the analytic situation. First of all, of course we *are* experts. Our patients are right to expect this and to pay us because of it. But equally, we are not the experts they expect us to be. We do not have to deny our expertise

[4] Jacques Lacan, *The Four Fundamental Concepts of Psycho-Analysis* (London: The Hogarth Press and the Institute of Psycho-Analysis, 1977).

to recognise an archetypal projection. I actually try to demonstrate my expertise at my very first meeting with a patient, not just to show off, but because to listen to someone and then to put what one has heard in a new way is better than saying, "You need an analysis" – it *is* analysis. Conversely, if I can't do this, I wonder if analysis is the best suggestion.

Secondly, we do need to diagnose. We need to reflect on such questions as – is he psychotic or borderline, is he demented, is there an underlying depression? – not only to assess his prospects (prognosis), but also to help us decide on an overall strategy, as well as moment to moment tactics in responding to him (treatment). These considerations apply not only to the beginning, but throughout the analysis.

Finally, we have to decide when it would be a good idea for the analysis to be terminated, and at this point to have some idea as to whether the analysis has been successful or not.

All these judgements involve use of the medical model. Now, of course one does not have to be making these judgements all the time. In most cases, one does not even have to think about them very often. Perhaps the best work is done when the analyst is not very conscious of these issues. But he should be able to switch models and to think in this way when he wants to, or when the need arises – however, there is plenty of time.

None of this implies that the patient be treated as a passive object. He can be consulted and a lot of the process can be shared with him. The analyst need not regard himself as the only expert. Much of the analyst's thinking in theoretical terms is, however, best kept private.

The question of the extent to which the analyst should be impersonal or 'human' and spontaneous is really a separate issue and, I think, a very complicated one. The association between clinical and cold is unfortunate. That the doctor can and must be detached does not mean that he has to be cold or mechanical with his patient.

Finally, of course, none of this implies abandoning a 'symbolic' approach. Understanding and interpreting symbolism are of the very essence of the analytic work. I should like, however, again to repeat a point I made earlier about scientific theories. There is no such thing as *the* meaning of a dream or any other unconsciously determined event. There is the meaning to the analyst and there is the meaning to the patient. The work of analysis is the bringing together of these points of view. We may say "the dream is telling us", but this is just a figure of speech. I make this point because the analyst relying on a 'symbolic approach' can be just as arrogant as any doctor.

The medical model has unchanging features and, in this respect, can be said to have archetypal roots. At the same time, even though retaining these features, which distinguish it from other models, it does not constitute a closed system, but a partially open one which can change. I am suggesting that the analyst should not deny that he is a doctor, but try to be a good one, perhaps even make an inner Hippocratic oath so as not to abuse his position. At the same time, perhaps the greatest abuse is to identify himself too concretely with this role. Avoiding this identification requires the awareness and use of other models. By this, I mean not only the enormous range of ways of conceptualising the mind or psyche,[5] but also other ways of viewing the dyad of the analytic encounter which I have focussed on in this paper. The doctor's approach to his patient is only one model. Others include that of a mother to her baby, a priest to his parishioners, an adept to his opus, a scientist to his experiments, an explorer to his unknown territory, an archaeologist to his site or even simply that of two friends sitting together quietly talking. Each of these models (and there are many more) has its good and bad uses. So, too, has what I have called Jung's individuation-model. None is right or wrong and each is one amongst many. Let us continue to argue about them, but to recall that our common object is how best to arrange them, combine them and order them. In this way we can, amongst many other things, try to be good doctors.

[5] see: Charles Hampden-Turner, *Maps of the Mind* (London: Mitchell Beazley, 1981).

# The Dirty Needle: Images of the Inferior Analyst

Robert Bosnak (Cambridge U.S.A.)

## The Dream of Psychoanalysis

"Here was revealed on July 24, 1895 to Dr. Sigm. Freud the mystery of the dream."[1] Thus Freud imagined a marble plaque on the house where the dream came to him: the dream of psychoanalysis, a meeting with Irma.

This is the core dream in Freud's *Interpretation of Dreams*. Freud says of it: "This is the first dream that I subjected to a thorough interpretation."[2] Thus this dream, usually referred to as "the dream of Irma's Injection", marks the beginning of modern dream analysis.

It is usually assumed that this dream is the beginning of psychoanalysis because Freud used it as a "specimen"[3] to demonstrate his method. The dream itself is treated as incidental, as if Freud could have chosen any dream to initially demonstrate method. For Freud and psychoanalysts after him, the breakthrough lies in the interpretation, not the dream itself.

I want to take a different inroad. To me, the dream is central and the interpretations incidental. I take the Irma dream as the *creation myth* of psychoanalysis: a revelation in the sense of epiphany, to the scribe Sigmund Freud; a genetic code of psychoanalysis clad in the day residues of First Analyst.

Jung describes the phenomenon of the initial dream as follows: "It frequently happens at the very beginning of the treatment that a dream

1 Erik H. Erikson, "The Dream Specimen of Psychoanalysis", *Journal of the American Psychoanalytical Association* (2, 1954), p. 7; citing the Freud-Fliess letters: S. Freud, *Aus den Anfängen der Psychoanalyse* (London: Imago Publishing Co., 1950).

2 Sigmund Freud, *The Interpretation of Dreams*, James Strachey tr. and ed. (New York: Avon Books, 1965).

3 Erikson, *loc cit.*

will reveal to the doctor, in broad perspective, the whole programme of the unconscious."[4] If the dream of Irma's injection is taken as the archetypal revelation of psychoanalysis, and not only as an expression of the person Sigmund Freud, then the images portray a preview *in nuce* of the psychoanalytic domain: the initial dream of psychoanalysis. In the metaphor of current genetics, a genetic code is a blueprint to be repeated in each ensuing cell; thus psychoanalysis would be an endless variation on the Irma dream.

## Dream of July 23–24, 1895[5]

A great hall – a number of guests, whom we are receiving – among them Irma, whom I immediately take aside, as though to answer her letter, and to reproach her for not yet accepting the "solution". I say to her: "If you still have pains, it is really only your own fault." – She answers: "If you only knew what pains I have now in the throat, stomach and abdomen – I am choked by them. "I am startled and look at her. She looks pale and puffy. I think that after all I must be overlooking some organic affection. I take her to the window and look into her throat.

She offers some resistance to this, like a woman who has a set of false teeth. I think, surely, she doesn't need them [that]. – The mouth then opens wide, and I find a large spot on the right, and elsewhere I see extensive greyish-white scabs adhering to curiously curled formations, which are evidently shaped like the turbinal bones of the nose. – I quickly call Dr. M. who repeats the examination and confirms it... Dr. M. looks quite unlike his usual self; he is very pale, he limps, and his chin is clean-shaven [beardless]... Now my friend Otto too is standing beside her, and my friend Leopold percusses her covered chest [on top of the bodice], and says: She has a dullness below on the left, and also calls attention to an infiltrated portion of the skin on the left shoulder (which I can feel, in spite of the dress)... M says: There's no doubt that it's an infection, but it doesn't matter; dysentery will follow [supervene] and the poison will be eliminated... We know, too, precisely how the infection originated. My friend Otto, not long ago, gave her, when she was feeling unwell, an injection of a preparation of propyl... propyls... propionic acid... trimethylamin (the formula of which I see before me, printed in heavy type)... One doesn't give such injections so rashly... Probably, too, the syringe [*Spritze*] was not clean.

[4] C. G. Jung, *CW 16*, § 343.

[5] Freud, *Interpretation*, pp. 138–140 in Strachey, but text cited is another translation: A. A. Brill, Great Books of the Western World, 54, p. 182/83.

(I have taken the translation of Brill – though inprecise in places – since he tells the dream in the present tense, as it is presented in the original, whereas Stratchey translates the dream in the past tense, losing a lot of immediacy of the drama. The words between [] are some literal renderings of the original. Since the word *Spritze* in German has several connotations, I have given the original word.)

## Birthday Reception

In his associations to the dream, Freud says that this reception* is for the birthday of his spouse. The creation myth starts out in a great hall where many figures are received to celebrate a day of birth. The day of birth of the spouse of Analyst, his feminine partner for life. Psychoanalysis, Freud's spouse for life, *in statu nascendi.* As we witness the creation of psychoanalysis, the day of birth of the spouse, we meet the *dramatis personae,* the characters in this myth:
– Freud, First Analyst, Archanalyst.
– Irma, Psyche-in-Analysis
and later three other Doctor figures. Among them, the drama of psychoanalysis is conceived.

## The Relatives

In the background of Irma, visible only in the preamble[6] to the dream, are her relatives, who are described as the ones who don't like the treatment. The natural solution in which Psyche-in-Analysis exists, her next of kin, resists analysis. On a mythical level, this indicates the fear that natural familiar soul has of analysis and her desire to resist it.

Therefore, the first movement Archanalyst makes with Psyche-in-Analysis is one of separation – "Irma, whom I immediately take aside". The exterior light Archanalyst has shed onto Psyche-in-Analysis – "I take her to the window" – is resisted, not only by Psyche herself – "she offers some resistance to this" – but by her natural *intimi* as well. This illustrates Jung's image of the *opus contra naturam.*

## Medical Quaternio

Our creation myth shows us four medical figures; imagine them grouped around Psyche, these masculine medical attitudes.

* The word translated as "receive" is the German word *Empfangen.* This word also has the medical meaning, "to conceive a child."

Of course there is Archanalyst, who says in his associations to the dream: "It is as if I looked for each occasion to reproach myself for a lack of medical conscientiousness." In the treatment below about the images of inferiority we'll see why.

Then there is Dr. M. In the preamble[6] he is described as an authority (this is Joseph Breuer).[7] The authoritative voice in matters of pathology and prognosis – "There's no doubt that it's an infection… dysentery will follow and the poison will be eliminated." In case of psychoanalysis, this diagnostic and prognostic authority, however, is limp and his chin shaven of the beard of virility.

The authoritative judgement in analysis is limp, uneven and not penetrating, lacking phallic dignity.

Leopold is the conscientious observant perspective, the one who looks carefully at the phenomena. He is the one attitude who, through careful observation of Psyche-in-Analysis, discovers the nature of the pain.

[6] Freud/Brill ibid., p. 182
Preliminary Statement:
In the summer of 1895 I had treated psychoanalytically a young lady who was an intimate friend of mine and of my family. It will be understood that such complicated relations may excite manifold feelings in the physician, and especially the psychotherapist. The personal interest of the physician is greater, but his authority less. If he fails, his friendship with the patient's relatives is in danger of being undermined. In this case, however, the treatement ended in a partial success; the patient was cured of her hysterical anxiety, but not of all of her somatic symptoms. At that time I was not yet quite sure of the criteria which denote the final cure of an hysterical case, and I expected her to accept a solution which did not seem acceptable to her. In the midst of this disagreement, we discontinued the treatment for the summer holidays. One day a younger colleague, one of my most intimate friends, who had visited the patient – Irma – and her family in their country residence, called upon me. I asked him how Irma was, and I received the reply: "She is better but not quite well." I realized that these words of my friend Otto, or the tone of voice in which they were spoken, annoyed me. I thought I heard a reproach in the words, perhaps to the effect that I had promised the patient too much, and – rightly or wrongly – I attributed Otto's apparent taking sides against me to the influence of the patient's relatives, who, I assumed, had never approved of my treatment. This disagreeable impression, however, did not become clear to me, nor did I speak of it. That same evening I wrote the clinical history of Irma's case, in order to give it, as though to justify myself, to Dr. M., a mutual friend, who was at that time the leading personality in our circle. During the night (or rather early in the morning) I had the following dream, which I recorded immediately after waking.

[7] Max Schur, "Some Additional 'Day Residues' of 'The Specimen Dream of Psychoanalysis'," *Psychoanalysis – A General Psychology: Essays in Honor of Heinz Hartmann* (New York: International Universities Press, Inc., 1966), p. 70.

Finally there is Otto, our healer, who causes the iatrogenic disease. If we take the Irma dream as creation myth, as our initiation dream, then we must see how each of these four attitudes is active in our therapy of psyche. The one who feels he's done something wrong, the one who limply states what's the matter and where it's going, the one who carefully observes, and most of all our therapist, who makes psyche sick. Each of them seems to be a necessary component in our drama.

## Psyche Covered

"Leopold percusses her covered chest", literally: "over her bodice". Of course we are in Victorian Vienna. But since we phantasize about each image in the dream as if it mattered to our psychoanalytic initiation, we can disregard history and look at mythical image. Two distinct emanations come to mind: – Psyche-in-Analysis is always under cover. We never see her unveiled; Psyche, a dance of endless veils. This ends the hope that we will *see* what is really going on. We must sense it underneath the cover-up. Then our language must cover what it tries to reveal; and all clear descriptions as to the true nature of psychic reality are dubious. A bodice of myth is woven around psyche.

There is material between Psyche and Analyst. The work of analysis goes through the material. This material is formed by the sexual tabu between Psyche and Analyst. This tabu is necessary since, as we will see below, the nature of their relationship is one of dirty sexuality. The tabu leads this porno-eros over from the literal naked enactment to the vivid sexual imagination of the transference, most clearly described by Jung in his *Psychology of the Transference*. This tabu on naked touch, on direct sexual contact in our creation myth gives an amoral indiction against naked sexuality as therapy.

## "Solution"

"reproach her for not yet accepting the solution"

When Oedipus, Freud's central hero, is asked a riddle by the Sphinx, he knows the solution. And knowing the solution to the riddle is the doorway to the incest. Riddle and solution belong to mother and incest. Psyche-in-Analysis does not accept the solution Archanalyst has found for the riddle of her illness. His Sherlock Holmes fails to unlock her doors. It is Archanalyst who does not understand the meaning of the word solution in the mysteries of psyche. Mother poses riddles, psyche is mysterious. For Psyche-in-Analysis, "solution" means turning into water, the stinking waters of dysenteric diarrhea that will discharge what poisons her.

In *Psychology of the Transference* in the chapter called, "Diving into the Bath" (par. 454 [my translation]), Jung says:

"this diving into the 'sea' means 'solutio'. Dissolution in the physical sense and... at the same time the solution to a problem. It is to be placed back into the dark initial state... This stinking water contains all in itself, of which it has need."

With the problem of *solutio* we have reentered the original Greek meaning of the word *analysis:* the process of dissolution; dissolution into stinking water, dysentery.

And, as Jung stresses at another point of the paragraph cited above, it is the waters from *below* that cause the process of dissolution. The waters from below rise and dissolve the fixed positions, the fixed boundaries, the clear distinctions. This intimates that we are not dealing with a distant and clean process of clear vision and detached treatment, but a dirty one where the distinctions between psyche and analyst dissolve. Both are drenched in the stench of stinking water, the experience of the low. Being dissolved in the feelings of lowly stench is the experience of the inferior: feeling lower than low. This feeling of inferiority is the experiential counterpart to the initiation from below.

## Images of the Inferior Analyst

In this section are collected those moments in our story of genesis in which Archanalyst or one of his colleagues is shown as inferior. One of these images we already referred to: limping, beardless Dr. M. The authoritative analyst is not one of strong posture and manly beard, but limping, devoid of virile regalia. The analytical authority is not firm and of masculine superiority (as a beard in 1895 would allude to), but dragging its feet and of inferior dignity.

This image is repeated in the Preamble: "In the Summer of 1895 I had treated psychoanalytically a young lady who was an intimate friend of mine and my family. It will be understood that such a [lit.: mixture of relationships] can become the source of manifold exitations for the doctor, especially the psychotherapist. The personal interest of the doctor is greater, *his authority less.*"

Archanalyst and Psyche-in-Analysis are intimate already before the onset of analysis. They are familiar to each other, calling each other *du*, before becoming the constituents of psychoanalysis. They are involved in a mixture of relationships, as in alchemy: a *massa confusa*. There is no clear single relationship, no cool detachment as the *a priori* of psychoanalysis, but an unnerving mix-up. Any attempt to remain disengaged and exclusively professional seems doomed from the outset. Personal involvement is intrinsic to analysis as there is no objective persona to hide behind. Between analyst and analysand there is not the relationship of the disinfected syringe administered detachedly by a white-coated doctor, but a dirty needle, laden with personal infection. Also, this mixture of relationships refers to the fact that there is an internal psychic relationship between psyche and analyst before any analysis. Psycho-analysis is an intimate familiar process that goes on constantly in the depth of soul as one of the archetypal processes. It is only socially formalized and structured by the literal psychoanalysis. It is this primordial psychoanalysis that forms the basis for literal psychoanalysis. It may therefore be important to establish in the beginning of literal, artificial analysis how the primordial analysis has been conducted to have a notion of which elements get mixed when primordial analysis and artificial analysis interpenetrate.

"... the reproach, that I had promised the patient too much..."

In the Preamble,[6] Archanalyst thinks he hears the reproach of having promised too much. Psychoanalysis is related to the Promise, the archetypal intimation of a Better World to Come. Since it is the nature of the Promise to never be fulfilled, Psychoanalysis is always a "partial success" (Preamble: "the treatment ended in a partial success...").

Hence the constant gnawing sense in the analyst of not living up to what was promised, since the natural relationship to the Promise is the failure to live up to it. This is the basis for the sense of charlatanism plaguing Archanalyst: the con-man who promises more than he delivers.

## Violation

Irma has been shown to coincide with, or correspond to, the victim of one of the worst-botched cases in the written history of psychotherapy: a dreadful incident. The following information is based on an article by Max Schur, Freud's personal physician. Schur gives "supplementary background material for the Irma dream which will constitute, so to speak, a preamble to Freud's preamble".[8]

"From a series of (unpublished) letters (to Wilhelm Fliess) the following facts emerged: Freud had treated a female patient, Emma, for hysteria. In the correspondence, this patient is first mentioned in the… letter of March 4, 1895. Like Irma, Emma had been examined by Fliess, at Freud's request, to determine if there was a partly "nasal origin" of her somatic symptoms. Fliess had come to Vienna, recommended surgery (apparently of the turbinate bone and one of the sinuses – compare Irma dream), and had operated her there, returning to Berlin a few days later."[9] The progress of the treatment is documented in the following excerpts of Freud's letters to Fliess:

March 4: "We really can't be satisfied with Emma's condition; persistent swelling, going up and down "like an avalanche", pain to the point where morphine is indispensable, poor nights. The purulent secretion has somewhat decreased since yesterday. The day before yesterday (Saturday) she had a massive hemorrhage, probably because a bone chip the size of a penny had come loose; there were about two bowlfuls… March 8: "…I arranged for Gersuny (surgeon) to be called in, and he inserted a drain,… he behaved in a rather rejecting way. Two days later… there was moderate bleeding from the nose and mouth; the foetid odor was very bad. R. (Dr. Otto in Irma dream)… suddenly pulled at something like a thread. He kept right on pulling, and before either of us had time to think, at least half a meter of gauze had been removed from the cavity. The next moment came a flood of blood. The patient turned white, her eyes bulged, and her pulse was no longer palpable. However, immediately after this he packed the cavity with fresh iodoform gauze and the hemorrhage stopped.… The following day the operation was repeated… So we had done her an injustice. She had not been abnormal at all, but a piece of iodoform gauze had gotten torn off when you removed the rest, and stayed in for fourteen days, interfering with the healing process, which it had torn away and provoked the bleeding. The fact that this mishap should have happened to you… Of course no one blames you in any way, nor do I know why they should…"

[8] Schur, *Ibid.*, p. 54.

[9] Schur, p. 55.

April 11: "Gloomy times, unbelievably gloomy. Mainly this business with Emma which is rapidly deteriorating... eight days ago she began to bleed... two days ago new hemorrhage... New packing, renewed helplessness... Yesterday... (the blood) didn't spurt, but surged, something like a fluid level rising exceedingly fast and then overflowing everything... Add to this the pain, the morphine, the demoralization resulting from the obvious medical helplessness, and the whole air of danger, and you can picture the state the poor girl is in... I'm really quite shaken that such a misfortune can have arisen from this operation, which was depicted as harmless. I am not sure that I should attribute to this depressing business the fact that my cardiac condition is so much below par for this year of my illness..."[10]

Freud bases his theory of the wish-fulfillment nature of dreams on this Irma dream. Namely, he says, the dream exonerates me from all wrongdoing by blaming Otto, who (as stated in the preamble) reproached Freud for promising the patient too much. Otto gave the injection with the dirty needle, causing all of Irma's pain. From the letters, we can see another reason why it should be Otto, Dr. Oskar Rie, onto whom the blame Freud felt should be displaced: Dr. Rie, Otto, is the one who discovers Wilhelm Fliess' malpractice. Schur remarks that this episode also marks the beginning of the end of the powerful transference Freud had to Fliess. At this time, as can be seen in the letters, Freud was by no means ready to blame Fliess for any wrongdoing ("of course no one blames you"). So the displacement of the guilt unto Otto has double purpose: to exonerate both himself and Fliess. Freud stresses how helpless he felt during all this to the extent of a deterioration of his heart condition. The inferiority is here heart-felt.

From his personal perspective on the dream, the wish-fulfillment aspects of the dream, moving the inferiority away from ego, shows clear. But what does this Emma image add to our mythical reading of the dream as creation myth of psychoanalysis? From this perspective, the movement of the guilt from Archanalyst to Colleague is not a displacement but a further specification of the imagery surrounding Archanalyst. Otto is Archanalyst in his dark and dirty aspect.

The added material introduces a new figure: Wilhelm Fliess. Who is Wilhelm Fliess? The word *Fliess* means "flow" and Freud says that he was "overflowing with ideas as long as (Fliess was) in reach". Fliess was Freud's ardently admired lover; the intercourse of this love affair was

[10] Schur, p. 55–59.

nasal; they constantly treated and worried over the state of each other's noses which they both acknowledged as an intimate sexual organ.

"In another (unpublished letter) Freud even begins with the salutation 'Lieber Zauberer' (Dear Magician)."[11]

Fliess is the healer who will cure the suffering by removing the fundamental cause of the disease, the nasal dysfunction.

Thus the figure of Fliess embodies the elevated magical healer at the source of the flow of ideation who promises the simple cure through the removal of the sexual dysfunction, thereby leading Psyche-in-Analysis to a moment where "within half a minute she would have bled to death".[12]

It is this cherished healer aspect of Archanalyst which leads Psyche-in-Analysis to her dreadful confrontation with death. The magical healer, the wellspring of ideas, makes psyche suffer the proximity of death gruesomely while intending a simple erotic cure. He is an unconscious dark eros who loves to play with ideas and phantasize about causes, and whose unconscious goal it is to lead towards a betrayal of Psyche-in-Analysis that drains her towards death.

According to the Preamble, Irma was suffering from "hysterical dread". Through the Emma material, we see how this *hysterical* dread is transformed into *realistic* dread in a process that looks like a sacrifice of Psyche-in-Analysis by the healer shadow of Archanalyst. If we take the Irma dream as an embodiment of psychoanalysis, as a description of what psychoanalysis *is*, then the foundation of our profession is tragic and the dark mission of our healer shadow is a necessary and repulsive element of the psychoanalytic drama.

The ugly way down is led by an inferior figure. The unraveling of Psyche-in-Analysis is a violation all the way, like the murderous tale of Hades and Kore.

## The Dirty Needle

One of the great dreams of modern medicine is that of sterility. The sterile disinfected whiteness is able, through clean injections, to cure disease. Now look at the dream of psychoanalysis:

[11] Schur, p. 67.

[12] Schur, p. 66.

Our needle is dirty with inferior motives, personal involvement, our filth. We infect. Our *cure* is dysenteric diarrhea. We turn to water with our patients through inferior feelings. Our treatment seems a debacle. Butchers of soul, inept surgeons, our ineptitude sticking in psyche's throat. Our love of healing magic all but kills psyche. Our love of ideas leads us not to the missing piece of a puzzle but to dissolute excretion. Our exalted purpose leads to the misery from below. And our dirty needle is filled with trimethylamin. Freud's association to this is that it is a sexual hormone, a sexual stimulant. That is shown in the dream to be the cause of the iatrogenic disease Psyche-in-Analysis is suffering from. She was penetrated by the unclean *Spritze,* which could also be translated as "squirter". The Latin word for unclean in the sense of unchaste is *incastus,* from which we derive the word "incest". So as to sexually stimulate her, Psyche-in-Analysis is incestuously entered by the dirty squirt which brings the iatrogenic disease as the cure, the dysenteric dissolution. Another aspect of the dirtiness of the needle that produces infection points to venereal disease. What is this incestuous sexually stimulating sickening process that leads to venereal infection and cure in psychoanalysis? We call it transference. The sick bond between Archanalyst and Psyche-in-Analysis sealed by the penetration of the dirty needle. Not a clean patient-doctor relationship, but a sickening, unchaste, highly personally involved and confused erotic bind: transference. Let us remember that the first talking cure, the case of Anna O., ended in a hysterical pregnancy.

Here again it is the inferior venereal ministrations that pervade psychoanalysis throughout. Ours is a sick story of love, a love story of sickness, the story of sickening love; excreting lovesickness in the stench of an outpouring of toxins.

## Conclusions

Inferior feelings are very hard to bear. By their nature, they feel horrible. According to the creation myth of psychoanalysis, Archanalyst and Psyche-in-Analysis dissolve in paroxisms of inferior feelings.

Since the beginning of my training, it has always occurred to me that I felt horribly inferior whenever psychic material was presented to me. I felt I couldn't understand any of it; that I should never have become an analyst; that I was stupid and in every way inferior to the material. In the beginning, I felt that more training would alleviate this. Then I found that my seniors felt similar things after decades of work. As in our creation myth, our seniors limp in unmanly fashion. Then I felt strongly pulled towards a scramble for academic credibility. More degrees, more respectability. Maybe as Professor Doctor Doctor I would feel less inferior. But now it has become clear to me that inferior feelings in the process of psychoanalysis are structural. They belong; they form the emotional experience of depth in the myth of psychoanalysis.

This could explain why, for the past century, psychoanalysts have reproached their colleagues for practicing an inferior blend of psychoanalysis and giving inferior training to their trainees.

How can we train ourselves in painfully gaining ever more precision in the differentiation between the many different kinds of inferior feelings? Such training would change our self-image to a lowly one, befitting the shadow of our endeavor.

The main enemy to such a training is the so-called inferiority complex. This complex puts a blanket of diffuse inferiority feelings over all our emotion, making a differentiation of all the different kinds of inferior feelings virtually impossible. And the inferiority complex takes all inferior feelings personally. That may be the biggest problem of all. Therefore, it seems to me of the utmost importance to study our myth of genesis and to know that Archanalyst feels terrible in many different ways, so that we can bear with him in order not to get lost in the trap that it is only us that feel this way. Because one of the most difficult aspects of inferior feelings is: they feel so damn personal.

# Children of Schizophrenic Parents: The Significance of Archetypal Processes in the Family for the Ego-Development of Children

Gustav Bovensiepen (Berlin)

Unfortunately, I am sometimes asked by child-welfare offices to determine whether a child should be taken away from his psychotic mother. In the course of this work, I have noticed that, in many cases, the child plays a central role in maintaining the stability of the mother, by which I also mean the stability of her delusional system, which I regard as an attempt at restituting of the ego by the self. In the course of this work, I have diagnostic, counseling and therapeutic contact with children ranging in age from 3½ to 17 years. I would like to share this experience with you and invite a discussion of some preliminary reflections on it. I have the impression that this particular constellation – the schizophrenic mother and her child – offers us a particularly good opportunity for a clinical test of our theoretical assumptions on the effect of the quality of early object relations on ego-development.

## 1. Description of the Children

In spite of the variation in their developmental stages, they have much in common with regard to their symptoms, their ego-experience, their ego-functions and the parental images.

*On symptoms:*

These children don't often turn up in child-therapeutic institutions. They are often "invisible" children, as Selma Fraiberg[1] once said. If we manage to find them anyway and take an interest, and if our own perspective is not too narrowed by the psychotic parent, we will often meet children whose experience and behavior is predominately determined by anxiety. This is not the typical developmental anxiety of children, such as separation anxiety, castration anxiety or object-loss anxiety. Nor do we often find specific and differentiated anxieties such as phobias, which require a certain degree of maturity and structure of the ego. This is more a diffuse and fluctuating anxiety, which forms the background of the child's experience. These children move carefully, as if permanently surrounded by dangers.

Many of them, particularly before puberty, have a high level of psychomotoric activity. This undirected and highlevel tendency to movement can be a physical aspect of the anxiety, as are also unspecific psychosomatic reactions such as headaches, stomach aches, psychogenic fever and sleep problems. These children act shy, withdrawn, well-behaved and willing; they are very sensitive and don't have much of a sense of humour. Sometimes they seem to be far away. Their attention seems to oscillate between inner and outer reality. They don't appear either clearly introverted or clearly extraverted. They have difficulty differentiating between ego and non-ego.

*On the ego-functions:*

I think we can assume that the ego of these children feels very threatened. Ego experience is largely dominated by the fantasy-ego which Kandinsky[2] described. Let us take a look at some of those ego-functions which, according to Fordham,[3] are particularly related to archetypal processes. Here I would like to add the functions of reality-testing to Fordham's list, because, for instance, the ability to distinguish between external and internal reality and to see relationships between them is an essential function of the self, as Lampert[4] pointed out. In

1 S. Fraiberg, "The invisible children". In: E. J. Anthony et al. 1978 (see note 21).

2 D. Kadinsky, *Die Entwicklung des Ich beim Kinde.* Hans Huber Verlag, Bern-Stuttgart, 1964.

3 M. Fordham, *Das Kind als Individuum.* Ernst Reinhardt Verlag, München-Basel, 1974.

4 K. Lampert, "Die Bedeutung von archetypischen Funktionen, Objektbeziehungen und internalisierten Objekten für die individuellen Erfahrungen des Kindes an der Mutter", *Analyt. Psychol.* 8, 1–14, p. 5, 1977.

any case, reality-testing was either functionally limited or not developed to the accepted level for an age-group in most of the children.

Some of the children I saw had definite disturbances of attention and concentration. They were highly distractable by outer stimuli and/or flooded by inner stimuli and had difficulties in selection and maintenance of attention. This neuropsychological problem may possibly be related to a surplus of unbound cathexis energy.

The children also had difficulties in discriminating feelings of their partners. It is hard for them to differentiate between their own standpoint and that of the other person. They are more strongly fixated in egocentrism, (in the sense of Piaget) an observation worthy of note in light of the concept of egocentrism which Lidz[5] has emphasized recently to explain regressive cognitive processes of schizophrenics. Anthony[6] has also paid particular attention to this aspect and made comparative studies of the children of schizophrenic and of manic-depressive parents. He says that the reason children of schizophrenic parents have more difficulties in discrimination of feelings and in reality-testing than do the children of manic-depressives is that it is easier for a child to recognize the unreality of the "private life" of a manic-depressive parent than the diffuse connection to reality of the schizophrenic.

As far as motor control goes, the previously mentioned motoric disquiet is not a problem of the regulation of motor impulses. In this respect, the children are normal. Many of the children, however, show a clear predominance of a body-scheme which is not adequately developed for their age and in many cases is fragmented, which may point to an unstable body-ego.

The most obvious defence mechanisms of the older children are denial and to do as if it never happened, as well as splitting. Fordham also lists an ability of the child to do without controlling and organizing functions. This obviously developmentally necessary function – for instance, in order to allow archetypal images to emerge – is difficult to estimate. The children of schizophrenic parents are subjected to the

[5] Th. Lidz, "Egocentric cognitive regression and the family setting of schizophrenic disorders". In: L. C. Wynne (ed.), *The Nature of Schizophrenia*, John Wiley & Sons, New York, pp. 526–533, 1978.

[6] E. J. Anthony, "Kinder manisch-depressiver Eltern", In: H. Remschmidt (ed.), *Psychopathologie der Familie und kinderpsychiatrische Erkrankungen*, Huber Verlag, Bern-Stuttgart-Wien, pp. 12–33, 1980.

archetypal fantasies and ideas of their parents to an unusual degree and they are permanently occupied with controlling and separating themselves from these fantasies. They also have to protect themselves from a strong inductive effect, a contagiousness, of the parental projections. This means that it is difficult to distinguish between the archetypal projections of the parents and the fantasies of the children formed according to an archetypal pattern.

Here, I have only discussed some disturbed or disturbable functions. I do not want to forget to point out, however, that these children also have many relatively autonomously developed and functional ego-qualities which I cannot go into at the moment.

*On parental images:*

Jung made us aware that parents and family members are mythologized in childhood, or that archetypes are experienced as personalized in the parents. This is, of course, also true for the children of schizophrenic parents. There are, however, differences between this experience and that of healthy or neurotic children: The psychotic parent is described extremely impersonally, either completely erased from reality or presented in the form of a threatening picture of a devouring animal, dragon, ghost, deathly monster and so on.

These children lack compensating positive archetypal images of the parents. They often have no interest in «typical» parental figures which are archetypally pre-determined but still human, such as kings and queens. The predominance of the threatening side of the Great Mother and the relatively reduced part of the "personal mother" agree with an observation made by Rubin and co-workers:[7]

They compared drawings made by children of schizophrenic mothers with those made by children of healthy mothers. When asked to draw people, the children of schizophrenics drew fantasy figures of monsters or vampires significantly more often. They also had a tendency to leave out family members when asked to draw a family. The object representations were significantly less "human" and personal. I suppose that the developmentally necessary process of "secondary personalization" as described by Neumann[8)] is retarded in the children of psychotic parents – retarded in favour of the persistence of arche-

[7] J. A. Rubin, N. Ragins, J. Schachter, F. Wimberly, "Drawings by schizophrenic and non-schizophrenic mothers and their children", *Art. Psychoth.* 6, pp. 163–175, 1979.

[8] E. Neumann, *Ursprungsgeschichte des Bewusstseins,* Walter Verlag, Olten-Freiburg/Br., 1971.

typally formed parental images. Difficulties in working through parental images which have been projected outside the family can be a result of this development in the course of the further individuational process of these children.

I should like to add an observation made by H.-J. Wilke when we discussed this topic in the Berlin Jung circle: In the reconstruction of the mother image during analysis of an adult patient who had a psychotic mother, she appears as strangely artificial, dummy-like and rigid, like an inanimate foreign particle. She is not capable of settling anxiety, or may herself be deeply threatening and anxiety-producing.

The experience and reaction of the children to the manifestation of acute psychotic symptoms on the part of the mother is of a different quality: the more subliminally predominating anxiety structures itself into concrete fear, for example, of being attacked, destroyed, or sexually molested. Older children become afraid of losing their identity or of becoming like the sick parent. The accompanying feelings are depressive: shame, guilt for the "craziness" of the mother and loyalty conflicts dominate their experience. Strong fantasies of melting and flowing together on the part of the psychotic mothers are particularly threatening to the children. These can also be expressed in delusions with incestuous content. Sometimes the actual acute psychotic phases can also lead to induced psychotic reactions on the part of the children. Since these occur in my cases (and in research literature) relatively seldom, however, I would assume that the self evokes compensating archetypes with a protective character. I don't know enough about this yet, but I see the problem as extremely important for the development of a theory of the psychodynamics of "health".

## 2. The behavior of psychotic mothers with their children

Now I would like to mention a few facets of the behavior of schizophrenic mothers toward their children.

In spite of the well-known fact that schizophrenic psychoses often become manifest in the period of pregnancy and birth, statistical comparison shows that this is less true of schizophrenic than of depressive patients. There are gynecologists (Gödtel[9], Pauleikhoff[10]) who are of

[9] R. Gödtel, *Seelische Störungen im Wochenbett*, G. Fischer Verlag, Olten-Freiburg/Br., 1971.

[10] B. Pauleikhoff, *Seelische Störungen in der Schwangerschaft und nach der Geburt*, Enke Verlag, Stuttgart, 1964.

the opinion that pregnancy and birth have a rather stabilizing influence on the psychotic or pre-morbid personality of schizophrenic women. Another fact seems to me to underscore the stabilizing effect of the transformative character of the Great Mother. The frequency of obstetric complications, still-born children and spontaneous abortions of schizophrenic women does not differ from the frequency in healthy women. It is significantly lower than with depressive women (McNeil and Kaij[11]). At the risk of a slight chuckle by my colleagues more oriented toward organic medicine, I might offer a psychological explanation of this phenomenon: As we know, the schizophrenic is under the domination of very destructive mother archetypes. I am convinced that disintegrative/integrative processes of the self set in motion by procreation lead at the same time to the constellation of compensating positive aspects of the Nature-Mother, which influence the psychosomatics of birth. The majority of these mothers I have met experienced pregnancy as particularly happy and satisfying. They describe this period of their lives as a unique phase of well-being and of an inner uroboric peace. We can suppose that they also developed "primary maternal preoccupation" as described by Winnicott[12]. A few of the mothers were under the sway of extreme ambivalence during pregnancy, expressed in fantasies and wishes for abortion, killing, or giving the baby up for adoption, or also in fantasies of eternal fusion with the child. Traces of Medea and Hecate on the one hand and identification with the Madonna and the babe in her arms on the other were the dominant archetypal images determining the experience of one mother during pregnancy.

If the positive aspect of the transformative character of the Great Mother determines the experience of most of the schizophrenic mothers, this is apparently because some needs from the period of early childhood are being met. This general aspect has unique meaning for the schizophrenic woman.

What happens when this situation is ended by birth and the gradual separation from the child in the first years of its life? What happens when the dissolution of the Dual-Union (Neumann) which continues after pregnancy is endangered? This can shake the entire personality of the schizophrenic mother, so that negative mother images are re-mo-

[11] T. F. McNeil, L. Kaij, "Obstetric factors in the development of schizophrenia: Complications in the births of preschizophrenics and in reproduction by schizophrenic parents". In: L. C. Wynne, op. cit. 1978.

[12] D. W. Winnicott, *Vom Spiel zur Kreativität*, Klett Verlag, Stuttgart, 1971.

bilized from the unconscious via projective identification and the ego is inflated. If acute psychotic symptoms should break out shortly after birth, it can happen that the child becomes a victim of total amnesia and is not accepted by the mother, as Biermann[13] reported. In the cases of mothers I saw, the conflicts with the children tended to break out toward the end of the first, and in the course of the second year, increasing as the child matured. I suspect that deintegrative processes with archetypal dynamics are triggered in the mother by critical developmental phases of the child and then take over her entire person. As we know, weaning, learning to walk, separation and rapprochement-crises, toilet-training and so on are such crises. This means that we must keep our eyes not only on the deintegrative and integrative processes in the child, but also on the mutually induced processes which become apparent in the mother.

*Some examples:*

A two-year-old child had to be taken away from a chronically paranoid mother partly because she had literally fed it sick from a delusional anxiety that it could starve to death.

The mother of eight-year-old Julia described how she enjoyed knowing that "there's a baby lying in the basket at home" because then she didn't feel so alone with her anxiety. She was completely perplexed when she started reacting to the increasing motoric expansivity of the child at the age of sixteen to eighteen months with rage and beating. Julia developed into a very good girl with relationships to everyone and no one at the same time. She was very well-behaved at school. But she was plagued by night-mares in which ghosts kept trying to force her to kill her mother.

The increasing maturity of the children can also lead to a situation in which the child itself is not seen as the one endangering symbiosis, but rather that the paranoid delusional systems are projected onto the father or other family members.

A mother projected her own symbiotic, i. e., incestuous wishes onto the father, his mother and his sister. She thought she was the only one who could protect the child from sexual molestation, which she had phantasized archaically.

[13] G. Biermann, "Die seelische Entwicklung des Kindes im Familienmilieu Schizophrener", *Schweiz. Arch. Neurol. Neurochr. Psychiat.* 97, 87–132, pp. 329–360, 1966.

Some mothers give me the impression that they and their children symbolize their selves in a concrete way. An inner separation of this close relationship calls forth self-loss-anxiety.

This became particularly clear to me in the case of a six-year-old boy whose mother, apparently stimulated by his oedipal approach to the father, accused the father, in a strongly fixed delusional system, of wanting to kill the boy with the goal of "destroying" her "mentally", as she expressed it. Every detail of daily life and of the father-son relationship fed her delusional system.

A mother with Christ-delusions clung to her 12-year-old son in the acute phase and pleaded with him to protect her from persecutors, saying he was a part of her own self anyway. This boy lived with his mother for years, and the mother and child roles were almost completely reversed: he cooked for her, did the shopping and took care of a large part of the relationships with the outside world. Nobody noticed until his school achievement started lagging somewhat. This mother had always been interested in philosophical, religious and psychological questions. Her main occupation with the boy when he was still a small child consisted in drawing "common-fantasy-sketches", as she called them. She probably did it to maintain the participatory relationship with the child as long as possible.

Here we see clearly an element of a schizophrenic mother, which reminds me of the description of the *mediale*-type of Toni Wolff:[14] the *mediale* is overpowered by the collective unconscious and formulates what is "in the air"; she identifies herself and others with archetypal contents. The distinction between conscious and unconscious, between I and Thou, and between personal and impersonal psychic themes is insufficient. She mobilizes psychic themes which others experience as foreign, often as threatening and dangerous. The children emphasize the unpredictable and irrational in their descriptions of their mothers, which makes them insecure and fearful. The *mediale* element is particularly clear when religious or political themes and events are built into a delusional system to which the entire family is subjected.

In conclusion, I would like to point out a very important element of the way these mothers act with their children: their reframing of reality. This is a common procedure in dealing with small children, for example, when a child has hit its head on the edge of the table and complains about the "bad table". It is easier to comfort the child if both complain about the bad table. This model, which actually is one of the

[14] Wolff, Toni, *Studien zu C. G. Jungs Psychologie*, Daimon Verlag, Zürich, 1981.

projective identifications, is used frequently by these mothers in later developmental phases in much more complex situations.

## 3. Discussion

Now I would like to try to summarize the above within a theoretical framework. First, I would like to remind you of the ego-experience I mentioned earlier. In this connection, I would like to quote the Swiss poet Robert Walser, who expressed in two short sentences what I was trying to describe. Robert Walser voluntarily withdrew into a psychiatric institution at the age of 51 because he no longer felt able to withstand the pressure of his archetypal images alone. He then spent almost 30 years of his life in the institution without ever writing again. In his fragment, "The Child", he has the child speak the following sentences: "No-one has the right to act toward me as if he knew me. If I should recognize anyone, I don't say so to his face; that would be untender of me and would call forth ill humour".[15]

Many of the children I have worked with have such an impersonal and distanced sensitivity. Yet I must emphasize that I have not seen a representative sample of the children of schizophrenic parents. I am speaking here of those who bear the mark of having spent an important part of their childhood with a psychotic parent.

The schizophrenic or pre-schizophrenic mother and her infant have some things in common: both have a weak ego and an undifferentiated self. The ego-self-axis is unstable and insufficiently structured. Both are primarily archetypally attuned to each other in their mutual expectations, perceptions and intentions. For the child, this is true because it is a child, and for the mother, because she is not only mother, but also schizophrenic. She is closer to the collective unconscious than a non-schizophrenic mother. Therefore the conditions are different than with a healthy mother: Neumann's[16] assumption that, in the case of normal development, the mother only "dips into" the uroboric "unitary reality" of the child in the early phases of development because the child only determines a part of her whole being, does not hold true for many schizophrenic mothers. They can become possessed of the child in their whole personality and existence. The child as a symbol of wholeness, a symbol of undifferentiation and chaotic drives, but also as a symbol of life, evokes in all of us – but more directly, faster and more

[15] R. Walser, "Das Kind" (III). In: Das Gesamtwerk, Bd. III, Kossodo-Verlag, Genf-Hamburg, p. 406, 1967.

[16] E. Neumann, *Das Kind*, Rhein Verlag, Zürich, p. 13, 1963.

intensively in the schizophrenic mother – a sense of the archaic and undifferentiated in its negative and positive aspects.

The transient feeling of extraordinary well-being and stability which many schizophrenic mothers experience in pregnancy and after birth may be an expression of the transient mobilization of the original self, as Fordham[17] used the term, as well as of the related uroboric ego-consciousness. This makes the stubborn clinging to a primitive identity of the mother and her child understandable. If this state is disturbed, either through maturation processes of the child or by changing relationships within the family, destructive archetypal fantasies can be stimulated. The ego of the mother becomes dominated by images of the threatening Great Mother. Fantasies of destruction, and abandonment of the child are either externally realized or contained within the construction of the delusional system. In the simultaneity or in the alternation of fusion and destruction fantasies, the deeper dependency problems of the schizophrenic become apparent. This means for the child that it grows up in environments which have matriarchal uroboric qualities even in their outer manifestations: there is more irrationality than rationality, communication fluctuates, the borders between ego and non-ego are unclear and changing, inside and outside are inseparable. The communication disturbances we know from research in schizophrenia also belong to this category. The background anxiety of the children which I mentioned at the beginning is comparable to the fear Neumann hypothesizes for early homo sapiens. He writes, "the defencelessness of early man against the dark superior power of the world and of the unconscious must lead to an existential feeling of permanent danger".[18]

Now the crystallization of the ego from the self, this necessary polarization, cannot be regarded as isolated from the formation of the first object relations. Lampert has correlated the views of Jung, Fordham and Winnicott on this matter in a very enlightening way. He summarized the via regia to object relations this way: "As a result of play and experiment, of hate and love, and with the help of a constant and cooperative mother, the child can relate the various archetypal expectations welling up from his inner world with a sufficiently real mother outside himself. Thus he can form a basis for object relations

[17] M. Fordham, "Primäres Selbst, primärer Narzissmus und verwandte Theorien", *Anal. Psychol.* 3, pp. 189–206, 1972.

[18] E. Neumann, *Ursprungsgeschichte des Bewusstseins*, Walter Verlag, Olten-Freiburg i. Br., p. 54, 1971.

which are not flooded by delusional fantasies from archetypal sources."[19]

The failure of this process, however, constitutes the basic disturbance of the schizophrenic mother herself. She is continually in retreat from real objects and reframes them delusionally following an archetypal scheme which forms the background of the incompatible complex which has inflated her ego.

The schizophrenic mothers seem to use their children as part objects. This means that her actual and concrete maternal behavior is determined more by her own archetypal projections than by sufficient adjustment to the real needs of the child. This is evident, for instance, when the child is drawn into the delusional system. The child as part object of the mother gathers immense meaning because it serves the restitution of the mother's self.

Now we can imagine how difficult it must be for an infant to perceive the mother as an external phenomenon and to differentiate between her and its own projections, because the schizophrenic mother blocks a process which Winnicott[20] emphasized: the attack on the maternal object, the repeated attempt to destroy the object, and the ability of the mother to "survive" this destruction and not "to take revenge" (as Winnicott says). Or one might say that the primary relationship between schizophrenic mother and child is their common unconscious and this is primarily determined by the mutuality of their archetypal projections, perceptions and expectations. The gradual maturation of the child and the physical and drive-differentiation related to it, stimulate deintegration with accompanying archetypal fantasies and impulses not only on the part of the child – the mother or her unconscious perceive these primarily archetypally or symbolically, but they are answered concretely. For instance, if the child projects annihilation fantasies in a separation phase, the mother will take these at face value. She reacts with annihilation or fusion wishes as a defence against her own anxiety, or with persecution. The child experiences this as a confirmation of his own annihilation fears which accompany his aggressiveness. As we have seen, sometimes she transfers those projections from the child to her husband or other family members. Secondary personalisation is only insufficiently successful: the mother image remains impersonal, and the emergence of the ego from the self does not pro-

[19] K. Lampert, ibid., p. 5.

[20] D. W. Winnicott, *Reifungsprozesse und fördernde Umwelt*, Kindler Verlag, München, p. 109, 1974.

gress. The border between mother and child is not drawn. The ego of the child is lacking in ability to structure and to polarize.

If the mother is completely identified with the archetype of the eternal nourishing mother, she can block the child from his illusion that the breast and the mother are parts of himself. The child who, according to Winnicott, feels sure of his magical control of his mother in this situation will become deeply insecure through a sudden change in the feelings and fantasies of the mother when she is abruptly identified with a negative aspect of the transformative character of the Great-Mother.

Without going into much more detail, we know that these disturbed processes in the child lead to problems in developing object relations and object constancy and ego-development, respectively, differentiation between ego and self.

In conclusion, I would like to point out that I have been describing the negative situation of these children and their mothers. When we remember that forty to sixty percent of the children of schizophrenic parents do not, as far as we know from current research,[21] develop severe disturbances in childhood, then a highly relevant question would be to ask what protective processes unfold when children are exposed to such unusual, or especially adverse, conditions while growing up.

I think especially this aspect should be an important challenge for us if we take seriously the idea of the archetypes and of archetypal processes in child development.

## Summary

A report is made on children whose mothers are suffering from a schizophrenic psychosis. The children display general anxiety, which is an expression of the instability of the ego-self axis. The ego functions which are related to archetypal processes are particularly disturbed or disturbable. Their ego-experience is strongly dominated by the fantasy-ego. Ego-development is a result of the special conditions to which the formation of early object relations is subjected with a psychotic mother. Since the schizophrenic mother is closer to the collective unconscious, the maturation steps of the child trigger deintegrative processes of the self in her too, which become apparent through destructive archetypal

[21] E. J. Anthony, C. Koupernik, C. Chiland, *The Child in His Family*, vol. 4, John Wiley & Sohns, New York, 1978.

fantasies, the archetypal background of which are aspects of the threatening Great Mother. Since the schizophrenic mother has a disturbed relationship to reality, she has tendency to make these archetypal fantasies concerete in the external world, or to live them in a delusional system, since her ego-complex is inflated by archetypes. This results in blockage of the processes of secondary personalization in the child, and in a persistence of impersonal mother images, which remain within the collective unconscious. This can become manifest in a strong denial and splitting of the personal mother. The children have difficulties in developing object constancy. And yet, they develop autonomous secondary ego-functions which allow them adequate adjustment in childhood.

# Success, Retreat, Panic: Over-Stimulation and Depressive Defence*

Peer Hultberg (Frankfurt-am-Main)

The concept of over-stimulation or hyperexcitement has until recently been used predominantly in connection with children. It has been discussed as an intense reaction of over-involvement resulting from too-strong stimuli from the outside, especially from over-close and over-taxing parents. However, in the past decade there has been a tendency to consider the concept also as an inner psychic phenomenon frequently observed in adults. This change of emphasis is mainly the result of the work of American writers on the so-called self-psychology, notably Heinz Kohut and his followers. Over-stimulation in this latter sense is, in the language of Kohut, defined as a "mobilization of archaic exhibitionistic libido" (Kohut 5, p. 5) which threatens to flood the ego. This process may be triggered off by something in the outside world, or an inner stimulus or phantasy may be externalised. It is, however, in contrast to the classical concept of over-stimulation, essentially an endopsychic process. In the language of Jung one might say that over-stimulation in this sense is a process whereby conscious or unconscious psychic contents of an inflationary or grandiose nature are aroused and threaten to overwhelm the ego. The ego, however, is strong enough and has sufficient reality sense, as it were, to defend itself against both identification with the grandiose content and general non-psychotic states of inflation, and against irreversible submersion psychosis. The process, however, does call forth an excitement which is felt as highly uncomfortable and which gives rise to strong anxiety. The

* Reprinted by permission of *The Journal of Analytical Psychology*, where it appeared in Vol. 30, No. 1 (1985). It also appeared in German in *Analytische Psychologie*, Vol. 15, No. 3 (1984).

manner in which the ego defends itself against this anxiety is mainly by retreating. An ego which is especially prone to become hyper-stimulated seems above all to protect itself by secluding itself from the wave or source of excitement. This is then generally experienced either as a state of resentful depressive hopelessness or as apathetic isolation and utter passivity, or both.

The process may be illustrated by the following story:

A young painter from a provincial town in Denmark held his first exhibition in Copenhagen. It was received well. Encouraged by this, he was soon afterwards able to arrange a second exhibition with a reception equally favourable, if not better. The young artist then went home to visit his parents in their idyllic little Danish town. As he was sitting in the train he suddenly felt as if he were about to burst, to fly into a thousand pieces. He was overwhelmed and entirely unable to control his phantasy that, when the little local train eventually pulled up at the station, a red carpet would have been laid out and a delegation headed by the mayor would be awaiting him with music and flowers. He got into a panic and started to pace frantically up and down the corridor of the train, imagining with dread the deafening sound of the brass band welcoming him. Overwhelmed by an inexplicable anxiety, he found his way to the small bar in the train. And when his parents met him at the station – needless to say, without any municipal delegation or brass band – their son literally fell out of the train, totally drunk. Curiously enough, however, apart from the alcoholic poisoning, his state of mind was tranquil and composed. He had mastered his excitement and the subsequent anxiety, and he no longer felt torn to pieces. Although his mood was somewhat sad and even resigned, at the same time he felt calm. However, for a very long time afterwards his creative powers seemed to fail him, and he was unable to paint properly for several years. He lived in something akin to a mild apathy and dejection and chose to finish a very conventional course of university studies rather than go on trying to make a career as an artist.

This small scene seems to speak for itself as an illustration of the problem of over-stimulation and retreat. Here was a man in his late twenties who, all of a sudden, sees the fulfilment of his most daring hopes. To become a painter and to be recognised as such was to him the supreme goal in his life. It had been so ever since he was a small, sensitive boy who, from the age of six, had to assert himself at school by means of his intellectual, and especially his artistic, talents. His parents never understood his situation. They did not see his plight and never considered his painting as anything of value. He quickly saw through his mother's superficial and sentimental praise of his efforts as a child and carefully kept everything he painted away from her lest she should use it for her own self-enhancement. The father was just not interested. And when he exhibited his pictures they were, in fact, both shocked and extremely embarrassed that their little boy could paint such big and such blatantly erotic canvases. On the other hand, they mildly flattered themselves at their son's success. The painter had thus never obtained any real recognition before the unexpected success with his first two exhibitions. But rather than finding strength and encouragement for further steady work, he became overjoyed and subsequently hyper-stimulated. And this tendency to be almost torn to pieces at the fulfilment of his most burning wish had to be defended against in such a way that over-stimulation gave way to apathy and dejection for a long time to come. He fell into a state of emptiness; his initiative was blocked, and he felt paralysed. In short, he experienced a condition close to depression.

It is, however, important to underline that at no point was there any question of his falling into a manifest depressive psychosis. His ego seemed to function with a certain degree of reliability as it had always done, and he kept up his fairly good work record. In other words, he seemed quite early in life to have acquired a minimum of psychic cohesion, or ego strength, which prevented any complete submersion in the world of his phantasies. All the same, his ego did appear frail and seemed protected only behind rigid walls, which then came under fierce attack through the realisation of his burning ambition. It was, however, strong enough ultimately to withstand and to defend itself against the onrush of over-stimulation. The psychic tension could be regulated and the falling-apart prevented, albeit by rather immature or even archaic defensive manoeuvres.

The manner in which the walls are generally rebuilt after a flooding of over-stimulation – especially in the non-analytical setting – is also illustrated by this case. However, the following brief extra-analytical account may show even more clearly the essential features of this restorative process.

A woman violinist, on the strength of a very successful first performance, was awarded a scholarship to go abroad to study with one of the most famous of violinists. She returned home to give her second concert, which was a startling success. The audience recognised her as the national equivalent of the eminent violinist and the enthusiasm was almost uncontrollable; people would hardly let her leave the platform. She reacted by getting into a panic after the concert. She hid in her dressing room, allowed no one to get near to her, cancelled immediately all further arrangements for concerts, and the following day decided to give up her career as a violinist entirely. It was impossible for anyone to persuade her to do otherwise. She broke away from her musical milieu and in due course obtained a post at a school as an ordinary music teacher, and she remained there for the rest of her working life.

For the young painter and for the violinist, the fulfilment of the greatest and most intense wishes of their lives led to a dangerous situation where the ego of each of them was about to be entirely flooded by grandiose phantasies. In both cases, the ego defended itself by retreat and apparent emptiness. But when it came to a restoration, it was, especially in the case of the violinist, unable to restore itself to its former dimensions. The young painter had to live for several years in a state much below the level of his artistic talents and possibilities, and was, in fact, only helped out of this condition through analysis. The violinist lived like that for the rest of her life, contenting herself with a job which she found rather mundane, although her decision was naturally supported later by other defence mechanisms such as intellectualisation, rationalisation, and ideological and ethical arguments.

From a Jungian point of view, one notices here the resemblance, especially in the latter case, of this sequence of events to Jung's concept of 'the regressive restoration of the persona'. Jung coined this term in his 1916 lecture, "Über das Unbewusste und seine Inhalte", and elaborated it in the enlarged version of the lecture, "The relations between the ego and the unconscious". He uses it to describe one of the possible reactions to the breakthrough into consciousness of unconscious contents, and illustrates it with examples taken from everyday life since:

> It would (...) be a mistake to think that cases of this kind make their appearance only in analytical treatment. The process can be observed just as well, and often better, in other situations of life, namely in all those careers where there has been some violent and destructive intervention of fate (Jung 3, p. 164).

The restoration of the persona in a regressive way means that the individual in question "will have demeaned himself, pretending that he is as he was *before* the crucial experience, though utterly unable even to think of repeating such a risk. Formerly perhaps he wanted more than he could accomplish; now he does not even dare to attempt what he has it in him to do" (Jung 3, p. 164). In other words, the person leads a life on a lower level than before.

The difference between Jung's description and the problem of over-stimulation as described here is that Jung uses the reaction to a catastrophe as an illustration of his concept: he takes as an example the case of a business man going bankrupt. In the context of over-stimulation, however, one is dealing with the reaction to an unexpected success, the fulfilment of a deeply nourished hope which threatens to upset the psychic equilibrium and create unmanageable inner tensions. The individual withdraws into isolation, either concretely, as in the case of the music teacher or into an alcoholic aloofness, as in the case of the young painter. But when they eventually emerge from their protective and calming isolation, it is not with an ego which is better able to defend itself; it is with a patched-up psychic equilibrium. They emerge with an ego which is able to defend itself against the onrush of over-stimulation only because it has given up the ambitions and wishes the fulfilment of which caused the almost uncontrollable flooding. The healthy part of the psyche has not been strengthened; on the contrary, the psychic scope has been reduced and apathy adopted as a major defence mechanism. It might perhaps be said that here is a defensive mechanism which is the reverse of the regression in the service of the ego, akin to Anna Freud's concept of ego-restriction.

Like the regressive restoration of the persona, the retreat after over-stimulation seems rarely to bring individuals into analysis. The retreat in itself is defence enough to keep them going. The avoidance of risks and of situations which may give rise to hyperexcitement generally assures a relatively smooth day-to-day functioning. And, as Jung indicated, the phenomenon is encountered perhaps less in analysis than among one's friends and acquaintances.

### *Over-stimulation in analysis*

However, there is a group of patients for whom over-stimulation appears to lie at the core of their problems. These are people who, in their youth and also as children, have frequently given the impression of being very talented, at times even exceptionally so. However, they never really seem able to live up to the promise they initially inspired. Instead of developing and realising their gifts, they appear, often fairly early in life, to slip into a somewhat mild depressive state; and they tend to remain in it forever, except perhaps for the odd short outburst of creativity in which they suddenly seem to rekindle the expectations they originally awoke. Generally, however, they live a reduced life, not in the sense that one feels that their intellectual powers or their creative talents have dried up, but merely that these never appear to have been led into channels where they may be fully and purposefully employed. The most typical feature, however, is that there is a specific task which they cannot accomplish, although they seem generously equipped to do so and also very well prepared for it. They may even come into therapy explicitly to be helped to perform this task, or it transpires very early in therapy that they are worried (or at times through rationalisations resigned to the fact) that they cannot finish their doctoral dissertation, that they have broken off their course of study a short time before the final exams (which naturally they had every reason to believe they would pass well), that they are simply unable to make the last preparations for their crucial recital, although the programme has been rehearsed for years. The rather absurd modern notion of concert abstinence seems to be a rationalisation for such an inner state. Here a performing artist may rather retire than expose himself to the enthusiasm of an audience, as in the case of the violinist mentioned above. The following account may serve as an illustration of overstimulation as a basic psychic problem.

Mrs. Lake is an American. She is close to forty and has come into analysis with a 'man's disease'. She has a bad heart. She is working overtime at her school without extra pay, is engaged in trade union activities, and in addition, gives courses in art history almost every evening. The weekends are spent organising political work, and she has not had a holiday for more than two years. However, she feels amply rewarded by the prestige she has achieved as an ardent environmentalist and by the small political organisation devoted to these problems which, she feels, she herself has created from scratch. Were it not for the heart, everything would be well. In the initial interview, she mentions a curious fact: she, the prizewinner at school and at university, she, who won some highly coveted scholarships and whom everyone thought would climb to the top of the university ladder, just cannot finish 'her book'. After a sabbatical year to do research in Europe, she even had herself posted back to Germany to carry on the work, which was supposed to assure her a top position in her former university department. "Mark you", she adds in the initial interview, "when I have written my book and proved my point, everyone working on Dürer will have to take it into account; and all the encyclopaedias in Germany and subsequently in the whole world will have to be revised".

In the following session, I try to test her claim, and as far as I can see, it is not just inflated madness. She explains her ideas to me painstakingly and accurately, showing me supporting reports from museum directors and professors. It appears that she really has a point which will throw an entirely new light on her topic and she seems able to prove it.

The sore point, however, is that her book cannot be written. She is now in her late thirties and it should have been finished years ago. Everyone around her is encouraging, everyone supports her; but the book stays where it has always been, in a box of neatly filled-in index cards. It has long ago ceased to be embarrassing to her. She has swallowed the hurt of disappointed expectation, she just plods on. But still she cannot write, although she has all the material she wants, and from an intellectual point of view nothing prevents her.

This problem, and not her heart, quickly became the focus of the sessions.

There was no difficulty in linking the problem up with Mrs. Lake's negatively experienced mother, but then everything seemed to stop. Mrs. Lake had been brought up by her divorced mother, who kept her, the only child, away from the father until his death. And it was not till she started analysis that Mrs. Lake really began to see *how* brutally she had been exploited by her mother from childhood up till the present day. So we both tended to search for the root of her problem in her relationship to her mother.

Was the reason that she could not finish her book defiance against the mother? Was it revenge and an expression of rage in connection with the early trauma that she had never been accepted as she was, but had always been exploited narcissistically in order to enhance the mother's self-esteem? Was she begrudging the mother the triumph of having a daughter who had published a book of her own? Or was it guilt over her succes, because, as the author of an important book, she would finally have superseded the mother? Could it be just defence against competitiveness with the mother? Or had she, through projective identification, incorporated the inferiority and incompetence against which the mother defended herself so vehemently? Was she merely treating her book with the same demands of hyperperfection with which the mother had treated her as a child? Was the thesis her child which she, unmarried and childless, would not permit to develop according to its own laws and of which she could not let go? Or was the block a deep prophylaxis against the shattering disappointment that the mother would after all *not* recognise her and accept her, but remain as indifferent to her achievements as she had always been, even after she had accomplished this, to her, tremendous feat? Did her block thus express deep doubts about her own worth and her own intelligence, which could not be counter proved by realistic self-esteem? Or was it just the *puella aeterna's* fear of entering the world of the grown-up? Or a fear that growing up might mean irrevocably leaving the mother, and thus finally having to give up the neurotic entanglement with her, which had been almost the only form of human relationship she had known, or, at any rate, the most important? Or could it be a question of identity, a fear of abandoning the identity of the daughter as such, of the *doctoranda*, the eternal daughter of the Alma Mater? Or had the book been the only means whereby she could confirm herself to herself and maintain an inner continuity? Was she then clinging to it as a child clings to a transitional object? Or was she clinging to it because she had *not* been able to transform it into a transitional object, but kept experiencing it as a gift to the mother? Was the book one of the few stabilising factors in her life; and would it then be possible for her to finish it if the analysis and I, in the transference, took over this stabilising function? And, conversely, was the inability to get on with the work in the present context of the analysis, and in spite of my various interpretations, a transference phenomenon: she feared that I, like the mother, might take the credit for her work if she were to finish it because of therapy with me, a fear that I, too, would exploit her for *my* narcissistic needs and treat her and her work as a feather in my analyst's cap? Or, worse still, a fear that I, like the mother, might choose just to ignore it and treat it as a matter of analytical course?

We looked into all these possibilities and all seemed quite convincing. There was something about them all, but none of them seemed to hit the mark. Only one thing seemed certain: Mrs. Lake was depressed in a restless, tooth-grinding way, not because she could not write her book, but in order *not* to write it.

It was not till the concept of over-stimulation was introduced that the reaction was more in the affirmative. It was even possible to speak about the classical "aha-experience". Things now seemed clearer. The book was the goal of her life. More she did not want from life; she had in advance decided against any further research. It was enough to her to think that, when she had officially proved her point, all the major encyclopaedias in the world would have to be rewritten, and that her name from now on would appear in the indexes of all works on Dürer. She would expect nothing more from life. Perhaps this limitation of herself was a kind of anticipatory and prophylactic restoration of her persona in a regressive way. However, it did not succeed in curbing her over-stimulation and the subsequent anxieties at the thought of what might happen when she had finished her book. On the contrary, the confinement of her life's work to this single book seemed to have the adverse effect: it appeared to accentuate the absolute character of the fulfilment of this most burning wish and to exacerbate her fears of the consequences to her psyche when she had fulfilled her task. She was not afraid of being drained, or of the emptiness which might come over a person who has reached the goal he has set himself, nor of the feeling of sudden bewilderment which one might suppose comes over the donkey when it has suddenly devoured the carrot which for years has been dangling before its nose. What she was really afraid of was simply of bursting with joy, of being overcome with excitement to such an extent that she could not control it. And her feeling of emptiness as well as her severe work inhibition was her way of coping with this anxiety and defending herself against it. In these overstimulating phantasies, the mother naturally also cropped up. One of the most hyperexciting phantasies was of an ultimate reconciliation with her mother. Through her success, she would at last have replaced and even superseded and surpassed the father whom the mother had castrated so effectively. She would finally be able to compensate the mother for the severe troubles which the father in her eyes had caused her in the marriage, and thus, in the end, she would win the mother's love.

It now transpired that over-excitement and hyperstimulation were very important features in the life of Mrs. Lake. She was, for example, totally unable to calm down if she had experienced some form of success in her professional life. She described how she would then talk incessantly to herself in her car or when walking in the street, where people would even turn round and look at her. At home, she would argue with herself for hours, either sitting on the edge of her bed or pacing up and down her study till five or six in the morning, when, from sheer exhaustion and by means of a couple of glasses of Dubonnet, she would at last collapse into bed for an hour or two. She was now herself able to connect this with her mother, who had never given her any admiration or recognition for her often exceptionally good achievements, nor any sympathy in her worries. Mrs. Lake then grew unable to feel any real joy in herself and in her accomplishments. Furthermore, she was provided with no measure by which to appraise realistically the value of her achievements. She thus had no inner joy in herself and in her activities and no inner criteria for judgement of herself. Indeed, many of her dreams pointed to this general depressive state of her soul; deep down, behind her often sparkling vitality and her 'green' environmentalist activities, there was a bleak psychic desert and a dream-ego deprived of any illusions. It was therefore understandable that she should react with terror to the thought of having to cope with the extreme happiness when she had reached her long cherished goal; and that she should prefer her subdued, somewhat depressive and blocked state rather than risk exploding from a joy which she had no means of controlling. In this way, she defended herself against the dread of over-stimulation, but at the price of a severe work inhibition.

Mrs. Lake appeared fully able to accept the interpretation of over-stimulation as being at the core of her problem. And as a result of this, she decided to abandon her ambitious project. The entries on Dürer in all the major encyclopaedias of this world are, after all, not going to be rewritten. Like most of her colleagues in the academic world, she chose to restrict herself to writing the occasional article. At the same time, as she gave up the attempt to write her book, she also approached her old college and was delighted to realise that she had not been forgotten. On the contrary, since she had always been an excellent and inspiring teacher, she was offered her old position and returned to the United States in a composed frame of mind. And when friends and colleagues suggest that she might, after all, write a nice little popular book on Dürer, she can now cope with the stimulation and stem the flood of phantasies – and refuse.

## Over-stimulation in the Transference

In the analytical process as such, over-stimulation seems, above all, to manifest itself in connection with the transference and probably also the countertransference. In the transference, it seems principally to evolve around an extreme sensitivity to the closeness of the analytical situation, especially at times when idealisation or projective identification are at their strongest. The highest goal of the analysand at times is to be as intimate with the analyst as he possibly can, and the feeling that this wish could be fulfilled may again be too overwhelming. Subsequently, the analysand has defend himself against this dangerous situation.

The manner in which the analysand experiences the perils of closeness is naturally highly varied and very subjective. The sharing of a joke can be as upsetting as the phantasies aroused when a confessing analyst feels he must disclose parts of his personal life as a reward for frankness, as a consolation, or as a surrender to more or less subtle emotional blackmail. A chance encounter outside can give rise to ideas of identical interests or identical life problems. Pleasure on the part of the analyst, as indeed his praise, can give rise to phantasies of being the chosen person, and so on. Behind all these phantasies lies the dread of being overwhelmed and of losing control as a result of reaching the unbearable state of intimacy and closeness. This may be expressed as a fear of being seduced by the analyst – seduction naturally understood in the broadest sense of the word, intellectual or ideological or theoretical seduction being often just as dangerous as sexual seduction. Here there is a dread that the analyst might abandon his self-control and initiate the wished-for closeness.

Kohut and his followers have pointed out an important fear in this context – the fear of being swept off one's feet by an interpretation which hits the centre of things (see, for example, Goldberg 2, pp. 9, 63, 83, 85). This fear has probably at least two main sources. It is naturally an expression of the fright at what might happen if an insight is suddenly achieved and hitherto unconscious contents are released and engulf the ego before it has had time to organise its defences. But it also seems to be a fear of being over-stimulated by the joy at having at last found a fellow human being who, seemingly by instinct or intuition or by extreme empathy, can feel the needs and the plight of the analysand even before he himself understands it. Many cases of prolonged silence in therapy may probably be put down to this anxiety, rather than being seen as an expression of unconscious aggression or defiance.

The following occurrence may illustrate this point:

A couple of years ago, I was presented with a copy of the first edition of T. S. Eliot's *Four Quartets*. Since I was very happy both with the book and the thought behind it, I let it lie on a table in my consulting room, so that I might read a little in it between hours. An intelligent woman patient with a strong, rather dependent transference immediately noticed the book and remarked on it. As she was very interested in literature, I fetched the book and read the passage about the wounded surgeon to her:

Our only health is the disease
If we obey the dying nurse
Whose constant care is not to please
But to remind of our, and Adam's curse,
And that, to be restored, our sickness must grow worse
(Eliot 1, p. 181).

We discussed briefly how Jungian, in fact, these thoughts are, and this led us, I believed, in a natural way into the hour.

As one too often does when breaking the rule of abstinence, I thought little of this and merely believed that we had discussed something of interest to her. I was therefore very much taken aback when she started her Monday session with a very earnest request: "Would I please, please in future, *please* never more break the analytical neutrality and not introduce matters from my personal life; she was just unable to cope with it." At first I was perplexed and did not know what she was referring to; I believed it could only be an anecdote, not even concerning me personally, which I had produced to drive home an interpretation. Only then did she explain that it had to do with the poem. It seemed to her that I had talked about it in a very special way, as if I had felt the need to communicate something especially private and personal to her and to her alone, and exactly at this point in her analysis. She had registered my pleasure in the poem and interpreted this to mean that I had no one at all with whom I could share my joy and my interests. In that way, I had made her my partner, I had seduced her, she felt, intimating a loneliness in my personal life, as well as deep problems, which were parallel to her own problems and her own loneliness. She had returned home after the hour overwhelmed by excitement and phantasies that, after all, she was the chosen one, that her feelings for me had echoed in me. She was, at the time, in a stage in her analysis where she did not retreat into an overt depressive mood as a result of the over-stimulation. However, she did feel that she was in danger of losing control over herself and experienced again a dreadful fear, almost like a fear of death, of losing herself to me, and thus entering into one of the fatally destructive relationships which she had previously known and in which she had entirely given up her own personality. For a couple of hours, she was trembling all over her body and it took her a full evening to calm down sufficiently so that she could write herself out of her excitement. Furthermore, she spent the whole weekend studying Eliot in the belief that he had been the subject of my doctoral thesis.

The defence and retreat phenomena connected with over-stimulation in the transference are naturally very varied but aim predominantly at avoiding the threatening closeness. This may happen in a phobic way, by increasingly incapacitating anxieties, for example. Or, especially early on in analysis, it may lead to the analysis being broken off, often exactly when the analyst feels that things are going particularly well and a really good relationship is about to be established. The fear of praise may lead to snarls at the analyst, who has perhaps indirectly given vent to his pleasure at the good cooperation. Or the analysand may ostentatiously, and maybe even in a hurtful manner, forbid himself any interest in the life of the analyst as a defence against overwhelming phantasies. He may, as indicated before, appear drowsy, passive, be silent in a bewildering manner, rather than dare to expose himself to the friendly warmth and empathic understanding of the analyst. Or he may defend himself against being overwhelmed by his own idealisation of the analyst by criticising him, or seemingly rejecting the school of analysis to which he assumes the analyst belongs. Long tirades against Jung, often of a political nature, or the belittling of Freud's Viennese *petit bourgeois* background seem to be instances of this, as do certain dreams, especially at the beginning of analysis, the contents of which poke fun at the analyst's theoretical framework or at the analyst as a person.

At this point, perhaps one specific type of defence against hyperexcitement ought briefly to be mentioned: the use of the age-old depressant, alcohol. When the previously mentioned young artist was caught by the possibility of a fragmentation of his personality by his overwhelming, grandiose phantasies, he retreated at first into an alcoholic stupor. Mrs. Lake likewise had, now and then, to lull herself to sleep with her glass of Dubonnet. This is almost a parody of the reality-orientated defence against over-stimulation, which is controlled retreat and organised withdrawall. But, when the source is internal, it is difficult to find a place to retire to and to do so in a regulated manner. It appears, however, that the healthy part of the psyche, in a highly inadequate way, uses alcohol to defend itself against disintegration. When people with alcohol problems are faced with deeply agitating phantasies and are about to be flooded by hyperexcitement, they seem able to quieten the intrusive grandiose phantasies by drinking. Alcohol appears here to have a certain ego-regenerating function. The individual is able to retire, regress and isolate himself, and subsequently to restore his personality through alcohol. Although drinking may naturally be the revengeful reaction to a disappointment or an imagined rebuff, it may also be caused by highly stirring phantasies released in the transference, for example, through a misunderstanding of the analyst's friendly warmth. And the only way, then, in which the ego seems able to defend itself against such floodings of joy and excitement is by staging a flooding of its own.

Such a drinking pattern seems, for example, to be the basis of the alcoholism of one patient who easily became severely hyperstimulated. On one occasion he was overwhelmed by the beauty of nature while wandering for days in an impressive Alpine landscape. His happiness at such splendid scenery was so great that he just could not contain it. The excitement grew so painful that it became unendurable and he had to have alcohol in order to calm down: "I just had to drink in order to become a normal person again, otherwise I don't know what I should have done for sheer joy", as he expressed it.

I am here reminded of Keats' "Ode to a Nightingale", where the poet "being too happy in thine happiness", wishes for "a draught of vintage... That I might drink, and leave the world unseen, / And with the fade away into the forest dim" (Keats 4, p. 207). Hyperstimulation seems to have been a psychic reality for many of the Romantics; and it was, in fact, observations concerning the Polish Romantic poet Adam Mickiewicz which initially gave rise to my interest in the phenomenon. In "Ode to a Nightingale", Keats also points to the ultimate regression in the face of hyperexcitement:

> Now more than ever seems it rich to die,
> To cease upon the midnight with no pain,
> While thou art pouring forth thy soul abroad
> In such an ecstasy!
>
> (Keats 4, p. 208).

Perhaps the equivalent in the late twentieth century to such sentiments is the experience of a recently married young woman who, on a glorious early summer morning drove her open car at very high speed in blazing sun down a motorway with her husband at her side. At a certain moment, she suddenly became obsessed with the desire to drive her car straight into the pillars of one of the motorway bridges: life was so overwhelmingly beautiful that death seemed the only consequence of her rapture.

It seems important to mention the use of alcohol as a combatant of over-stimulation, since alcohol is so often mentioned in general discussions as the bringer of spirit. This might lead to a false understanding of some of the problems lying behind alcoholism or heavy drinking. In cases where over-stimulation plays a part, one may even say that alcohol is used in its opposite, depressant way, to combat a surplus of spirit, as it were. And to see the alcohol problem as an expression of a thwarted spiritual search would be misleading, to say the least. On the contrary, alcohol here enables the ego to retreat in a defensive manner and thus withstand the threat of being swamped by spiritual contents. In other terms, it appears that, just as one talks of anal defence against orality, one might here talk of an oral defence against an even deeper regression, a defence against the entire breaking up of the psyche. This mixture of defences seems clearly illustrated in the last case I will bring of the man who "just had to drink to become a normal person again".

T. was a very meticulous and extremely hard-working and ambitious natural scientist – a true anal character, as one usually calls it. He had the habit of working late in the evenings at his laboratory. At a certain point, he would start to drink. This, he felt, would enable him to work on a little longer. Soon, however, the quality of the work would be such that it was quite useless, and then he just drank on in a rather guiltless state, at times feeling that he was rewarding himself for being a genius. Hence he was able to muse about life for some hours, he could abandon himself to happy phantasies, or he was lost without anxiety in joy at having found a mistake or a fault in his calculations. Finally, in an alcoholic haze, he returned home from the laboratory. In the end, his wife refused to accept this as "the way scientists work"; she confronted him with the alternative of divorce or therapy, and this brought him into analysis. Here there seemed to be a defence against orality which, however, at a certain point broke through and clearly came to the fore when the scientist permitted himself a little drink, rationalised partly as a reward for his industry and partly as an excuse to get the energy to work on a little longer. At the same time, the drinking itself defended him against a feeling either of void or, more probably, of over-stimulation, when, for example, he finally found an insidious mistake; these feelings would invariably have overwhelmed him if he had finished his day's work without drinking. Without drink, he would either feel exhausted and start doubting the meaning of all that he was doing, or he would get carried away by grandiose and anxiety-inducing phantasies. He had, for instance, terrifying phantasies of making an absolute fool of himself when receiving the Nobel Prize from the hands of the Swedish king. When he drank, however, he was able to control these phantasies, and they were not experienced as overwhelming. And rather than being terrified, he would, in fact, enjoy them and could safely abandon himself to them, knowing that they would wear off as the amount of alcohol increased. Drinking in T.'s case is thus not only to be interpreted as a reward for industry (orality breaking through anal defences); it seems even more to be a defence against the hyperexcitement induced by phantasy products springing from what may be called anal industry. In this connection, it also seems possible to argue that the well-known everyday phenomena of nightcaps and 'unwinding' after a day's work may be understood in this way. This may be a more fruitful interpretation than merely seeing them as oral compensations for the difficulties of life.

## Countertransference

As regards the countertransference, a certain parallel seems observable to the situation of hyperexcitement in the transference, although the basic anxiety of attaining intimate closeness to the analysand may not be so pronounced. However, it can certainly not be ruled out entirely. There might, for example, be moments where the analysand is experienced as a parental figure whose approval and even admiration is sought through a strikingly correct interpretation or a convincingly good piece of advice. This may well happen if the analyst as a child has been called upon to advise his parents rather than being advised by them and to win their acceptance in this way, a situation which probably is not so uncommon for children who later become analysts.

In the countertransference, two factors above all seem conducive to a flooding of the analyst's ego: admiration and success. They may naturally be defended against in many highly different ways. The analyst may, for example, attempt to keep the analysis under tight control, guarding himself against getting too much from the patient, as it were. In this case, he may play down the patient's achievements, either in the sense of not properly acknowledging material brought to the sessions, or not recognising things achieved outside the analysis, either as a response to the analytical work or directly to gain praise from the analyst. This control may be rationalised as 'preventing acting out', or 'refusal to give narcissistic gratification'. All in all, such analyses may seem grey and dull or unduly severe, and the analyst will continually feel inadequate and complain that he never seems to achieve anything – feelings which naturally sooner or later will be picked up by the patient and damp all enthusiasm for the work.

It also appears that boredom in the analysis may at times spring from a similar source. It need not only be the analyst's response to resistances on the part of the patient. I remember a patient whom I found unbearably boring; I dreaded the three weekly hours with him and could hardly restrain myself from confronting him with this. Only when I realised that it was, in fact, mainly my own problem and that I was defending myself against archaic idealisation on his part, could I cope with my boredom. This was so much more excruciating, and hence highly defensive on my part, as the patient's idealisation was of the type which is intensely intrusive, and thus it was felt by me as being very aggressive. I had simultaneously to defend myself against something both intrusive and idealising, and for some weeks that was too much for me.

I wonder whether the fear of closeness on the part of the analyst, which may arise as a reaction to a patient's overstimulating admiration, might also find expression in a certain apprehension regarding inquiries into the patient's personal life, or directly in avoidance of phantasising about him. This would naturally mean that the analyst was depriving himself of one of the best tools for interpretation. In any event, it does appear that fear of over-stimulation can hamper interpretation to a great extent. The analyst may fear the impact of the correct interpretation in the same way as the patient, either because of the consequences which it might have on the patient, or because he is afraid of the over-stimulating effect on himself of his skill in hitting the mark. This is a dread that his own virtuosity may finally bolt away with him and flood him, an anxiety which it seems is also felt by many artists.

The fear of admiration or of idealisation, that is, the fear of being praised, with the resulting avoidance of closeness, is likely to lead to rather uninspired analyses where not much happens. This is often rationalised as steady work on the part of a reliable analyst. Over-stimulation, however, may also take the form of fear of being flooded in the case of evident success. This could lead to an unconscious avoidance of success altogether. One of the many ways of preventing success is to terminate analysis prematurely, or even break it off, an act which might again be rationalised, for instance, by advocating principles of not binding the patient too strongly to the analyst, of not believing in over-long analyses, of wishing the patient to take the responsibility for his own life.

The following example, not of an analyst but of a physiotherapist in her early thirties, may illustrate the problem of over-stimulation in the helping professions, that is, the fears aroused in the helper by his own powers. Mrs. Nielsen was highly gifted in her field. However, like all people whose skill approaches virtuosity, she was also an exceedingly hard worker who had gone to great lengths to improve her skills and training. As a result of this, she was able at times to achieve cures which were almost miraculous: people condemned to the wheelchair were able after some months of treatment to get up on their own and take their first steps; a spastic baby whom everyone had given up and who had given himself up and turned all but autistic, gained control of his motor apparatus, started smiling at his mother, expressed frustration and understandable rage, and became very curious about the world around him. At a certain point, Mrs. Nielsen grew frightened of her own powers. The events taking place in her practice were nearly too much for her to contain or to cope with. They seemed uncanny to her, and she felt that she possessed almost supernatural powers or, conversely, was possessed by such powers. She was partly fearful lest she should "grow into the skies and become a megalomaniac", as she expressed it, and partly afraid that something fundamental was wrong with her since she could achieve these stunning results. In her worries about her successes, she was at a point where she wished to put an end to it all and just become an ordinary run-of-the-mill physiotherapist. She did not know where the whole thing would lead to otherwise, she said.

After a thorough discussion of her cures, she and I agreed that there was, in fact, nothing supernatural about them. She had not consciously or unconsciously entered into a pact with the Devil, whatever shape he might take in the psyche of a late twentieth century woman. Her seemingly miraculous successes sprang from a combination of conscientious hard work and an uncommonly good training combined with an excellent diagnostic intuition based on her trust in her subliminal or unconscious perceptions. She felt her situation had also become worse during her analysis because she had achieved an even better contact with her unconscious. Moreover, her enthusiasm for her work, combined with her confidence in her unconscious, especially in her unconscious observations, gave her pronounced suggestive powers which contributed further to her fears. She could carry people with her and awaken their own trust in themselves and in the possibility of what they had hitherto believed was impossible. And this naturally was a necessary condition for a cure. Because of this insight into her inner and outer reality, it was possible to halt her tendency towards retreat in the face of hyperexcitement at her astonishing cures. She built up a realistic self-esteem which prevented her from flight in terror from her own successes or from thwarting them. She no longer saw herself as being like a faith healer in the grips of mysterious powers which would grow or wane without her control. She realised that she was simply a highly-skilled professional woman who had a fine career ahead of her.

It seems then that the main defence mechanism against over-stimulation on the part of the analyst is the well-known device of ego-restriction, be it in the form of a restriction of his human response, his empathy, his attention and vigilance, his interpretative, skills, or his general performance. However, one feature might be particularly considered in this context, and that is the rejection, if not the direct rebuff, of the patient's feelings. This may take place as a reaction to idealisation where the analyst in the countertransference, for example, may reject parents who have idealised him as a child instead of letting him idealise them, thus depriving him of guidelines and leaving it to him to fend for himself and perhaps for the parents too. But, naturally, a rebuff of the necessary idealisation from the analysand may also be a question of idealisation felt as too much, that is, as the fulfillment of the most cherished wish. In this connection, one specific aspect of the rejection and rebuff should be pointed out – the rejection of gratitude. Melanie Klein was certainly right in emphasising the importance of both envy and gratitude for the human being. However, in general, too little attention has been paid to gratitude. This may certainly be felt at times as exceedingly uncomfortable. In the case of Mrs. Nielsen, the physiotherapist, the worst moments for her came when patients, especially ordinary simple people, expressed their profuse thankfulness to her for her remarkable cures. Often these patients were extremely moved, and she had the greatest difficulty in not belittling their feelings as well as her own achievements. The embarrassment was aggravated because, like Mrs. Nielsen herself, the patients generally had no particular religious beliefs. Hence they could neither thank their God for their cure, nor could Mrs. Nielsen thank hers for her gifts. Her ego had thus to carry the full weight of the gratitude, which in former times might have been bestowed on God or on a saint as well as on the healer. And it seemed very understandable that she should cringe away and retreat from this task with its inherent possibility of gross inflation.

In the analytical setting, over-stimulating may manifest itself not only because the analyst senses that he has been successful in his work with the patient, but also because he fears being swept away himself if he allows the feeling of gratitude as such to emerge in the analytical situation. Maybe he himself has never really experienced this feeling, either in his personal life or in his analysis; hence he is forced to perceive it as dangerous and threatening to his psychic equilibrium. Perhaps it should be emphasised that rejection is being discussed in connection with over-stimulation and the subsequent dangers of flooding of the ego and not in connection with cases where the analyst thwarts his own success out of envy of the patient for the feelings which the patient experiences as a result of his analysis with him. There are probably quite a number of analysts who envy their patients their good analysts, in the same way that certain parents may envy their children their good parents.

The analyst's rebuff of the patient for fear of his own over-stimulation induced by gratitude may thus have very serious consequences for the outcome of an analysis. It may again be rationalised; for example, by advocating conformity to rigid rules of not accepting tokens of gratitude, of not giving narcissistic gratification. However, it may be argued that gratitude is one of the most important feelings to emerge in analysis.

One of the goals, if not even the principal goal, of analysis might be said to be an experience of the feeling of gratitude. It is one of the feelings associated with the experience of a relationship to something greater than the ego. It may not necessarily be the aim of an analysis for the patient to experience this feeling solely in relation to the actual parents. There will always be cases in which this cannot be achieved, however profound the analysis. The parents may have to remain rejected. But the important thing is that gratitude is experienced at all.

Speaking in Jungian terms, one might say that the feeling of gratitude is very close to being the feeling equivalent to the experience of the psychic totality, of the supraordinate personality, the conjunction, or whatever name one uses. This transcending factor may initially be projected onto the analyst. But even thus, the feeling of gratitude seems to be a step not only towards the realisation of good inner and outer objects, but also towards self-awareness.

However, the feeling of gratitude also implies a corresponding degree of ego-awareness. And thus it seems that a relation between the ego and the self may be built up which is not a merger of the ego into the self, with the corresponding danger of grandiosity or inflation. Gratitude appears to ensure that the two psychic instances are kept apart, but at the same time, remain intimately related.

Over-stimulation and the related depressive defence may be observed in connection with a very wide range of psychic phenomena. It is encountered within analysis but perhaps even more often outside. The defence, in other words, seems to be particularly effective, especially, perhaps, in cultures where qualities like modesty, self-effacement and non-competitiveness are considered primary moral values. The defence against hyperexcitement ranges from shyness and a general tendency to hide one's light under a bushel, to an attitude of humility on principle, to fears of healthy competition and fear at one's own achievement, to severe doubts about the value of oneself and of one's accomplishments, and it may end in serious work inhibition, sterile regression, and empty depression. The defensive manoeuvres may be supported by a whole arsenal of secondary rationalisations and of references to ethical, social, and religious ideals; and even psychological self-labelling may be employed, like references to one's introversion or one's sadistic super-ego.

Jung has called attention to the important phenomenon of the regressive restoration of the persona. This concept is extremely valuable when one considers the subsequent reactions to the defence or retreat against hyperexcitement. Jung has shown how the walls are rebuilt after a flooding of consciousness by unconscious contents, and how the individual lives a life on a lower level than before, being "smaller, more limited, more rationalistic than he was before" (Jung 3, p. 166). One may, however, be entitled to ask whether it is possible to observe a manic defence against the depressive defence against over-stimulation and against the regressive restoration of the persona. The question may sound sophistical, yet it appears that a characteristic feature of the regressive restoration of the persona and of the depressive retreat after, or prophylactically before, over-stimulation is often an almost compulsive manic activity. And this hectic activity may then secondarily be used as a rationalisation for avoiding situations which might cause hyperexcitement. In the cases mentioned above, for example, Mrs. Lake entered therapy with heart difficulties as a result of her exorbitant political engagement, and the young painter also developed heart problems during his later university career. In these instances, where it is directed against the depressive state connected with over-stimulation, the manic defence appears to be particularly fierce and even virulent. There seems little doubt that this may be explained only by assuming that it is reinforced by an intense narcissistic rage of a highly self-destructive nature. Neither the regressive restoration of the persona nor the retreat phenomena connected with over-stimulation thus imply a state of lethargy. On the contrary, appearances may be strikingly deceptive. Behind the smiling façade of the astonishingly energetic but self-effacing individual who merrily labours himself to death, claiming no reward, there may be a frail and deeply anxious ego which fears the unmitigated onslaught at any moment of its own grandiose phantasies, if it has not already experienced this.

## Summary

Over-stimulation is discussed as an endopsychic process, whereby psychic contents of an inflationary or grandiose nature threaten to overwhelm the ego, thus causing anxiety. The ego under consideration is, however, able to defend itself more or less successfully against this anxiety and does not succumb irreversibly to it. The defensive mechanisms employed by the ego have the character of a retreat which is experienced as a state of empty depression. This depressive defence is linked with Jung's 1916 concept of the regressive restoration of the persona. The phenomenon is treated theoretically with reference to Jung and to the modern American writers on self-psychology, notably Kohut. It is illustrated by extra-analytical occurrences, where the depressive defences seem to function. Subsequently it is considered as a focal point in analysis, and it is then discussed in the context of the transference and the countertransference. The connection with the use of alcohol is specifically underlined. In conclusion, the concept of a manic defence against the depressive defence is briefly sketched without being further elaborated.

## REFERENCES

1. Eliot, T. S. (1969). *The Complete Poems and Plays.* London. Faber & Faber.
2. Goldberg, A. (Ed.) (1978). *The Psychology of the Self.* New York. International Universities Press.
3. Jung, C. G. (1928). "The Relations between the Ego and the Unconscious". *Coll. Wks,* 7.
4. Keats, J. (1982). *Poetical Works.* Oxford University Press.
5. Kohut, H. (1971). *The Analysis of the Self.* New York. International Universities Press.

# Analysis in Training*

Thomas B. Kirsch (San Francisco)

Jung was the first to recognize the necessity of the training analysis, and did so while still a Freudian psychoanalyst. Freud acknowledged the importance of this contribution when he stated: "I count it one of the valuable services of the Zurich school of analysis that they have emphasized this necessity and laid it down as a requisition that anyone who wishes to practice analysis of others should first submit to be analyzed himself by a competent person" (p. 116). One year later, Jung wrote the following: "Just as we demand from a surgeon besides his technical knowledge, a skilled hand, courage, presence of mind, so we must expect from an analyst a very serious and thorough psychoanalytic training of his own personality before we are willing to entrust a patient to him" (1913, p. 200).

Thus, the importance of the personal analysis for analytic training was central for both Freud and Jung from the beginning, before the First World War. In Jung's later writings, he continued to place the personal analysis of the analyst at the core of training, all the while recognizing its limitations: "... anybody who intends to practice psychotherapy should first submit to a 'training analysis,' yet even the best preparation will not suffice to teach him everything about the unconscious... A complete 'emptying' of the unconscious is out of the question if only because its creative powers are continually producing new formations" (1946, p. 177).

In the field of analytical psychology, before the formation of training institutes, the way to become a Jungian analyst was through personal analysis with Jung and/or one of his assistants. An analysand usually attended seminars, but a letter from Jung saying that the individual was

* Reprinted by permission of Open Court Publishing Company from: *Jungian Analysis*, ed. Murray Stein (La Salle, Ill.: Open Court, 1982).

ready to practice analysis was virtually the only way to become a Jungian analyst prior to World War II. The first generation of analysts came to analysis primarily out of personal need, with little conscious thought of becoming analysts themselves. The early analysts were quite literally transformed into practitioners of their profession through their analyses. I would refer to this transformative aspect of the analysis itself as the individual calling to become an analyst.

Today's potential candidates have some notion of what it means to be an analyst before starting training. Usually they have been exposed to the analytic community through seminars, public lectures, workshops, and so on. They also have some idea, however filled with projections, of what the professional analytic community is like, and they want to become part of it. It is my hope that the individual sense of vocation will not get lost through all the group exposure to Jungian psychology. This paper focuses on the personal analysis of the candidates as a feature of their training. A discussion of the academic requirements, goals, and selection of candidates may be found elsewhere.

Prior to entering training, the potential candidate's analysis is not very different from other therapeutic analyses. When the analysand applies for candidacy, some changes may take place. What role does the analyst play in either encouraging or discouraging the analysand to apply for training? The task is somewhat easier when the analyst in good conscience can encourage the applicant. The analyst is an ally of the candidate, which has implications for the transference-countertransference. Sometimes an apprentice model is constellated, in which the candidate becomes a "disciple" of the particular analyst.

However, what happens if the analyst does not believe the analysand would make a good candidate? Should the analyst be the one to tell such analysands that they are not suitable to become analysts? When I definitely feel that the person would not be suitable, I have discouraged the analysand from making application for training. Often, the analysand then realizes that being an analyst is not what he or she really wanted. In one case, the analysand knew that he preferred dealing with psychotic patients using medication and short-term treatment. He realized on his own that he did not need or desire analytic training after having initially thought it would be good for him. When I do not have a sense of whether particular analysands should be candidates or not, I encourage them to apply and let an admissions committee evaluate them. Naturally, in all cases, the decision is up to an admissions committee, but here we are examining the role of the personal analysts vis-à-vis their analysands in the application process.

Jung's statements, quoted above, emphasize the importance of the personal analysis of anyone wishing to become an analyst, but they do not elucidate what a training analysis is, nor is a distinction made between it and other types of therapeutic analysis. In the English-language Jungian literature, only one article specifically addresses itself to the subject of training analysis (Fordham 1971). I define the training analysis as the analysis of a person who is in analysis for the express purpose of becoming an analyst. The person generally has entered analysis because of some form of suffering, but at some point has decided to become an analyst.

In addition to training analysis, the institutionalization of training has produced "training analysts", which implies that some analysts are better suited to train candidates than others. This adds another goal to the increasingly hierarchical structure of training, which I strongly resist. Ideally, analysands or candidates should be free to choose their own analysts based upon the personal characteristics of the analysts, rather than being limited to certain preselected analysts, no matter how qualified they may be. The argument usually given against this freedom is that trainees will pick analysts who have the same defenses they have and thus will not work out their neurotic conflicts. However, I have noticed that in reality candidates usually work with more than one analyst during their training, and that this problem takes care of itself. It is also true that in analytic societies candidates tend to gravitate toward a select few analysts who see most of the candidates in a given institute, but the choice seems to be based upon the psychological authority of these analysts rather than on their political power.

Unfortunately, I have seen among my psychoanalytic confreres the situation in which a potential candidate had to change analysts because the first was not a training analyst. In one case this change was extremely disruptive. For these reasons, San Francisco, Boston, Chicago, San Diego, and the Inter-Regional Society do not have the category "training analyst". In New York and Los Angeles, one applies to a local certifying board to become a training analyst, although the importance of the training analyst category has diminished. One may point out that this step presents another hurdle for young analysts to pass in the pursuit of their own psychological authority.

Regardless of whether the analyst is called a training analyst or not, the process of being in analysis is considered central in all Jungian training programs throughout the world. What this central process of analysis involves varies tremendously from place to place. An enormous range of differences exists in such matters as the frequency of sessions, the couch versus the chair, the relative importance of transference, and the reductive versus the prospective aspects of analysis.

The length of time of an analysis varies, of course, from individual to individual. Most training institutes demand a certain minimum time in analysis before application for training. The usual minimum number of analytic hours required to complete training is approximately 300, and the maximum is unlimited. Some institutes require candidates to be in analysis throughout their training. From my point of view, this requirement is an intrusion of institutional demands into the individual analytic relationship. Analysis cannot be legislated. If the person no longer requires analysis, he or she should be free to terminate it. For instance, some potential candidates have had long and deep analysis prior to their training, and it makes no sense to require further analysis. On the other hand, in order to circumvent a resistance to analysis, the termination of an analysis during training should be with the approval of the personal analyst. As the analytical process is a lifelong pursuit, analysts themselves will go back for further analytical work from time to time, often many years after they have finished formal training.

Once training has begun, what role does the analyst play in promoting the ongoing candidacy? This seems to be one of the issues in which there is a real divergence of opinion. Hillman stated the central position of the Zurich Institute, which was the pioneer Jungian training center:

> At the Institute in Zurich this clear separation of training and analysis does not exist. Training analysts, seminar leaders, supervisors, examiners and curatorium have been and still are, more or less, the same people. This reflects the attitude that training is analysis and so cannot be separated from it... But the analyst gives in writing to his colleagues his opinion as to the suitability of the candidate. This opinion remains crucial. If the analyst is opposed to the candidate's further candidacy, the curatorium will not override his judgment... the primary training takes place in the dialectic between candidate and analyst. (1962a, p. 8)

Today, however, the personal analyst no longer has such a central role in the evaluation of the candidate in Zurich.*

* A. Guggenbühl-Craig 1980: personal communication.

The earlier Zurich approach to training analysis would seem to overburden the already difficult work of analysis. If the training analyst has the power to pass judgment upon the candidate, it seems that candidates might withhold information, fearing that it could be used against them. I am told that this has been a problem in psychoanalytic training. Many newly qualified psychoanalysts will choose to have a posttraining analysis, just so they can have an unpressured therapeutic experience no longer under the scrutiny of an analyst who is also an authority figure.

For this reason, the San Francisco Jung Institute has taken a position opposite to the Zurich one. In San Francisco there has been a complete separation of the training analysis from the rest of the training process. The training analyst is not allowed to give any specific information to the certifying committee. The philosophy behind this is that no matter what happens, the candidate is entitled to an honest analysis. The task of evaluating the candidate then falls to a certifying body that collects information from seminar leaders and supervisors, and then has personal interviews with the candidate. Not having the input from the personal analyst of course makes the task of the certifying body more difficult. Since the training analyst does not have an evaluative function in training, there is a freer exchange and a more genuine analytic experience. Other American Jungian training centers are divided in their approach to this issue. In the beginning, New York and Los Angeles followed Zurich's example, but these societies moved to a position closer to San Francisco's as they began to find the training analysis overburdened, for the reasons mentioned.

Even if the analyst does not have an official voice in the evaluation of a candidate, the analysis of a candidate is different in many ways from an ordinary therapeutic analysis. Persons who enter analysis with the idea of becoming analysts have a definite aim or goal beyond their own therapy. They wish the analysis to serve the end of their becoming Jungian analysts, an ego aim. Such an aim is clearly different from that of a person who comes with no specific goal other than to get treatment for suffering. In the nontraining analysis, there is an end point at which the analyst and analysand separate, whereas in the training analysis there is continued connection in their shared professional world.

As a result, in the latter situation, unconscious material is constantly being influenced by the pressure of ego demands, such as seeking inclusion in the professional community and the training program. These ego demands may be quite similar to those of the analyst him- or herself. Some candidates' dreams may deal only with personal unconscious material, for example, and they may be concerned that their dreams do not include enough archetypal material, so that they doubt their "Jungian identity". Or, candidates may strongly resist having their material interpreted in a Jungian way. This resistance may manifest itself in several ways. In order not to conform to collective expectations, they may not want to discuss dreams or other unconscious material. If they do present dreams, they may be resistant to their symbolic meaning, again, so as not to conform to the Jungian expectation.

What we are dealing with in the analysis is the archetype of initiation (Henderson; Micklem). The analysand as initiate may have a resistance to emerging unconscious material. The analyst as one of the elders may be seen as the wise old man or priestess in the initiation process. Furthermore, the analyst is a member of the group into which the candidate as initiate wishes to enter. There is a necessary ordeal and trial of strength that the analysand as initiate must undergo in order for the *rite de passage* to take place. It is an archetypal situation in which both the personal analyst and training institute carry the projection of the group of elders or *communitas*.

Von Franz has discussed the vocation of analyst in the context of shamanic initiation. In primitive tribes, the shamanic initiate is the one who experiences a breakthrough of the collective unconscious and is able to master the experience, a feat many sick persons cannot achieve. Von Franz emphasizes that such an experience must occur in the analysis of a candidate as part of the training of an effective analyst. It is the perspective of initiation that differentiates the Jungian point of view from that of some Freudians. The latter often see resistance as the product of the parental introjects, now projected onto the analyst and institute. For the Jungian, resistance includes not only those aspects, but also the dimension of shamanic initiation, which evokes the collective unconscious.

The persona of the analyst, as well as the sum of collective, conscious attitudes that have developed toward the profession of analyst and toward the local training institute, may become critical concerns to a candidate. In every training analysis, questions about a particular seminar leader, or about how a certain person ever became a Jungian analyst, will surface. The candidate may question why the institute has a particular rule or a certain seminar topic and not another. These issues tend to surface within the training analysis, but in my experience they are often used as a form of resistance to some more personal issue for the candidate. Although one must deal with their content, it is important for the training analyst to recognize the resistance aspect and deal with it. My own tendency, out of my concerns about the training program, has often been to focus on the content issue and miss the resistance aspect.

An even deeper issue involves the tension between individuality and collective responsibility. Training analysts must, on the one hand, honor the individual expression of the analysand; on the other, they have a collective responsibility to the Jungian community to affirm certain values basic to the practice of Jungian analysis. Candidates are in a profound search for their own identity and will often question the value of becoming analysts. Eventually, the candidate may cause the training analyst to question the value of analysis itself, with thoughts like these: after all, analysis can help so few people; some are not helped at all; analysis itself may be just a luxury. Training analysts must be secure enough in what they are doing to stand the "test".

More agonizing still for the candidate is that he or she, like all analysands, must eventually realize that there is no point of security outside the analysis itself to provide a sense of direction, and whether a personal transformation will take place cannot be known beforehand. All training institutes say that they honor the individuality of the candidate, but at the same time they emphasize certain collective values and attitudes about the meaning and importance of Jungian analysis. Beyond that, the different institutes embody certain styles and emphasize certain aspects of the analytic process, and individual candidates have to come to terms with these nuances of emphasis with which they may not agree.

A further complexity in most training analyses is the fact that the majority of candidates are in the first half of life when they enter training, even though Jungian psychology often emphasizes changes that take place in the second half of life. The usual training analysis therefore deals with problems of the first half of life. This creates a tension between the candidate's own experience in analysis and certain aspects of Jungian theory and practice. Moreover, the institute wonders how the candidates will develop as they mature. What one hopes for in the training analysis is that enough genuine dialogue with the unconscious will be experienced to foster a commitment to continue the process. This does not always turn out to be the case.

A large issue in any analytic relationship is the transference-countertransference. In a training analysis, this phenomenon has many complications not found in a normal therapeutic analysis. Training analysts are potential models for the candidates. In their analyses, the candidates experience how their particular analysts work. If there is a transference, the trainees will introject the analyst and will begin their own practices by using a similar style. After all, who else's work has the candidate experienced at such close hand and so intimately?

The problem is, though, that the training analyst's style may not work for a particular candidate. Differences in psychological type and personality may mean that the analyst's style cannot be imitated by the trainee. If, for instance, an introverted thinking type is attracted to an analyst whose typology is extraverted feeling, the experience may be good for the trainee but will serve poorly as a model for the trainee's own analytic practice. The training analysts, on the other hand, may have considerable difficulty in letting the candidates go in directions that are not consonant with their own dominant attitudes and orientations. It is hard for an analyst to judge whether differing attitudes derive from differing psychological typologies or from unresolved transference-countertransference issues.

Fordham has offered insight regarding the irreducible pathological core in any transference-countertransference situation. All analytical psychologists value the individuating factor, but the shadow of human nature surfaces when candidates' individuation contradicts their mentors' most sacred tenets. How the training analyst and candidate handle this complex impasse is extremely important, not only for them but for their institute. If genuine differences are not accepted, they can lead to splits within the training institute after the candidate becomes a qualified analyst. The training analyst therefore is both a role model and a person against whom the trainee can react.

Extraanalytic contacts, rivalry with "sibling" patients, and decisions about self-disclosure by the analyst are factors that frequently generate psychological issues in training analysis. Although the relationship to the analyst is initially restricted to the consulting room, this situation often changes when analysands become candidates. It is then probable that they will have contact with their training analysts outside of analytic hours. Candidates' experiences of seeing their analysts as seminar leaders are often initially fraught with difficulty. One typical reaction of the candidates is to feel exposed. They feel as if their analyses are continuing right there in the middle of the seminar, and that everyone else is noticing how vulnerable they are at that moment. They may feel as if their analysts are talking directly to them, while in reality they are addressing the whole group. It may also be hard for training analysts to talk to their patients in a seminar.

Sibling rivalry is often constellated in candidates who "share" their analysts with other students in a seminar. In the analytic hour, the trainees have their analysts all to themselves and do not have to share them with anyone else. They may have the fantasy of being the analyst's only patient, or perhaps at least the most special one. In the seminar situation, on the contrary, trainees see others who are in analysis with their analysts, and fantasies of rejection or of being less preferred than others may surface under these conditions. Furthermore, how others in the seminar react to their analyst becomes an issue. The candidates want their analyst to look good in the eyes of their peers. Thus transference issues are carried out of the consulting room into other areas.

These transference factors, inherent in training situations, allow more contact between analyst and analysand than in the therapeutic analysis. As a result, the candidates tend to have more real knowledge about their analysts than ordinary analysands, and consequently there are more "hooks" on which to hang projections. Now there occurs a temptation for the training analysts to be more self-disclosing in an effort to validate their patients' perceptions and to welcome them prematurely as colleagues. A certain collegial attitude can enter into the analysis, which affects the transference-countertransference relationship. Perhaps this temptation also reflects the isolation and loneliness of being an analyst and the desire to share one's experiences. Casualness may mask deep unresolved problems.

Personally, I find that my increasing sensitivity to the problems posed by the collegial attitude have led me to become less self-revealing with potential candidates than with other analysands. I have become more conscious of the transference-countertransference level of interpretations with candidates. I want to minimize the differences between the training analysis and the therapeutic one, and especially to lessen the effects of the extraanalytic contacts.

Such emphasis on the transference and countertransference causes the analysis to last longer, as more of the unconscious material is interpreted in the light of the transference. In London, where one group of Jungians practice analysis using the couch, a regressive transference is fostered, and hence more infantile psychopathology is evoked. This can be extremely helpful to trainees, for they can experience certain psychopathological states in themselves within the transference relationship rather than merely learning about them from textbooks and clinical exposure. Fordham specifically encourages providing conditions wherein psychopathological states can be experienced in the training analysis (1971). His thesis depends upon the concept that psychopathology is the result of quantitative, not qualitative, variations in the experience of unconscious conflicts. The hope is that the candidates can experience and transform their own areas of psychopathology so that they can help patients who have similar problems. Equally, the trainees can learn what parts of themselves are healthy and therefore do not require analytic work.

In line with the view that the training analysis should involve the maximum exposure of a candidate's complexes, it has been suggested that training should include more than one analyst/analysis, as they would most likely emphasize different aspects of the analysand's psyche according to the dialectic that is established. On the other side, it has been argued that this dilutes the intensity of analysis. Proponents of both points of view expressed themselves in a "Symposium on Training" published in the *Journal of Analytical Psychology* (Fordham 1962, p. 26; Plaut, p. 98; Hillman 1962b, p. 20). A review of the debate was published by this author (Kirsch).

Multiple analyses – that is, the practice of seeing more than one analyst during training – has long been an accepted pattern among analytical psychologists. It dates back to Jung, who would often refer his analysands to a female analyst at the same time that he was seeing them himself (Wheelwright). Multiple analysis has two main advantages. First, if carried out with a male and a female, it may activate the inner polarity between male and female components of the psyche. A man's anima will be experienced differently with a woman analyst than through the anima of a male analyst. Obviously, sexual fantasies will also be experienced differently depending upon the sex of the analyst.

In addition, seeing a second analyst gives the analysand an opportunity to experience a therapist of a different psychological type. As mentioned earlier, an analysand often starts analysis with someone who is of a similar psychological type. Later on in the analysis, it may be important to have the experience of someone of an opposite type and function. Theoretically, therefore, a wider consciousness of anima and animus and of one's psychological type will be experienced through multiple analyses. Since a future analyst should have the widest possible analytic experience, multiple analyses are to be recommended.

On the negative side, there is the justified concern that this practice leads to transference "leakage". Any analysand may transfer to another analyst when an unconscious block develops with the first analyst. Analyst and analysand may, with the best of intentions, work out a transfer or an addition of another analyst without realizing that they are avoiding a resistance.

An extremely important issue is how a candidate's analysis ends. The ending of analysis is a difficult and complex subject in its own right. There is the realization that an analyst needs to continue self-analysis forever, and that there will be periods of returning to one's original analyst or going to another one. Fordham has described the termination of a training analysis as depending upon:

> (1) the patient's history, embodying past separations, capacity to feel grief and gratitude, (2) the overt transference situation, (3) clues obtained from one or a series of dreams, (4) the reality situation of the new Society member, (5) an assessment of the ongoing individuation processes at work in the unconscious, and last but not least, (6) the training analyst's countertransference. (1971, p. 181)

Fordham emphasizes the idea that an unresolvable pathological nexus exists between any patient and his or her analyst, consisting of the irreducible part of certain complexes in both analyst and patient that cannot be analyzed away. Fordham discusses this idea in terms of the actual traumatic situations that have occurred for both analyst and analysand that can be elucidated but cannot necessarily be changed, and also to the theme of the "wounded healer" referred to by Jung. Fordham maintains that the full elucidation of this pathological nexus is frequently overlooked through insufficient concentration on reconstructing infancy and childhood. I would point out that the elucidation of the pathological nexus is critical in a training analysis, since it may be the only way to help potential analysts recognize the damaged parts of themselves that are likely to come up in their future professional work.

Fordham states that a candidate's pathology is all too often displaced into the local society in which the future analyst will practice. The local professional society carries the projection of family, and members react to it as such. Concurrent with this are all the individual transferences and countertransferences among the individual members that can never be fully resolved. These mutual projections flare up from time to time, and it is hoped that they can be contained within the local society. But, when that unresolved pathological nexus is too large, it becomes a nidus out of which hatch tendencies for one or more members to split off from the larger whole. This situation is what makes the basically rewarding job of being a training analyst disillusioning as well.

This paper has encompassed a delicate subject. Personal analysis of the candidate is the core experience in the making of a Jungian analyst. It needs to be the most individual and subjective of experiences, and yet, at the same time, candidates are evaluated by a certifying body that probes their relationship to their own psyches. How does one protect the individuality and creativity of the analytic process, and yet at the same time produce analysts? The very mention of the word "training" constellates complexes, because analysts all have their own strong ideas of what the analysis of a candidate should be. It may seem that I have here focused too much on some of the problems of the analysand in training. If that is the case, it has been because of my desire to retain as much of the core analytic experience as possible for the candidate, and not have it diluted by the institutional demands of training.

## REFERENCES

Edinger, E. 1961. Comment. *Journal of Analytical Psychology* 6/2:116–17.

Fordham, M. 1962. Reply. *Journal of Analytical Psychology* 7/1:24–26.

_____. 1971. Reflections on training analysis. In *The analytic process,* ed. J.B. Wheelwright, pp. 172–84. New York: Putnam.

_____. 1976. Comment. *Contemporary Psychoanalysis* 12:168–73.

Franz, M.-L. von. Beruf und Berufung. In *Die Behandlung in der Analytischen Psychologie,* ed. U. Eschenbach, pp. 14–32. Fellbach: Verlag Adolf Bonz.

Freud, S. 1912. Recommendations to physicians on the psychoanalytic method of treatment. In *Standard edition,* vol. 12, pp. 109–20. London: Hogarth, 1958.

Guggenbühl-Craig, A. 1971. *Power in the helping professions.* New York: Spring Publications.

Henderson, J. L. 1967. *Thresholds of initiation.* Middletown, Conn.: Wesleyan University Press.

Hillman, J. 1962a. Training and the C. G. Jung Institute, Zurich. *Journal of Analytical Psychology 7/1:3–18.*

_____. 1962b. A note on multiple analysis and emotional climate at training institutes. *Journal of Analytical Psychology* 7/1:20–22.

Jung, C. G. 1913. The theory of psychoanalysis. In *Collected works*, vol. 4, pp. 85–226. New York: Pantheon, 1961.

_____. 1946. Psychology of the transference. In *Collected works*, vol. 16, pp. 163–321. New York: Pantheon, 1954.

Kirsch, T. 1976. The practice of multiple analyses in analytical psychology. *Contemporary Psychoanalysis* 12:159–67.

Marshak, M. O. 1964. The significance of the patient in the training of analysts. *Journal of Analytical Psychology* 9/1:80–83.

Micklem, N. 1980. Paper read at *Symposium on Training*, Eighth International Congress of Analytical Psychology, 5. September 1980, San Francisco.

Newton, K. 1961. Personal reflections on training. *Journal of Analytical Psychology* 6/2:103–6.

Plaut, A. 1961. A dynamic outline of the training situation. *Journal of Analytical Psychology* 6/2:98–102.

Spiegelman, M. J. 1980. The image of the Jungian analyst. *Spring* 1980:101–16.

Stone, H. 1964. Reflections of an ex-trainee on his training. *Journal of Analytical Psychology* 9/1:75–79.

Wheelwright, J. B. 1975. A personal view of Jung. *Psychological Perspectives* 6:64–73.

# On Cultural Anxiety

Rafael López-Pedraza (Caracas)

During a discussion on the problems of Western man, Borges remarked that so-called Western man is not just a Westerner, since we have to take into consideration a particular book in his culture – the Bible – which comes from the East. The Bible is an Eastern product; but no one in the Western culture can avoid the influence of this book and the consequences it has wrought.

The Bible begins with a creation myth.[1] Creation myths can be found in the literature of most cultures, but we have to accept that this Biblical creation myth, which in other cultures would not occupy such a predominant place, gives something special to our culture because it is at the base of what we call our religious belief. Religiously speaking, Western man is a believer; he has to have faith. God created man in his own image. This belief has been central to Western man's religious life and, of course, central to holding his psyche and his madness.

As a Western man, living in the historical traditions of my geography and race, I feel this Eastern product very much in me, and I accept that it covers a great part of my life. This is so because the essence of the Bible is monotheism: the worship of one God, and the jealousy and wrath of that God if there is any other worship. This belief has pervaded *in extenso* the world in which we live: our religious belief; our way of life; the ideas of our culture; our politics; the sciences; and, last but not least, the study of psychology. Monotheism is deeply ingrained in the psychology of every Westerner, no matter what his geography, social condition, or education.

[1] For the psychology of creation myths, see Marie-Louise von Franz, *Patterns of Creativity Mirrored in Creation Myths* (Zürich: Spring Publications, 1972).

Thus, the Bible, the book of monotheism, though geographically alien to Western man, has such a predominant place in his psychology that other books which could be considered to be more truly Western have receded into what we call the unconscious, or are important only to scattered minorities. In fact, the Bible is basically in opposition to Western books, an opposition most evident in the books of mythology: the pagan polytheistic books; the books of the many gods with their images; the wealth of the many forms of life. Greek mythology offers the most complete catalogue of images ever produced: forming the stuff of tragedy; the sources of poetry and literature; feeding life poetically; peopling the earth with images; the foundation of philosophy. We must include as well the many other mythologies of the Western world: the Northern European mythologies; the hidden tradition and legends of the Celts; the mythologies, legends, and poetic conceptions of the autochthonous American peoples, etc. These are the books which have to do with what, in Jungian psychology, we call the collective unconscious.

And then there are the books concerned with the origins of life on earth, the evolution of man, with their provocative discussions about the human race, man's behaviour, etc. They are the books which tell us about man's most remote and primitive history, and they make the more humble proposition that humankind is not the crowning achievement of God's creation, but simply another species of animal at a certain level of evolution; this last very much in opposition to the creationism of the Bible.

Western man has written many books during his history: books which actualize the old myths; which tell the story of the history he has lived through; and the great achievement of his literature, in which essential aspects of his psyche are revealed – all of which are the concern of today's psychological studies. Nevertheless, all this wealth at the level of collective consciousness does not match the Bible – the foreign book from the East – because the latter has a special effect: it provokes an identification with the text, a collective identification, something the other books do not do; or if there is an identification, it remains mostly at an individual level, or at that of a small group.

In the Medieval Spanish tradition, there seems to have been an awareness of this identification the Bible provokes. It has never been a book for the majority. In the Church, it has been rather a book which erudites consulted, and a source of amplification for the saints. Cervantes, in the most important book of our literature, advises us about the madness into which our Lord Don Quijote fell through reading "The Book of Knights" too intensely. I sense in this awareness an old and complex tradition which prevents any literalization of the written word.

Westerners, more since the Reformation, have been reading these Eastern Biblical tales, and they have reacted in different ways, ranging from a foolish identification to a tactful or brusque rejection, enabling them to take a distance to the book. The point is that the Bible, due to its Eastern ingredient, upsets Western psychology precisely because it triggers off a collective response. It seems the conception of the one all-powerful, imageless God whom the believer has faith in, provokes this kind of psychological identification.[2] And because the Bible moves toward identification, it is difficult to talk or write about it psychologically. It is a religious book actuated by faith, and millions of people today identify with it. But it is also the religious book of the Jewish people, the centre of their life and tradition, and because of its religiosity, there is little or nothing that can be worked out as a psychology. I wonder whether psychology, the individual movement of a psyche, could have anything to do with it. I have always been puzzled by the fact that, in spite of so many Jewish students of psychology, they have not done any work on the psychology of Judaism. If there has been some contribution,[3] it has been very little, especially if we consider its huge importance for our culture. But perhaps a psychological study of Judaism is impossible; what has been done is more a sort of psychological exegesis of the Bible, or to include it rather indiscriminately in studies of comparative religion, down to the amplification method of Jungian psychology.

During the last fifteen years, Jungian studies have paid more attention to monotheism and polytheism, seeing them in terms of polarities that are tremendously relevant to Western man's psyche and to the dynamism of psychotherapy. This is a very different approach from the Jungian amplification method which distracts the focus from what

[2] I have always thought the Freudian conception of the transference has the same element as the old Hebrew dependency on an imageless God.

[3] A relevant contribution to the material of this paper is offered by Rivkah Schärf-Kluger in *Psyche and Bible* (Zürich: Spring Publications, 1974), Part I, p. 3, where she writes: "... one must also take seriously the idea of the chosen people, for it belongs to the main stock of fundamental religious experiences in the Old Testament. The danger of this idea, its 'shadow' so to speak, is hubris, i.e., the danger that the ego of the people, carried by the individuals identified with it, may take possession in an inflationary way of this content that originates in the Self, or may be overwhelmed by it."

should be our most urgent concern as Westerners: to differentiate between the monotheism and the polytheism in our Western psyche. Moreover, it is a differentiation to be undertaken with an acute awareness of the historical cultural conflict which exists between these two main streams in the Western psyche. What has been done in this respect has been very meagre, in terms of a rather shy mentioning of the difference between monotheism and polytheism. But my intention in this paper is to discuss this issue in terms of a *conflict*, a basic psychological conflict. Further, I consider that it is essential to bring the issue of this conflict out into the open, because it is to corner the studies of psychology where they really are (whether people are aware of it or not), where our psyche is most afflicted, an affliction we disguise in the shape of history, religion, or politics. It is as if a tabu has been operating in the studies of psychology. Attempts to get down to this basic issue have begun only relatively recently, so there have been very few real repercussions of all its implications.

We know that, in the seventeenth century, the foundation of the study of the natural sciences was based, psychologically, on the premise that science had nothing to do with religion. Actually, what gathered together the men of those times to talk about science was precisely that, historically, it had become impossible to express religious differences. Modern science is the child of religious wars full of anxiety, blood, and cruelty. The scientific dialogue allowed them a possible way to relate at a distance from the madness of the major religions. We know also that the cradle of modern psychology was natural science. Moreover, even if we presume that the baby is no longer in the cradle, nevertheless it seems our baby has not grown up enough to be very far from it.[4] So it is understandable that it is rather tabu, as I mentioned, to talk about living religion in psychology. Though I am sure we do not need to be reminded that it was Jung who started to push psychology along the path to religion. But besides these historical complexes, one feels there probably exists some deeper resistance in us which prevents us from viewing our psyche in terms of the polarities of monotheism and polytheism; it is as if, besides the historical complexes we have

[4] We insist in talking about and discussing psychology with the attitude of the natural sciences, using the same rhetoric, a rhetoric which does not belong to the complexities of psychology. This same way of thinking is also applied to the humanities: essays on poetry, for instance, which deal with poetry as if it, too, belonged to the studies of the natural sciences. This makes for a tremendous confusion. And, at least in the studies of psychology, what comes out of this confusion, most of the time, is a boring codified jargon pervading the majority of psychological papers.

inherited, there is an intimate inner tabu, as if the conflict were afflicting our basic nature.

Monotheism and polytheism make up the two basic components in the Western psyche; and we need to be profoundly aware of them both. We need to be more astute at recognising what emanates from the monotheistic side of life – collective consciousness, beliefs, faith (the influence of the Eastern book), – and what emanates from the more repressed pagan polytheistic side – the archetypal images. But even more important, we have to become aware of the *conflict*, with its resulting anxiety, which, from the beginning, these two streams have produced in the Western soul.

E. R. Dodds, in his *Pagan and Christian in an Age of Anxiety*,[5] discusses the religious experiences and conflicts during the first centuries of Christianity, calling those times an 'age of anxiety' after a poetic phrase coined by W. H. Auden. It was a time when the conflict between traditional paganism and the new Christian monotheism openly broke out, a time which, in some ways, can be likened to our own time, that is likewise an 'age of anxiety'. Dodds's essays, on what for him was historically an age of anxiety, stimulated me into having a wider view of anxiety and enabled me to see what he says within a more psychic context. I would say that the Western psyche has always lived with the anxiety produced by the constant conflict between the pagan mythologies – the many gods with their differentiated images – and the one imageless God of monotheism. It is an anxiety that arises from a conflict of cultures. There has always been what I would like to call *cultural anxiety*. Man's deepest conflicts are cultural, something that psychology cannot evade.

Dodds' book gives a historical perspective, emphasized by taking the title of Auden's poem, implying that the feeling of cultural anxiety is more apparent, more acute, in times of historical extremes. But it is from extremes that reflection begins with regard to what has always been there and taken for granted. And here I would like to promote some reflection over this issue of polytheism and monotheism by pointing out the *obviousness* of these two sides in the Western psyche, and then to ask a question: Why has it taken psychology so long to start thinking about the monotheism and polytheism in ourselves and to realize that these two historical realities are at the base of our con-

[5] E. R. Dodds, *Pagan and Christian in an Age of Anxiety* (Cambridge: Cambridge University Press, 1965).

flict? I am aware that this move attempts to reflect the basic standpoint of Jungian psychology from another angle. The study of psychology has been conceived in the dualism of ego consciousness and the unconscious, both being concepts that we might view as imageless cover-ups for the real underlying conflict. Nevertheless, this dualism has been inherited by psychology: one way and only one way of looking into psyche.

What, in fact, we have inherited is a monotheistic bias. It is as if a camera-man were shooting a film with a lense that focuses only on the vertical perspective of ego consciousness and the unconscious. But one wonders, whether what comes out in the film, once the film is developed, is inevitably by way of concepts and symbols, not images.[6] I would say, the ego/unconscious dichotomy conceptualizes and symbolizes what arises from the unconscious. *Whatever conception we have concerning the ego,* it is impossible for me to imagine the ego as the receptor of images. Traditionally, it is the soul that receives images; and this is valid for psychic processes and psychotherapy. Now I would like to propose that, without burning the old films, we change the lense of the camera. Then, when shooting our film, we can catch with a sharper focus what comes out of the Judaic monotheistic side of the psyche and what comes out of the pagan polytheistic side, for then it follows that we can begin to differentiate and have a clearer picture of the individual psyche, situated between the two poles, which suffers the anxiety

6 The structure of the studies of psychiatry and psychology has been mostly based on concepts derived from empirical clinical observations of mental illness. From the beginning of the century, the symbol appeared as dominant in the studies of the unconscious. Freud evidently arrived at his use of symbol, understood by Jung as mere sign and symptom (semiotic), from his studies of conversion hysteria at the turn of the century; on the other hand, Jung began his work as a psychiatrist with psychotic patients, in which he made his great discovery of the religious symbol in the unconscious of those patients. Here the word symbol is appropriately applied, because the original *symbolon* means the union of something previously divided; and symbolism is at the base of most of Jung's ideas on the opposites and the reconciliation of the opposites. In *Psychological Types,* I sense that Jung used symbol and image in an undifferentiated way, giving to them the same value. Later, he became more specific and clearer concerning archetypal images. Images began to be more differentiated, and so provide us, today, with a wider field for exploration, where I consider the more relevant psychological work is going on, and where the symbol is taken as an attribute of the image. A psychotherapy of the image offers a new perspective to hysteria; in the case of psychosis, we sense that the imaginary response to the patient's unconscious symbolism propitiates a better therapy; and a new finding of the image in psychosomatic ailments brings an entirely new approach to the psychotherapy of these complaints (see, in this volume, pp. 81 ff, Alfred Ziegler, "*Horroris Morbus:* Unit of Disease and Image of Ailing").

engendered by the conflict. But for this to happen, we have to be particularly aware of what the monotheism in us is doing while we are busy focussing on the polytheism, because our monotheistic ego lense is so automatic and given.

The change from an ego point of view to having an awareness that embraces both monotheism and polytheism is, for me, of immense importance. And it is a change of view which can only be reached through awareness. In his *Re-Visioning Psychology*, James Hillman says that the last works on Judaic monotheism were done by Freud in *Moses and Monotheism*, and by Jung in *Answer to Job*.[7] When discussing this, Hillman somehow transmits a feeling of boredom, implying that the Judaic source has been exhausted and that now the exploration has moved into pagan polytheism. Now to follow this shift is one thing, as it is undoubtedly where the treasury of images is stored, and where the scholarly aspect of psychology has moved. But we must not confuse the scholarly work, fine instrument though it is, with the aim of the study of psyche which, following my thought, would be to catch the psychic conflict.

For we can do a lot of research into the pagan myths and remain unaware of the cultural anxiety generated by these two powerful forces of monotheism and polytheism in the psyche. We can do a lot of research comfortably insulated by our monotheistic bias and repeat what one inheritor of the studies of natural science – Freud – did when, due to his monotheism, he picked out a single polytheistic myth – the Oedipus myth – and made it the original cause of neurosis. He remained unaware that that polytheistic myth has in itself an endless polytheistic imagination to deal with that myth, an imagination very remote from his monotheistic and scientific standpoint.

Personally, I find it difficult to view the psyche in terms of an ego/unconscious opposition. It seems to me very unpsychological and belongs to the inheritance from the monotheistic tradition of the ego's identification with monotheism, and thus the repression of what is *not* monotheism. Whereas the other perspective I am proposing – to retain an awareness of both monotheism and polytheism – seems to me more fitting for the study and discussion of psychic processes and for psychotherapy. At least I find myself more at ease with this standpoint. Sometimes one wonders whether the word 'psychology' has been rightly applied to the studies which carry that name. We have to realize that to

7 James Hillman, *Re-Visioning Psychology* (New York: Harper Colophon Books, 1977), p. 226.

study psyche from an ego point of view is more absurd than we think.

So let me explain my point of view on this a little more: When, instead of staying in the ego, we embrace the psyche's point of view, we can be more aware of our monotheism and more able to detect when it is operating. Obviously, we cannot have this awareness when we are in the ego, for the ego inevitably carries the monotheistic point of view. We need to recognise the monotheistic rhetoric, to read the monotheistic discourse. We are far too prone to take the monotheistic side for granted. As I said, it is what contributes to a great deal of the cultural anxiety we live. We cannot go on speculating about psyche, longing to 'make soul', without having an appreciation of the complexities and ramifications of monotheism in our psyche and life.

For the analyst who might be interested in the proposal to become aware of both monotheism and polytheism, the challenge would be to learn how to become more aquainted with the difference between the monotheistic and the polytheistic rhetorics: to build up as abundant a memory as possible of their different styles. What for the Renaissance man was the achievement of a 'unified memory',[8] for the modern analyst might be a differentiation, by way of its rhetoric, of the material emanating from the strong monotheistic side of the culture and of that emanating from the more repressed pagan side. From the viewpoint of psychology today, the Renaissance man's achievement would be a mess for the modern man, because there would be no basic differentiation of his cultural anxiety. The art of psychotherapy would be to reflect to the patient from this kind of memory that can both memorize and at the same time differentiate between monotheism and polytheism, and, by bringing an awareness of the conflict, break through the patient's cultural anxiety.

If we shift from identification with the ego point of view and move toward a differentiation of monotheism and polytheism in the psyche, we can begin to have an idea of how *guilt,* which in our culture manifests in terms of a strong identification, can now, thanks to a new psychological distance, be insighted as a rhetoric. Guilt, with its endless variations of guilt-feelings and its embroidery of guilt-making, can be approached as one of monotheism's basic rhetorics, its most obvious

[8] This is a reference to Giulio Camillo's notion to unify memory, a memory comprised of the Judeo Christian tradition and the rediscovery of the pagan images, and which expressed the longing of the Renaissance man to cope with his cultural anxiety. See Frances Yates, *The Art of Memory* (London: Routledge and Kegan Paul, 1966), p. 155.

one. One can almost say that monotheism can be equated with guilt. The weight of guilt carried by Christianity comes from its dominant Judaic side, from the religious identification in the Jewish tradition (anxiety over keeping within the laws of the religion): "In the beginning was guilt." We know that, in Greek paganism, guilt was not at all important. I remain with Nilsson, who pointed out that it was basically alien to the Greek spirit.[9] When guilt did make an appearance, it was reduced to certain sects – the virginal and puritanical Pythagorean and Orphic sects. Guilt was a sectarian business – anxiety over keeping the rules of the sect. But it was never swallowed by the Greeks in general, who rejected ideas of guilt.

With all its variations, Western culture is an unconsciously guilt-ridden culture and, inevitably, our psychology has a strong guilt-ridden aspect. In our lives, we can detect the complexities of guilt operating autonomously. We all know people who are successful, refined and cultured, and yet any conversation with them about any subject becomes dominated by guilt. There are people who manage to see the events of their life only within the spectrum of guilt, who are skilled at keeping guilt in the foreground, either in themselves or in others, for whom it is out of the question that they might conceive of life as anything else than deeply pervaded by guilt. A whole life can become paralysed because of guilt projections upon seemingly rather banal events: the paralysis of a life rotating systematically around guilt.

As a psychotherapist, one is accustomed to listening to what are often bizarre projections of guilt. If one listens to this kind of autonomous guilt-making with a certain distance and without being caught by that same guilt, if one is detached enough to avoid making a judgment, what one is listening to is a rhetoric of the absurd. So to approach guilt in terms of a rhetoric is immensely valuable, because it is only through discerning the rhetoric of guilt as an absurdity and an inflation, that some degree of awareness occurs. I see guilt as a tremendous inflation, therefore, in itself, awareness is a deflation of guilt. I realize that this proposition of mine to treat guilt as a rhetoric is not an easy one to accept; even I have some difficulty with it. Personally, guilt bores me to death, and makes me feel its psychological uselessness. If it is the image that really moves the psyche, the reading of the psychic image, then I cannot conceive that it is possible to read that image when in a guilt-

[9] Marin P. Nilsson, *A History of Greek Religion*, trans. F. J. Fielden (Oxford: Clarendon Press, 1949), p. 217.

ridden state, because the image invariably becomes distorted by a feeling which does not belong to it.

We cannot avoid the conclusion that cultural anxiety comes into psychotherapy exacerbated by millenia of all-pervading autonomous feelings of guilt. Monotheistic speech is invariably guilt-ridden and, of course, guilt-making, and is in psychic opposition to the endless variety of the archetypal consistent images. Monotheistic guilt is imageless, as is the one God, the source of guilt in our Western culture. For the analyst who accepts cultural anxiety – the conflict between monotheism and polytheism in the psyche – the answer is the painful one of learning to discriminate between the rhetorics: the conceptual imageless rhetoric of monotheism and the imaginative rhetoric of polytheism, to withstand the conflict between the two, and to reflect on and value the difference between them.

James Joyce was a great example of a life lived under the pressure of cultural anxiety; in his case, the friction of it generated an energy which transformed it into art. *Ulysses,* that *tour-de-force* of Western literature, expresses what I have been trying to get across about cultural anxiety: the hero, the modern Ulysses, is, paradoxically, a Jew married to an Irish Catholic woman. The guilt-ridden Jesuitical Catholicism and the different kinds of paganisms – the Mediterranean and the author's own Irish Celtic – are the sources of the book's complexities. It is a great work that reveals the fragmentation and the madness of the cultural anxiety in the soul of a genius who was able to transform that anxiety into a religious syncretism. With reference to Bloom, W. B. Stanford wrote: "Originally a Jew, then vaguely Protestant and Catholic in turn, Bloom is now an agnostic humanist."[10]

*Ulysses* is only comparable to another *tour-de-force* of religious syncretism (at its best, cultural anxiety is transformed into religious syncretism): Jung's alchemical opus, in which his cultural anxiety was worked out and insighted through Medieval alchemical material. For me, Medieval alchemy was an expression of cultural anxiety, a religious syncretism contained in the alchemical vessel. Jung's cultural anxiety, the con-fusion of the two main sources – the Judaic and the Mediterranean pagan – were worked on in the alchemical retort in a soul which was able to hold that confusion being based, at a deeper level, in a Swiss, Celtic, Roman, Germanic paganism.

[10] W. B. Stanford, *The Ulysses Theme* (Oxford: Blackwell, 1968), p. 213.

The involvement of Jung's cultural anxiety can be felt when he quotes Paracelsus, who said: "...I write like a Pagan though I am a Christian",[11] an observation which describes the anxiety of many men during Western history. According to Jung, the psychic position of being more pagan than Christian contains a feeling of inferiority. It is the position of one who is living from and for the soul, a soul that makes no concessions, no explanations, no conceptualisations – like that of Joyce or Jung. I guess Jung himself had this feeling of inferiority to which he alluded. He transmits it in his desire to have no followers; his avoidance of falling into criticism; his respect for the other peoples' complexes; his connection to the other person as the other person was. He was never in the inflation of considering himself a leader. The resistance he felt against founding the Jung Institute is well known. One feels Jung's anxiety in his conflict with the scientific world, so alien to his pagan soul. The notion of Paracelsus concerning each person with his or her own star finds an echo in Jung's main concern: individuation.

Joyce and Jung, who happened to be acquainted, who both suffered and made their two different *opi* under the extreme pressure of what I like to call cultural anxiety, both had the strange stamina given by the mysterious ingredient of the old European Celt, and both reveal to modern man the main complexities of the cultural anxiety he lives.

Whereas Joyce and Jung are examples of men who lived more at the pagan end of the spectrum of cultural anxiety, Sigmund Freud, on the other hand, is an example of a man who lived at the extreme monotheistic end. He was a child of the Old Testament, of the Chosen People, that literalization leading to fantasies of racial purity. He was also a child of the natural sciences, and thus under the spell of the search for scientific truth. He has left us the image of a founder and leader of a school, with followers who had to accept the scientific psychological discoveries of the leader as dogmatic truth. Instead of each person with his own star, he imposed on his followers the monotheistic notion of one star for everybody. This, in itself, gives us a view of a monotheistic psychology, a psychology which rejects what does not fit into its monotheistic conception.

Nevertheless, though he occupied that extreme monotheistic end of the spectrum, it is striking that the elements Freud chose for expressing

[11] CW 13, para. 148. I recommend a reading of Jung's "Paracelsus as a Spiritual Phenomenon" to gain an insight into the double cultural anxiety lived in the 16th century: on the one hand, the schism in Christianity itself and, on the other, the Judaic pagan conflict, expressed by Paracelsus as *Pagoyum*, which was one of his favorite neologisms, compounded of *paganum* and the Hebrew word *goyim* (para. 148).

his researches into psychology were taken from the pagan polytheistic side of the psyche: the Oedipus complex; the polymorphous perverse child; Eros and Thanatos, etc. In choosing a polytheistic pagan myth as the base of his theories, Freud revealed his own cultural anxiety, and this gives us an impression of the conflict between monotheism and polytheism in a predominantly monotheistic mind. His opus is a product of cultural anxiety, too, showing the historical and cultural abyss between his monotheistic position and the polytheistic sources he was dealing with. We can appreciate the effort and drama experienced by a man ostensibly in a position of monotheistic superiority, trying to deal with pagan inferiorities and feeling all the discomfort of such a position. One cannot but be moved by the stamina needed for such a task.

However, there is no question that Freud was not sufficiently aware of what was going on below the surface of the time in which he was living. He was blind to the forces gathering in the unconscious of the people among whom he lived. He was, perhaps, not immune to that strong Jewish fantasy, in the Germanic countries, of assimilation, an odd fantasy in that it did not take into account the dilemma of being assimilated, and yet remaining the Chosen People. It is impossible for me to equate social assimilation with religious syncretism. Religious syncretism moves internally; it is a product of cultural anxiety and a historical and psychic mover. Assimilation at the racial and social level always remains a collective political problem.

By pointing to these three very representative men of the century who made their opi through cultural anxiety, I have been trying to show its creative aspect. Now, let us take a look at the other side of the coin of cultural anxiety; when, out of deep unconscious roots, it erupted into devastating collective madness and destruction. Let us turn to the history of the Jewish people in Germany at the time of National Socialism and the Second World War. Fortunately, in this respect, we are the inheritors of Jung's "Essays on Contempory Events",[12] essays that lead the way to the study of collective madness; so to tackle a delicate issue of this sort is well within the Jungian tradition. Moreover, Jung did not leave a dogma concerning these events; he said they should be reflected from many different angles. Therefore, I believe it will never be out of place to discuss the Holocaust, either in the context of Jung's essays or with a more secret interest motivated by the fears which have increased in us all since Jung left the world.

[12] CW 10, Part III.

We have to learn again and again from the inexhaustible past, from its complexities that can never be reduced. For, if we can learn from the past, then there is the chance to enrich our present consciousness and maybe even our future. And, when I say we, I am referring to us Jungians today, but in no way thinking that what we learn can pervade the world or anything like that. The difference between Jung's generation and our own is that they believed psychology could influence collective events, and we can detect some inflation in that pretension. In any case, we have learned from Jung's "Essays on Contemporary Events", and we can learn still more from them. So let me offer my own personal reading of three of these essays within the framework of cultural anxiety.

The first essay, "Wotan", is a masterpiece on collective psychosis, demonstrating how an archaic Northern European mythological figure took over the German consciousness. In Jungian psychology, this phenomenon is termed possession, or psychosis. But when we study a psychosis, something we are accustomed to doing, we are studying the conflicts which provoked the psychosis. Wotan is an elusive figure, appearing only when the times are propitious and then vanishing. Jung leans on a monograph on Wotan by Martin Ninck, who, writes Jung, "... describes him... as the berserker, the god of storm, the wanderer, the warrior, ... the lord of the dead..., the master of secret knowledge, the magician... [Ninck] assumes an inner affinity between Wotan and Kronos, and the latter's defeat may perhaps be a sign that the Wotan-archetype was once overcome and split up in prehistoric times [like Kronos]... At all events, the Germanic god represents a totality on a very primitive level, a psychological condition in which *man's will was almost identical with the god's and entirely at his mercy*."[13]

This connection between Wotan and Kronos gives us an appreciation of the archaic forces unleashed by Wotan in the German people. Kronos was the father of the Titans, which puts those archaic forces in the mythological realm of the Titans, therein deepening our sense of Wotan, who disappears for millenia and reappears when the times are propitious, as a chronological phenomenon. The being of Wotan is in Kronos' time; so we can say that this special collective psychosis is Titanic.[14] Jung says that these archaic forces erupted because Christian-

[13] Ibid., paras. 393, 394 (Italics mine).

[14] See my paper "Moon Madness – Titanic Love: A Meeting of Pathology and Poetry" in *Images of the Untouched*, The Pegasus Foundation Series 1 (Dallas: Spring Publications, 1982), for my approach to the psychology of Titanism.

ity was unable to hold the conflict.[15] There was no religious syncretism to catch and hold in its net the forces of the eruption.

With his discussion on Nietzsche, Jung conveys an image of cultural anxiety, by suggesting that Nietzsche's ostensible confusion between Christ and Dionysos was, in reality, Wotan, that "fundamental attribute" of the German psyche, operating in Nietzsche's psyche. Evidently Nietzsche was not keen on German literature, implying that he could not directly explore the psychological sources already there in his own backyard, so to say, with the result that his own Germanic complexes fused with his studies of classical philology, his involvement with Dionysos, and the monotheistic thorn in the name of Christ the Saviour.

The third picture of cultural anxiety appears in a footnote about Wilhelm Hauer.[16] Jung knew him, and one senses that Jung had very ambivalent feelings toward him: on the one hand, Hauer was a scholar of Kundalini Yoga and, on the other, he was a Nazi. As the founder and leader of the German Faith Movement, he became possessed with the demented idea of making a German religion of faith without the Christian ingredient. It was a new and even crazier rejection of the possibilities in historical religious syncretism: the rejection of the monotheistic book from the East, as if this book, which his own Luther had brought to the people, had become an intolerable image. He was proposing a pure *virginal* German religion, uncontaminated by the Judaic Christian influence.

Jung's essay on Wotan is a diagnosis, impeccably worked out, of a collective psychosis, the psychotic condition of the Germans at the time of National Socialism.

In the second essay, "After the Catastrophe", a masterpiece for the study of the psychopathic personality and collective psychopathy, there is no longer even the remote possibility of an image: only anxiety and guilt expressed at the psychopathic level. There is no longer the unconscious dynamism of an archaic figure taking over the situation. After reading "After the Catastrophe" several times, one comes to the conclusion that guilt and psychopathy are so closely linked that you cannot talk about one without the other. I would even go so far as to say that psychopathy equals guilt and guilt equals psychopathy. If we accept this kinship, then it follows that whenever guilt appears, there

15 CW 10, para. 384.

16 Ibid., para. 387, 16n.

is, at the least, a psychopathic component. From Jung's reflections in this essay, one gets the impression that the only way to deal with psychopathy is through guilt. It seems, when confronted with the psychopath, guilt is invariably there. We put the guilt onto the psychopath, and the psychopath projects the guilt onto someone or something else. Psychopathy is rife with guilt. First, Jung puts the guilt for the catastrophe onto the Germans – onto the psychopaths – but then he goes further and places the guilt onto the whole of Europe. We are introduced to the first grand vision of psychopathy: it is part human nature; we all have a psychopathic part in varying degress; it is in each person, and it can manifest collectively.

It is in this essay that one feels Jung's cultural anxiety as in no other of his papers.[17] One senses it the most when he puts the guilt onto the Germans, as if guilt is the inevitable language when the psychopath jumps into the foreground. In my paper on Titanism, I tried to work out guilt as belonging to the imageless part of the psyche, guilt coming from the lacuna where no image is possible. And now, in this present paper, we have discussed guilt as being at the core of the monotheistic imageless God. I consider Jung's "After the Catastrophe" to be a great research into the imageless part of human nature, what I associate with the psychopathic component. However, one feels that Jung, in writing his paper, was at the most extreme point of his own cultural anxiety, when it could no longer be contained and worked upon imaginatively, but rather was spilled over into anger and guilt. It was a desperation which could only be expressed by way of the language of guilt. Guilt was constellated. Jung is telling us that one of the reactions to psychopathy is anger. He did not place the guilt onto the Germans in a manipulative or guilt-making way, he placed it with all the honest anger and rage he was able to express in writing, and he moves us to accept our own anger and rage as a natural response to psychopathic behaviour.

"Fighting with the Shadow", the third essay, has an enticing title. If "Wotan" is about the eruption of a Northern European archaic figure and "After the Catastrophe" is about the horror of the psychopath, then we can only engage in what the third essay is all about: fighting the

[17] One is deeply moved by Jung's cultural anxiety. When thinking about the wonder of the Renaissance, he said that, had it not been for that little German priest, the Renaissance would have given us the most extraordinary rebirth of ancient culture. But then, in "Wotan", he implies that Protestantism would have been the right Christian answer. All his cultural anxiety is in this contradiction: his mess between Protestantism and Catholicism, not to mention the fainting at the *Hauptbahnhof*; we can faint when in extreme anxiety (Kolb).

shadow. It is, too, a precise title, particularly for those of us who learn psychology from the study of the shadow, which, as far as I can see, is the only way to expand psyche and the study of psychology. The fight with the shadow allows us to free ourselves from the strait-jacketed view of Wotan only as psychosis, and the catastrophe only as psychopathy. Between these two extremes – psychosis and psychopathy – lies the psychic possibility of fighting the shadow or, at any rate, becoming a bit more aware of what we mean by shadow, namely, what we do not know about human nature.

All that psychosis and psychopathy made possible the Second World War with its eighty million casualties, among them six million Jews. But it was the killing of those six million Jews – what is called the Holocaust – that makes the Second World War quite different. And the Holocaust is central to cultural anxiety, because, without the extermination of six million Jews, the other deaths would have been counted as in any other war, the war of always, of generals fighting generals. Furthermore, *viewed from the perspective of cultural anxiety*, it is precisely the Holocaust that can teach us about shadow. The Holocaust is indeed very relevant to the subject of this paper – cultural anxiety – because it was the result of a religious and racial conflict; and relevant also to fighting the shadow, because there was the mad fantasy of destroying a shadow, utterly, out of the impossibility of assimilating it. The Holocaust was a shadow conflict.

So if there was an archetype at work in all the psychosis, psychopathy, and horror of the Holocaust, it was the archetype of purity: the virgin.[18] The virgin is an archetype that constellates intolerance and thus casts a dark shadow. And we can establish an affinity between monotheism and virginity in that they are both exclusive: they do not tolerate any form of life other than their own. There is no doubt that a peculiar affinity exists between monotheism and virginity (we have only to think of the history of Christianity and the Christian missionaries). Euripides, the poet of the irrational, reminds us of the bloody butchery that went on in Tauris to find the victims offered to Artemis, presenting us with an image which can be seen as a prototype of massacre: in the sense of offering human sacrifices to the Virgin Goddess of purity. So, without going into the history of the Jewish diaspora in Germany, a subject beyond my scope, in what follows, I believe I can put forward a view of the Holocaust in terms of virginity that is not terribly

[18] This paper, "On Cultural Anxiety", was written as part of a work in progress on Artemis, the archetype of virginity and purity.

difficult to accept: the Holocaust as the horrifying result of two peoples driven by the madness of virginal purity. It is this virginal fantasy of two pure races that gives to the Second World War its psychological peculiarity and makes the cruelty of the Holocaust a unique episode in Western history.

But, first, let me make a small digression: One of the most misused terms in this century's psychology is 'aggression'; its abuse is convincing enough. Until just the other day, the ideas concerning aggression, found in studies of animal behaviour, anthropology, etc., were that man has an instinctual aggression like the animals. According to these ideas, what goes wrong in man is that the so-called primitive complexes break out and take over the 'self-controlled civilised' individual. The blame, with a certain hypocrisy, is projected onto the primitive man we all have in us somewhere. All sorts of theories were elaborated in this connection, even the one concerning the old brain and the new brain; the new brain being threatened by the old primitive brain. However, today, the latest books on evolution[19] offer us more sophisticated psychological ideas, more in keeping with the spirit of our times. If man only had an instinctual aggression, then it would be contained within the ecology of his instincts. But it is more complex than this. Aggression at the level of so-called primitive man, who knows more or less how to deal with it, falls too short for explaining what we see in the world today.

Throughout recorded history, so-called human aggression would seem to spring from cultural conflicts, an expression of man's cultural anxiety; and if the recent books on evolution present primitive aggression as being more than just instinctual, but rather a product of culture, then there is nothing to compare with today's so-called civilised man, applied to whom the word aggressive is no longer valid. It is out of context and one could even say, simply not strong enough. As aggression is lived at the more primitive level, for the civilised man with his excess of cultural conflict, I prefer to use the word cruel.

In accepting the Jungian term of shadow as the field for exploration, depth psychology has to include cruelty, a by-product of culture and civilisation, as an essential component of shadow. I think of cruelty as being within the human possibility of fighting the shadow, as something accessible enough to keep within our daily awareness: cruelty is cultural, and therein lies its possibility to become psychic. It is as if history were constantly modifying our view of this issue. We cannot have the same view of this human trait as we had fifty years ago: cruelty

19 For instance, Richard E. Leakey, *The Making of Mankind* (New York: Dutton, 1981).

increases. Historically speaking, Jung, as well as his followers and collaborators, worked on this part of human nature in terms of evil. They tackled it mostly within the Western religious tradition of the polarities between good and evil, or evil as the part of our nature we cannot deal with and have to reject.

To summarize: Bearing in mind these three facets of human nature, we are trying to differentiate what belongs to the darkest part of our shadow. Aggression is an instinctual attitude appearing in the conflicts of primitive man, and also at the primitive level of the psyche and our complexes. (We could perhaps use the word aggression for some of the attitudes and behaviour of children and the mantally ill.) Cruelty is a product of civilised man's cultural anxiety. Of course, aggression and cruelty overlap. And lastly, in the studies of Western religion and philosophy, evil remains in the polarities between good and evil, the latter, in Jungian psychology, being the part of our nature we cannot assimilate and have to reject.

But, for our personal survival, for the protection of our souls, cruelty is the facet on which to concentrate. It is our most immediate concern, an all too evident part of our daily lives, of the world, and of our practices, where we are accustomed to seeing cruelty disguised in psychiatric diagnosis and treatment. Cruelty is an element of our constant cultural anxiety. We are all cruel somewhere. The political tortures and murders of today are closer to us than we care to admit. Indeed, we are far away from those Socratic days when, in spite of cruelty, Eros was the main concern. Borges put it very clearly when he said that you can know everything, even be a great poet, but if you do not know about cruelty, you do not know anything.

This attempt at a differentiation will not withstand much criticism, but its purpose was to arrive at a part of the psyche where we can perhaps tackle this dark shadow aspect of human nature: to concentrate on cruelty. Moreover, after this digression, I think we can now have a better perspective from which to view the Holocaust as a shadow conflict; this has little to do with the way in which it has been basically seen in terms of victims and victimizers, but rather as a manifestation of cruelty as a by-product of cultural anxiety.

"Being victim seems to be the destiny of Jews",[20] said a modern Jewess, Golda Meier, to a modern Jew, Henry Kissinger; as if this is the price to be paid for the fantasy of being the Chosen Ones. Her statement even implies an unconscious longing. There is a strange psychol-

[20] Quoted in *Time Magazine*, February, 1982.

ogy in this acceptance of being the victim, a psychology of being driven by a destiny that unconsciously precipitates the search for the victimizer. It is a destiny which has an extraordinary strength and the skill to find the portion needed for the living forces of that destiny. If the goal of one's destiny is to become a victim, then all a person's energy goes into that. If the final purpose is to be a victim, then one imagines that this is what really brings fulfillment. Such a sense of destiny turns a life into becoming the vehicle for the drive of that force. This is how I prefer to view the history of the Jewish diaspora in Germany: the Jewish people, driven by the force of their destiny – their racial purity – down the centuries propitiating and building up to the final consequences of the Holocaust.

Being chosen and being the victim are the same, and being chosen is a paradigm for purity. Let a twentieth-century writer, George Orwell, in his *1984*, written at another time of extreme cultural anxiety, describe the kind of monotheistic rejection which makes the madness of racial purity possible; he was actually concerned with how purity appears in the latest monotheistic conception of life: today's state monotheism:

> What was required in a Party member was an outlook similar to that of the ancient Hebrew who knew, without knowing much else, that all nations other than his own worshipped 'false gods'. He did not need to know that these gods were called Baal, Osiris, Moloch, Ashtaroth, and the like: probably the less he knew about them the better for his orthodoxy. He knew Jehovah and the commandments of Jehovah: he knew, therefore, that all gods with other names or other attributes were false gods.[21]

The shadow, this madness of racial purity, this exclusiveness, cast, in turn, constellated the German madness of racial purity: racial purity constellating racial purity. What history revealed in Germany was the killing of 'pure' Jews by 'pure' Germans: the pure Aryan race versus God's Chosen People. Two virginally dominated conceptions of life, the outcome of which was insanity. The impact of two virginal psychologies resulted in a mass destruction, a massacre. Victims and victimizers, victimizers and victims, dancing together in a hellish ballet of death. Moreover, it was in this demented appearance of virginity that the most destructive element lay, where seemingly the destruction focussed, almost as if the whole terrible war were a mere pretext to make possible the shadow meeting of two racial purities.[22]

[21] George Orwell, *1984* (Harmondsworth: Penguin, 1981), p. 246.

[22] If we read the documents on the war, we come to the conclusion that the Nazi High Command was more obsessed with the Jews than with what was going on at the war fronts.

We are accustomed to finding no madness in the Jewish conception of their religious and racial purity. But, from the psychological angle, we are obliged to see it as a madness. For, we have been trained to perceive in terms of Jung's equation of religion equalling madness. As a religious people, we feel how religion is a net to catch and hold our madness. But Jung also trained us to see religion as the field of the unconscious, where the shadow lurks, where cultural anxiety is most evident; in other words, the field to study.

In this paper, I have offered a psychology of the Holocaust which seems to me a more profitable way of studying it at this point in time. It is a psychology well rooted in Jung's legacy of the collective unconscious, the historical complexes, and the shadow. I prefer to view the Holocaust in terms of cultural anxiety and the constellation of two shadows, both with their cruelty, than at the guilt level or that of victims and victimizers.

E. R. Dodds, in *The Greeks and the Irrational*, says, rather convincingly, that when paganism was in decline before Christianity took over as the one ruling religion, the dominant attitude, in the Western soul, was a "fear of freedom".[23] So the fear of the many was assuaged under the protection of the One. But if, in our own times, we find a parallelism to Dodds' 'age of anxiety' (times which herald big changes in the world), we cannot say that today's soul finds much of a refuge in monotheism: because it is that self-same monotheism which is producing the fear; which does not respect the right to be different; which has the fantasy of making one monotheistic world. Today, the world is caught in the ultimate terror of the clash between two predominant monotheistic systems: one, the North American monotheism conceived from that same mixture of racialism and religion, the white Anglo Saxon Protestants (the WASPS), readers of the Bible (the Eastern book); the other, the monotheistic excess of Russia, the monotheistic conception of the State. In spite of any awareness they might have of each other's shadow, these two monolithic systems seem bent on destroying each other. They both have that dangerous virginal ingredient of purity – the one Biblical, the other ideological – and in their struggle, they produce today's fear. It is a historical situation which touches everyone, notwithstanding their history and geography.

[23] E. R. Dodds, *The Greeks and the Irrational* (Berkeley: University of California Press, 1968), Chapter VIII, "The Fear of Freedom".

In writing this paper, I would like to finish by stressing how much I have taken into consideration my own immediate historical complexes.[24] I am a Caribbean man, a historical product of the Caribbean section of what is called the Latin American Baroque. It is a mixture of Christianity in its Spanish version – a rather good balance between a Trinitarian monotheism and the old images rooted in the Mediterranean, plus a strong Celtic component. This is, in itself, a religious syncretism, producing its own anxiety and dynamism. But it is a religious syncretism which made an even wider syncretism possible: the fusion with the many different autochthonous American religions, not forgetting the religions the Africans brought with them in their souls. In this brief summary of the syncretism called the Latin American Baroque, I do not want to leave out the cruelty of our history – the piracy, the constant tyranny. We are a people who have to put a lot of energy into balancing our cultural anxiety: between the poets and the tyrants, the tortures, the shadow I want to call cruelty. And ours is a brand of cultural anxiety that occupies a wider space in the spectrum spanning monotheism and polytheism. What is more, it obviously leans more toward the polytheistic end and shows that inferiority when seen in relation to the monotheistic end. It is out of these complexities that I have written this paper; and it is out of these complexities that I feel the fear of monotheism and see it more as a menacing excess than as a challenge to the images in my soul, the images that nourish one's sense of life.

Cultural anxiety is my way of reflecting the inherited historical conflict, in any Westerner's psyche, between monotheism and the many paganisms of the Western world. Cultural anxiety could be seen in many other ways, and I presume each person has his or her own way of accepting and dealing with this anxiety. It is not difficult to think that Jung's concept of the Self was his way of holding the One and the many. But, as a man who has learned from Jung's teaching, I would say, in this respect, that to follow the tracks of one's own individuation is what is really valid. I personally feel that, in the world we live in, tolerance, as a way of understanding, is basic. However, I am also aware that inside me there are elements prone to tolerance and elements prone to intolerance; I have to suffer the anxiety these two opposites bring about in me, and I feel the challenge of trying to tolerate what is, in itself, intolerant.

[24] In most psychological papers, Jungian analysts tend not to acknowledge openly the historical complexes behind their papers.

# Anima-Animus in a Changing World

Norah Moore (London)

This paper reexamines the archetypes anima and animus and their images in the light of present day culture, and trends in social psychology and anthropology. It does not present a feminist point of view.

Students in London, men and women, often have difficulty in grasping Jung's theory of anima and animus because they find his classic descriptions sexually chauvinistic and unsympathetic to their own inner experience of both masculine and feminine.

It is important to remember that Jung developed his ideas in a different age from ours. Male and female gender roles and attitudes are now less polarised than then, and gender orientation has changed with the culture. Now men are increasingly involved in traditionally feminine work such as child care and house work, and women educated more widely, functioning as wage earners and in the professions and politics.

Gender should be distinguished from sexuality, which is linked to actual differences in physique, hormones and genes, although hormonal changes at different times of life make for some overlap and there is also individual variation.

Gender differences, on the other hand, although often considered innate, vary from age to age and between cultures, and concern social roles, occupation, ownership and inheritance of property, and rights over children, all factors subject to many influences, to which I will return. Gender differences have been linked to personality also.

Jung defined anima and animus as counterparts of the persona: "The anima is by and large *complementary* to the character of the persona. A very feminine woman has a masculine soul, and a very masculine man has a feminine soul – the more masculine his outer attitude is, the more his feminine traits are underrated: instead they appear in his unconscious. The character of the anima can be deduced from the persona." (Jung 19, p. 469)

If men's and women's personae are tending to become less gender polarised in recent times, it is but a step to recognise that the images of anima and animus must change also so that they, too, are less polarised genderwise, since they depend on the persona in a complementary way.

The point I wish to explore is that images of anima and animus are dependent on culture, and are becoming less polarised, more fluid, and partly overlapping, so that, as the roles of men and women approach each other, so images of anima and animus appear not as opposites, but as different aspects of one archetype: *anima-animus.* I distinguish here between archetypal images which we can observe, and archetypes themselves, which cannot be seen, but only postulated or inferred.

I will clarify gender roles and images first, as determined through culture and nurture, and second, as manifestations of a single archetype – *anima-animus,* that is both male and female and exists in both sexes. I see it as bipolar in its images (as are all archetypes), having spiritual and bodily poles and positive and negative aspects.

## Jung and Variable Anima and Animus Images

Jung lays the foundation for the notion of variable anima and animus images when he says that the character of the anima, deduced from the persona, can be either male or female, according to where the individuality is experienced. If this is felt as joined to the persona, then the anima is female, but if the individuality is unconscious, the anima is masculine and is not necessarily projected. The main orientation is then towards the perception of inner processes. "In every case where the *individuality* is unconscious, and is associated with the soul, the soul image has the character of the same sex. In all cases where there is an *identity* with the persona, and the soul is unconscious, the soul image is transferred to a real person. It may happen that a soul-image is not projected but remains within the subject, and this results in an identification with the soul because the subject is then convinced that the way he relates to his inner process is his real character." (Jung 19, p. 470) Jung says that this applies to father transferences in men and mother transferences in women, and to some instances of homosexuality.

A patient exemplifies this: he had idealised his father as great, but he in fact was unsympathetic, pompous and overbearing, inflated with self-importance and never at home. He had not despised his son for being poor at games and interested in poetry, but could not understand him. My patient, when I knew him as an adult, was timid, given to gossip and to indirect manipulation of interpersonal relations. He wore soft, velvety, furry clothes and flowery shirts. His persona thus had many "feminine" qualities (if we take the classic view), while he identified in dream and fantasy with a "masculine" anima, often dreaming of himself as a tough commando. He was attracted to managing, driving women, one of whom he married.

## Can the archetype change?

Can the archetype change and its images be fluid? Tillich clarified that, although archetypes themselves are fairly constant, their images differ with culture. Symbols are the infinitely variable path through which archetypes are translated into human terms, through images that are conditioned by the individual and social condition. (Tillich 48) Hubback, too, pointed out that the way we interpret symbols varies according to the opinions current at the time. (Hubback 18) The assessment of the role of biology itself depends on interpretation associated with any culture's mode of life. (Rosaldo 40)

Jung spoke in accord with his time when he said, "the anima is not to be found in the imagery of women". (Jung 21, p. 129) Today we see that our patients of both sexes experience soul images in both "anima" and "animus" terms.

What is the *anima-animus* archetype in itself? Archetypal gender orientated images cluster round the archetype, which is their centre of organisation. The images vary with the way the persona is conditioned. Some (including Jung) have said that male images are directed towards outside physical reality and imply a conscious attitude. But orientation towards the outside world is mostly conditioned and not innate, as I shall show. Moreover, consciousness includes (and perhaps is defined as) a relationship of ego to unconscious (through archetypal images and symbols). The notion of male consciousness, i. e., awareness and insight, has historical antecedants in male ascendency in western culture. To the man, his unconscious anima, when projected onto a woman, has made her seem to him relatively unconscious, this becoming an accepted view. This attitude is met, for instance, in many of Shakespeare's plays. (French 13) But conversely, a woman's animus, projected, makes men seem to her more unaware and unconscious, so that each sex tends to regard the other as the less conscious.

Jung speaks of a male-female pair of archetypes: "the mother-complex is caused in the first place by the assimilation of the mother to the pre-existent feminine side of an archetypal 'male-female' pair of opposites, and secondly by an abnormal delay in detaching from the primordial image of the mother. When projected, the anima always has a feminine form with definite characteristics. This empirical finding does not mean that the archetype is constituted like that *in itself*. The male-female syzygy is only one among the possible pairs of archetypes, albeit the most important one in practice and the commonest. It has numerous connections with other pairs which do not display any sex difference at all and can be put into the sexual category only by main force. These connections are found in the spontaneous fantasy-products in neurotic and psychotic case material. When one carefully considers this accumulation of data, it begins to seem possible that the anima in its quiescent unprojected state has no exactly determinable form but is in itself an indefinite structure which can assume definite forms only in projection." (Jung 20, p. 69)

The important point is that these pairs of opposites are not gender-linked, one of them remaining a possibility and the other embraced. Examples are thinking and feeling, often considered gender-orientated. Although Jung found both functions in men and women, in his day, thinking was considered to belong to males and feeling to females. That attitude does still occur, but is becoming less common and men may show feelings and women think and hold opinions without the censure they once risked, for this gender-link has worn thin.

Jung also attributes many other pairs to the original syzygy. Among religious and philosophical ones, he mentions: One-Other, cosmos-chaos, morality-temptation, Christ-Devil; and among personal and psychic pairs, man-child, subject-object, doubt-credulity, extroversion-introversion and consciousness-unconsciousness. He also refers to pairs from Buddhist philosophy, such as nonself-impermanence, and nonexistence-suffering. (Jung 22) Others might be left-right, going-returning, or northness-southness from the *Tao Te Ching*. (Moore 32)

None of these pairs is inherently gender-linked, but many have become so in one age or another. For instance, woman has at times been seen as the Devil, treated as a child, as temptress, as an object, as lacking consciousness or being only capable of chaotic thinking, having had rejected shadow content of the male ego projected onto her.

## Clinical example

Before exploring influences that affect gender differentiation, I cite a patient as illustration.

T., handsome and austere, inwardly felt a vulnerable girl. She was the younger daughter of a wealthy race horse owner, clever but educated only in social graces, having never been allowed serious study. One summer while he was abroad in the army, a bomb fell on an air raid shelter where she and her sister were. The mother was outside and was killed outright. The babies, aged one and two, were dug out alive, but no one explained why their life had suddenly disintegrated. T. was reared by an aunt until enrollment at a second-rate genteel school at five, spending holiday's with father, who had remarried and adopted a son.

T. did badly at school. Her father had told her that, "you do not train hacks for the Derby", often calling her a useless silly girl, sending the adopted brother to a good school and university, bringing him up to expect to inherit the property and control of the stables.

T. married an older man, but it failed, since she did not attempt to hide contempt for his poor ability compared with hers. In midlife, she remarried a penniless youth who let her dominate him. She was rivalrous with her brother, with many bitter quarrels, thinking she could run the stables better than he. This seemed realistic, since she was the more incisive and clearer-headed but merely lacked training, accepting this as normal for a woman of her class.

By the time she was in analysis, she was crippled by asthma and depressed. She felt I lacked insight and ability to understand her poetic and religious feelings. She thus kept me at a distance from her innermost thoughts, because she could not trust me not to go away, taking her good things with me. But in her dreams, I was seen accompanying her on a journey to a paradisal garden where time stood still (and sessions did not end), the sun shone, roses grew round the door and her habitual sense of doom was not yet known. In these dreams, she was a pretty, curly-haired baby in a frilly dress. Sometimes she was a poor little vixen trapped in a hole, who escaped into a beautiful meadow.

In spite of asthma, she was a fine horsewoman, equalling her father and excelling her brother and she rode to hounds. She avoided the duty of social life, and wore old corduroy trousers and men's shirts.

T.'s upbringing had denied her a chance to develop her natural business ability. Because of her mother's early death, she had not been able to separate from her and (as Jung described) the primordial mother image remainded as a "feminine" soul image, while her outward orientation was more "masculine". This usurped the false "feminine" persona she had acquired as a child.

T. exemplified many cultural influences that affect gender-orientation: education, example, suggestion, imitation, permission, conditioning, mirroring and identification. Such influences vary between classes and between generations.

Deutsch, writing of women's low self esteem, said that western women present themselves to their children as passive, dependent, lacking orientation to reality, but the fathers present themselves as progressive, active, independent and orientated to reality. (Deutsch 9) This governs the way their childrens' gender persona develops.

## Innate or conditioned gender differences

How do these influences act to bring about gender differentiation (for it is on this that images of anima and animus depend)? Social psychology helps this question and is particularly relevant to Jungian thought, since it offers objective observation of behaviour in early infancy- a time of prime importance when archetypal images originate.

Several workers have investigated mothers' handling of infants. Moss found that mothers showed a tendency to reinforce the behaviour of boys and girls differently. They fondled the boys more and held them longer each day, so that they were more stimulated and aroused by tactile and visual contact, crying more, and were less tractable than the girls. Moss thought this mutual behaviour might have been initiated by greater vulnerability of boys to perinatal trauma, which made them more irritable than girls, so that the mothers picked them up more often. He found that mothers responded more to the girls by mirroring their expression and baby talk than they did boys. He thought these differences in handling initiated a pattern of socialisation in keeping with social expectation, according to which females are more responsive to socialisation and less aggressive than males. Moss also considered kinaesthesia important in conditioning, gender identification being acquired through body contact at the earliest stage and not through words or discipline. (Moss 35)

Hartley, too, thought the first process in sex role identification kinaesthetic through body manipulation, like fussing with a girl's hair or fondling a boy's genital. He also listed canalisation, verbal appellation and activity exposure as effecting gender differentiation. (Hartley 15)

Rabban, in a study of sex role identification in young children in different social groups, said that canalisation directs the attention a certain way. For instance, a boy may be discouraged from playing with dolls as 'girlish' and a girl from playing football or with trains. By the age of three, most children have learned to choose toys and play in accordance with adult expectation of gender role. (Rabban 38)

A girl may be told, "boys are rough" or, "what a pretty girl you are", and be scolded for fighting and praised for staying clean, but her brother be admired if he defends himself "like a proper boy", enjoys a rough and tumble and gets a bit dirty. So, girls must repress spontaneous behaviour earlier than boys because of verbal appellation.

Mothers relate to baby girls according to how they experience their own bodies, giving permission to be like them. But a depressed or neglectful mother may not give permission, or, if envious, may try to make her daughter unlike her. A childish frigid mother who may not even admit to menstruation may not give her daughter permission to be a woman, so that she feels unclean when she matures.

A father's mirroring and permission is also vital to both sexes. In his paper on paternal deprivation in relation to narcissistic damage, Carvalho drew attention to the father's role in the differentiation of the original mother-father pair. (Carvalho 5)

Sometimes a child is given permission to value his or her contrasexual side, and here I was lucky, one result being that I have not felt a drive towards the womens' movement, although I see the need for it. When I was a small girl, my father, a very 'masculine' man, used to talk to me about the time "when he was a little girl". This was, I suppose, his way of making a link with me. I knew he had not been a little girl (although he had worn petticoats as a baby), just as I knew my brother was not a girl, and that I would not grow into a man but into a woman, like my mother, as I longed to do. It was a story, a make-believe between us, and yet, in a sense, true: my father was telling me that he had a little girl inside him somewhere and that I had the makings of a man, and that this was quite as it should be; we were of the same nature, not different.

The gender reinforcement a father gives his children depends on his view of himself; this varies in different historical times.

Cross identification may occur if a father plays boy's games, with his small girl if he has no son, or a boy is mollycoddled by his mother because he is pretty or the youngest.

## Gender, personality and complex

Gender has often been considered linked to innate differences of personality, particularly aggressivity and passivity, and objective studies have been attempted of this. For instance, Erikson described differences in the play of three-year-old children, boys building high walls with towers and cones, and girls making low enclosing walls. He linked these differences to the shape of the childrens' genitals, to male aggressivity and female domesticity. (Erikson 11)

That study raises two questions. First, is the difference innate or acquired? A large body of work throws light on this problem. Sears et al, in a study of young babies, found that mothers allowed boys more aggressive behaviour from birth, and subsequently made less attempt to check it in them than in girls, accepting that greater aggressivity is to be expected of males; but they remained unaware of their part in conditioning it. (Sears et al. 44)

Schaeffer et al., in a study of patterns of response to physical contact in neonates, found that some newborn babies disliked body handling and became irritable and aggressive, but sexes did not differ significantly. They noticed that mothers reacted differently to the sexes, confirming any tendency to aggression and irritability in males, but discouraging it in females. (Schaeffer et al. 43)

Kagan and Moss, in a prospective study of the relation between childhood and later behaviour, followed children from birth to maturity, finding that boys tended to become relatively aggressive at adolescence and girls more passive, whatever their nature had been in infancy. That is, while aggressive boy babies and passive girl babies remained so, those with the opposite nature to the expected social norm changed during childhood, passive boys becoming more aggressive, and aggressive girls more passive. (Kagan & Moss 23)

Witkin, in his book on psychical differentiation, supports the view that differences in aggressivity between boy and girl babies is only small, and much less than that between one male and another, or one female and another. (Witkin 49)

Money, in a comparison of developmental differentiation of masculinity and femininity, drew these views together, saying that, while biology may point the direction of psychical gender differences, it does not govern their extent, which is influenced more by conditioning and social training. (Money 31)

A second question raised by Erikson's study is whether the observation itself was influenced by the observer's theoretical and subjective viewpoint. For instance, in a study of the use of language by men and women, Spender found that observers were rating similar words such as 'maybe' or 'perhaps' differently, according to which sex was speaking. Male usage was classified as an absolute or strong form, but female usage as a qualifier or weak form. (Spender 46) It can be argued similarly that, in Erikson's study, a value judgement was being made about the patterns the children made with the bricks, because of a preconceived idea of a girl's role and a boy's aggressivity, and that this may have altered the observation made, or the way it was interpreted.

The way we interpret observations about gender role and personality is subject not only to the sort of conditioning we have had and the theories we adhere to, but also to cultural influences. The concept of anima and animus comes under the same influences.

As well as to aggressivity and passivity, gender identification has often been considered linked to other personality traits, such as creativity or argumentativeness, and psychic functions, like feeling and thinking. This we see reflected in Jung's description of anima and animus.

Anthropological studies show that this distinction is not universal. Many years ago, Mead described how, among the Arapesh of New Guinea, gender was differentiated by occupation and inheritance of cult objects, not by personality. Women made decisions and had authority over children; men did not, but could earn status by nursing them. It was laughable among them to ascribe any particular personality trait to a person because of sex, or to think him or her as womanish or mannish because of traits more often found in the other sex. (Mead 30) In a more recent study of the regulation of sexual patterns amongst the same people, Henry found similar gender patterns, and that they were not linked to temperament. (Henry 16)

Mead found among another people, the Tchambuli of New Guinea, that, although some temperaments were thought allied to sex, this was in a manner surprising to western eyes. Men were coquettish and artistic, women more domineering, sexually urgent and adventurous.

Some people had the so-called wrong feelings, or worse, the feelings of the other sex, a woman being a creative fickle flirt, or a man dominant, and this caused censure or ostracism. Davenport more recently confirmed Mead's findings, describing how the men decorated themselves with flowers in their hair and women had more power. (Mead 30, Davenport 8)

Complexes and maladjustments arise from the kind of society we live in. "Any society that specialises its personality types by sex, which insists that any trait – love for children, interest in art, bravery in the face of danger, garrulity, lack of interest in personal relations, passiveness in sex relations: there hundreds of traits of very different kinds that have been so specialised – is unalienably bound up with sex, paves the way for a kind of maladjustment." (Mead 30, p. 273)

Malinowski long ago proposed the same argument, reasoning that psychic complexes (referring to the Oedipus complex) are not general phenomena, but are linked to the culture in which the child grows up; Oedipal rivalry is less evident in societies where the father has less authority, and has no universal application, since Freud framed it without reference to wider sociological or cultural settings. (Malinowski 29)

Since Jung's concept of anima and animus presents a similar cultural difficulty to that of the Oedipal complex, its case can be argued in a similar way. His paper, "Anima and animus", seems to modern eyes very clearly based on gender roles and prejudices of patriarchal society of many decades ago. (Kirsch 24) This concept cannot be extended to all cultures. For instance, we would expect a Tchambuli man to have an overbearing decisive anima, and his wife a passive flirty animus, in compensation to their gender personae, quite the reverse of Jung's images.

It can also be said that Jung's images do not apply to any culture for ever, but must be reassessed as gender roles vary from age to age.

Gender differentiation is global, but follows no universal rule, whether in family structure and mothering, or political activity, although anthropological studies show that, in general, women's role is seen as less important, less interesting, less public. (Rosaldo 40)

In a wide, cross-cultural study of women in Indonesian, American Indian, African and Spanish American cultures, Sanday found that gender roles depended on the amount of energy each sex expended on three major activities: reproduction, defense and subsistence. Since bearing children fell to females, the probability was that the other tasks fell to males, who thus had main control of resources. She found domestic and public roles commonly varied, although high status (such as control of material, demand for produce and political participation) in one often implied high status in the other also, as it does in our culture. Any move towards greater equality of the sexes must be a late development in a culture, when the economy allows better education and correspondingly wider choice of occupation for all. Sanday's point was that political and economic factors affected the view taken of women's nature. (Sanday 42)

A century ago, Engels proposed that women's position varied between societies and epochs according to the prevailing economic and political relationships of the society, basing his views on historical and ethnographical data. (Engels 10)

Anthropologists have long recognised that gender patterns differ between cultures. Benedict, an early pioneer in this field, distinguished patterns having to do with exchange and ownership of property from those having to do with procreation. In western civilisation, these two aspects are linked, but not universally; for example, among Zuni Indians of New Mexico, men are acknowledged as procreators, but women own all the property. Among the Dobu of New Guinea, on the other hand, the husband is chosen from a hostile tribe, where he continues to live, visiting his wife in secret, having no property or family role apart from his sexual one. In certain tribes, such as the Trobriand, descent is not reckoned from the father, no connection being seen between intercourse and the birth of a child. This may be from ignorance of fatherhood; or because of a power struggle between the sexes, or for economic reasons, even when the father's procreative role is known. (Benedict 2)

Development of gender roles is subject to three factors: biology, the nature-culture dichotomy and mothering. (Chodorow 6)

The question of the biological factor, often considered primary (Levi-Strauss 26), has been confused by male bias in interpretation. Freud's theory of girls' penis envy presupposed that the penis is superior, so envy would be natural. Bettelheim, on the other hand, suggested that either sex envied the function of the other, but women expressed it more because of this bias that deems the envy natural. (Bettelheim 3) Lomas has drawn attention to the envy a man may have for a woman's capacity to bear children. (Lomas 28) Balint preferred to call penis envy jealousy, because it is people with penises that mothers love, not those without. (Balint 1)

Biological resemblance of a girl to, and a boy's difference from, the mother means differing patterns of identification and separation. A daughter is influenced by the mother's concept of her body. This is not merely the lack of a penis; she may feel commanded by mysterious powers within that are a source of life, and vulnerable to external magic that threatens it, as Guatemalan women do. (Paul and Paul 37) A European woman, too, may know the lunar periodicity of her menses and speak of them as 'the curse'. Colby, in a study of Mesamerican Indians, suggests that, because of the experience of penetration and of the growing child within them, women may have a permeable body boundary (not a weak or inadequate one). This may produce a feeling of comparative lack or personal identity or of less distance from nature, which is passed from mother to daughter. (Colby 7)

Chodorow saw four stages in a boy's separation from his mother. First he realises that his body is different; next, he asserts that he is not a female, and later he represses or devalues his 'feminine' traits. Finally, he asserts that he is a male and identifies with father. Until recently, he had only slight contact with his personal father, who was rarely seen; he would see more of him, now that he takes more part in child care, but less of mother, who may have a valued outside role. (Chodorow 6) Male identification is now more personal and continuous and less archetypal.

An opposition between man and woman has often been deduced (stemming from eighteenth century thought, notably of Rousseau), related to one between nature and culture. Levi-Strauss, an exponent of this point of view, postulated the following pairs: woman/man, domestic/culture, nature/culture, unconscious/conscious, making an extrapolation that woman equals nature. The widely followed corollary is that woman is subordinate because nature includes that which should be controlled. He also suggested that incest taboos were crucial because they led to exogamy, and exchange of women. He thought language played a central position in kinship and gender, men having capability for symbolisation but women not, and that in exogamy, exchange of women was symbolic, like exchange of words. (Levi Strauss 27)

Lacan, following Levi-Strauss, said that the phallus was a key signifier, possesion meaning power in discourse, command over language and a consequent prestigious place in society. (Lacan 25)

Subsequently the Stratherns studied the Hagen people of Papua, New Guinea and found these pairs: nature/culture, wild/social, mountain/cultivated. These opposites were not gender-linked, but antithetical and somewhat ambiguous. The mountain, for instance, was the source of rain and streams, but also of thunder and destructive of wild animals. It was a male deity, as was the god of cultivation, but female consorts mediated them. (Strathern 47)

In an interesting parallel, Harris found that the Laymi of the Bolivian Andes had all male deities who represented similar opposites, incarnating them in their most specific forms. Female gods and women in their tribal and marriage roles were seen as mediators between the contrasting pairs, e. g., between nature and culture. (Harris 14) Ortner also discusses the position of women as mediators. (Ortner 36) This is a different conception from the opposite gender based pairs seen by Levi-Strauss and has interesting repercussions on the way we think about the anima, so often seen as a mediator between ego and unconscious (and appearing as such in men's dreams, like Beatrice to Dante). The position of the animus is less clear, perhaps because this concept was more of an afterthought for Jung.

## Anima-animus Images and other Archetypes

Images of *anima-animus* are affected by other archetypes, for instance, the personal shadow tends to be linked to images of the contrasexual archetype if anima and animus images are polarised. Thus, a man may evaluate his feeling function (if inferior) as weak, messy, and seducing like the negative side of his anima. Similarly, a woman's shadow may be linked to oppressive overbearing images of her animus. (Moore 34)

We have seen how gender persona is influenced by many cultural factors. We also see in our patients how such contemporary changes are echoed in the way a man tolerates his femininity better today, and a woman her masculinity. Attitudes to gender identification change, too, at different times of life and as a result of individuation.

Such polarised anima and animus images may be hard to separate from other archetypes, for instance, anima images from parts of the great mother. The link is not usually with her feeding, caring or holding aspects, or with images that are in general part of an acceptable good-enough mother image; but the anima receives those unacceptable images of the mother archetype that are usually met transpersonally, such as a divine perfect or nasty starving one, an ethereal inspiring maiden or beautiful seducing enchantress, a weak fallen woman or evil witch. That is, bad or unattainably good images of the threefold mother

(mother, maiden and witch) become linked to anima, while good, caring, holding and loving images are put onto the acceptable wife. Similar links between animus images, the great father and acceptable husband can be traced. (Moore 33)

Anima, animus and trickster images are also closely linked. A woman often sees a man as tricky and unreliable because her animus is projected onto him, and a man a woman as fickle and treacherous because of his projected anima. Thus, each sex may have contrasexual trickster images and so aver that the trickster is of the sex opposite to themselves.

Idealisation and reversal of images may occur, the animus appearing as a golden holy youth rather than a jealous petty tyrant. For instance, a driving, ambitious woman had several love affairs with parish curates, seeing men as holy saints. She undermined her partners' masculinity and made them impotent, remaining unaware of her own aggressive animus.

## Splitting and Individuation

Reappraisal of anima and animus does not mean, of course, that Jung's formulation ceases to be vitally important. It does mean that mutual projections on partners (and falling in love) are experienced more fluidly and involve much more than stereotypic gender based ones. For instance, a logical, clear-thinking woman and a poetic, impractical, vacillating man may fall in love. My point is that, although conjunction of opposites are needed for the release of psychic energy, these need not be gender based, but counterparts (not necessarily opposites) in different related *persons*.

Yesterday's patterns may be a problem if perpetuated: this couple illustrate the difficulty of accepting polarised gender roles too well: The husband was a stereotypical business man whose mother had proudly told his fiancée that he could not even boil an egg and (of course) had never set foot in the kitchen. His wife remained dutifully at home, waited on him and the children, did not drive, read what he told her to, and listened to selected news he read from the newspapers. She seldom ventured any opinion, since such stepping out of her role upset him, and "of course" there was no question of her working. The children saw their parents as figures of fun, a source of embarrassment before school friends, for what had been the norm in the early part of the century (when Jung wrote "Anima and animus") was now an anachronistic problem.

SPRING PU
P.O. BC
DALLAS, T

| | | | |
|---|---|---|---|
| YOUR ORDER NO. | 241 | INVO | |
| DATE SHIPPED | 11-30-88 135 | SHIPPED VIA | |

SOLD TO James S. Witzig
3690 Knob Hill Lane
Eugene, OR 97405

| QTY. | TITLE |
|---|---|
| 1 | Spring 1988 |
| 1 | Women's Dio |
| 1 | Sybol & Clin App |
| 3 | Books Shipped Total |

PLEASE PAY FROM THIS INVOICE

LICATIONS №  35475
222069
XAS 75222

| | | | |
|---|---|---|---|
| DATE 11-17-88 | | CODE | PD |
| kpost | TERMS | | prepaid |

HIPPED
O

| | EACH | TOTAL | | |
|---|---|---|---|---|
| | | 15 | 00 | |
| | | 17 | 50 | |
| | | 32 | 00 | |
| | | 64 | 50 | gr |
| -10% dis | | 6 | 45 | dis |
| | | 58 | 05 | |
| | | 3 | 00 | P+H |
| | | 61 | 05 | net |

241

An example of people whose gender personae are less polarised was a woman who was a leader, ambitious, a good organiser and original writer. Much had been expected of her less able brother and little of her, and her school successes did little to compensate the mother for disappointment in him. Because clever, she was educated to think logically, contrary to her dominant feeling function. She loved grappling with strong waves, high winds and mountains. In spite of mixed pressures, or perhaps because of them, she was able to live equably with so-called masculine and feminine elements in her make-up, marrying a man with a similarly fluid anima-animus, warm, caring and intuitive, who was successful but not ambitious.

Another example was a man who, although an intrepid explorer, was also a poet. He married a rather prosaic aggressive woman, not as interested in sex as he, conservative and distrustful of creative ability. These two examples show how marital partners of people whose anima-animus images are not very polarised complement them in an atypical way.

In her book, *Androgyny*, Singer examined recent redistribution of gender roles from a view of comparative religion, seeing there the achievement of a new androgynous inner world. (Singer 45) I do not agree with those assumptions. As we know, the original syzygy deintegrates into opposites, one of the pair being identified with the persona and the other projected onto persons. However, the extent of this splitting into opposites is subject to cultural influence. The syzygy is reached again as a result of individuation. I do not think that it is either the original or an individuated syzygy that is found in today's social change. What *is* found is more fluidity and less polarisation of the images of opposites such as anima and animus. Nor can we say that more or completer individuation is found in the populace (unless one takes the dubious view that a culture can individuate, not just people). The change does mean, however, that contrasexual sides of the archetype need not be so completely opposed (and, as a consequence, projected) as when Jung wrote, it now being possible to interpret anima and animus as different images of one bipolar archetype, *anima-animus*. The archetype has not changed; but rather our images of it and the concept inferred from them.

Anima-animus differs from the original syzygy, for it is contained in it and deintegrates from it. Syzygy itself is expressed in creation myths, in ideas of the nature of God, and in self images that are indistinguishable from symbols of God and may be androgynous. In the Old Testament, masculine qualities of Jehovah predominate. He is often shown as volcanic and avenging, but the prophet Hosea spoke of God's loving kindness, mercy and long suffering, and his nurturing, healing side:

> I drew them with bands of love and I was to them as they that take off their yoke, and I laid meat unto them. I will heal their backsliding, I will love them freely. I will be as the dew unto Israel: he shall grow as the lily and will cast forth his roots in Lebanon. I am like a green fir tree. From me is thy fruit found.

The Gnostics followed a tradition that God was androgynous. In Genesis also, according to the Priestly Creation Cycle of the fourth century B. C., the word for God is a plural one, Elohim, the Gods, as in the passage, "God created man in his own image: male and female created he them", suggesting that God himself is both male and female. (Campbell 4) The individuation process also, is sometimes pictured as male-female; when, for instance, Herakles became a female slave, Ramakrishna changed into a girl and Tiresias into a woman.

Jung took the more usual view that syzygy is not male-female, but a state of relationship between diverse opposites that give birth out of their mutual tension and capacity for reversal. (Jung 22) The earliest images a baby has of the syzygy may be the safe, holding, androgynous, parental couple. (Samuels 40) The diad between this pair, and the baby may be the first incarnation of the syzygy in flesh and blood terms, and the beginning of individuation.

We know from Fordham's work that individuation is a recurring event from infancy. (Fordham 12) It is spirally recurrent in Jung's view, and reunites male and female as, bit by bit, projections are taken back and owned; but the images are also closer together because of changing culture, their images overlapping. If the contrasexual archetype is kept inside (because it is less necessary to project an image if less polarised), the anima and animus act more as an internal pair of opposites, not necessarily gender based, in communication with each other rather than split off, so a man may link his individuality (in Jung's terms) to his tender caring side, and a woman take possession of her logical assertive side.

As Christian Rosencrautz puts it in the Chemical Wedding:

> This day, this day, this, this
> The Royal Wedding is. (Yates 50)

There can be a greed in wanting to be both male and female, enviously grasping at the role of the other sex. (Hubback 18) Lady Macbeth exemplifies such women. She could slightingly say the following to her bloodthirsty, warlike lord, spurring him on by her mettle to further ambition, at the cost of her own femininity:

> Thy nature is too full of the milk of human kindness,
> I may pour my spirits in thine ear
> And chastise with the vigour of my tongue.
> Unsex me here, stop up the senses and passage of remorse,
> That no compunctuous visitings of nature
> Shake my fell purpose.

Another patholological wish is to protect oneself from the mother by identifying with the father as well, or vice versa, as did the following patient: Margery was tall and gawky, wore clothes suited to a prepubertal girl, talked intellectually and had read most of Jung, which she said she understood and might have written herzelf. She was neither interested in men nor in feminine pursuits. Her sister, a year younger, had been premature and needed much maternal care; Margery was fed by her father, whom she grew to idolise. She reached puberty early, but the frail immature sister still had most of mother's attention, who expected considerable personal support from Margery and did not help her over pubertal problems. The girl identified with her father, but was not clever enough for a career and drifted into being an unappreciated home daughter. I soon realised that she did not have a false self, as I had first thought. She could feel, but was much more at home with organising and thinking, although not good at it. She had identified with masculinity as a defence against her rage at her mother's rejection and demand, and to protect mother from damage. Her natural persona should have had some masculine qualities, but she was driven to exaggerate them. After some years in analysis, she started to show a colour sense and dress well, trained as a secretary, married, and had a family of boys.

There is a standpoint where one may legitimately allow oneself to have both 'masculine' and 'feminine', as in some of the patients described above. Instances used to be seen where a girl had hidden her intellect because that was not acceptable; it may have challenged her brother too much, or frightened men, so that she did not find lovers, or have made her unsure of herself as a woman. For instance, one woman refrained from earning more than her husband or excelling him by taking a post graduate degree, thus trying to preserve the conventional power balance. Such reactions are less frequent now. There may, however, be a fear that the partner will be not only deprived, but sucked dry and destroyed: a negative result of taking back the contrasexual archetypal images.

Gender roles may polarise or split in ways in line with current culture, but inappropriate to a person. A man with a not very differentiated persona may find this hard to accept, and strive to maintain a false façade of strong masculinity against his natural bent. For instance, a teacher made a conscious effort to maintain strict discipline, dressed very correctly, and played rugby football, but his leaning was to poetry, music and religion. He repeatedly lost his job and picked quarrels because he saw any headmaster as inflexible, bigoted and envious (like the rather masculine anima that appeared in his dreams).

Hesse was another who rebelled. In 1919, he reached a crisis between the expected manly role in post-war Germany and his own inclination to introspection and poetry, and was no longer content with the false persona of his upbringing; he fled to Montagnola in the Swiss alps, hoping to escape. His words express the conflict between that conventional role and his inner world, where, as for the Hagen people, both the masculine mountain and the mediating woman are found:

> Often I tried the frightening way of reality,
> Where things that count are profession, law, fashion, finance,
> But disillusioned and freed I fled away alone
> To the other side, the place of dreams and blessed folly.
> A mountain range in the night,
> On the balcony a silent woman.
>
> (Hesse 17)

## Summary

Anima and animus images depend on gender persona. This varies at different times of life, with changing hormones, and shifting roles in later life, with new emphasis on values and meaning. It varies between cultures and is influenced by conditioning and other factors, and from age to age.

Splitting and projection of images occur world wide and in all ages, but do not all follow our present western pattern of differentiation, or the patterns current during the early part of the century, which influenced Jung in his classical description of anima and animus.

Because of the variability of gender persona, the images of anima and animus (that are their unconscious counterparts) are seen as polyvalent, fluid and interchangeable to a degree not taken into account by Jung, so that they appear as images of a bipolar pair of archetypes, *anima-animus,* occurring in both sexes.

## References

1 Balint, A., 1954 *The early years of life: a psychoanalytic study,* New York.

2 Benedict, R., 1935, *Patterns of society,* R. K. P., London.

3 Bettelheim, B., 1954, *Symbolic wounds; puberty rites and the envious male,* New York.

4 Campbell, J., 1964, *The masks of God: occidental mythology,* Viking.

5 Carvalho, R., 1982, "Paternal deprivation in relation to naıcissistic damage", in: *J. Analyt. Psycho 127.2.*

6 Chodorow, N., 1974, "Family structure and feminine personality", in: *Woman, culture and society,* ed. M. Z. Rosaldo and L. Lamphere, Stanford Univ. Press.

7 Colby, B. J., 1967, "Psychological orientation" in: *Handbook of middle American Indians,* ed. M. Nash, Austin, Texas.

8 Davenport, W., 1965, "Sexual patterns and their regulation in a society of the southwest pacific" in: *Sex and behaviour,* ed. F. M. Beach, Wiley.

9 Deutsch, H., 1945, *The psychology of women,* New York.

10 Engels, F., 1891, *The origin of the family, private property and the state,* Foreign Language Publishing House, Moscow.

11 Erikson, E., 1965, "Inner and outer space: reflections of womanhood", in: *The woman in America,* ed. R. J. Lifton, Houghton-Mifflin.

12 Fordham, M., 1978, "The maturation of the ego in infancy", in: *Lib. of Analytic Psychol, Vol. 1,* ed. Fordham et al.

13 French, M., 1982, *Shakespeare's division of experience,* Cape.

14 Harris, O., 1980, "The power of signs" in: *Nature, culture and gender,* ed. C. MacCormack and M. Strathern, Cambridge Univ. Press.

15 Hartley, R. E., 1966, " A developmental view of female sex role identification" in: *Role theory,* ed. B. J. Biddles and E. J. Thomas, Wiley.

16 Henry, J., 1964, *Jungle people,* Vintage books.

17 Hesse, H., 1972, *Wandering,* Cape, London.

18 Hubback, J., 1978, "Reflections on the psychology of women", *Int. J. Analyt. Psychol 23.*

19 Jung, C. G., 1921, "Definitions: soul image" in: *Coll. wks 6.*

20 Ibid, 1936, "Concerning the archetype" in: *Coll. wks 9i.*

21 Ibid, 1937, "Psychology and religion" in: *Coll. wks 18.*

22 Ibid, 1942, "Transformation symbolism in the Mass" in: *Coll. wks. 11.*

23 Kagan, J. and Moss, R. A., 1962, *Birth to maturity,* Wiley.

24 Kirsch, J., 1973, "Woman's changing image of self", in: *Psychological perspectives,* vol. 14, 1.

25 Lacan, I., 1977, *The four fundamental principles of psychoanalysis,* Harmondsworth, Penguin.

26 Levi-Strauss, C., 1969, *The elementary structure of kinship,* Eyre and Spottiswood, London.

27 Ibid, 1977, *Structural anthropology,* Allen Lane.

28 Lomas, P., 1964, *Childbirth ritual,* New Society.

29 Malinowski, B., 1927, *Sex and repression in savage society,* R. K. P., London.

30 Mead, M., 1935, *Sex and temperament in three primitive societies,* R. K. P., London.

31 Money, J., 1963, "The developmental differentiation of femininity and masculinity compared", in: *The potential of women,* ed. S. M. Faber and H. D. Wilson, in: "Man and civilisation symposium", McGraw-Hill.

32 Moore, N., 1983, "The archetype of the way: *Tao* and individuation" in: *Int. J. Analyt. Psychol 28.3.*

33 Ibid, 1983, "The archetype of the way: the ego self relationship", in: *Int. J. Analyt. Psychol., 28.3.*

34 Ibid, 1984, "The left hand of darkness: aspects of the shadow", in: *Int. J. Analyt. Psychol., 29.3.*

35 Moss, H. A., 1970, "Sex, age and state as determinants of mother-infant interaction" in: *Readings in child socialisation,* ed. K. Danziger, Pergamon.

36 Ortner, S. B., 1974, "Is female to male as nature is to culture?", in: *Woman, culture and society,* ed. M. Z. Rosaldo and L. Lamphere, Stanford Univ. Press.

37 Paul, B. D. and Paul, L., 1963, "Changing marriage patterns in a highland Guatemalan community" in: *Southwestern J. of Anthropol., 19.*

38 Rabban, M., 1950, "Sex role identification in young children in two diverse social groups", in: *Genetic psychology monograms,* McGraw-Hill.

39 Reiter, R. R., (ed), *Towards an anthropology of women,* Monthly Review Press, New York.

40 Rosaldo, M. Z., 1974, "Theoretical overview" in: *Woman, culture and society,* ed. M. Z. Rosaldo and L. Lamphere, Stanford Univ. Press.

41 Samuels, A., 1982, "The image of the parents in bed", in: *Int. J. Analyt. Psychol., 27.499.*

42 Sanday, P. R., 1973, "Toward a theory of the status of women", in: *American anthropologist, 75: 1682–1700.*

43 Schaeffer, H. R., Emerson, P. E., 1964, "Patterns of response to physical contact in early human development", in: *J. Child Psychol. and Psychiat. 1964, 5.*

44 Sears, R. E., Macoby, E. E., Levin, H., 1957, *Patterns of child rearing,* Harper and Row.

45 Singer, J., 1977, *Androgyny,* R. K. P., London.

46 Spender, D., 1980, *Man made language,* R. K. P., London.

47 Strathern, M., 1981, "Self interest and the social good: some implications of Hagen gender imagery", in: *Sexual meanings,* ed. S. Ortner and H. Whitehead, Cambridge Univ. Press.

48 Tillich, P. J., 1962, "Memorial lecture" in: C. G. *Jung 1875–1961,* Analytical Psychology Club of New York.

49 Witkin, H. A., 1962, *Psychological differentiation,* Wiley.

50 Yates, F. A., 1972, *The Rosicrucian enlightenment,* R. K. P., London.

# The Age of Plastic*

Kenneth D. Newman (Jerusalem)

The movement and development of Time was once envisaged as Four Ages: the Golden, the Silver, the Bronze and finally the Age of Iron. Each epoch is a material, and symbolically, a nature of the human condition; or, if you will, a collective spirit. Today we live in a new Age, a quality of Time until now imaginally unmanifested, a Fifth Age, the Age of Plastic.[1]

Within the ruling spirit of this newest of Ages are characteristics that identify and distinguish it from all the others. For one, unlike its predecessors, plastic is not found in nature. It is a non-natural product, but, what is more, a non-natural force, for the term plastic, deriving from the Greek *plassein*, 'to form', denotes a formed material as well as a formative principle. Plastic, as both an end-product and a process, stands outside of Mother Nature.

Unlike gold, silver, bronze or iron, plastic is made solely by man. It is a materialization of psychic chemistry. In this post-modern Age, mankind has succeeded in manifesting something made almost exclusively of the chemistry of the soul. The forms, colours and uses this imaginal material and creative force take are dictated only by the imagination of those who mould it.

[1] In 606 B. C., Nebuchadnezzar, King of Babylon, had a dream where he saw, "a great image... mighty and of exceeding brightness" (Daniel 2:31). "The head of this image was of fine gold, its breast and arms of silver, its belly and thighs of bronze, its legs of iron, its feet partly of iron and partly of clay" (v., 32–33).
The prophet Daniel interpreted the lower elements of the colossus as the increasingly inferior kingdoms that shall follow that of Nebuchadnezzar's, which is represented by the head of gold. We might generalize these kingdoms in time as the Five Ages, which terminate in a strange fifth substance identified as "miry clay and iron" (v., 41), and which I am suggesting anticipates plastic.

* Reprinted by permission of the *Cahiers de Psychologie Jungienne*, where it appeared in No. 38/3 (March 1983).

The term plastics in chemistry is very loosely used to denote a wide class of organic material. Plastics are based exclusively on the chemical element carbon, which joins together into complex molecules in the shape of hexagonic rings. The discovery of carbon's uroboric molecular shape in 1865 and the subsequent birth of organic chemistry was made by the German chemist F. A. Kekulé. What catalyzed his theoretical formulation was a dream in which Kekulé imagined he saw a snake seizing its own tail.

Extrapolating Kekulé's serpent dream, Thomas Pynchon, in his book *Gravity's Rainbow*, appropriately returns us to the Garden of Eden, for what eventually transpires through plastic is nothing less than a new myth of creation. Pynchon writes:

> Who sent this new serpent to our ruinous garden… something that Kekulé's Serpent has come too – not to destroy, but to define to us the loss of… we have been given certain molecules, certain combinations and not others… we used what we found in Nature, unquestioning, shamefully perhaps – but [Kekulé's] Serpent whispered, "*they can be changed*, and new molecules assembled from the debris of the given…" Can anyone tell me what else he whispered to us?[2]

Michael Adams, in his fascinating article, "The Benzene Uroboros", speculates that what the Serpent whispered was the word 'plastic'. He convincingly supports this by citing what Pynchon calls "Plasticity's central canon: that chemists are no longer to be at the mercy of Nature. They could decide now what properties they wanted a molecule to have, and then go ahead and build it".[3] Thus what further discriminates plastic is that it has nearly no natural boundries and no limits to what it can and cannot do or be.

Although not directly comparable, there is a certain interesting analogy between plastic and its Aristotelian antecedent, ether. Ether was the fifth 'element' following earth, fire, air and water. Presumably this fifth dimension of archetypal space must be occupied by the imaginal, for both ether and plastic are products of the imagination. What differentiates the *Zeitgeist* of Plastic from the prototypal element ether is that while ether is non-existent on any level other than the imaginal, plastic transmutes into matter. Einstein's formula, $E = mc^2$, has now been partially accomplished in reverse, as the theory would have it; not

2 Thomas Pynchon, *Gravity's Rainbow* (New York: Viking, 1973), cited in M. V. Adams, "The Benzene Uroboros" in *Spring 1981*, p. 156f.

3 Michael Adams, "The Benzene Uroboros", p. 157.

matter transformed into energy, as in radioactivity, but energy (psychic) transformed into matter, as found in plastics.

What further illustrates the non-naturalness of plastic is that it does not comply to the reality of 'from dust to dust'. Not coming, in a sense, from material reality, it does not decay, decompose, rust, rot or return to any primal, elementary form through its 'death', for it does not belong to any natural cycle. The ecologists, otherwise called 'nature lovers', especially despise plastic for being non-bio-degradable. Similarly, clothing made of any of the many synthetic fibers, celluloid bags, deoderants and the like do not 'breathe'. This again alludes to the 'unnatural' character of this material.

In its capacity as a plastic force, the post-modern spirit of plasticity has altered a fundamental axiom of the life-process symbolized in the *opus alchymicum*. As Roland Barthes so astutely put it, "for the first time, artifice aims at something common, not rare".[4] No longer a search for the most valued, the noblest of the natural: the golden. We find now a different quest with different procedures: a whole new alchemy.

Originally alchemy sought the transmutation into gold. The higher sense of value contained in and accorded to this element has something of the same primal value found in the earliest of Ages. The first often associates with the highest and the purest, the genuine and the pristine. In this sense, the medieval alchemy of the soul was fundamentally reductive in its efforts to make gold out of non-gold, comparable to analytical psychology's occupation with transforming material to its purest form: the archetype. The new alchemy seeks a synthetic transformation into that which has never been. It is a process of transformation that fully recognizes the artificiality of its man-made construct: consciousness. For while the alchemy of gold is a non-natural process, its end-product is perceived as natural. The alchemy of plastic, too, is concerned with transforming something into something else and thereby conforms to the traditon of an *opus contra naturam*; however it does not perceive that which it creates as natural.

What further distinguishes these two fundamental imaginal processes is that plasticity does not give any inordinate value to its created product. Like plastic artifacts, plastic consciousness is used with no overwhelming sense of awe. Its greatest value lies precisely in this, for it stops worshipping and hoarding, warring and envying its possession.

[4] Roland Barthes, *Mythologies*, Annette Lavers trans., (London: Granada, 1983), p. 98.

The alchemy of plastic appreciates that consciousness or any myth of meaning does not have any absolute, greed-producing sense of value.

For example, if one understands an event (= the *prima materia*) from an Adlerian perspective, and what otherwise would be a meaningless happening, i. e., lacking meaning, transforms into an instance of a will-to-power, let us say, the artificiality of this construct is seen without feeling one has found the golden answer, for there are other moulds that might equally hold, shape and transform this event into something of value.

Reshaping our plastic metaphor, we identify yet another characteristic that distinguishes the alchemy of gold from that of plastic. While the former involves a romantic quest for a practically unattainable symbol that integrates all the elements of the personality, the alchemy of plastic reveres a post-uroboric, unintegrated state of existence. This is really the commonplace, the usual, the ordinary state of man and the valuing of this without romanticism's disparagement is what polymorphous plasticity is about.

Although C. G. Jung developed an entire psychology of totality and completion, he also felt the inadequacy of this formulation. Not just that it was practically unattainable, but that the concept of totality *per se* is suspect. In a letter,[5] Jung wrote: "I doubt the genuineness of the 'complete man'." In his extremely brief but brilliant exposition on the development of the anima-figure, Jung concluded, "the fourth [and last] stage illustrates something which unexpectedly goes beyond the almost unsurpassable third stage. Presumably only by virtue of the truth that the less sometimes means the more."[6] Jung spent a lifetime expounding on another golden state of totality: the *mysterium coniunctionis*. He supports the validity of this psychological union between the masculine and the feminine principle in many ways in innumerable images. One of the most impressive and convincing of these images is that of the hermaphrodite. Yet Jung goes on to write (in spite of efforts, I have failed to relocate this citation) that he never came across this image in the dreams or unconscious material of any person, himself included, presumably.

It is difficult to imagine today unified totality. For one thing, we know too many things that cannot be experienced because they are *sinnlos*

[5] Gerhard Adler, ed., C. G. *Jung Letters* (Princeton: Bollingen, 1975), Vol II, 21 July 1927, p. xxxii.

[6] Jung, C. G., CW XVI, § 361.

(literally 'without sense', and hence, senseless). There is no way to reconcile perceiving the sun setting, feeling the firm, stationary ground beneath my feet and experiencing being at rest with the knowledge that I am twirling in space while hurtling along at fantastic speed. I can know one thing and feel another and be assured that both are correct, while contradictory. Psychologically, this situation makes for an irreconcilable split where body, soul and spirit exist in a condition of non-unity. Consequently, fantasies of psychological totality achieved through a unity of diversities must be discarded. What remains is a pluralism of realities, each with their own and different perceptions, interpretations and evaluations.

Plastic is slippery, cold, hideous and disgusting – like the skin of a serpent (no wonder it was born in Kekulé's reptilian fantasy) – but this is only the swan song of a dying Age. It is the earth and air, gold and iron in our soul rejecting the new. The sound and sights, the feel and values of this new soul are doubly offensive to the senses and sensibilities of the old. Firstly, because this is always the reception of the new by the old, and specifically, because this new is so different from what came before it, being contrived and unnatural.

Today's music is played on fiberglass and transistors. We have a flourish of plastic arts and plastic food, plastic surgery and surgery of plastics, as well as plastic sex with its condoms, IUD's, diaphragms and vibrators. Our soul winces. Is it really the end? Or is it another cosmic pregnancy we are in the midst of, our souls squeezed in involuntary peristaltic constriction?

This new Age will be so different from the past, so iconoclastic that it will make the Renaissance and Reformation look like a garden party. Revolution-for-the-sake-of-revolution (Marx, terrorism); revolutionary in ideas ('Black is beautiful', synchronicity); revolutionary socially (open marriage, zero-population growth); revolutionary economics (floating currency and, although gold is still the cornerstone of world economy, it is not the same gold of old having no fixed, singular value).

And perhaps with the same emotional reaction that the world of plasticity engenders within many of us today, we find the many different shapes and sizes that psychotherapy has taken. *For modern psychotherapy is one of the many products of plasticity.* As I have written elsewhere,[7] the alchemical image of the *temenos*, otherwise connotated

[7] Kenneth Newman, "The Riddle of the *Vas Bene Clausum*", in *Journal of Analytical Psychology*, 1981.

as the *vas bene clausum*, serves admirably as an image for psychotherapy, as both a vessel and a process. "The bottle", Jung wrote,[8] "is an artificial human product and thus signifies the intellectual purposefulness and artificiality of the procedure… As the *vas Hermeticum* of alchemy… it has to be made of glass." The glass bottle that both holds the process and is the process is a product of plasticity. In a word, psychotherapy is a plastic art form.

It is evident that not all "hermetic bottles" are the same nor intended to house the same processes. Nevertheless, in spite of these differences, the plastic nature of psychotherapy is witnessed in that *all forms of psychotherapy are involved in movement.* Alterability is not merely a characteristic of plasticity, it is its very definition. The scientific encyclopedia identifies two types of plastics: those bodies which are ordinarily rigid, but which, when subjected to increased temperature or pressure, become pliable, e. g., glass, and those other bodies which, in the process of working, soften sufficiently to be made to fill moulds, e. g., rubber.

Some psychotherapies identify this plasticity as expansion, others as the attainment of greater depth, still others as behavioural modification or symptom alleviation. Whether the means to attain these therapeutic goals be by an additive or subtractive process,[9] all entail movement. Movement is the bottom line in all forms of psychotherapy.

If each therapy has a different direction of movement, nothing could be said about a general typology of psychotherapy using movement as a parameter. However, these movements are neither random nor as diverse as one might imagine, considering the myriad forms psychotherapy takes today. In point of fact, *the entire field of applied psychology can be divided into four movements: up, down, to the right, and to the left.* Within this scheme, the essential difference between various psychotherapeutic schools can be located, while at the same time holding them together.

To the 'uppers' belong the encounter groups, touch therapies, marathon sessions, enlightenment workshops, primal scream, psychodrama, gestalt, some non-directive therapies, as well as the increasing number of existential schools, which include, among others, Rolfing and Dasein. By different and various techniques, each involves itself in exploring and expanding the personality. For this group of psychother-

[8] Jung, C. G., CW XIII, § 245.

[9] Newman, "Counter-Transference and Consciousness" in *Spring 1980*, pp. 125f.

apies is concerned with raising new material, new experience and/or different levels of awareness.

Among the 'downers' we find all the major schools of depth psychology, which includes, most notably, the Freudians and the Jungians. This approach seeks to ground the individual in some conceptual structure by providing a cognitive *temenos* for what is envisaged as the raging chaos, the *prima materia*. Placed within the *vas bene clausum*, or 'well-sealed vessel', the therapeutic process endeavours to contain and hold the psyche of the analysand so as to enable the transmutation from disorder to order to procede. It is not surprising that downers regard consciousness highly and are fearful of psychosis, for the structuring or ordering of "the confused assortment of crude disordered matter"[10] is the vector of this psychotherapeutic movement.

One might object that analytical psychology, with its concern for the transpersonal and the non-ego, dreams and flying saucers, parapsychology and religion, is anything but a 'downer'. Yet, in the final analysis, the criterion in determining this is not the content, but the attitude towards that content, which for analytical psychology is one of giving a cognitive shape through meaning to inner and outer primal material.

Thus, however different their means and intent, both uppers and downers, as artificial plastic agents, participate in a *mytheme* of movement. The validity of this psychotherapeutic axiom is placed in relief when we consider its exception, namely, the absence of movement in therapy. Toni Frey makes note of the sometimes incurable qualities in both patient and analyst. And what diagnoses incurability is immovability.[11] Raphael López-Pedraza makes this even more specific when he writes: "the idea of human nature having two parts – a part that does not change and a part that moves – is valuable for psychotherapy. It is of obvious practical value in psychotherapy to have an awareness of these two elements, so that we can detect what in human nature does not change, so as to localize our psychotherapeutic aims in that part which moves."[12] James Hillman, in his article, "On the Necessity of Abnormal Psychology",[13] is primarily challenging an image of perfection that leaves no place for imperfection as presented by psychopathology. However, if I may take this somewhat out of context and use

10 Jung, CW XII, §185, n. 59.

11 Toni Frey, "The Treatment of Chronic Psychosis" in *Journal of Analytical Psychology*, 1978.

12 Raphael López-Pedraza, *Hermes and His Children* (Zürich: Spring, 1977), p. 89.

13 James Hillman, "On the Necessity of Abnormal Psychology" in *Eranos 1974* (Leiden: Brill, 1977).

it to our present purposes, we might be able to conclude the following: if pathology, or certain instances of it, at least, is that which is not given to movement, then this suggests that there is place for a pathology of one's personality that is neither amenable nor intended for transformation – even as the downers understand it, i. e., beyond interpretation and hence, meaning. A simpler argument would be to address ourselves to healthiness and normalcy, which no one assumes should move, be transformed or understood.

I would like to carry on with this discussion of movement and its antinomy, because it is crucial to psychotherapy; and yet it has received relatively little recognition. Astrology makes a very telling comment on the matter of movement and non-movement, for astrology gives place – inherent, irreducible, unavoidable place – to both. The eighth house of the natal horoscope relates to the unconscious. It is associated with sex and death, being the house of Scorpio, but it is ultimately the house where deep soul transformations can, need, and ought to take place. So, if it is the place of death, it is so only in so far as the old, the rigid, the time-worn dies to give place to the new. The twelfth house of the Zodiac is another story. This 'house' is usually cited as the prison, hospital, insane asylum, connected with diseases of fate and fatal diseases, isolation, suffering and deep introversion. Some commentators believe the house of Pisces stores inner, primal knowledge known, but unlearned, from a previous life. Others say it refers to that in this life which will be lived in the next, or similarly, the aspects of one's personality to be redeemed in the next Karma, for, in this life, they are irreconcilable, irresolvable and damned. Precisely which formulations of this and the eighth house are 'correct' is not the issue. What is is the fantasy captured, developed and reflected back to us in astrology. A fantasy that finds and gives place to those types of psychic contents designed for movement and transformation and those which reside in a place of immovability. Both places are honored, each has its respective deity-world-reality.

Now movement need not necessarily be equated with development, for movement can be change as well as progress. And in the three types of movement – progression, development and change – the four directions of therapeutic movement are identified. Jung made something of a similar psychic distinction between progression and development. Progression is a life-movement or natural life-flow; consciousness and differentiation do not enter here. Development, on the other hand, is an evolution of personality brought about by material realized and related to by the ego consciously.[14] While progression is based upon the archetypal process to experience life, development is grounded in a different archetypal process, namely, the instinct for meaning. *Progression* and *development* therefore best describe the therapeutic movement of uppers and downers, respectively, while I have reserved the term *change* for 'horizontalists'.

Among the 'righters' and 'lefters' which form the other two directions of psychotherapy, we find all the colours and shapes making up behaviour modification. These therapies involve themselves in changing situations and circumstances in a horizontal fashion, as, for example, changing the compulsive smoker to the compulsive non-smoker. Systematic desensitization therapy, biofeedback, aversion conditioning therapy and cognitive therapy are all examples of this branch of psychotherapy.

What differentiates horizontalism from verticalism (taking the uppers and downers together now) is that the horizontalists are not – nor do they feel it necessary – involved in enlarging the personality. In contradistinction, both the uppers and the downers are concerned with psychological growth, for each sees as its goal some new or renewed contact with the unconscious. While the uppers stress opening up experiential capacities through a release of the unconscious, the downers place the emphasis on an ever-increasing understanding of the conscious and unconscious aspects of the personality, thereby creating a new order of being.

We see this tendency among the downers to ground phenomena in meaning exemplified in one of Jung's most profound formulations, that of synchronicity. Of the three fundamental criteria identifying synchronicity – acausality, simultaneity and meaning – it is really only the latter that must be present for an event to be synchronistic. In the last analysis, "the value of synchronistic occurrences lies in the deep sense of meaning they give to people."[15] Since every single moment is made

[14] Jung, CW VIII, § 70. For some practical psychological examples of the employment of this distinction, see my book, *The Tarot: A Myth of Male Initiation* (New York: Quadrant, 1983), ch. 7.

[15] Mary Ann Mattoon, *Jungian Psychology in Perspective* (New York: Free Press, 1981), p. 149, modified. I have omitted one word in this citation, for Mattoon actually writes: "the value of synchronistic occurrences lies in the deep sense of meaning they *can* give to people" (underlining mine). But if a person does not have that sense of meaning we cannot legitimately speak of synchronicity. Anything *can* be synchronistic and probably everything is, but it is only those events recognized as 'meaningful coincidences' that become identified as synchronistic. For further critical discussion, see my article, "An Overview of Jungian Psychology" in *Psychological Perspectives*, 1983, pp. 104–111.

up of endless coincidences, if we could but see meaning in them, they would be truly synchronistic experiences. For this to happen, one must find what the alchemists called 'the stone'. With it, the world would be just exactly what it is: a continual miracle of meaningful experience.

The phrase, 'meaningful coincidence', captures the basic tenet running throughout analytical psychology and, by extension, all depth psychologies. The quest for soul is the quest for meaning to life, which, for the downers, constitutes life's meaning. The alchemy of this branch of psychology is the search for that psychic faculty which will give life and its endless phenomena an absolute, subjective meaningfulness. Thus the alchemical quest culminated with realizing the Philosophers' stone, one of whose formulations was the *anima rationalis.*[16]

It is not due to a lack of differentiated thinking that the alchemists claimed the process begins with the *prima materia* and ends with it. Or, reversing this, that "the stone is without beginning and has its *primum Ens* from all eternity."[17] Or, as Jung elsewhere stated it, that "the *lapis* is... the beginning and the goal".[18] In other words, redemption is the seeing of meaning in all matter of things and this is no less present at the beginning of the *opus* than at the end. The problem is the difficulty in seeing it, which is why it is named, 'the stone of invisibility (*lapis invisibilitatis*)'.[19] Consequently, the stone is the *prima materia,*[20] and the *prima materia* is the stone,[21] though they are not identical.

It is also not due to any lack of differentiated feeling that the alchemists claimed the stone is everywhere and everything. "What we are seeking", said one alchemist, "is sold publicly for a very small price, and if it were recognized, the merchants would not sell it for so little".[22] Another alchemist wrote: "the philosophers tell the inquirer that... everyman has [the *lapis*], it is every place, in you, in me, in everything, in time and space."[23]

The transformation into gold, which defined the *opus,* was the development in attitude that could see the value in the vulgar (*vili figura*)

16 Jung, CW XII, § 368 and § 423, n. 52.

17 ibid., § 431.

18 ibid., § 427, n. 4.

19 ibid., § 243.

20 ibid., § 337.

21 ibid., § 433.

22 ibid., § 159, n. 33.

23 ibid., § 433.

and the ever-present. We can, therefore, appreciate the reasoning behind the valuing Jung took towards psychopathology, which is something depreciated by psychology collectively and the person individually.[24] Jung wrote: "We should even learn to be thankful for [the neurosis], otherwise we pass it by and miss the opportunity... We should not try to 'get rid' of a neurosis, but rather to experience what it means, what it has to teach, what its purpose is... A neurosis is truly removed only when it has removed the false attitude of the ego."[25] It is this transformation in attitude that cures the "neurosis of psychology", as Wolfgang Geigerich terms it,[26] and proves the main contribution of the downers.

What differentiates the natural stone from the plastic one is that, in the original vision of alchemy, what was valued was always the same meaning. So by psychosexologizing phenomena, as the Freudians do, or archetypalizing it, as do the Jungians, both work to see the essence beyond corporal or common sense.[27] And this essence is monistic. Whatever form the vision of meaning, i. e., myth of consciousness, takes, whether this be an eternal archetype or omnipresent sex, the soul of the downers is in evidence. This attitude culminates in the narrowing of focus onto 'the gold', to have *one* system of values, to value only one type of interpretation, emotion of experience. "Where as all gold looks alike", a plastic mentality favours discrimination, where "each complex has its own smell",[28] and maybe more than one.

Descartes envisaged the human body as a fluid system. The brain, Descartes contended, drives a fluid through the body, which drives the muscles as it might turbines. This is a mechanical image of man. Since man's discovery of electricity, the brain is imagined to be a computer with a major telephone line (the spinal cord) carrying numerous electrical wires to all parts of the body. This is an electrical image of man. After Copernicus imagined a heliocentric, circulating universe and broke thereby with a 1500 year tradition, Harvey found the circulation of the bloodstream, employing a fire-extinguisher as his model.

[24] Jung, CW XVI, § 11.

[25] Jung, CW X, § 361.

[26] Cf. Wolfgang Giegerich, "On the Neurosis of Psychology or the Third of the Two" in *Spring 1977*.

[27] Cf. Newman, "The Shadow of the Shadow", lecture delivered at the 8th Intl. Congress of Analytical Psychology, San Francisco, 1980, unpublished.

[28] Patricia Berry, "On Reduction" in *Spring 1973*, p. 82.

What these few examples are intending to illustrate is how plasticity operates. In each instance, a mental construct is materialized – turbine, computer, fire-extinguisher – and then employed as a metaphor. While nature once provided the inspiration to man's imagination and was the source of his understanding, artificial constructs now fulfill this service. So, in a circular process, a technological artifact manufactured by man transforms into a metaphor by which he comprehends his world and himself. It follows that, with different artifacts, our understanding would be different, and in this artificial non-absolutism is the essence of plasticity. Truth is not something given, but an art-form imagined by a psyche that is not a piece of nature like the flowers and the animals, but is human and capable of creating in its own image that which is not natural.[29]

It follows that, although different, the alchemy of gold and plastic each belong to the spirit of the downers.[30] The transformation into plastic, which embodies the new alchemy of the soul, is the transformation in attitude that can see polyvalent meaning in a pluralistic reality. Synchronizing with the Age of Aquarius ruled by the planet Uranus, which, in the Zodiac follows Capricornian Saturn, pluralism and equality supercede a traditional, monolithic hierarchy of meaning and meaningfulness. "So we can understand why the figure of the protecting circle [i. e., the *temenos,* the mandala, etc.] was seized upon. It is intended to prevent the 'outflowing' and to protect the unity of consciousness from being burst asunder by the unconscious."[31] In this monistic spirit, the alchemy of gold turns everything into the same thing. Plasticity, on the other hand, takes us away from a unitarian view

[29] Even when we approach the issue of the non-naturalness of the psyche from the opposite direction, we arrive at a similar conclusion. Take, for instance, instincts: these very deep emotional patternings are often imagined or imagified as animals. Yet instincts do not equate to animals; they only take this imaginal form.
Commenting on Apuleius' book, M.-L. von Franz said, "if a human being behaves like an animal, he is not in harmony with his instincts. An animal which behaves like an animal is in harmony with itself. If a tiger behaves like a tiger, it is, so to speak, individuated… If we sink to an animal's pattern we deviate from our own… The tragedy of Lucius-Apuleius is that, within his donkey's skin he still feels like a human being." *(A Psychological Interpretation of the Golden Ass of Apuleius,* M.-L. von Franz (Zürich: Spring, 1970), IV, 7f.) That the psyche is something outside of the natural is implicit when Jung wrote: "Although biological instinctive processes contribute to the formation of personality, individuality is nevertheless essentially different from collective instincts; indeed it stands in the most direct opposition to them." (CW VI, § 88).

[30] As a derivative of oil, plastic originates in what has come to be called 'black gold'.

[31] Jung, CW XIII, § 47.

of the natural to the infinite possibilities of the artifice. Concurrent is also the lack of pretension of plastic as we get away from the obsession with the noble. We might speculate that it is even in reaction to this King Midasian nightmare that the psyche introduced plastic.

Breaking the monotonous tyranny of the *unus mundus,* where only that which is natural and goldenized is ultimately valued, as in the tradition of the self, plasticity values everything... for what it is. This does not suggest nihilism nor any other Saturnalian-type psychosis, because the Age of Plastic is not a state of mind or psychological condition where nothing has meaning, but one where everything has meaning. This, nevertheless, does not negate meaning, because nothing has the same meaning. The same thing even means a multitude of things, as well as having a multifactorial aetiology. In short, a postmonotheistic a-naturalism emerges.

If I may employ a vulgar amplification, this new collective soul is illustrated in the increasing appearance in movies and television of actors and actresses who are common looking, ordinary-behaving and unusual in their usualness. The language found in books, magazines and newspapers, not to forget the mass celluloid media, is likewise more and more the common, everyday vernacular. Comparably, when Lovejoy set forth his theory of history as a development of 'units of ideas', he examined the minor philosophers and poets, who, he contended, gave more vibrant representation of these units than the great thinkers.

It was an alchemical dictum that "[the stone] is found in every place and at any time and in every circumstance, when the search lies heavy on the searcher".[32] Commenting on what the condition – "when the search lies heavy on the searcher" – refers to Jung wrote, "this remark can only be understood as meaning that a certain psychological condition is indispensible for the discovery of the miraculous stone".[33] We might only add that this "certain psychological condition" *is* the stone... or plastic, depending upon the specific psychological condition that prevails. Perhaps it is a meaningful linguistic coincidence that when one gets 'stoned' or 'is stoned', presumably a modern equivalent of 'having the stone', the otherwise ordinary is mira-

[32] Jung, CW XII, § 360, n. 37.

[33] Ibid.

culously experienced for what it always is: special and kalidoscopically meaningful.[34]

It would take us too far afield to enter into a full discussion of the psycho-mechanics of plastic, but I would like to give its main points. In his essay on the dogma of the trinity, Jung writes that it is trinitarian thinking which enables the human mind to "think in opposition to nature, thus demonstrating its godlike freedom".[35] The infinite possibilities of plastic have not a little to do with triadic thought processes. Ordinarily, however, trinitarian thinking is marked by being non-realistic and non-realizable. Hence, von Franz writes, "the difficult step from three to four would also be the progression from the infinitely conceivable to finite reality".[36] "This peculiar dissociation [of a triadic state from a quaternal mentality] is, it seems, a product of civilization, and it denotes a freeing of consciousness from any excessive attachment to the 'spirit of gravity'. If that... can be left behind and even forgotten, then consciousness has won for itself a new and not entirely illusory freedom. It can leap over abysses on winged feet; it can free itself from bondage to sense-impressions, emotions, fascinating thoughts and presentiments by soaring into abstraction."[37]

Plastic, however, is very unique indeed, for plastic is realized fantasy and thereby it is insufficient to identify it solely as trinitarian, for it partakes of all the criterion of the quaternius. Yet, it is somehow different.

Classically the quaternal element in masculine psychology is contrasexual, meaning it images itself in men as the feminine: "Four signifies the feminine, motherly, physical; three the masculine, fatherly, spiritual. Thus the uncertainty as to three or four amounts to a wavering between the spiritual and the physical."[38] (In women, the reverse is the

[34] An appreciation of the inherent potential remarkability of what is otherwise perceived as common and usual is found in the following statement by Pascual Jordan (*Verdrängung und Komplementarität*, Hamburg, 1947; cited in M.-L. von Franz, *Number and Time*, Rider, London, 1974): "We become aware that in everyday waking life, situations are present which are fundamentally just as amazing as the more infrequent unusual manifestations of telepathy." By 'telepathy', I assume Jordan is including all of so-called parapsychology, which, with less resistance and repression, would be less paraphenomenological than most people like to believe.

[35] Jung, CW XI.

[36] Von Franz, *Number and Time*, p. 122.

[37] Jung, CW XI, § 245.

[38] Jung, CW XII, § 31.

case.) What makes the psychology of plastic so different is that the archetypal image residing in this outwardly projected psychic realization is a femininity that is oddly masculine. It is finite and materially existing while, at the same time, abstract and non-natural, dynamic and infinitely variable.

During a great feast, King Belshazzar of Babylon "drank wine, and praised the gods of gold and silver, bronze, iron, wood and stone".[39] When called upon to interpret the mysterious handwriting on Belshazzar's wall, Daniel upbraided the king for polytheism – "you have praised the gods of silver and gold, of bronze, iron, wood, and stone".[40] As a Hebrew monotheist, the claim of the prophet Daniel is that these gods that reside in matter are inferior to his god, because they "do not see or hear or know".[41] Like God's words in the first of his Ten Commandments: "You shall have no other gods before me",[42] God himself recognizes the existence of other, however supposedly inferior, gods. Without the acceptance of a materializable polytheism, the words of the Second Commandment that, "you shall not make *for yourself* a graven image... for I the Lord your God am a jealous God",[43] make no sense.

And what is more to our point, in this chapter of the Book of Daniel, you will note that there is no god of 'miry clay'. As has been suggested above,[44] the element clay, as it appears in the Book of Daniel, might well be anticipating at that time the still imaginally unmanifested material plastic. It should, therefore, follow that clay, and, by extension, plastic, also has its god. In a word, but for reasons that would take us still further afield, I believe that plastic is a product of the collective unconscious mind that can be imagined in the divine figure of Athena.

We are here at this congress in Jerusalem, a city in a state of tense, but generally peaceful, dissociated union, looking at a stew in our own therapeutic vessel. With the typology of psychotherapy outlined

[39] Daniel 5:4.

[40] V., 23.

[41] Viz.

[42] Exodus 20:3.

[43] V., 45, underlining mine.

[44] Supra., note 1.

above, the affinity between a clinical and symbolic approach becomes readily evident, for both quite simply belong among the downers. What each provides – in its own idiom – is an interpretation of the world. Although that interpretation differs in its content and style, it does not differ in its essence or its intent, for both are equally products of a plastic imagination in service of the spirit of the downers.

Although a symbolic approach has a somewhat lighter feel to it than a clinical approach, the specific density of each plastic does not intrinsically change its substance. Although a symbolic approach has a more open-ended form to it, the shape also does not fundamentally alter matters. While the clinical approach takes on darker hues, like browns and grays, and the symbolic imagines itself in whites and pastels, the colour again does not change the *mytheme* of meaning that each participates in. In brief, the clinical and symbolic approaches are brothers belonging to an interpretative approach to psychotherapy and this places them in the fraternity of downers.

## Conclusion

This paper began with an introduction on plasticity and led into a general dissertation differentiating schools of psychotherapy according to movement. Attempting to illustrate the plasticity of soul, it sought to define and appreciate the various types and directions therapy takes. It ended, however, doing precisely the opposite. When it came to examining the clinical and symbolic approach, the archetypal attitude of the *unus mundus* took over, devouring plurality in unity, creating a sense of oneness that is as frightening and repulsive to plasticity as plastic is to its predecessors.

# Attacks on Analysis* +

Barry D. Proner (London)

A feature of child analytic therapy is that actions which replace thought, or reflection, can take a significant, even central position. What may at first glance seem an obnoxious hindrance to analysis is in fact worthy of our careful consideration. The sources and uses of these actions are as necessary to analyse as any words or pictures presented to the therapist. There are many reasons, of course, for their existence and a number of them initially come to mind.

First, there is the problem of symbolising, which children are learning about but have not yet acquired to the degree adults may have. Despite their use of drawing and play materials in treatment, children in analysis do not naturally behave as if they experience the frame as a symbolic world. In other words, the distinction between inner and outer realities is often a fine one, as it is of course with many adults, particularly those in regressed states. In their play children are negotiating this divide between internal and external reality all the time. Jung, in the Foreword to his important paper, "Psychic conflicts in a child" (Jung 9), emphasised that childhood sexuality is the predecessor of concept formation, and that conflicts around sexuality can prevent the development of what later came to be called symbol formation (Klein 12).

Secondly, there is the fact that ideas and feelings which relate to the analyst, however obscurely, the components that seem to be transfered from living figures in the inner world, seem to me to have a peculiar aspect in childhood. In contrast to what is usual in adult analysis, the real, living parents are very much at the centre of everyday life. What we call 'the transference', therefore, is very close to its source in the imagery built from the meeting of inner archetypal elements and the

* Reprinted by permission of *The Journal of Analytical Psychology*, where it appeared in Vol 28, No 3 (July 1983).

+ I wish to express my appreciation of the invaluable assistance given me by Dr. Michael Fordham in understanding Benjamin.

external parents. States of love and hate, persecution of placation, sexual states, states of defiance or of extreme dependency, concern or indifference, dreaminess, sadistic or compliant behaviour, the grateful, loving, jealous, envious, generous or excited states which can and do come about in the consulting room – these elements may have little or no distance from the physical drama which at least to some extent generates them. Jung seemed to have placed considerable stress on these patterns being a direct result of the parental conflicts, as well as suggesting the importance of archetypal elements. Now we know much about the individuality of the child right from the very beginning of extrauterine life which appears already in intrauterine life according to recent research findings (Liley 14). But in any event, the interactions with which analytic work is concerned are concrete physical experiences and symbolic equations of everyday life in the child's inner world. As Freud said, "The internal resistances, against which we have to fight in the case of adults, are in the case of children for the most part replaced by external difficulties" (Freud 7). Although this paper is concerned with what are, in fact, internal resistances, I hope to show that they are not so much replaced by, as made manifest in the form of behaviour.

The factors which I have thus far suggested contribute to expression through *action* rather than *reflection* in child analysis, can, nonetheless, be accompanied by mental components, latent or formed, whether conscious or unconscious. In contrast, a third possible basis of these activities which one sees in psychotherapy ensures that no such mental operations take place. Although ontogenetically realistic in an attempt to preserve at all costs the self (see Lambert 13, pp. 52–79; Fordham 5), the outcome of this form of functioning is generally severely pathological. I am referring now to a mode of dealing with the analyst and his setting wherein the actions or activities are attacks on all thinking or imagining.

When I say this is for the preservation of the self, it is because it seems that what might be thought or imagined by the patient and/or the analyst, is (a) so horrible or alien and (b) there is an insufficient sense of an internal mother who makes it safe to bear overwhelming effect, that existence itself is at risk. To quote Bion in another context, "Fear, hate and envy are so feared that steps are taken to destroy awareness of all feelings, although that is indistinguishable from taking life itself" (Bion 1). It is certainly seen in babies, as we have observed, and as the following examples will show. The description is of a baby who, when faced with an unmanageable degree of affect would 'switch off'. At 3½ weeks of age, the following was recorded. The baby was flooded with stimuli and remained in a 'mindless' state, seemingly unable to represent his needs mentally. I am grateful to Miss Elizabeth Urban for the following extracts:

> The mother and I were standing over the carry-cot and Lily (the older sister) was peering in as she patted Ted (the baby), and then pulled him towards her by the cap that was tied around him, treating him like an inanimate doll. The mother jumped a bit to see this and told Lily she had to be gentle with Ted. Ted during this slept, except he scowled a bit at being pulled by Lily. We went into the kitchen, where the mother put Ted in the bouncer next to my chair. He continued to sleep as he was placed in the bouncer and slumped down in his seat. The mother asked me if I wanted some soup, which I declined, and she poured herself some and sat down, and spread some cheese on some toast. As Lily sat down she reached for the mother's toast and was allowed to take it. The mother spread some more for herself.
>
> Ted lay in the bouncer and grew increasingly restless. He frequently turned his head from left to right, and raised his hands and arms. He raised his arms outward in front of his face, and he screwed his face up and turned it from side to side (still eyes closed and sleeping). He held his arms tensely, and then would relax them, still holding them out in front of himself. Then he would drop his arm, and his hands clenched the strap of the chair that went across the front of him to hold him in. He began to make vocalisations: little eh, eh, ehs, and opened his eyes. When the vocalisations intensified the mother went over and picked him up, and unclenched his left hand from the strap and commented on the grip. She sat him on her lap; his head was over her right elbow. She lifted her pullover and briefly massaged her right nipple, then turned Ted's head with her left hand towards the breast until he began to suck. He sucked heartily two or three times and then turned away and fell asleep. He then turned his head towards the breast, and the mother helped to direct him and again he sucked followed quickly by his going to sleep, while the mother was trying to finish her lunch. She seemed to feel that Ted had finished that 'course' and prepared to take Lily and Ted downstairs to change Ted and read to Lily and finish Ted's feed before the two children settled for the afternoon.

At eight-and-a-half months the following was observed:

> While Lily and her mother were talking and the mother was anticipating rather than doing anything about getting Ted's breakfast, Ted sat quietly looking down at the table top sucking his two middle fingers. He seemed to be deprived and left out. At one point he talked through the fingers that he was sucking in his mouth. I noticed there was a *little shuddering movement* around his mouth.

This was a baby who suffered intense stimuli and affects, often with very little recognition of them conveyed to him by his mother. In the first extract, the baby was impinged upon by his older sister and he had various direct physical responses to it; his mother responded by directing him to the breast. In the second description, a feeling of hunger was not recognised or met and was probably not mentally represented at that point. The shudder was perhaps in its place. The recognition of feelings and any attendant efforts to give back the intense experience in a digested form, such as a sound, a gesture, or giving it a name, seems to be of considerable importance for the conversion of purely non-mental states into some form of 'thinking' or imagery. We call this a form of maternal 'holding' or 'containment'. The idea of a container comes from Jung (10) with which certain ideas of Winnicott (17), Bion (2), and Klein's concept of 'spaces' can be fruitfully compared.

It seemed Ted did not have the experience of a sequence of need, anticipation of fulfilment, holding, satisfaction, and a tapering-off transition. His experience was fragmented, he would 'cut off' and only feel things when they were actually happening. Often he did not seem to develop mental imagery of his needs. We have an example with Ted of a point where this maternal containment does, however, occur; in this case in regard to intense pleasurable affect. At 10½ months:

> The mother arrived back from her errand and came into the kitchen, whereupon Ted livened up considerably. He kicked, smiled broadly, squealed, laughed and babbled. She acknowledged Ted and smiled at him, and on more than one occasion he waved his hands excitedly in the air – reminiscent of a motor-cyclist revving up – and kicked his legs and squealed. He babbled and squealed and at one point made whispering baby talk. He also "blew a raspberry", sucked on his tongue and otherwise carried on a quite cheerful conversation while playing with his hands and the cup. The mother sat next to him and put her arm around him, and he smiled up at her lovingly in his love-struck, starry-eyed look.

It has been suggested, as I will show later, that one critical reason for the long period of dependency of the human infant is that during this time the mother must do the thinking (Meltzer 15). This therefore provides the baby with much more to incorporate than just milk, in the form of a mother who, for instance, converts a purely physical phenomenon into something which can be thought about, and thought can be taken in by the baby and form the basis of an inner world. Without such a basis, we have one of the roots of the well-known adult complaint of 'emptiness'. Incidentally, this idea is not inconsistent with the idea that "thought springs from experience of a non-existent object, or in other terms, of the *place* where the object is expected to be but is not" (Bion 3). Jung said, "I lay stress on the significance of thinking and the importance of concept-building for the solution of psychic conflicts" (Jung 9). Especially in the case of overwhelmingly intense affects, the alternative to mental representation is 'mindlessness'. So in analysis, no less than in mother-baby relations, a 'processing' is essential. We do it through 'giving it a name' with our interpretations, at times in concert with physical management, so that things do not get overwhelming, and with our providing a 'containing' setting or framework, also both in physical and mental terms (i. e. our 'frame of mind' – our analytic attitude) (Fordham 6).

It is this form of non-thinking in analysis and the approach to it with which my paper is chiefly concerned. In child analysis, actions or activities of the sort that are specifically there to make nonsense of your work can be your daily fare. Moreover, our own individual responses to these activities, wherein we ourselves can equally unwittingly adopt the same sort of mindless or destructive postures as our patients, can be a hazard. Or, they can provide positively invaluable information in the understanding of the process that is taking place. These activities need not be confined to the consulting room; the patient may engage in them elsewhere and the behaviour can still pertain to the analysis.

This process may be difficult to tolerate both because of the actual physical and mental stress involved and because the experience apparently runs counter to that of the ideal analyst in our minds. His efforts are unflaggingly directed towards the breaking down of complex structures into their simple components and he thereby arrives at something approaching psychological 'truth'; we call this the 'analytic attitude'. These actions threaten to prevent our doing this work. But it is the very understanding of them which is utterly relevant to the problems for which the patient has come. We can only suppose that, as the patient continues to come, he does wish to understand, and that the actions are a communication to be understood. Analysis, therefore, requires the exposition and understanding of these operations, particularly with reference to the mother-baby or the analyst-patient as a good working couple. If we are successful, we can facilitate not only the analysis of other mental operations, but also the capacity to *think* under ordinary circumstances, including being able to think the unthinkable.

Benjamin's analytical treatment took place in a hospital department of child and family psychiatry. He came five days a week for just over three years. From the beginning, there was an unceasing but ever-changing sequence of actions which were to come into the analysis (and elsewhere). His first session gave me an indication of what I was to expect. He was particularly regressed, and in the material his body and others' were the centre of his interest, as for a tiny baby.

> When I met him he looked more like a six-year-old that an eight-year-old. He was small but sturdily built, with dishevelled dark hair and large, sad, blue eyes. He had an outgoing, mischievous way of relating. He lost no time in actively exploring the environment in a rushed, excited way, checking windows, door, an upper gallery with spiral staircase which was in the room and, finally, the box of toys I had provided. He was particularly interested in the light switches and operated them over and over in rapid succession. He removed the glass switch plate,nearly breaking it. He wanted to open the windows, which led out on to a mansard roof, four storeys above the ground. He said he wanted to go out on the roof to look at the people below and begged me to unlock them. He placed a chair on the couch and stood on it, to try to reach the windows. I commented that he wanted to look and was being looked at here. He could not reach the windows and went up to the iron balcony and leaned over. He slid down the bannister. He again went upstairs and kicked on the floor. He pulled the window blinds up and down. I remarked that he was exploring to see whether it was safe here and if I was safe to be with. It was frightening to be in a new place with someone new and to leave Dr. A. behind (who had referred him, having seen him several times in assessment). He told me he had not finished his Lego model he was making with her and that she had nice games. My Lego was small and he wanted Dr. A. back. He asked if he was going to go to her again. He then completely unravelled a ball of string I had provided him with – about thirty metres – and tied it to the iron balcony, getting it all tangled up. I said perhaps he wanted to tie me up to Dr. A. He said he wanted to tie the string to me to bring me to the other clinic or to use it to bring Dr. A. here. He explored the room again and climbed up to some high windows again, this time reaching them. I had to stop him opening them and he pouted, with tears welling up in his eyes. I said I thought he was really angry that I would not let him do all the things he wants and frightened that sometimes he might need me to do things for him and could not make me be what he wants. He said, "Don't talk about sad things. I don't like sad things." He asked if his father was right next door, how much time we had together, and whether he could have adventures down at the bottom of the house where the lift is (in which he came up when he arrived) and where he said all the games are. He started to go out of the door. I followed him but as he went towards the lift I guided

> him back to the room, saying he wanted to get away from sad things, of not being in charge of me and his fury over that. He wanted to go into the bottom, of mummy/the house and have exciting feelings and get away from where he is stopped. He sat down on the sofa and pouted again and began to cry, saying he did not like it here. Dr. A. had many toys and better Lego and his model there. He said, "Nothing is good here and I'm not coming back again". He banged on the wall with his fist several times, then kicked the wall lightly two or three times. He got his string and tied it all around me and between the stair railings and the chairs. He used Sellotape to stick down the string. I said perhaps he was tying me up to make me not dangerous. He checked on his father and said he needed to go to the toilet. I said our time was up and perhaps he wanted to get rid of something worrying that had got into him, as well as comfort from his bottom. I said I would show him the lavatory on the way out.

I realised after this session that both Benjamin and I were extremely anxious. His anxiety was expressed in excited activity and attempts to explore, feel in power and omnipotently control my room and me. Mine was expressed in trying to stop him, both with my actions and my interpretations. He thought me to be a prohibiting, controlling object who became something bad which threatened to take him over and he had to tie me down, get away from me forever, or evacuate me. In fact, his analysis became very much a question of how I could deal with his manic, omnipotent states while both analysing the need for them and, without becoming bad, controlling their more intolerable manifestations enough to make analysis possible. I felt that ideally the key lay in my behaving like a strong, containing father who keeps things safe without being frightening or retaliatory, at the very same time as being the caring, tolerant and durable mother who can make sense for the baby of the senseless states. In short, I hoped, like a good parental couple working together, with my hands which stopped him hurting or getting hurt, at the same time as my words found meaning in his intense states.

This first session contained much action and little reflection. Very slowly, however, B. and I seemed to be having a dialogue which entailed rather more mental representation. Two months after the first session, following the Easter holiday break, we had the following series of sessions which I think show some progression from a dominance of the severely non-mental to the beginnings of mental processes where conflict is concerned, or from mindlessness to play. Incidentally, we had changed venue early in his treatments; he now came to my consulting room at the hospital which was on the first floor. (Please note that we use his word for the body parts and functions.)

B. came into the room and went to the basin with the cup from his box, getting some water. He went to the window, opening it and began spitting out and dropping water out. He came towards me, hitting me and rubbing against me. He climbed up on to the mantelpiece, jumped down and had 'fights' inside the cupboard (where the basin is).
Dr. P.: "You're not sure you're the big one doing the beating or the little one getting beaten up. Here with you and me you may feel we are battling over who is in charge and that our words are like weapons."
B. stared at the lights and then switched them on and off.
Dr. P.: "The lights are your mummy's eyes which you looked at when you were feeding at her milk bottles and you feel safer when you can turn them on and off and be in charge of them yourself" (I said, "The lights are your mummy's eyes" rather than "are like", because I thought he was in a state of symbolic equation rather than metaphoric imagining. "Milk bottles" is B.'s word for his mother's breasts.)
B. (made some comment about having a big cock and Dr. P. has only a small one). Then he said: "I have to do a pooh."
Dr. P.: "You do every time you come."
B. came back saying he had a lot of farts.
Dr. P.: "And you want a big pooh in your bottom like a big cock that tells you you have power, and to make me the little baby who has to wait for you, and also to get rid of all my words down the loo."
B. rubbed against me making excited sounds.
Dr. P.: "You want to make us mummy and daddy when they make love which gives us together the good feelings they must have, when you feel like only a little baby with a little cock."
B. could not settle, going out of the room several times. He came in, standing around me and went to play with water. He tried to take my shoe off.
Dr. P.: "You want to take my trousers off." (He had said this in a previous session.)
B.: "Yes, so I can see your cock. I'll take mine off and show you mine." He unzipped his trousers, displaying his genitals, saying he was going to pee on me.
Dr. P.: "You want me to know you have got a good, big penis and for me to be frightened so you can make me do what you want and need, as if I'm mummy's milk bottle."
B. went out of the room, came back and set up a lorry with the chairs and table, making big, dramatic roaring sounds. Finally he came to me, trying to hit me and also snuggle into me. I said he wants good loving things from me, like from mummy, but he has to be a big daddy penis to frighten or control me into giving anything good, and not to be horrible to him.

The following session.

> B. came up the stairs saying he will bring draughts and beat me like he beat Dr. A. He sat in my chair, grinning broadly.
> Dr. P.: "You are imagining yourself to be right inside mummy-me, feeling strong and safe."
> After three or four minutes, B. climbed on top of the mantelpiece, then on top of the tall cupboard (over two metres high) built in next to the fireplace.
> Dr. P.: "You are going way up on top of things to feel high and make me low."
> B. came down and began climbing on me.
> Dr. P.: "Climbing on me like the high places, on top of me and in charge of my body, like the room." As he pressed himself against me, I said, "You want to be right inside me so I can't go on holiday and leave you – I'd carry you around inside wherever I want." (This was just after the Easter break, as mentioned.)
> B. began staring at the lights, then at my face, then my genital area.
> Dr. P.: "You want to take all my good parts in with your eyes and be in charge of them."
> B.: "I came here when you were away and I swung on the strip light." He asked, would I see Anthony (his younger brother) once. "You have shoes like Anthony."
> Dr. P.: "Maybe that means to you that I like what Anthony has and want to let him take your place here."
> B. went in the cupboard and said he was going to pee.
> Dr. P.: "Like peeing inside my body – to control me, perhaps." (He then pretended he got thrown out.) "Maybe that's what you think I'm doing to you when I tell you what you are doing – that I'm throwing you out."
> B. hit me and wanted me to hit him.
> Dr. P.: "So we are the same."
> B. climbed on top of the cupboard and lay there sucking his thumb. He got his hands and clothes filthy and wiped his hands on the wall and ceiling.
> Dr. P.: "You are wiping pooh on my body when I seem not to let you be the same as me or inside me, and I seem to throw you out with my words that try to explain what you feel. When it's like that, it is so hard to feel safe outside me, and to play with other things like the toys in your box."

Gradually Benjamin began to have brief moments of sitting still and looking reflective and sad in response to a comment of mine. He seemed to be allowing space inside for reflection where, however briefly, good and bad could meet. This meant (a) that at times the badness was not so great and powerful that all good would be annihilated if they were contained together; and (b) that I could be allowed to have some good to give and he could let himself take it, rather than relying strictly on his own food in a uroboros-like way. The sessions began to have more symbolic play in them, although still manic and violent in nature much of the time. Over the course of the analysis, Benjamin did a great deal of throwing cushions at me; shouting; bringing in food and eating it in front of me with a triumphant grin and all the accompanying noises of having a great, blissful feast; he did a lot of the bodily thrusting himself or pushing himself onto and into me; taking his clothes off and prancing about; flooding the floor with water; climbing; hanging out of the window and shouting or dropping things out; and of course, going to the toilet, to which I eventually decided to accompany him, as it was part of the session. He almost invariably had an extremely foul-smelling bowel movement and, as we were enclosed together in a rather small lavatory, it was certain to evoke feelings of revulsion in me, which was undoubtedly exactly what he feared and yet wished to confirm. He also frequently came late, refused to leave at the end, and on two occasions, begged to borrow some money from me for the bus, as he had spent his on sweets on the way to his session. There were also reports (from him or from his parents) of various 'occurrences' outside the therapy, although these diminished in time. For instance, he got lost when in a large park with his parents and was not found for four hours. But by far the most striking activity and one which came to be characteristic of his sessions was what I call 'jamming' my voice, and indeed my ability to think. It was evident that he created at those times mindless states in himself. This had a perverse nature which so twisted and maimed the quality of our relation that I found myself often feeling rather hateful towards his behaviour. What he did was a form of wild, frenzied caricature of rock singing and performing, on a stage which he made of my desk, using my curtains behind it in all sorts of ways. He pretended to have a guitar and screamed anarchic 'songs', or what appeared to be parodies of love ballads, while thrusting and gyrating wildly about with his body with an excited grin on his face. In fact, it was quite brilliantly executed. But so often did this kind of behaviour take up most, if not all, of the session that I became despairing as to what to do. It was so terribly unpleasant and intrusive as to make me acutely uncomfortable much of the time. Bion wrote: "The attempt to evade the experience of contact with live objects by destroying alpha-function leaves the personality unable to have a relationship with any aspect of itself that does not resemble an automaton. Only beta-elements are available for what ever activity takes the place of thinking and beta-elements are suitable for evacuation only – perhaps through the agency of projective identification" (Bion 1). Yet eventually it appeared there were lyrics, in so far as I could distinguish them, which expressed some rudimentary form of image, usually about being jilted by a lover. I was treated to the names of the various rock groups that Benjamin believed he was representing, such as 'The Arrow', and after some time (I was convinced by then that my interpretations and my remarks about his 'rock music' were having no effect whatsoever), he began to introduce another element, that of 'playing the piano'. Benjamin had an ingenious way of using the few bits of furniture at our disposal to evoke a very vivid image of what he was recreating, be it lorry, caravan, fort, camp, or schoolroom. In this case, it was a piano and concert hall, and this, I felt, had a quality of repairing the violent triumphant and largely successful attacks on thinking and on our even being together. During those moments, he began to talk to me, telling me what he was doing, in contrast to the insensible screaming moments before.

Here are two excerpts from sessions later in the analysis, one shortly after the other. In the first, I am exasperated about the rock screaming/singing and unfortunately say and do what I can to stop it. In the second, we both have proceeded into a more verbal area. My intervention seems more attuned to the 'good' impulses as well as the 'bad' ones and I get an outpouring of direct verbal communication.

> B. sat on a 'throne', which he constructed out of all the chair cushions and said he is a king who is so powerful he could make anything happen.
> Dr. P.: "Like getting rid of daddy and having mummy to himself." (This was to do with something that had gone before in his play.)
> B.: "No, it's to get rid of mummy and have daddy to myself."
> Dr. P.: "You mean there are better things to get out of daddy's body than out of mummy's?"
> B. sat in his chair for a long time, thinking. He turned out the lights and sat in my chair. He said he is afraid of the cost of electricity. It also would cost thousands and thousands of pounds to replace the strip light if it got damaged.
> Dr. P.: "That's how difficult it feels to make it better when you've got rid of the good-mummy-milk-bottle-me in your mind."
> B. switched on the lights. He went to the lavatory to pee, switching off the lights before going. He came back and went to my desk, and standing on it began a long sequence of singing in a slow way, gradually getting more and more frenzied. The only word I could make out was 'generation'.
> Dr. P.: "I think you are getting lots of excited pleasure from your own body, especially your penis, and getting rid of my words because they are bad food which causes bad and sad feelings." I said I wondered what the words meant in his songs.

B.: "It's secret. It means 'love'."
Dr. P.: "It's a way to love yourself with excited feelings and keep bad-mummy-me out. It may also mean you love the good me and you have to keep it a secret."
B. sat down and played with the things in his box. He put a boy doll on a bear and had a crocodile bite a tiger.
Dr. P.: commented about him having a strong bear-penis and biting up the dangerous tiger me.
B. hung a length of string out of the window all the way to the ground. He got me to hold both his legs so he did not fall out.
Dr. P.: "You are getting me to be a mummy you allow to hold you and keep you safe and you can ask for it with words."
When the time was up, he ran out and waited while I packed up, which he usually did himself. I said he was letting me clean us up.

## Three weeks later…

Before this session, I was in the toilet. Someone banged on the door, having tried to open it, banging as if he was going to bash the door down. When he heard the toilet flush, he stopped. I came out and B. was crouching on the floor near the lavatory door, smiling sheepishly. He went into the lavatory and I said he could come up to the room when he had finished. He grunted. I waited in the room for five minutes then went to investigate. He was back in the waiting room and looked up from a book when I came in. As we went upstairs, he prevented me from going up, saying with a big grin, "Where are you going? You're a stranger. You can't come up to my room." He rushed into the room and sat in my chair and I sat opposite.
Dr. P.: "You are me and I am a stranger-Benjamin that I don't want in my room."
B.: "Yes, I am you and I don't want you in here."
Dr. P.: "You saw I didn't want you in the toilet with me. That we are not part of each other."
B. began violently singing his rock music, standing on the desk. He mentioned the name of some groups he was 'being'.
Dr. P.: "If you can't *be* me, you will be an excited rock group that makes its own good feelings."
B. listened, saying nothing.
Dr. P., after a gap: "I wondered what happened in your mind when you were having a bash at the door and I came out."
B.: "I was frightened. I was afraid someone would come out and hit me."
Dr. P.: "That you might have seen something."
B.: "Yes – I might see a lady naked."
Dr. P.: "Like when Mummy is in the toilet and you want to go in."

B. began singing loudly and wildly as before.
Dr. P. (after five to ten minutes of the singing): "You want to do the things you are good at like rock songs to show me your good bits, not your worries."
B. stopped suddenly and said: "I got into trouble at school. I wrote in my book for my friend to see, 'I don't want to do any work today – too hard!' The teacher walked around the room and saw it and sent me to the headmaster. He gave me a note to show to my parents which they had to sign. I hate getting into trouble," he said with much feeling. "I am a vicar's son. My daddy is a clergyman and it's terrible if I get into trouble."
Dr. P.: "Especially because you worry that you've hurt mummy and daddy by what you've done."
B.: "Sometimes I get the cane. Daddy gives me a good hiding."
Dr. P.: "I think that is a bad daddy in your mind. Not real daddy, actually."
B.: "I know he doesn't look like he would, but he hits me really hard with the cane that mummy has."
Dr. P.: "Then he is the naughty hurting one and you feel not so worried about hurting mummy and daddy."
B.: " I feel really upset when I sing, 'Lord Jesus cut his ass on a bit of glass', which the others all sing, because it's blasphemy. Because Lord Jesus is with you all the time and he loves you. He is right here now and he loves you."
Dr. P.: "I am right here now and you are worried you hurt me, and that is when you need to sing the rock songs, to put all that out of our minds."
B. then began to sing violently manic rock songs, e. g., "You belong to me", which he made up, and others of various groups he likes. He then drew flags of various countries on the blackboard and didn't seem to hear me when I said, "It is time to go". He left me a mess to clean up rather than have his usual compulsive tidying ritual, and I said, "You mended me with nice drawings of flags."

In the above extract we can see that a rapport had begun to get established in that I could be permitted to be a mother who can receive the baby's affects, leaving me to give them a name. Perhaps the violent attacks on our thinking with 'rock' music thrown at me was therefore also an attempt, as in the case of the baby I described, to find a container for unmanageable affects. In addition, B. wished to determine my capacity to mediate archetypal impulses before they could become connected up with any sort of mental imagery. Only then might there be verbal expression. As Plaut put it, "The analyst as container should function both for the purpose of expulsion of worthless material... but also for ingestion" (Plaut 16).

From the first session of treatment, B. indicated he was seriously depressed beneath his excited façade. He was extremely anxious lest any thinking occur to do with feeling helpless and vulnerable, or alternatively, uncontrollably powerful, rageful and damaging. A central defence, beside his precocious verbal ability and lucidity at times – such as when he told me in the first session, "Don't talk about sad things" – was the use of manic violent and/or sexual bodily activity either connected to, or cut off from, me. This activity seemed to serve the purpose of neutralising and rendering useless any analytic function which was going to identify the so-called 'sad things' and result in their becoming mentally known.

In addition, my interpretations came from my inner world and might have roused terrible envy had they been allowed credence. Hubback writes about this in connection with the shadow (Hubback 8). My ideas were prevented from being good milk which was mine to give or to withhold. They might have represented to B. 'inner treasures' of mine in complete contrast to the desolate internal world B. believed was his and which he could not successfully disown. No interaction, no dialogue between the good and the bad states was possible, lest all goodness be swamped and spoiled. No combination of opposites could occur, only confusion. I noted many sorts of confusion in B.'s material – of bodily zones, of gender, of boundaries, of time and place, light and dark, etc. He managed through a reversal of 'him' and 'me' to keep out the bad (my thoughts) and preserve the good by taunting me triumphantly with mock good feeds, such as chomping on his wonderful apples and crisps with a victorious leer. He wanted to make me into an empty, helpless baby with a small 'minkle', as he called it once (a mini-winkle?), who greedily sucks at my girl-friend/mummy's bottom and breasts and is very naughty. She, incidentally, was known as Miss Eggyboggle, who had eggies and bottles which I desperately depended upon.

I think experiences such as mine with Benjamin are not uncommon in child analysis. They present enormous problems of management. At the same time, they are great treasure-houses of analytic material. In adult analysis, we of course encounter the same conflict between what some psychoanalysts might call the life instinct and the death instinct, the conflict between allowing the creative penetration of the analyst and attacking it. I would see this rather as a defence to *preserve* the self. The occurrence of this in various adult patients comes clearly to mind but is not within the scope of this paper.

One of the problems of management is the analyst's own mindless responses. This can occur in physical form, such as stopping the session, pushing the child away or allowing certain forms of behaviour and not others (e. g., letting him cuddle up to you but not to hurt you), feeling tired of the case, going off to sleep, or even hating the patient. It can also take verbal form, such as using your interpretations to stab or to stop the child, or otherwise to give permission to the behaviour. An incomplete interpretation, for instance, can generate further confusion between inner and outer realities. Any of this can happen with words or even one's tone of voice.

The thread which runs through these actions and reactions of patient and therapist, one of mindlessness, could perhaps be encompassed in what Jung referred to as psychoid processes. They may be closely compared with what Bion termed beta-elements. In the use of the term 'psychoid' by Driesch, which Jung refers to, there was, interestingly, the idea of the "prospective potency of the germinal element". In other words, they are elements which can be the progenitors of psychic processes. Bleuler also used the term to refer to everything sub-cortical, non-mental, the physical, life-preserving functions. Jung, in discussing the dissociability of the psyche, and the meaning of 'psychoid', stressed the indivisibility of psychological processes (Jung 11, para 3). His idea was that psychic events can be likened to a spectrum of light or sound, with a lower and upper threshold, psychoid processes being at both ends of the psychic scale.

In Bion's terms, the process which may occur then is that beta-elements may get converted into alpha-function, which is required for thoughts. As we would understand it, this is a function of the original self having de-integrated and re-integrated successfully enough in relation to the object (the mother, or bits of her in accordance with the limited cognitive apparatus of the baby), for the baby to develop the reality of a sufficiently good, caring and dependable internal mother-object. This having been accomplished, she can be bitten up, gouged out, bashed up, defecated into, left behind, or worse – and survive. At that stage, the baby (or the patient) can afford to take the actual body of his mother (or his analyst) for granted and replace it with a symbol, thus opening out the vast new prospect of abstraction in play and in cultural/creative development. Edwards, summarising Fordham's idea, states: "In our field it is the pathology of the original self, and of the de-integrative-re-integrative archetypal processes, the fixations of, and regression to, the early internalised self-object relationship and the interference with the development of identity, which are of concern" (Edwards 4). The ego function of mental representation is, it seems to me, an essential component in this development of identity, in that it permits the baby or the patient to realise their status as wholly separate from the object. This is no more and no less than the realisation of an archetypal potential in the original self as Fordham has defined it, free of the pathological developments which Edwards has concisely summarised.

I cannot precisely define what I did with Benjamin to facilitate this process occurring, if indeed it did, but it seems to be important that both the mothering and fathering functions I described earlier should be combined to form a 'holding environment' – the hands which physically contain the explosions of affect, when the patient *must* be stopped, and the mind which intangibly holds the affects, and perhaps in some way transforms them. Meltzer gives a clear description of this:

> Klein's was a model in which development unfolds and in which the mother more or less presides over it by modulating the baby's mental pain. Bion took the view that the mother has to perform functions for the baby, mental functions, which the baby then can learn to perform for itself by internalising her. He formulated in terms of the baby's relationship to the breast: essentially the baby, in a state of confusion, and having emotional experiences about which it cannot think, projects distressed parts of itself into the breast. The mother (experienced by the baby as her breasts) and the mother's mind (experienced by the baby as the breast) has to perform the function of thinking for the baby. She returns to the baby those disturbed parts of itself in a state that enables thinking, and particularly dreaming, to commence... By linking dependence with the experience of the absent object as the 'first thought', Bion suggested a new, highly adaptive meaning for the long period of infantile helplessness, implying it is necessary for the internalisation of the mother as a *thinking* object, not merely a *serving* one (Meltzer 15).

Kenneth Lambert's work on the activities of the analyst in this regard is highly illuminating (Lambert 13).

Then, as in the alchemical vessel, a development can occur in this frame and something vital to the growth of the ego can perhaps occur, which is that the good-enough parent, or part-parent, can be genuinely taken inside, rather than pushed into a swallowed whole, out of fear and a need to control.

## Summary

A commonly noted feature of child analysis is the centrality of actions which take the place of mental operations, be they conscious, as thought, or unconscious, as phantasy. These actions can have their origins in the course of both 'normal' and 'pathological' personality development. In the case of the latter, the infant's need to protect and preserve the Self can interfere with his actually developing the capacity for mental representation, and in the personalities of these individuals we can see a preponderance of what Jung termed the 'psychoid' pole of the archetype, or what Bion seems to have meant by 'beta-elements'. Examples are given from infant observation and from the analysis of a young boy in which the responses of the analyst as well as those of the child were of considerable importance in understanding the processes involved. This can equally apply to work with adults. Adequate development in this area is crucial for symbolisation and for creativity.

## References

1. Bion, W. R. (1962). *Learning from Experience.* London. Tavistock.
2. Bion, W. R. (1963). *Elements of Psychoanalysis.* London. Heinemann.
3. Bion, W. R. (1965). *Transformations.* London. Heinemann.
4. Edwards, A. (1978). "Schreber's delusional transference – a disorder of the self." *J. analyt. Psychol.*, 23, 3.
5. Fordham, M. (1974). "Defences of the self." *J. analyt. Psychol.*, 19, 2.
6. Fordham, M. (1978). *Jungian Psychotherapy: A Study in Analytical Psychology.* Chichester. John Wiley & Sons.
7. Freud, S. (1933). "New introductory lectures in psycho-analysis." Std. Edn. XXII.
8. Hubback, J. (1972). "Envy and the shadow." *J. analyt. Psychol.*, 17, 2.
9. Jung, C. G. (1915). "Foreword to 'Psychic conflicts in a child'." *Coll. wks*, 17.
10. Jung, C. G. (1925). "Marriage as a psychological relationship." *Coll. wks*, 8.
11. Jung, C. G. (1947). "On the nature of the psyche." *Coll. wks*, 8.

12. Klein, M. (1930). "The importance of symbol formation in the development of the ego" in *Contributions to Psycho-Analysis, 1921–45.* London. Hogarth (1948).

13. Lambert, K. (1981). *Analysis, Repair and Individuation.* London. The Society of Analytical Psychology.

14. Liley, A. N. (1972). "The foetus as a personality." *Aust. N. Z. J. Psychiat.,* 6, 99.

15. Meltzer, D. (1981). "The Kleinian expansion of Freud's meta-psychology." *Int. J. Psycho-Anal,* 62, 2.

16. Plaut, A. (1969). "Transference phenomena in alcoholism" in *Technique in Jungian Analysis.* London. The Society of Analytical Psychology (1974).

17. Winnicott, D. W. (1963). *The Maturational Process and the Facilitating Environment.* London. Hogarth.

# The Winning of Conscious Choice: the Emergence of Symbolic Activity

Joseph Redfearn (London)

In this contribution I hope to describe how unconsciousness (unconscious acting, unconscious identifications) can be given up and thereby replaced by conscious awareness and choice. I shall notice how 'symbols' emerge into consciousness as part of this change.

For example, I shall describe how a little boy was able to stop behaving in a restless, aggressive, unsatisfiable way, and how a 'lion' symbol emerged at the same time in his analysis. In other words, 'lion-like' behaviour gave place to the lion symbol.

This ability to 'give up' behaviour or unconscious identifications is necessary before we can speak meaningfully of responsibility or of a responsible attitude towards one's own behaviour. It is of the utmost importance for politicians, lawyers, and those concerned with education thoroughly to understand the facts about responsibility and the ability to use symbols and exert conscious choice. Much or most of our corporate and group behaviour being of the pre-responsible, choiceless sort, it seems vital for the future of mankind to take these facts to heart, rather than as at present functioning on choiceless unconscious acting-out and on the use of moralistic platitudes and concretized, externalized self-symbols such as the group, the nation, the ideal society, and so on.

In his *Alchemical Studies* (CW 13), Jung (p. 45) says that his chief aim in therapy is to labour with the patient towards the detachment of consciousnees from the object, towards the dissolution of *participation mystique*, whereby unconscious contents are projected into the object, in a state of unconscious identification. When Freud said, "Where id was, there shall ego be", he was saying the same sort of thing in his own terminology. They are voicing the hope of culture and civilisation in the fact of blind instinct, but they both know that the hope depends, paradoxically, in giving full value to instinct and the unconscious, and not in the one-sided (and therefore blind) worship of ideals and idols.

And both Freud and Jung were great clinicans who, on the whole, knew when it was wisest to let the dragon slumber in its lair, and when not to go disturbing forces in the face of whose power they were themselves impotent.

A symbol has to be defined in terms of the use that can be made of an image, act, etc., by the person or persons concerned, rather than in terms of the image or act itself. Thus defined, the symbol is at the growing point of therapy or personal development. Symbols arise when an individual is preparing to give up a bit of unconsciousness, or, put in another way, when the unconscious is preparing to yield up one of its treasures.

Whether or not the 'I' can gather, work on, and eventually enrich itself from this world of potential value which we now tend to call the unconscious, depends on the working relationship between 'I' and unconscious, a talent, a gift, and a skill which can be learned and which is the most priceless thing in life. Jungians may often refer to it as the ego-Self relationship. (For an introduction to the topic, the reader is referred to Jung, CW Vol. 7, especially "The relation between ego and unconscious"). The ego-Self relationship is essentially an 'I-Thou' relationship and is at the basis not only of the relationship between 'I' and unconscious, 'I' and God, 'I' and one's potential creativity, but also at the basis of deep personal relationships, starting with, and being greatly dependent upon, the first relationship with the mother (see, for example, Newton and Redfearn, 1977). When this relationship is destructive or uncreative, work on the relationship between the partners in the analysis is often necessary in order to lay the foundation of a more satisfactory I-Self relationship.

The difficulties and obstacles we have in benefitting from unconscious products are themselves largely unconscious. These difficulties are of the same general sort as those we have in relating creatively to other people. As I have said, the prototype of the ego-Self relationship, including these difficulties, is the infant's relationship with his/her mother; or at least, the relationship with the mother as remembered, reconstructed, and fantasied by the analysand, which is a somewhat different thing, of course. This assertion seems to me to be supported by the following empirical fact. We find that the analyst's holding, validating, and reflective behaviour towards the analysand can eventually be introjected by the analysand and thus modify or transform his ego-Self relationship. This suggests very strongly that the infant introjects his mother's holding, validating, and reflective behaviours and that these latter form an important part of what we call the ego and/or the self, and even of those integrating and harmonizing functions associated with the Jungian Self. The mother reflects upon and reflects back the child's communications and behaviour, allowing the child essential space in which to act and experiment, and thus lay the foundations for the 'I'-Self relationship and the ability to play and to use symbols.

In therapy (hopefully less and less as therapy proceeds), the therapist may have to mediate for the analysand this symbolic capacity, this 'transcendant function' between conscious and unconscious. Dependence in the relationship between patient and therapist, Jung said, can be seen as a measure of the degree to which the patient is lacking in his ability to relate his consciousness with his unconscious (CW 8, p. 74). Combined, I should add, with the degree to which he, the patient, is able to use the therapist to compensate for this lack.

Jung considered that the consciousnesses of children, primitive man, neurotic and psychotic persons are relatively weak and permeable. The barrier function of consciousness may be lacking altogether. There is a localized or general lack or deficiency of the 'as if' attitude of consciousness towards the unconscious contents. Thus the Cameroons witch-doctor wearing the lion mask is not just pretending to be a lion, he '*is*' a lion (Jung 1964, p. 44). Similarly, for a schizophrenic patient of mine, when I prevented her from rushing out into the street, I was not just *like* the Devil, I *was* the Devil (or so she said, in a way which I experienced as literal and very chilling). The same may apply to the young child, and to the neurotic person in certain areas.

As the consciousness of the child, in this sense, is relatively undeveloped, and the symbolic function likewise in a rudimentary state, it is in children, and in our child analysands in particular, that we may most readily and simply observe the development of the symbolic capability, the emergence of symbols, and of the way symbols are used.

The function of holding-together or containing opposing or conflicting wishes is itself often symbolized by a container or cimcumscribed area. For Jung, the alchemical vessel in alchemy, the protective and protected parts of the Self where transformative experiences can be rehearsed and resolved symbolically, represents an important development in the consciousness of mankind. The temple, the walled city, the stage of the theatre, and the frame of the picture are all examples of the same thing.

This containing capacity, at first mediated by the mother, is experienced and hopefully finally introjected by the child and becomes the child's ability to contain his impulses and conflicts to the extent that useable images and symbols arise in consciousness. Urinary and other sorts of continence may be an important bodily expression of progress in this holding capacity. But what does this holding and containing mean in parental and therapeutic practice?

Some of the clearest and simplest examples of the process of symbol formation, showing the various factors involved, are provided by child analysts (e. g., Fordham 1969, Chapter 10). Let me quote from a paper by Dorothy Davidson (1979, pp. 36–37), a London child analyst, showing how the analyst's 'holding' behaviour enabled restless, aggressive, hungry and unsatisfied (lion-like) behaviour in a four-year-old child to be given up and replaced by concern for the analyst, with the concomitant emergence of a 'lion' symbol. In my terminology, the 'lion' is here an oral sadistic complex which shows itself in behavioural terms, but which with therapy comes to be experienced as, or represented by, a lion symbol and related with the 'I' of the child.

> John was a very disturbed and restless child of four when he started analysis with Mrs. Davidson. There was "a search for something... someone to contain him. He tried various chairs and a couch but could only remain on them for a few moments. Then he would hurl himself off or out of the chair, creating the impression of having been thrown out. This theme culminated in the following way. John made what he called a cage for himself out of some furniture. He now spent the great part of his sessions inside his cage and said he was a lion. From time to time he would rush out of his cage and attack me, but then there was a change; prior to it he had *really* attacked but now he was *pretending* to scratch and bite me. These attacks seemed to belong to his oral impulses and phantasies represented in the image of a lion who came out for a feed. One day, John, sitting in his cage as usual, said "The lion is hungry – don't let him out". There was a new note in his voice and an expression in his eyes which I had not seen before, and I recognized it as concern. He had been able to put his dilemma into words. I responded to this by saying that I knew the lion was hungry and needed to come out and eat me – but that he, John, loved me and did not want to eat me up. He smiled and said "Feed him in his cage". Accordingly I gave him pieces of Plasticine, which he pretended to eat. At the same time I talked to him about having been held in his mother's arms and being fed by her. He replied "Like this". After another feed John enlarged the cage; then he

> announced "The lion wants to come out – he needs a lead". I tied some string to John's buttonhole at his request, then he said, "He needs a label" and asked me to write on it 'John Lion'. He now came out of his cage with me holding the string. When the session ended he went off holding my end of the string and said he was leading his lion home. Only later did I discover that he had also taken a small police car! This seemed to symbolize his growing ability to manage the affects represented by the lion."
> The next day, John made Mrs. Davidson pretend to be a witch who could turn him into a lion, but this was alright if he could hold on to a 'John' label. From this play, Mrs. Davidson understood that John was searching as if for a feeding breast and also for containment, and that through finding these at least in a token way within the transference, he was able to enact the fears, phantasies and destructive impulses which up till then had overwhelmed him.

Of course there are a lot of questions, left unanswered here, regarding what constitutes an effective token satisfaction. How non-concrete or non-literal can or must it be in order to push forward the therapy? The answer, rather maddeningly, I am afraid, depends on the stage of development of the consciousness of the child or patient. Parents and therapists develop a fairly unerring feel for this.

This account of six weeks' play therapy conveys the relatively complex, skilled and sensitive talk and behaviour subsumed under the simplistic heading of 'the analyst's containing function', or 'the analyst's holding behaviour', and so on. I should like to emphasize a few of the features which seem to be important in this 'holding'.

1. A warm, mutually caring relationship had been established. It is implicit in John's concern for the analyst.
2. The analytical setting, and Mrs. Davidson's friendly tolerance, gradually resulted in the 'cage' play. The cage having been established – an additional safety boundary within the therapy room – the hungry lion can now be enacted in play and the oral aspects of the restless behaviour and dissatisfaction worked on.
3. Mrs. Davidson's own play responses were sufficiently concordant with John's feelings and play as to enable John to go forward in his play. She did not give oral interpretations until these were initiated by John's intimation that the lion was hungry. Even this short extract contains many examples of how she was able to meet and gently push forward the play and hence the therapeutic process.
4. The restless, aggressive behaviour – the lion behaviour – is 'tamed' by Mrs. Davidson's fortitude (in coping with the real attacks), thera-

peutic skill and the warmth and security of the therapeutic relationship and setting. John's concern for the therapist then enables him to do his own containing (caging), a benevolent caging learned directly from her behaviour towards the restless lion. This degree of concern may of course not be there and may take a long time to develop, but it may be an essential stage in the replacement of acting-out behaviour by symbolic activity.

5. Mrs. Davidson's interpretation of a 'lion' part and a 'John' part was intended to help John to differentiate out and at the same time contain two opposing sub-personalities in his Self. The ability to differentiate out and contain (roughly) opposing tendencies and wishes is often referred to by analysts as the ego function of 'containing ambivalence' or 'containing the opposites'. No choice is possible until containment ('continence') is achieved, i. e., until Mrs. Davidson's containing behaviour has been taken aboard by John.
6. The lion's lead, the link between the tamer and the lion – later the tamer is John himself, John's ego – is worth noting. String and other symbolic links are often of crucial importance in the process of symbol formation. Once the container is securely internalized, the external string can be relinquished and the internal link between the ego and the symbolic activity is sufficient. Mrs. Anne Brown, a child analyst trained at the S.A.P. in London and now working in Australia, told me of a case of hers (personal communication) of a four-year-old child who, at the beginning of therapy, was virtually mute. His play at first largely consisted of the use of string in linking with Mrs. Brown and binding them together. As the relationship was established, the string play was relinquished and replaced by other forms of play, and talking was now possible.
   In therapy, token links are often necessary in the transition period in which the therapist's mediation and containing function is being gradually internalized and taken over by the patient.
7. The confusion of, and about, John's initial behaviour was gradually clarified as John was helped to distinguish and separate out the 'lion' part of himself that wanted to burst forth and eat up the analyst (which emerged more clearly as it was caged and became a 'pretend' part), and the John part (the ego part), who was responsible and who cared for the analyst. In other words, the symbol only emerges clearly out of the unconscious matrix of acting-out once the 'as-if' aspect is clearly established. The 'as-if' aspect ('I am only *pretending* to kill you, eat you, be dead, etc.) enables play to go forward and the

symbolic image to develop fully. If this essential boundary of the awareness of metaphor is not yet established, the individual *behaves* as if the metaphor were a fact. John, for example, might be acting out the lion and hallucinating a witch. But of that we can never be sure, as the metaphor – in-action, the 'unconscious fantasy', can only be inferred from the behaviour, including the verbal behaviour.

It would be unwise to advance this observation to the status of a general hypothesis. For example, clear images may emerge into consciousness before the corresponding behaviour is anywhere near to being able to be given up or not be given up as a matter of choice. There is often a splitting between image and corresponding affect which is used defensively (intellectually, for instance) in order to delay affective (moral) responsibility and autonomy.

There may, of course, be various reasons for not acting out our impulses, e.g., fear as well as love. But it seems to me that impulses inhibited because of fear become incorporated into the shadow along with the hated part of the person responsible for the fear, whereas impulses inhibited because of concern become a part of the self available to the normal adaptive 'I' and are 'I'-enhancing. It goes without saying that choiceless behaviour (the unintegrated 'subpersonality') can be 'given up' for the sake of other persons than the mother or analyst, and for the sake of idealized or loved 'internal objects' and abstract principles, such as democracy, liberty and of ethical considerations.

So much for the emergence of symbol and conscious choice in a particular child. The achievement of 'consciousness' in the sense in which I have used the term consciousness is always a relative affair. One could never be 'completely conscious' of a lion sub-personality, any more than one could be in complete charge or in complete rapport with a lion. A certain amount of wisdom, a certain amount of courage, a certain give-and-take, will help enormously, but the relationship between oneself and one's lion is never settled once and for all.

The taming of the lion may become a habitual act, and in this sense, the lion will go back into the unconscious. Only when restlessness or appetite are stimulated (by fatigue, hormonal changes, dissatisfactions and frustrations) may the lion then be awakened from its slumbers and become a problem. Much of our everyday behaviour is unconscious in this sense of being habitual. I do not believe there is any essential (neurophysiological) distinction between the unconsciousness of the way we walk about and open and close doors and go upstairs or downstairs without counting the steps, and the unconsciousness of John's lion-like behaviour before the lion symbol emerged. The symbolic activity (consciousness of the sub-personality in question) only arises when necessary, when the unconscious activity is called into question for one reason or another.

Of course repression and other 'defences' are very real phenomena. They reflect negative feelings between sub-personalities, for example between the present 'I' and a given sub-personality. The negative relationship can be of many different kinds and the concept of repression is too general to be of much use in therapy at our present more sophisticated stage of development.

In therapeutic work, symbols do not arise in the patient so much as in the inter-action between patient and therapist. They do not emerge out of the patient's unconscious into the patient's consciousness, but they arise out of a shared unconscious into a shared consciousness, so to speak. Shared consciousness and shared responsibility is often how progress comes about.

To illustrate this, I should like to describe the emergence of a symbol in the relationship between one of my analysands and myself. There is nothing remarkable about it. Its everyday nature gives a fairer idea of the work of analysis than the occurrence of a shattering experience or revelation, although these latter certainly occur. The 'symbol' was of a rapist/robber who later developed into an ant-like creature who was trying to break down a barrier and reach a treasure.

For my own convenience, I asked my patient if he could come an hour later each week for his Friday morning session. He raised many objections and the atmosphere between us became very tense. I felt I had to say that I was not going to make an issue of it, but it seemed necessary to discuss our feelings about it. It emerged that he was experiencing me as a robber-violator in asking for the change in times. In fact, any demand on him to change himself or his arrangements, etc., was experienced by him thus. I, on my part, was experiencing him as a somewhat selfish person incapable of considering other people's needs or of 'putting himself out' for anyone else. When we were able to get some sort of picture of the robber-rapist which had pervaded the emotional atmosphere between us, we had arrived at a useful symbol, symbolic both for him and for me, which we often later used in our analytic work. We were able to compromise on the matter of times of sessions. We were able to go on and relate the robber image with real aspects of his father. The robber was also prominent in the mutual projections between his parents and in the quarrels between them over money, etc. He was also present in the victim/persecutor relationships affecting his family throughout the generations.

A few weeks later, she dreamt of trying to go to a Jungian seminar given by an elderly friend of his who actually gives such seminars. His somewhat free associations with this friend included references to his friend's bedroom in which were photographs of the latter's late husband, and comments on his friend's large double bed. In the dream, my patient could not get to the seminar but ended up in a cul-de-sac called Anterix Road. His associations with this word 'Anterix' were with the vagina, seen as a forecourt to the cervix and womb. He could reach the forecourt but could not penetrate into the womb, the inner place where the source of value and rebirth lay, which was also the parents' bedroom. So he associated this dream with feeling kept out of what is of most value in life.

The next day, he came to the session saying that he felt agitated and felt like screaming. I invited him to look into this feeling. He said he imagined himself as an ant with long antennae trying to get through a thick wall. On the other side of the wall there were red and green jewels shining, and a white light was present in their vicinity. He was able to identify the ant with the rapist-robber; and the wall with her own defences against the rapist robber in himself. The ant, of course, represents that which, when projected, his defences are trying to keep out. When his feeling of 'I' is inside the wall or temenos, he has a feeling of self, but often feels insecure and projects the robber on to his environment. When his 'I' is outside the wall, he has no feeling of self and is a mass of sensations and murderous impulses, is possessed by envy.

The image of jewels and light surrounded by a relatively impenetrable defence is, of course, a mandala. Let us digress in order to clarify the meaning of this symbol. As I have just indicated, the meaning of such a symbol depends very much on where the 'I' is located relative to it. If the 'I' is identified with the treasure or with the mandala as a whole, it means a 'self' which hopes for continence and security. The wall or barrier surrounding the contents serves to defend this 'self' from outside threats and to stop harmful contents and treasured contents from getting out. The thickness of the wall, therefore, is a measure of his insecurity against imagined and real rapist-robber attacks. But the great strength and intensity of his own needy, excluded feelings is what constitutes the strength and subjectively felt danger of being invaded, broached and plundered. When his 'I' is located in the ant/robber, the treasure inside the barrier is experienced as unattainable, and is, in fact, unattainable because of the strength of his own defences against his robber sub-personality. How this insecurity came about, how the defences had to be erected against invasive (needy) parents, is another story.

These thick barriers in the personality constitute important blocks against freedom and happiness. We have a situation of envy, in which what is on the other side of the barrier is idealized and unattainable, and subject to envious, destructive attacks.

If I and my treasure are constantly under threat from the robbing invader, I may, for example, try to make my house beautiful, always finding things wrong in it that have to be attended to. I may always be worrying about my financial security and my professional status in the face of envious colleagues, and I may always be worrying about pains and other hypochondriacal threats. These fixed aims and attempts to concretize the mandala may motivate my life long before the mandala is constellated. Only when the mandala is constellated and really reflected upon can security become a possibility, because it can now be given up. The attainment of the treasure is now a possibility because the ant no longer has to be kept out. In other words, one can now give up one's paranoid defences. Of course, not everyone who dreams of mandalas or paints them does give up his paranoid, envious sub-personalities. But with help or therapy, it would be more likely to happen.

In the mental sphere, a feeling of stupidity, thickness, inability to get at the desired knowledge or take things in, may result from the same barrier in oneself.

After this work, my patient was more able to empathize with others. This represented an increased ability for his 'I' to cross the self/not-self barrier, now less impenetrable.

The treasure of the transformation inside the container represents *both* the ultimate regression (to the 'good breast', even to the womb) *and* the highest and ultimate attainment in life.* These goals should not, of course, be conceptualized in rigidly concrete terms, but as the working out of one's sub-personalities in life and in oneself. However, these goals are in fact, usually and tragically, expressed in concrete terms.

* This pair of opposites, i.e., ultimate regression and highest aim, is one important aspect both of the *proprium* and of the Jungian Self.

The image of the rapist-robber was first produced by my patient when I was able to help him in taking an analytic attitude towards our difficulty over times. It developed into the ability to see himself as the robber ant. I am not saying that the containing function was solely carried by me in this instance, any more than I believe that in childhood it is solely the mother who has the monopoly of the containing function in her transactions with her child. Mutual respect, devotion to the work of analysis and an understanding of the work developed over years of work together, all eventually resulted in a greater ability to reach a working symbol each time a difficulty of this kind came up. Previously, we had both acted much more unconsciously, that is, more emotionally and with less understanding, but this had gradually changed in the direction of greater ability to analyze, so that more of an analytical 'ego' was present each time these misunderstandings occurred, not just in me, not just in him, but in the relationship. Previously, there had been a greater tendency on my part to react either passively or over-firmly in these conflict situations – these had been the only reactions possible for me at those times. And the same had been true for him, in much greater degree – he had reacted either very passively – obsequiously and frigidly, one might say – or with hardness and litigiousness, reminding me of rules and principles and of things I had previously said and promised and so on. His legalistic and moralizing reactions to the threats to his well-being from persecutors had figured very prominently in his social and professional behaviour in the earlier parts of his analysis, but were gradually mitigated in the way I have indicated.

When it is fully developed (if that were possible), the symbolic attitude involves giving full value to the emerging unconscious contents, as well as fully recognizing their 'as-if' quality. The full recognition of their 'as-if' aspect involves the abandonment of primary identity and of the delusory one-ness which denies psychic reality to the other in personal relationships and to the not-me as part of the personality. In childhood, it is chiefly the mother, or parts of the mother, with whom one at first unconsciously identifies in the boundaryless sense of primary identity. From the mother, the child, we postulate, gradually learns to differentiate 'himself'. He separates out a self image from her image and, at the same time, builds bridges of communication back to her and back to his own unconscious 'roots' (the parts of himself which are not differentiated out from the mother image). The symbol reaches out to the real mother and also connects him with his primary, non-differentiated self. Symbolic activity involves the giving up of these unconscious identifications, which are now felt to be illusory or delusory in character (otherwise there would be no spur towards abandoning them).

The London group of Jungian analysts has done valuable work in this field, whereby illusory or delusory identifications with the analyst can be given up and creative symbolic activity initiated. One of the first contributions was by Jackson (1963), describing an adult psychotic transference and its resolution. A little later, Dorothy Davidson (in 1965) described how a fantasy of being inside the analyst-mother was the beginning of her patient's ability to give up an unconscious identification with a damaged mother image (symbolized by a blitzed site). At the same time, the patient was able to deal with her envy of the idealized mother, and her wish to destroy her. Many London Jungians have stressed the connection between the giving up of unconscious identification or of idealized images of togetherness or wholeness, and the acquisition of personal identity and the symbolic attitude. Among those cited in this connection by Newton (1965) are Gordon (1965), Hobson (1961), Plaut (1959) and Strauss (1964). This motif is a London variation on the theme of individuation as the separating out of the ego from the collective unconscious. The London variation makes use of the work of psycho-analysts such as Klein, Segal, Milner, Mahler and Searles (see Newton 1965, 1975 for references).

Paradoxically, this giving-up of unconscious identifications is accompanied by the creative loss of boundaries, the creative illusion, the regression to animism, underlying the formation and the sharing of symbols. Language and all human intercommunication using symbols depends on this, as well as the creative process itself.

All this work was neatly summarized by Rosemary Gordon (1967) in the sentence, "(The) transcendent function can come into operation only when the original self has been allowed to de-integrate, when uroboric union has been sacrificed and when the opposites have been constellated".

This 'London' approach to symbol formation was taken further by Norah Moore (1975) with clinical examples of important stages in the ability to use symbols in adult patients. She describes this developing function as follows: If the relationship with the real mother carries enough of the experience of original wholeness, the infant is able gradually to give it up and to differentiate between 'inner' and 'outer'. The bridge between inner and outer is at first a symbolic equivalence, but representations of the lost primal self may then occur. As the ego develops, it defends itself against the unconscious from which it is emerging, but also relates to it by participating in the transcendent function. Later on, the formed ego is able to be an observer because defences have developed, and it has now to make some effort to get in touch with the unconscious, as in active imagination.

In times of regression, the unconscious is all around without much barrier, and no special effort is needed to encounter it. The symbol forms a bridge between inner and outer, relating always to the wholeness of the self. The conscious mind reaches out to whatever is unknown to it, whether in the unconscious or without, where the inner images are met as projections.

Thus the transcendent function is first encountered as a projective mechanism, which gives way later to creative formulation and imagination; the experience of the opposites is at first discontinuous, but later the opposites confront one another and a capacity for ambivalence develops. The developing transcendent function forms a bridge between the opposites as they collide: the gap between real and imaginary widens; here, the symbol is born; it allows conscious and unconscious to take hold of each other in a *coniunctio,* at once tangible and infinite.

Summarizing in our own way, we might say that the symbol reaches out to an original wholeness, a primary identity, a delusion of oneness, and also reaches out to adaptation to reality, to the other person, to the not-me part of the Self. It tends to occur precisely when the delusion of unity is (through the experiences of oneness and also of conflict) being given up. This 'giving up' is often accompanied by considerable anger, the anger of frustrated omnipotence, or by sad feelings. One usually learns to cope with this anger and pain by using the example of respected persons who have already learned to do so.

But it is not just a matter of foregoing blissful one-ness with the idealized mother, matrix, analyst, or anima figure. It is equally a matter of separating from the dead or damaged mother or Other, the blitzed site, the dead lover, etc. And that is the liberating aspect of separation. Paradoxically, the patient is only able to give up his delusory one-ness when the delusory one-ness, the infantile omnipotence, of the patient is given enough value by the analyst. It seems to be a fundamental law of analysis, perhaps of parenting and perhaps of human relationships in general, that the individual (patient, infant, etc.) can only yield up his pertinent bit of unconsciousness when this bit is given (or maybe feels it is given) enough recognition, value, sympathy (exactly which and what varies, of course) by the analyst, parent, etc. This is the essence of the effective counter-transference attitude which has to be worked on by the analyst in connection with unconscious aspects of himself, as well as of his patient. I hope this was made clear in the example I gave from my own work.

In this chapter on the symbolic attitude, I have confined myself largely to a synopsis of the London contribution on symbols in relation to the transference and the developing ego. There are many considerations I have omitted, which have been emphasized by Jung himself, as well as by workers in other schools of analytical psychology. For instance, as I write, I am watching two kittens at play on the hearth rug, 'playing at' stalking their prey, fighting their enemies, fleeing from danger, and so on. All these things they have never actually done. Their claws have never been extended in anger, their teeth have never closed on an enemy, they have never been really frightened by any real danger, they 'fight' and pat each other with a delicacy which is always fun for each other. It is obvious that an 'as-if' element has to be there from the start (in practice rather than in the conscious awareness of the kittens). The reaction of the mother cat, or of the other kitten, may be important in modifying the playful attacks as they occur. The human infant is the same. He never seriously sets about devouring the breast. Similarly, the most delinquent child, as well as the most fanatical witch-doctor, does not *actually* behave like a lion, even though he 'knows' himself to be one. In other words, the nature of play and of the inhibitory functions and boundaries which eventually result in adult symbolic activity are far more complex than the above formulations suggest. But these formulations are based on clinically important changes in our patients as they develop the symbolic attitude. Furthermore, they are useful to our trainees, and work done by our trainees on their control cases in recent years has shown a deep understanding and ability to use these ideas, with gratifying changes in their patients and their patients' relationships with their inner lives.

My own contribution (Redfearn 1965, 1970, 1973, 1978, 1979, 1980, 1982) has mainly concerned the integration of the subjective body and the mind in the symbolic experience, and of the role of the therapist in holding the opposites in the sense used above. This has involved training oneself in the use of the feelings and experiencing their basis in bodily experience, particularly in countertransference feelings and impulses. One uses oneself as a sensitized instrument in the work of paying attention to the patient.

I do not claim to be alone, or even a pioneer, in this area. It is all very much part of the stock-in-trade of modern analysis, at least of the London Jungians and of many, or most, psycho-analysts, too. But to illustrate what I mean, let me give another everyday example of this sort of skill, this time from work with a young professional man.

In a recent session, we were discussing my custom of charging for missed sessions, even when he had to miss them because of his work, and even when he gave me ample advance notice. He felt this to be unduly rigid, and said that he was much more flexible with *his* clients. I certainly saw his point and we agreed to talk over the matter further.

At the next session, to my interest, he did not bring up the subject, but instead he said he wanted to be more disciplined in his life and his work. He spent evenings in the bath instead of preparing work for his students next day. He needed pressure to make him work – pressure of time or the pressure of guilt. Once he had succeeded in getting into a working frame of mind, he could not stop. If he stopped, he became ill. So he needed self-discipline in order to be able to start work, and also in order to be able to stop work and avoid over-working.

He continued in the same vein about his inability to write scientific papers. When trying to do so, he makes tea, goes for walks, needs the stimulus of dialogue, is unable to do it himself. He had masses of material, had invented his own innovative method of working professionally which was found invaluable by his trainees, but had not managed to publish a single paper about it. He got into a similar difficulty with his doctorate thesis at university. The masses of material he accumulated simply got out of hand, so that he could not substantiate his brilliant ideas, which gave him grandiose fantasies and feelings of genius.

I replied to this by saying there seemed to be a difficulty in gripping, grasping, biting and digesting his material and his mental contents, and that he needed to fight them every inch of the way down on to the paper. Instead, he let the material swallow him. I said there seemed to be an inhibitory force at work, inhibiting the full and free use of his hands, nails, and teeth. He said that seemed exactly right. He then remembered a dream of the night before of torturing a woman to death by scratching and tearing the skin off her with his nails, and biting her.

On his way out, he said that he wondered why we had not discussed fees during the session, as we had hoped. I said jokingly that he needed to scratch and tear at me, and that maybe we could discuss fees some more soon when he had done that.

My interpretation about the inhibition of hands and teeth was based on my own bodily impulses and sensations when he was outlining his difficulties in coping with his own mental contents, in particular his inability to write papers.

This young man was at the end of his first year of twice-a-week analysis and we had achieved a good working relationship, in which (at least at times) his dreams, the transference-countertransference relationship, the bodily impulses and sensations and mental metaphors of the therapist, and the symbolic experiences were all being interpreted and seemed to be very much at the same psychic level. This occurs when the working relationship is, in some sense, a primal relationship where symbolic, archetypal experience and bodily experience are not split off from each other.

To a large extent, this skill can be learned. It is obviously a skill not just of the analyst, but of the relationship. But trainee analysts can be taught to learn this skill in their analytical relationships. For example, if a trainee in supervision with me says his client hurt him when he said so-and-so, he is encouraged to notice what sort of hurt it felt like and where the hurt was experienced. Was it a stabbing, a scathing, a crushing or whatever kind of attack, and so on? Training can help us use attacks on our narcissism to our own and the client's advantage, and our interpretations are directed towards helping the client in realizing why he attacks in these ways. The same use is made of positive affects which are reflected back to the client in a similar way. All this sounds far more systematic and deliberate than it actually is. Emphasizing just one aspect of the work is responsible for this.

This working relationship in analysis is referred to by Winnicott (1971) as an area of mutual play, in the sense that client and analyst are each giving the other the necessary space in which creative activity can occur, and each can use the space between subjective and 'objective' reality, illusion and 'reality', in a creative way. The approach and the theoretical formulations of the London Group of analytical psychologists owe a good deal to our proximity to Winnicott and the Tavistock Clinic. This gives a peculiar flavour to the London kind of Jungian teaching, which this paper tries to convey.

## References

Davidson, D. (1965) A problem of identity in relation to an image of a damaged mother. J. Anal. Psychol. 10, No. 1, 67–76.

Davidson, D. (1979) Playing and the growth of imagination. J. Anal. Psychol. 24, 31–43.

Fordham, M. (1969) "Children as Individuals", London. Hodder & Stoughton.

Gordon, R. (1965) The concept of projective identification: an evaluation. J. Anal. Psychol. 10, No. 2, 127–150.

Gordon, R. (1967) Symbols: content and process. J. Anal. Psychol. 12, No. 1, 23–24.

Hobson, R. F. (1961) Psychological aspects of circumcision. J. Anal. Psychol. 6, No. 1, 5–34.

Jackson, M. (1963) Symbol formation and the delusional transference. J. Anal. Psychol. 8, No. 2, 145–159.

Jung, C. G. (1956) Symbols of transformation. C.W. 5.

Jung, C. G. (1958) Prefatory note to "The Transcendent Function", C.W. 8.

Jung, C. G. (1964) "Man and his Symbols", London, Aldus Books.

Moore, N. (1975) The transcendent function and the forming ego. J. Anal. Psychol. 20, No. 2, 164–182.

Newton, K. (1965) Mediation of the image of infant-mother togetherness. J. Anal. Psychol. 10, No. 2, 151–162.

Newton, K. (1975) Separation and pre-Oedipal guilt. J. Anal. Psychol. 20, No. 2, 183–193.

Newton, K. & Redfearn, J. W. T. (1977) The real mother, ego-self relations and personal identity. J. Anal. Psychol. 22, No. 4, 295–315.

Plaut, A. (1959) Hungry patients: reflections on ego structure. J. Anal. Psychol. 4, No. 2, 161–168.

Redfearn, J. W. T. (1965) The patient's experience of his 'Mind'. J. Anal. Psychol. 11, No. 1, 1–20.

Redfearn, J. W. T. (1970) Bodily experience in psychotherapy. Br. J. med. Psychol. 43, 301–312.

Redfearn, J. W. T. (1973) The nature of archetypal activity: the integration of spiritual and bodily experience. J. Anal. Psychol. 18, No. 2, 127–145.

Redfearn, J. W. T. (1978) The energy of warring and combining opposites: problems for the psychotic patient and the therapist in achieving the symbolic situation. J. Anal. Psychol. 23, No. 3, 231–241.

Redfearn, J. W. T. (1979) The captive, the treasure, the hero, and the 'anal' stage of development. J. Anal. Psychol. 24, No. 3, 185–205.

Redfearn, J. W. T. (1980) Romantic and classical views of analysis: primal relationship or working relationship? J. Anal. Psychol. 25, No. 1, 1–16.

Redfearn, J. W. T. (1982) When are things persons and persons things? J. Anal. Psychol. 27, No. 3, 215–238.

Winnicott, D. J. (1971) "Playing and Reality". London, Tavistock. Now available as a Penguin paperback.

# The Split in the Clinical and the Symbolic Approach – Social and Political Implications

Anita von Raffay (Hamburg)

People going into analysis today have different needs than they had half a century ago or even a few years back. They look less for a cure and healing; they rather want to become more conscious and get connected to the needs of their soul. They want to know why they are the way they are – they come for the process of self-discovery. This is, of course, a good old Jungian idea which gets lost when the analyst is dependent on third party payment and insurance schemes, as we are in Germany.

If we are to meet these needs, we have to be conscious of the splits that go through us as individuals and also through society. I believe that the needs of analysts and analysands correspond or parallel the outer social needs. And I also think that the dissonance in our souls corresponds to the discord within society. I would like to describe this dissonance as the irreconcilable split between the feminine and the masculine in the soul and in the outer world. This breech exists not only between the patriarchal masculine and feminine, it also exists within the feminine itself. There is a real confusion of what the feminine is, the role women are to take.

So the needs of those coming into analysis, as well as our own needs and those of society, are to heal this split by liberating the feminine from its role of being an outcast and by newly understanding and redefining it. The women, like the Jews, have been outcasts for thousands of years. *Adorno* and *Horkheimer* said that one can notice and see from their looks that women and Jews have not been in power for thousands of years.[1] So that powerlessness, standing aside, away from life, silence, being wounded and not saying anything – all this belongs to the old ideas of the feminine. Naturally, the feminine is an outcast not only in women, but in men too. And it is with this split and with the need for new images of the feminine that clients come into analysis.

The dilemma with feminine identity is that feminism sees itself in a position of having to find radically different criteria for feminine identity, but often lands in old patriarchal patterns. The feminine has been projected into the neglected and disparaged sides of life like sexuality, body, powerlessness, spontaneity, irrationality, but all those are qualities which patriarchal thinking has *constructed* as being feminine because they seem opposites to the masculine. But masculine and feminine are not opposites. I admit I don't know really what the feminine is, and I think it is probably impossible to know that in our time of change. So I will use these old terms, knowing that they they are maybe no longer valid, or only in a biased way. There is an unresolved and probably unresolvable ambivalence between the masculine and the feminine, and it is still difficult to imagine forms of relationship other than of power, subjugation, jealousy, possessiveness, or utility.

I believe it to be of immense urgency that the feminine does not retire to the role which patriarchy has assigned it, namely to represent sensuality, emotionality, liberated sexuality, the body. This is femininity ending in a dead-end alley. Instead, the new form of feminism lies in the direction of accepting the dark, the underworld on one hand, and on the other hand, of using the imagination to create new models of feminine identity. Serious feminists like *Heilbrun* in the United States, *Luce Irigaray* in France and *Marlies Gerhardt* in Germany agree that what women are not using enough is the imagination to work on a new model of the feminine for themselves.

I think this new model must come from women *and* men. Since I have begun to work on this subject, my own dreams and those of my analysands (women and men) seem to develop new images for the feminine and for the relationship feminine-masculine. Actually I think women are more radical than men, but women used the masculine model for their own identity for thousands of years. Nothing else was imaginable, but it was a model which represented a *masculine projection* of the feminine.

[1] Adorno, T. W., Frenkel-Brunswik, E., Levinson, D. J., Sanford, R. N., *The Authoritarian Personality* (W. W. Norton and Co., Inc., New York, 1969).

In our analytical work, it is the symbolic approach which admits diverse images for the feminine, including the outcast side. In Archetypal Psychology, the dark side is accepted without wanting to change it, without wanting to make it light. It goes away from heroic ideals, is not out to strengthen the ego, to make it available for the functioning in the day world, but to stay with the dark, the night. *Hillman* wrote: "We must go over the bridge and let it fall behind us, and if it will not fall then let it burn."[2] This symbolic approach of sticking to the dream image, to the dark phantasy, without promise of redemption or development, stands in contrast to the clinical approach. The imaginal, the symbolic approach in analysis, holds that not only the dark, but also the pathological, the sick are integral parts of our soul that cannot be analyzed away.

The clinical approach, on the other hand, works with the concept of the sick patient and the healthy analyst ('clinic' comes from 'bed'). This creates a power problem. In Germany where I work, e.g., most analysands and also trainees come into analysis believing that the analyst has solved most of his or her problems, or is about to do so, and they hope eventually to come out of analysis the same way! The distance-creating effect implied in this model isolates the analyst and stimulates his or her omnipotence phantasies. With admiration I heard *Toni Frey*, in the Berlin presentation of a paper, saying that he works in the Zürich Clinic because it does him good. When clinicians talk together about 'cases', or generally in supervision, they always seem to talk about the patient, but never, or very rarely, about how the analyst feels, or if so, only in the countertransference model, so that again only the patient is meant.

It has become evident that the clinical model is a heroic masculine one, working on ego strengthening, on making the sick well, making them more balanced, more in harmony, less depressed, sending them towards individuation. But the killing of the dragon and the going on the night-sea-journey (which is always only done by *male* heroes!) are masculine tasks which promise light and resurrection. The symbolic or archetypal way of doing analysis and the model of thought lying behind it is more sympathetic to the feminine spirit and to the dark. Moreover, the idea of development is a nineteenth century concept and it did not exist before that time.[3] It is an idea giving rise to a great deal of unwar-

[2] Hillman, J., *The Dream and the Underworld*, (Harper and Row, New York 1979), p. 13.

[3] Giegerich, Wolfgang, ideas he expressed in a private seminar.

ranted hope for healthier and better life, and it strengthens what is strong already.

In order to find radically different ways of feminine existence corresponding to our present needs, we must get away from the Fatherworld. *Jung* said that separation from the Fatherworld means: carrying guilt. I believe that today it is our urgent task to separate from the Fatherworld, the patriarchy, the masculine and what we habitually associate with it. I want to mention only a few Fatherworld ideas: the heroic element, the power that does not permit weakness, the healthy which does not want the pathological, the light which excludes darkness, the eternal resurrection which excludes death.[4] The heroic appears in the outer world and in dreams as the Terrible Father driving the individual to ever greater activity, while joy and fantasy disappear. *Murray Stein* has shown that the Devouring Father is responsible for a materialization of spiritual things as well as a spiritualization and psychologizing of *materia.*[5]

The masculinization of Western Civilization has progressed rapidly to ever greater destructiveness. To separate from the Devouring Father side means more than carrying guilt. It means being able to endure conflict, submit to anxieties and live in the dark. It is an expression of our masculine existence that we do not want to live with conflict and that we think we have a right to be free of problems and fear. The result is that everything becomes more flat, more dry and that everything irrational, spontaneous, all that is a little crazy, chaotic or even disorganized is excluded. The Fatherworld has us in its claws. This also causes a split between the feminine and the masculine: "Those who suppress their anxieties see in those who admit them their worst enemies", writes *Horst Eberhard Richter.*[6]

Another manifestation of the Terrible Fatherworld is the setting down of rules and principles, of using techniques. We in Germany, embedded in the clinical model, have more rules and regulations concerning training than probably most other countries. We are caught in the medical model. And ever more meetings are held where training is discussed and more and more formalized. We are far away from *Jung's* saying which I saw pinned on the blackboard of the *Los Angeles Institute:* "If you must have a training center, for heaven's sake, have it as

[4] cf. Hillman, op. cit.

[5] See Stein, Murray, "The Devouring Father" in *Fathers and Mothers,* (Spring Publications, Zürich, 1973).

[6] Richter, H.-E., *Der Gotteskomplex* (Rowohlt, Reinbek 1979), p. 156 (my translation).

disorganized as possible." Connected with this is the fact that clinicians regret that *Jung* has not written a theory of neurosis. It is hard for them to see that Archetypal Psychology, staying close to the image, conjuring up mythology, has developed a far more precise, imaginal, and a more feminine model, where pathology and neurosis are more vividly described than in any theory that could have ever been written. Writing a *Jungian* theory of neurosis would mean yielding to the Fatherworld, staying with the old, not leaving familiar grounds. Similarly, I see in the clinicians' reductive use of genetic material a conservative element, again a fear to relinquish the known and a defense against the underworld, the unknown, the dark, death.

It is often difficult to convince control-analysands that the eternal reduction to Mother and Father is a defense used by the analysand, and sometimes by the analyst, against darkness. *Hillman* wrote: "Down there the healing is a deeper wounding and the new born infant is death."[7]

I said that the patriarchal, the masculine, is conservative and afraid to leave the known, while the feminine, if not tied into patriarchal patterns, is more radical, I believe, and more ready to leave the familiar. Women are more inclined to go down to the dark goddess, where hate, rage, disorder, left-overs, remnants reign. All that conflictual material, full of opposites, can more easily be accepted by them. *Walter Jens* wrote: "Only the feminine can bring about reconciliation because it is ready to go there where it can also be destroyed."[8]

In analogy to these facts, the 'archetypal analyst' with his/her symbolic approach containing feminine elements, works more radically, more confrontatively than the clinician. This is only possible if one is willing and able to bear conflicts. Confrontation is connected with equality, with the idea that one is talking to, and working with, someone who is your equal. I have had analysands tell me later, after I had confronted them, that they felt I had taken them seriously, that I treated them as equals. *Perera* writes that confrontation without equality is imossible.[9] Working reductively, on the other hand, takes away edges and minimizes the possibility of a personal relationship between analyst and analysand. Non-confrontation is a defense against equality.

7 Hillman, op. cit., p. 82.

8 Jens, Walter, in a program bulletin to the opera *Ariadne auf Naxos* (my translation).

9 Perera, S. B., *Descent to the Goddess*, Studies in Jungian Psychology 6, (Inner City Books, Toronto, 1981), p. 80.

I have found that the use of the feminine confrontative approach, allowing for more equality and liberality, goes with a certain personality structure. And this, again, is politically significant. *Emilio Modena*, A Freudian analyst, has stated that confrontative interpretation à la *Kernberg* is linked with a radical, liberal political standpoint, while the mirroring à la *Kohut* denotes a conservative attitude. *Adorno* already told us that to be confrontative is to be anti-authoritarian. So the fear of challenging the analysand would be unnecessary if the analyst directed the confrontation emotionally toward the analysand as a subject. *Adorno* writes: "The genuine liberal character cannot keep silent, he is impulsive, not repressed. His emotionality is not blind but directed towards the other person as a subject. His love is also compassion."[10] *Adorno* helps us to understand the connection I have made between the conservative heroic masculine and the liberal, dark feminine when he writes: "The identification of the authoritarian character with strength is concomitant with rejection of everything that is 'down'."[11] The 'down' is the feminine, the dark, the pathological, that which we have to confront ourselves with, and our analysands.

For women and also for men it is of vital importance today to be initiated into the dark, the feminine. "Depth psychology has too long insisted that the hero integrate the shadow, whereas maybe the heroic is actually a product of the shadow",[12] says *Hillman*. I believe it no longer represents the needs of our clients and of our age to work on the old analytic model of getting away from the motherworld. The dragon-killing is not so important anymore – maybe it is no longer valid. For it is a one-sided, typically masculine affair. And, by the way, the fight against the mother really means fighting the feminine. It is a defensive resistance, it is hostility towards feminine nature. The wounds of analysands are healed today by a reconciliation with the motherworld, not an escape from it.

We have heard a great deal about the dark goddess lately. To descend to her would also have important political and sociological consequences for both women and men, aside from the inner ones connected with our soul. For one thing, it would take the thousand years' burden off women, who were, until recently, the sole carriers of emotions, affects like rage, hatred, the dark, and were persecuted and ridiculed

[10] Adorno, op. cit., p. 781.

[11] Adorno, op. cit., p. 762.

[12] Hillman, J., "Notes on Opportunism" in *Puer Papers* (Spring Publications, Dallas 1979), p. 159.

for it, burnt as witches in the Middle Ages or treated as hysterics in this centruy.

By working with, and accepting, the feminine as an equal, men too would again be able to endure conflicts and suffering. Misery, darkness, weakness, fear would again become what they are: part of human existence, and not pathological conditions to be analyzed away. *Richter* speaks of the illness of not being able to be ill.[13] And just as the killing of the dragon is unnecessary because heroic, the search for Unity, Wholeness, Health also belongs to the monotheistic patriarchal world which is fading. It is the archetypal approach, the polytheistic one that lets the *many*, the *different gods* come and go and live in the soul without insisting on union and unity.

An important point in this monotheism-polytheism question to me is again its political implication. Monotheism, Oneness, Wholeness, the One always imply a power relationship, not one of equality. The monotheistic in a political sense does not tolerate the many, it is fighting plurality. The polytheistic view is multiple, in the depth, darker,[14] where disintegration, fear and loss exist. The polytheistic mentality, I believe, is non-authoritarian, just as in a democracy *many* views, *many* problems can be tolerated, and *many gods* served. In a democracy, we know that many problems can never be solved which could be dealt with easily in an authoritarian state. It is the same in our soul: in keeping to polytheism, we acknowledge that many things are there, also the sick, the pathological that never get well. We may have to tell our analysands that they might always be lonely, poor, rejected, or sad, that there is something cold and resentful which will never change.

That we are not a unity, not one, and that this has political consequences has been stated by *Kirchhoff*, a German writer who interpreted *Lacan* in terms of political thinking. *Lacan* said that the small child has irrevocably lost its unity with the mother when it is no longer being totally cared for. However, when the child looks into the mirror and sees itself as a totality, it is passionately fascinated with its own image and so succumbs to the illusion that he or she is a totality. The child is caught in this illusion and true reality, which would be diversity, disunity, is lost to him or her. So the mirror stage is less a narcissistic problem than it is a political, a totalitarian one. From this, the inclination

[13] Richter, title of a lecture given in Hamburg in 1982.

[14] Hillman, cf. *The Dream and the Underworld*, op. cit.

to totalitarianism develops. This illusion of totality and unity is a life-long fatality, says *Kirchhoff*.[15]

Let me say one last word about monotheism-polytheism which I linked to the clinical and archetypal approach, respectively. I think the polytheistic one corresponds to the extraverted, the monotheistic to the introverted character structure. The clinical model, with its emphasis on personal biography, on unity, on the self, on individuation, tends toward introversion, while the polytheistic imaginal approach, with its multiplicity, is an extraverted, and as I have shown, a more social and democratic model. We know that *Jung* placed a higher value on introversion than on extraversion. It is the Judeo-Christian heritage and prejudice with its idea that the good, the valuable life is *away* from society, is a life in introversion. This caused a split between spiritual values, which are locked up in introversion and mundane affairs, leaving thus all activities of political, social and public life in the hands of anti-spiritual forces, an observation made by the German psychoanalyst, *H.-E. Richter*, who quotes the philosopher, *Max Scheler*, who calls this phenomenon: "Hochmut der Innerlichkeit" – the arrogance of introversion.[16]

Now back to my initial idea that the needs of clients coming into analysis have changed. You will have understood that I believe the symbolic or archetypal approach with its feminine, polytheistic qualities fulfills these needs better, for it takes the client as our equal, with the same darkness and pathologies the analyst suffers from.

I don't believe that we can escape loneliness or guilt, but we can pull out of old models of introversion, we can maybe sacrifice the One, go down to the diversity of the underworld and come up and live in society by going into groups, working in and with therapeutic communities, extraverting in an emotional way. We will need not less id, but very strong emotions in order to survive.

A woman Marxist philosopher, *Agnes Heller*, reinterprets revolution, seeing it not as an economic event; the revolution to come will be an emotional one, she says. And I believe the feminine will be leading it on.

[15] Kirchhoff, B. "Lacan", in *Die Zeit*, 1980, No. 49, 28. 11., p. 49.

[16] Richter, H.-E., *Zur Psychologie des Friedens* (Rowohlt, Reinbek 1982).

# The Concept of the Pathological Shadow and its Relationship to the Concept of Defense Mechanisms within a Theory of Symbolic Psychopathology

*In memory of the creative relationship between Freud and Jung*

Carlos Byington (Rio de Janeiro)

## Foreword

After many centuries of brutal and systematic cultural persecution and repression, the Western Cultural Self emerged in the 18th century with a pathological dissociation between its subjective and objective perspectives. Whenever we try to formulate concepts which involve both the subjective and the objective levels, we come across this dissociation and our reasoning becomes prone to suffer the attack of psychological defense mechanisms which for centuries were built around it.

During the period of repression, any questioning about the nature of the Soul was thought dangerous and liable to be condemned as heretical. After two centuries of liberation, sanity and insanity are still indiscriminate. Is this a necessity or, like any other symbol which has been pathologically dissociated, must Psychology, too, work through many defenses within its own concepts to attain discrimination? Or is it still impossible for our dissociated Collective Consciousness to become aware that concepts are also symbols?

Does the Unconscious have a Death Instinct which naturally destroys life, or is this concept a symbol of our culturally repressed Shadow, which has become destructive due to our puritanical and rationalistic attitude toward life?

Does this fearful Unconscious need defense mechanisms in normal development, or are the defense mechanisms conceived for normal development a symbol of how incapable we have become to deal with the Psyche openly without defense mechanisms?

Is a Psychology which conceives a Death Instinct as "acting normally" in the Psyche and defense mechanisms as indispensable for "normal development" a scientific Psychology or just another rationalization which continues the work of the Inquisition, forging theories to justify the perpetuation of repression?

## Introduction

Modern humanism is becoming more and more ecumenical and its diffusion has contributed to the breakdown of barriers of specialized fields of knowledge which then became open to general analysis and criticism. At the same time, these specialized fields have made themselves much more available to everyone. One of them, Depth Psychology, is going through a period of critical transformation due to its own overexpansion into modern culture. In just about every cultural dimension, the dynamic Unconscious is considered in one way or another, and this has overburdened concepts which were conceived originally to deal with more limited reality.

The clinical field of mental disease is being submitted to intense analysis and criticism by the social sciences and this has shown us that in General Medicine and mainly in Psychiatry, the reductive medical model inherited from the nineteenth century has to be transformed. The critiques of the cultural movement called anti-Psychiatry, for instance, were more than pertinent and represented a serious challenge to many fundamental concepts of mental disease. At present, however, we are left with little more than good intentions and an immense theoretical confusion about the fundamental nature of mental disease, which affects its being understood and treated.

The usage of psychological methods and concepts in the fields of art and education have interwoven these areas so closely that it often becomes difficult to sort out what their real activity is and whenever pathological manifestations show up, this difficulty may become a great professional and moral challenge. The psychological discovery that creativity and learning are normal functions of the mind, together with the discovery that mental disease is so culturally dependent, created a new interrelationship between Psychology, Psychiatry, Education and Art which, on the one hand, proved immensely fertile, but which turned upside down the established notions of creativity, education and mental disease and threw their basic theoretical principles into chaotic confusion. This threatens many great discoveries of the past, which become drowned by waves of theoretical questioning and confusion, and in many instances favors ignorance and quackery, as in all times of change. A frequent counterreaction to such anxiety-raising indiscrimination is to reaffirm orthodox behaviour defensively. The result is that creativity and transformation become endangered and must try to get through between the Scilla of inflation and irresponsibility and the Charybdis of reactionary orthodoxy.

If we are to face these circumstances within the theoretical postulates of Jungian Psychology, we have to question many of its basic postulates and be free to change our way of understanding them. Someone heard Jung once say that he thanked God he was not a Jungian. Perhaps he was intuiting the situation we find ourselves in today at a 'Jungian Congress'. Are we to repeat and stagnate or are we to continue individuating and therefore creating? And if we create, shall we be able to preserve Jung's great discoveries as we review many of his basic concepts?

It seems to me that the backbone of Jung's psychological theory is that psychological events are creatively subordinated to archetypal organization, which coordinates the mind towards individuation. This relationship of the part to the whole makes the former a symbol which will always be the best expression of itself because *only in that way does it express wholeness.* It is especially this essence of Jung's work which I shall try to preserve and to follow as I try to formulate concepts in symbolic developmental Psychology and Psychopathology in this paper. It has always seemed to me that the denomination of Analytical Psychology was chosen as a synonym for Psychoanalysis to mark the separation from Freud, but that it did not identify the Jungian perspective adequately. On the other hand, the denomination of Archetypal Psychology used by many Jungians, and which seems much more pertinent, lays unilateral emphasis on the Unconscious. In this sense, the name Symbolic Psychology seems more appropriate to Jungian Psychology, mainly if we apply the archetypal perspective to Ego development expressed through symbols which unite meaningfully conscious-unconscious processes inside the concept of the Self.

Our congress theme, 'The Clinical and the Symbolic', invites us to reflect initially on the meaning of concepts implicit in the title words, clinical and symbolic, and this gives us the opportunity to present a theory of psychopathology based on the archetypal, i.e., symbolic developmental perspective. Traditionally, the word clinical is related to Medicine and disease, deriving from the Latin *clinicus* and the Greek *kline*, which means bed.[1] Symbolic, on the other hand, comes from the Greek *symbolon*, meaning a part from which one infers a whole; it derives from the verb, *symballein*, literally, to throw together.[2] Every branch of culture which deals with the dimension of meaning has studied and worked through ways to operate with the concept of symbol. Jungian analysts have done so extensively,[3] pursuing a main preoccupation of Jung himself.[4] The application of the concept of the symbol to developmental Depth Psychology has led me to the concept of symbol as the structuring symbol.

## The Structuring Symbol

When we observe symbols and search for their function in the personality in relationship to the total conscious-unconscious Self from the viewpoint of developmental Depth Psychology, we become aware that every symbol which is constellated in the individual or collective psychic field functions as a structuring symbol, transforming the Psyche and Consciousness by condensing psychic energy through archetypal patterns. In this way, a mental symptom may also be seen as a symbol and thus, the concept of the structuring symbol unites the concepts of the clinical and the symbolic. The concept of the structuring symbol is complementary to Jung's concept of the transcendent function[5] and is the central concept of Symbolic Psychology, from which will derive all the ideas herein presented on mental pathology.

1 *Webster's Collegiate Dictionary*, 5th edition.

2 Idem.

3 Stein, L. (1957) "What is a Symbol Supposed to be". J. Anal. Psych, 2, 1.

4 Jung, C. G. (1921). *Psychological Types*. Coll. wks., 6; definition of Symbol, n. 51.

5 Jung, C. G. (1916). "The Transcendent Function." Coll. wks., 8, pp. 132–219.

Symbolic Psychopathology unites the clinical and the symbolic dynamically around the concept of the structuring symbol. This paper is a theoretical research to derive psychopathology from normal developmental Symbolic Psychology. In order to do so, we have to review the concepts of the Self, the Central Archetype, the Ego, the Shadow and the Persona, to establish their dynamic normal interrelationship around the structuring symbol, and only then try to formulate pathology. If we fail to do this, we shall either tend to fall again and again into the formulation of pathological concepts from some static clinical point of view which will not correspond to the symbolic perspective and will imprison the Psyche into reductive formulations, or else we shall tend to remain in archetypal amplifications, generalizations and abstractions, unable to relate them coherently to Persona, Ego and Shadow development, and the specific historicity of their here and now.

If we consider the structuring symbol as a concept which theorizes on the development of the Soul through its archetypes, and if we want to maintain the central consideration of the Soul as essential to any psychopathological theory, then the structuring symbol must be given central importance both in normal development as well as in psychopathology. This is the same as to say that in such a theoretical approach, the clinical is just as symbolic as any other aspect of the Psyche, or else the sick Soul would not be considered Soul anymore.

These considerations create a new theoretical challenge, which is to discriminate between the normal and the pathological within the symbolic dimension. If we do not do this, our conceptual gain will bring with it a great loss. A gain because we have a Soul-centered approach to health and disease, and a loss because we have no differentiated theoretical approach for dealing with mental health and disease. It will not help us much if we question traditional Psychiatry for its diagnostically reductive and therapeutic impersonal approach but fail to create a substitute theory to differentiate adequately between mental health and disease in a more human, profound and intelligent way. If we do not have a theoretical reference to deal with the Soul differently in health and disease, we shall leave it to the fate of ignorant good intentions, which cannot then offer to the sick and the suffering the discriminating efficiency of the scientific method. The concept of the structuring symbol calls attention to the fact that everything which becomes active in the psychic dimension does so by taking part in the growth process of the whole Psyche. It is this structuring function of events which makes them psychically symbolic, whether we are conscious of this or not. In this sense, there is no essential difference between symbols and signs, for signs are also symbols used in a very codified and restricted way. The signalization of symbols is a very common feature of Consciousness in general, but it occurs most frequently in patriarchal Consciousness, due to its functioning essentially through abstraction, classification, codification and legislation. The structuring symbol is herein conceptually centered inside Neumann's Ego-Central Archetype Axis.[6]

## The Self and the Central Archetype

The concept of the Self as psychic totality, which encompasses the conscious-unconscious polarity, is not used in this paper as a synonym for the Central Archetype in order to avoid conceptual indiscrimination. This is part of a general effort towards clear formulation to avoid much of the unnecessary confusion which exists in psychological writings due to the ambiguous usage of concepts. In this respect, it seems important to discriminate between formulations through paradox, which include some specific logical contradiction in order to express a deeper meaning of concepts beyond their traditional meaning, and ambiguous formulations, which unintentionally encompass more than one meaning. Ambiguous thinking is the Shadow expression of paradoxical or antinomial thinking. When the alchemists refer to their process through many paradoxical formulations as, for instance, a warring peace *(bellica pax)*, a sweet wound *(vulnus dulce)* or an agreeable evil *(suave malum)*, they are expressly formulating that the process necessarily contains these antinomies.[7] They specifically mean to convey that it is through opposition that the opposites come to unite (warring peace); that it is through constructively wounding one another that they come to enjoy the sweetness of their union (sweet wound), and that it is through exposing themselves to one another, including their 'evil' non-accepted parts, that they will finally enjoy the agree-ableness of completion (agreeable evil).

6 Neumann, E. (1970) *The Child.* New York, G.P. Putnam's Sons, 1973.

7) Gower, J. *Confessio Amantis,* 57, 11, pg. 35 in C. G. Jung (1946). *Psychology of Transference.* Coll. wks., 16, pp. 353.

Thus, paradox is logical, although it has a logic of its own, which includes opposition and identity together in the process and is therefore more developed than classic Aristotelian logic, in which identity excludes opposition. This does not make the logic of paradox unscientific; on the contrary, it creates a more complex and difficult type of thinking. Antinomial thinking has been highly considered and extensively employed in esoteric teachings and in the wisdom of ancient civilizations, such as Hindu and Chinese, as well as in the West since the Middle Ages.[8] Jung employed antinomial thinking and its benefits extensively, as, for instance, when he established the rule that, "every proposition in Psychology may be inverted to advantage".[9]

Antinomial thinking, however, is more difficult than conventional thinking and so must be employed combining concepts even more clearly expressed than in Aristotelian logic. Whenever we use antinomial thinking combining ambiguous concepts or mix it unadvisedly with traditional logical thinking, indiscrimination of speech and confusion in communication is liable to occur. Therefore, if we describe the concept of the Self as the total conscious-unconscious psyche,[10] and an archetype as an unconscious matrix which can never become wholly conscious,[11] the only way in which we can use Self and Central Archetype as synonyms is as an antinomial expression. In such a case, the paradox could be used within an even greater paradox which says that, "the Self is smaller than the smallest and greater than the greatest, the Self is the whole and the parts and therefore the Self is also the Central Archetype". This, however, can only be said in antinomial speech. In this paper, whenever I employ antinomial expressions, they will be used between quotation marks. Normally, therefore, the concept of the Self and that of the Central Archetype will not be used as synonyms. A more detailed discussion of this ambiguity will be found in Fordham's discussion of the concept of the Self.[12]

This does not mean that the subjects to be discussed will not contain indiscrimination. Although I shall try to use concepts as discriminately as possible, the subjects dealt with are in themselves symbols and,

8 Jung, C. G. (1946). *Psychology of Transference.* Coll. wks. 16, pg. 307, footnote 9.

9 Jung, C. G. (Idem, pg. 268, footnote 5.)

10 Jung, C. G. (1921) *Psychologische Typen.* Coll. wks., 6, definition of "Ich", n. 26.

11 Jung, C. G. (1917). *The Personal and the Collective Unconscious,* Coll. wks. 7.

12 Fordham, M. (1963). "The Empirical Foundation and Theories of the Self in Jung's Works." J. Anal. Psych., 8:1.

therefore, always contain an indiscriminate part, which continues to be discriminated as we deal with them.

## The Methodological Problem of the Developmental Perspective: Structuralism and Evolutionism

In formulating a theory of development of the personality from the beginning of Ego formation, and following the researches of Michael Fordham[13] and Erich Neumann,[14] the main methodological pitfall we have to avoid is the loss of the structural archetypal perspective when we adopt the evolutionistic perspective. This has happened systematically with the application of the evolutionistic concept in Anthropology and in Psychology, and has practically invalidated this application. Whenever we set an intensely structural or archetypal phenomenon such as Levy-Brühl's prelogical thinking, Tylor's animism, Frazer's magic mentality, Freud's oral phase or Backofen-Neumann's matriarchal phase exclusively in stadial succession within the evolutionistic perspective, we mutilate the structural-archetypal perspective. From then on, we can only explain manifestations of these structures appearing later on if we reduce them to a regressive manifestation. This fatal pitfall of the usage of the evolutionistic perspective is then easily used by critics to invalidate the evolutionistic perspective itself; when this happens, we lose an enormous amount of valuable data. This pitfall has led to the invalidation of the usage of the evolutionistic perspective in Anthropology[15] as well as an in Psychology.[16]

Straight-line or reductive (non-structural) evolutionism which mutilates the structural dimension of reality is so difficult to avoid that Lévi-Strauss claimed the methodological impossibility of joining evolutionism and structuralism together in the same discipline. He goes on to say that, on account of this impossibility, Ethnology and History,

13 Fordham, M. (1976). *The Self and Autism.* London. William Heinemann Medical Books.

14 Neumann, E. (1970). The Child. op. cit.

15 Boas, F. (1930). "Some Problems of Methodology in the Social Sciences" in the New Social Sciences, Chicago, 1930, pp. 84–98.

16 Hillman, J. (1973) "Anima" in Spring 1973, Zürich, Spring Publications.

although two parts of the same whole, must remain separated, like the two faces of the God Janus.[17]

It seems, however, that the symbolic perspective, used in Jungian Psychology methodologically to express the union of polarities, can also be used to unite and operate meaningfully the evolutionistic and the structural-archetypal perspectives without reducing one into the other. And no other symbol can help us to illustrate this better than that of the Roman god Janus. His name is linked with the word 'door' (Latin *janua*). Among many of his attributes is that of the watcher. For this reason, his image was carved on doors looking both inwards and outwards, so that he could exercise his protection thoroughly.[18] So the same example which was used by Lévi-Strauss to operate this polarity separately can also be used to operate it meaningfully together. In the same body, we have two heads, or in the same head, two faces. The psychological function of the Symbol is to unite polarities and discriminate them into Consciousness. It is this symbolic function so well represented by the god Janus that can be used to unite History and Ethnology or Evolutionism and Structuralism *methodologically*. Indeed, we can say that if there is an initiation into Symbolic Psychology, its threshold is the concept of the Symbol, which opens the door to the reality of the Soul. The Symbol of the god Janus expresses the possibility of combining in the same head not only opposite points of view, but even opposite ways of seeing reality, i.e., opposite ways of observing and becoming conscious of the world. This uniting doublefaced head is the divine, mythological or, in our case, symbolic dimension. The unconscious side of the structuring symbol leads to the structural-archetypal dimension and the conscious side leads to the Ego, Persona and Shadow dimension (Diagram 2).

## The Four Archetypal Cycles of Ego Development

The Ego is the end result of the actualization of the Central Archetype.[19] This actualization of the Central Archetype is mediated by other archetypes, such as, for instance, the Hero Archetype, but by all

[17] Lévi-Strauss, C. (1949) "Historia e Etnologia" in *Antropologia Estrutural,* Rio de Janeiro, Tempo Brasileiro, 1975, pg. 13–44.

[18] Frazer, J. *The Golden Bough*, Book 1, *The Magic Art* 11:383. London, Macmillan, 1911.

[19] Whitmont, E. (1969). *The Symbolic Quest.* Princeton, New Jersey, Princeton Univ. Press., 1978, pg. 236.

THE DEVELOPMENTAL STRUCTURE OF THE INDIVIDUAL SELF

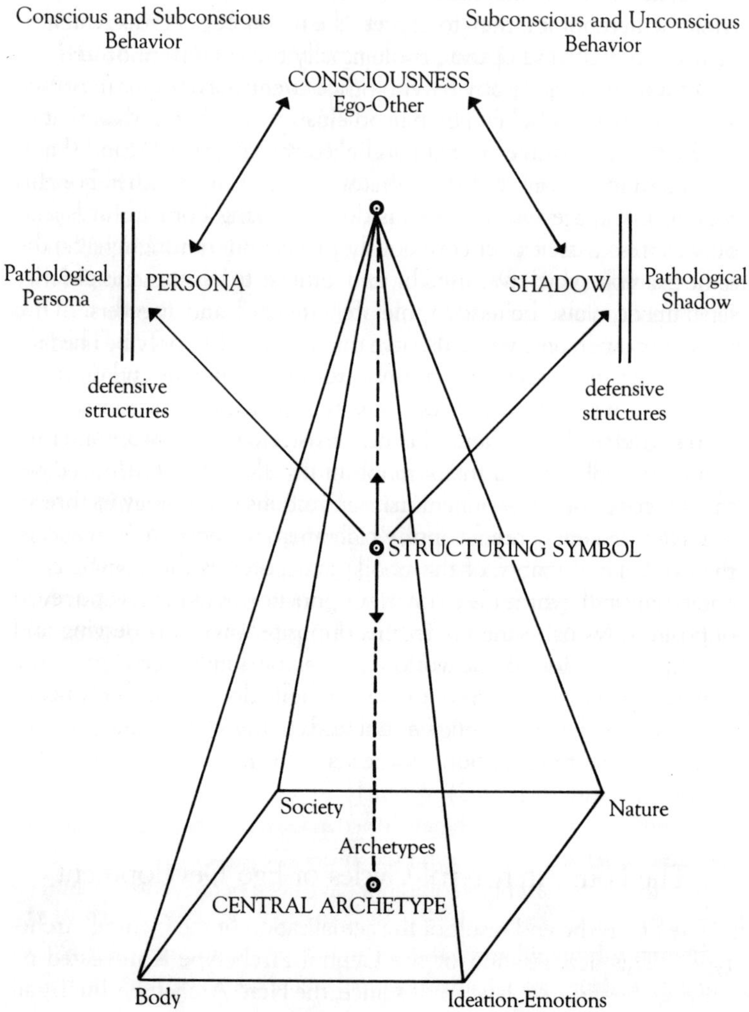


Diagram 2 – Modified from Byington, C. "The Symbolic Development of the Personality". Rev. Junguiana, Revista da Sociedade Brasileira de Psicologia Analitica, I:16, 1983. Complementary to Diagram 1.

other archetypes as well. The important thing to realize is that no archetypal action can possibly exist without Ego involvement, and vice-versa. To favor unilaterally Ego activity or archetypal activity in Symbolic Psychology, therefore, reveals a psychological bias which is incompatible with the phenomenological attitude of scientific methodology. We know that many psychological events express more of the conscious aspect of symbols, while others express more of their archetypal side, but this does not allow the psychologist to conclude that such an event or symbol is only conscious or egoic and the other only archetypal. On the contrary, because, when a symbol or psychological event expresses itself more consciously, the difficulty and the challenge to the psychologist is to search for, and understand the function of the veiled unconscious archetypal pole of the symbol, and vice-versa. The concept of a personal and collective unconscious can only be used in this relative way. The personal unconscious expresses symbols in which the conscious polarity is relatively more exuberant than that of the Collective Unconscious. In this sense, it seems a psychological misunderstanding to say that symbols of the Collective Unconscious have no conscious component. Is there, for instance, anything more personal than one's parents or one's identity, and yet is there anything more archetypal than those symbols? Is it possible to dream about something with which our conscious function has no relationship whatsoever? When someone dreams about an 'unknown' dragon, for instance, we can say that this is a very archetypal symbol from the Collective Unconscious of which we were not conscious before. However, if we examine this situation carefully, we realize that the categories of size (gigantic stature), of ferocity (potential danger), and of animality (extraordinary animal) through which we perceive and remember the dragon, are categories which developed in Consciousness by means of countless other structuring symbols. Indeed, without these conscious aspects, the dragon symbol could not have been perceived at all, much less remembered afterwards.[20]

Theoretically, we all know that an archetype cannot express itself by definition except through an archetypal image, i.e., a symbol which has some conscious part. In practice, however, we frequently see symbols interpreted exclusively from their archetypal aspects, as if they could exist without Consciousness and the Ego. Not only are consciousness and the Ego always somehow present in symbols, but the Ego always

[20] Williams, M. (1963). "The Indivisibility of the Personal and the Collective Unconscious", J. Anal. Psych., 8:1.

functions through some archetypal pattern. To say that, in the course of life, the Ego first separates from the Self, then finally relates to the Self is not only an oversimplification, but a dangerous one, for two reasons. First, because it falls head first into reductive evolutionism, and second, because it does not explain archetypally how the Ego arrives at such positions and functions in them.

As mentioned above, all symbols are archetypal and modify Consciousness as structuring symbols. There are archetypes which coordinate Ego development and Ego functioning throughout life, forming not phases but cycles which begin in stadial succesion, but from then on, continue to structure the Ego side by side (Diagram 1). These are the Great Mother Archetype, which coordinates the matriarchal cycle of Ego development, the Father Archetype, which coordinates the patriarchal cycle, the Anima-Animus-Coniunctio Cycle, which coordinates the third cycle, and the Central Archetype, which directly coordinates the Cosmic Cycle of Consciousness and Ego development. The Central Archetype and its quaternary structure must first begin its actualization through the matriarchal cycle, where Consciousness and the Ego function in a binary pattern, then through the patriarchal pattern, where they function in a ternary pattern. Only in the Anima-Animus cycle will Consciousness and the Ego be able to function in the quaternary pattern, which, in turn, will allow them to function in the unitary pattern of the Cosmic Cycle. In this sense, Maria Prophetissa's saying about the alchemical process that, “the one becomes two, the two becomes three, the three becomes four which is again one”, can also be applied to the development of the personality, of Ego and of Consciousness.

In this symbolic perspective, we employ evolutionism in the concept of the successive stadial appearance of the four archetypal cycles, and in recognizing their successive dominance during lifetime, but we do not mutilate the structural perspective by reducing it to a specific life stage. As can be seen in Diagram 1, each of the four archetypal patterns, once constellated, lasts throughout life. As adults, for instance, we continue working through symbols of the matriarchal cycle whenever we care for our children, our body, our home and… our planet. The second phase of our matriarchal cycle is just as important as the first. What we do for our children and for Mother Earth as adults is as important for the structuring of our Consciousness through the Great Mother Archetype as what we received from our parents and our planet in the beginning of life. We should not forget that life one day

THE DEVELOPMENTAL STRUCTURE OF THE PERSONALITY
THE FOUR ARCHETYPAL CYCLES
THE FOUR EGO-PERSONA-SHADOW PATTERNS

Second Phase of Cycles (polarity inversion)
Ego Shadow and Persona
continue developing actively
working through structuring symbols
in each archetypal pattern

First Phase of Cycles
Ego Shadow and Persona
Develop through Structuring symbols
in each archetypal pattern

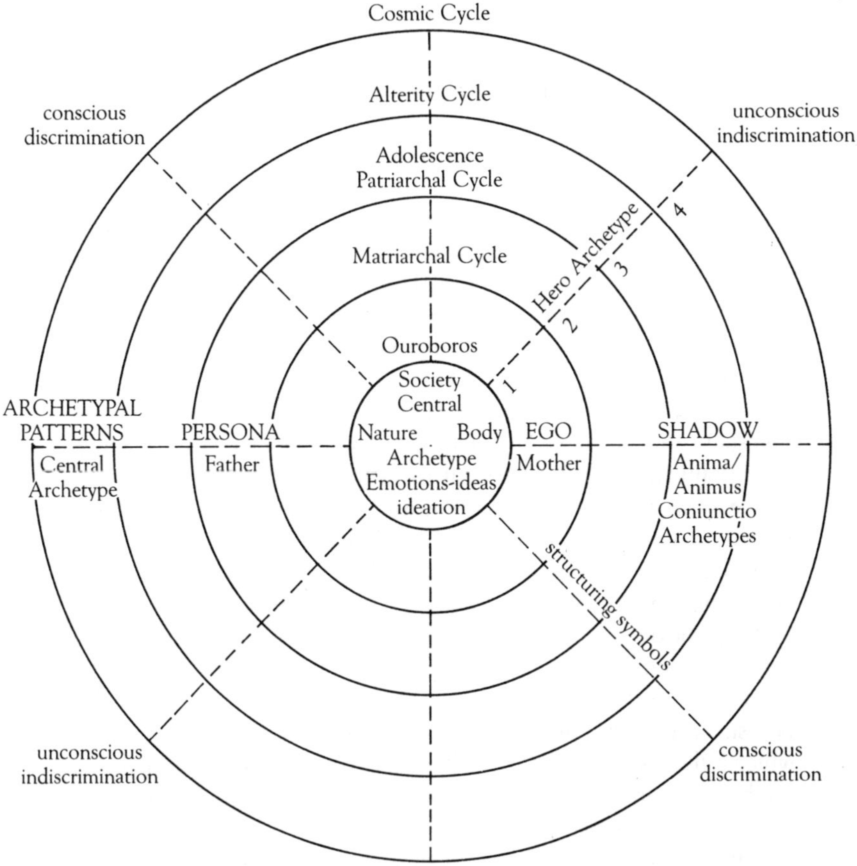


The four archetypal cycles begin in stadial succession but function side by side throughout life. Their psychological dominance also occurs in stadial succession but this does not prevent each dynamism becoming again dominant whenever necessary.

Diagram 1 – Modified from Byington, C. "The Symbolic Development of the Personality". Rev. Junguiana, Revista da Sociedade Brasileira de Psicologia Analitica, I: pg 12. Complementary to Diagram 2.

became possible on Earth, and from this life, our species originates. However, thousands of years had to pass while human Consciousness underwent enormous differentiation from nature, expressed through the adoration of the great fertility goddesses, until one day human Consciousness integrated this structuring symbol and the first great cultural revolution began through planting. It is important to understand these structuring symbols normally functioning through matriarchal dynamism rather than in terms of regressive behavior. Today's ecological symbols, for instance, should be discriminated as a matter of survival of our species. Their structuring potential in the differentiating process of matriarchal Consciousness is of great urgency since it will be an acquisition of Collective Consciousness which cannot possibly be understood in terms of regression. When we associate evolutionism and structuralism in personality development, we are able to conceive the Psyche through archetypal patterns which act simultaneously after their stadial successive appearance. Diagrams 1 and 2 together form a spiral, a mandala which according to Jung well illustrates psychic development as it interrelates the image of permanent growth with an unchanging permanent center.[21] The spiral composed byDiagram 1 and 2 should be perceived as a living spiral where archetypal dominance in one stage not only does not exclude other archetypal patterns which were dominant before, but needs them to function properly.

The application of the evolutionistic and structural perspective to normal and psychopathological phenomena in Symbolic Psychology thus becomes a common procedure. The father or mother imago appearing in a dream, for instance, can be approached either to evaluate the development of our Ego as to its acquired 'mothering' and 'fathering' capacity or to study the meaning of the constellation of the archetype in that particular moment. It is this combination of evolutionism and structuralism, of Ego development and archetypal reality, which is the essense of Symbolic Psychology and makes the structuring symbol its central concept. This concept expresses through the structuring capacity of every symbol in the here and now, the permanent structural reality of the archetype, together with the unique historical dynamism of its constellation.

In such a Symbolic Psychology, we may conceive the Neumann-Bachofen stadial succession of Ego development through a matriarchal and patriarchal stage and even become conscious of its analogy

[21] Jung, C. G. (1950) "Concerning Mandala Symbolism", Coll. wks. 9, part. I, pg. 648.

with Melanie Klein's pre-Oedipal dualistic child-breast stage (matriarchal) and Freud's Oedipal triangular stage (patriarchal) without losing the structural or archetypal perspective. This can be achieved if we do not simply dismiss each structure or archetype when the succeeding stage becomes dominant but, on the contrary, admit and search for its structuring function throughout the whole process. When we do this, we discover that the four main archetypes, Mother, Father, Anima-Animus and Central Archetype have a typical structuring-developmental life cycle with two phases, which become first activated in successive stages, but then last throughout life, acting simultaneously side by side (Diagram 1). In the first phase of every cycle, the Ego is structured through the cycle's pattern and in the second phase it will participate actively in the structuring function as it continues to be structured. Typical examples are the 'child-breast' relationship (matriarchal cycle), which the parents will go through again with their newly born in the second phase of their own matriarchal cycle. Another typical example is the further working through of the Oedipal triangle from the parental position in the second phase of the patriarchal cycle. As the process advances, more parts of the Ego tend to function in the second phase of the archetypal cycles. However, this fact has to be considered dynamically and in no way can it be used to equate the first phase of the cycle with the first half of life. Many parts of the Ego already in the first half of life function in the second phase of the archetypal cycle and parts of the Ego still quite undeveloped very late in life may begin functioning in the first half of the archetypal cycle.

One of the major contributions that this evolutionistic-structural perspective brings to Jungian Psychology is to realize the importance of the interrelationship of archetypal patterns during personality development. The archetypal psychodynamics of adolescence, for instance, is centered on the conflicting interrelationship of the Anima-Animus-Coniunctio Cycle with the parental cycles. With this perspective, we can see that, although this third cycle will become really dominant in what Jung described as the Process of Individuation in the second half of life, it already begins in childhood with the roots of individuality. The great problem inherent in symbols of the Anima-Animus-Coniunctio pattern is not only their constellation but the urge to struggle against matriarchal and patriarchal dominance. Much of what has been attributed to the 'negative Animus' in women or to 'Anima possession' in men has yet little to do with these archetypes and is the expression of patriarchal and matriarchal dynamisms. It is practically impossible to develop archetypal and, above all, symbolic psychopathology if we do not first discriminate the intense indiscrimination now present between the Great Mother Archetype and the Anima in man's Psychology and between the Father Archetype and the Animus in woman's Psychology, particularly in regard to the natural conflicting interrelationship between these archetypes.

In this respect, what Jung saw as a differentiation between the individual and the collective during the Process of Individuation can also be seen as the differentiation of the Anima-Animus-Coniunctio pattern from the patriarchal pattern, which can occur in Individual as well as in Collective Psychology. If we fail to see this, we shall naturally tend to limit Archetypal Psychology to the individual and also tend to identify collective values with something static, from which we should best free ourselves. Such an attitude prevents us from applying symbolic developmental Psychology to Politics, Sociology, Ethnology and History, and from subordinating them conceptually to Symbolic Anthropology.[22] The Anima-Animus-Coniunctio pattern is being differentiated in modern society on the individual as well as the collective level. We cannot understand archetypally anything at all of the change in the political map of the world from the 19th to the 20th century if we do not admit that society can also develop the Anima-Animus-Coniunctio pattern of Consciousness. The social quest, which is archetypally equivalent to the individual quest described by Jung in the Individuation Process, is already exuberantly expressed in the Christian Myth. The social quest for the democratic socialist state representing secular power as an expression of Christian humanism, appears in countless historical manifestations as, for instance, in the Symbol of the Round Table, which inspired the dialectical relationship of knights to their king during the transition from feudalism in France and England in the beginnings of the modern idea of State and Nation.

The evolutionistic-structural symbolic pattern of development is most useful for a symbolic *Weltanschauung* because it can be employed to understand the development of Individual as well as of Collective Consciousness. This, in turn, can be used to understand the Pathological Shadow of the Individual as well as of the Cultural Self. In this

[22] Byington, C. (1983) "Uma Teoria Simbolica da Historia". O Mito Cristao como Principal Simbolo Estruturante do Padrao de Alteridade na Cultura Ocidental". (A Symbolic Theory of History. The Christian Myth as the main Structuring Symbol of the Alterity Pattern in Western Culture.) Junguiana. Rev. Soc. Brasil. Psic. Anal. 1:1, pgs. 120–177.

sense, we can understand that 'modern man is in search of a Soul' in the same way as modern society also is. The social quest for democratic socialism which dominates modern history follows the same pattern of transformation of Collective Consciousness within the Social Self as we find in Jung's theoretical formulation of the Individuation Process. In this sense, the dialectical relationship of the Ego to the Central Archetype, which is characteristic of this pattern of Consciousness, is equivalent to the social-democratic relationship of individual and government in the development of the Cultural Self. This search for wholeness, which involves primarily facing the Shadow, is valid for Society as well as for the Individual; inspiring their common quest is the Anima-Animus-Coniunctio archetypal pattern and its archetypal conflict with the parental cycles of Consciousness. Let us now review the four archetypal cycles of symbolic evolutionistic-structural development of Consciousness.[23]

In the matriarchal cycle of personality development, the Ego and Consciousness tend to function in a binary pattern, due to the intimate and close relationship of Consciousness to the Unconscious. Matriarchal dynamism functions according to the fertility principle of sensuous necessity and desire inherent to the Great Mother Archetype and the Ego-Other polarity tends to function with the 'negative' Other or 'positive' Other in separate situations. This is not due to a split in the personality, since in matriarchal dynamism there exists no such discrimination to bring about a coherent relationship of opposites which could then be split, but rather due to the 'island' type of Consciousness of matriarchal dynamism which propitiates binary dynamism. The separation, for instance, of the Ego-bad breast relationship from the Ego-good breast relationship, and good mother from bad mother, is quite natural and does not need any split or defense to establish it. The difficulty in matriarchal dynamism is to associate, according to traditional logic, polarities which have already been discriminated, rather than to separate them.

In patriarchal dynamism, the Ego and Consciousness function in a ternary pattern because the deep separation of Consciousness from the Unconscious acquired through the dogmatic, delimiting, organizing, classifying, and hierarchic functioning of patriarchal dynamism tends to establish a coherent relationship of the Ego with polari-

[23] Byington, C. (1983). "O Desenvolvimento Simbolico da Personalidade. Os Quatro Ciclos Arquetipicos". (The Symbolic Development of the Personality. The Four Archetypal Cycles.) Junguiana, Rev. Soc. Bras, Psic. Anal. 1:1, pgs. 8–63.

ties. The Ego relates to one pole in one way and *simultaneously* learns to relate to the other pole also in a codified way. This essentially delimiting and organizing feature of the Father Archetype becomes frequently repressive; its dogmatically established classifications propitiate its orientation according to the principle of causality. The concepts of Psychoanalysis are mostly formulated inside patriarchal dynamism and, therefore, the relationship of Consciousness to the Unconscious is basically explained by repression. This tendency is increased due to the indiscrimination of pathology and normality in the medical psychological model, which has historically derived normal Psychology from pathological mental states. This limitation of Psychoanalysis, which intensely contaminated Analytical Psychology with the common usage of concepts such as projection to refer to normal and pathological dynamisms, is one of the main theoretical difficulties we meet in formulating concepts in symbolic developmental psychopathology.

The Oedipus Complex, which is the core of psychoanalytical theory, is a very important structuring symbol of patriarchal dynamism and well illustrates its ternary pattern. The Oedipus Complex structures the personality through a triangular codified relationship in which mother is defined not only by what she must be, but also by what she must *not* be, which, in turn, is dogmatically associated with what father must and must not be.

Matriarchal and patriarchal dynamisms are characterized by asymmetry in the Ego-Other relationship and between the opposites in general. The Ego always relates either in a privileged or unprivileged position to the Other and we can therefore say that matriarchal and patriarchal dynamisms are always somehow narcissistic.

The Anima-Animus-Coniunctio pattern of Consciousness is quaternary because in it the Ego can relate symmetrically to the polarities of the Other and associate them with its own polarities. I call it the Otherness or Alterity Cycle (from *alter,* which means 'other' in Latin) because in it, the Ego attains the prime of individuality which is simultaneous to the acquisition of the capacity to realize fully what *otherness* is. In this pattern of Consciousness, an analyst can identify someone's Shadow, for instance, but also realize how it is related to his own. This can only be achieved when the Ego transcends narcissism and becomes able to give up its power position sufficiently to relate in equal terms with the Other. When it does so, the Ego *simultaneously* acquires the capacity to realize that itself and the Other are equally important inside the whole process and, indeed, that the relationship of the Ego and the Other is the main expression of the activity of the whole. The finality of psychological development is not merely Consciousness, but quaternary Consciousness, which means Consciousness of the meaningful interrelationship of the Ego and the Other and their respective polarities as the necessary expression of wholeness, and which is the indispensable foundation of the unitary pattern of Cosmic Consciousness. Without the capacity to function in the quaternary pattern, Consciousness is not able to function in the unitary cosmic pattern, and its attempts to experience totality directly will sometimes tend to lead it into indiscrimination with intense Unconsciousness, bringing dangerous consequences to the personality.

Therefore, in the Anima-Animus-Coniunctio cycle, the Ego and Consciousness acquire the capacity to relate dialectically and creatively with the Other inside wholeness. This is the acquisition of the capacity of the full symbolic function by the Ego when it apprehends the relationship of the part to the whole which encompasses itself. Only in this pattern of Consciousness can the Ego experience the Self as encompassing the Ego-Other polarity in a meaningful relationship. This is the equivalent of saying that only in this pattern of Consciousness can the Ego conceive and deal with the principle of synchronicity. To formulate this differently and make it more clear, we can say that synchronicity is not exactly an event and not only a principle to explain reality, but rather an archetypal pattern through which the Psyche and Consciousness may function in certain situations. The capacity to become aware of synchronicity phenomena comes from the Anima-Animus-Coniunctio structuring pattern of Consciousness, which can be seen as a principle to explain reality beyond causality.

In this sense, synchronicity should not exclude causality, but rather function side by side with it in such a way as to understand reality. It does not seem correct to say that the causality principle is the main principle at the core and root of modern science. The great basic discoveries of modern science were made by individuals who were capable of operating the synchronicity principle and who then employed also the causality principle to check, analyse or induce that perception which had entered their Consciousness through synchronicity. Causality normally tends either to close the field of Consciousness in a coherent whole or to expand Consciousness and apprehend the new fact of knowledge by subordinating it to the old. Synchronicity, on the other hand, allows the mind to be open to the new, which can freely interact with the old and transform Consciousness as a necessity of the whole. Causality is the window of certainty and synchronicity, of mystery. The great advantage of the principle of synchronicity over the principle of causality is that it can contribute directly to symbolic knowledge because it apprehends the function of the Ego and of the Other simultaneously and this allows Consciousness to apprehend much faster the interaction of the Ego and the Other as an expression of the Self. This makes synchronicity the ideal pattern of Consciousness to apprehend the function of the Self through the meaningful interaction of polarities. The statement that synchronicity is not simply an extraordinary event but also a structuring pattern of Consciousness may be easily tested by interpreting reality synchronistically to someone whose mind functions predominantly according to the patriarchal pattern. This person will not understand anything at all and will try to force reductive explanations through the causality principle. Someone else who has developed the alterity pattern of Consciousness, however, can apprehend this special understanding of reality quite easily. In order to further understand the patterns of Consciousness, it is important to realize that the Ego functioning inside the matriarchal pattern will also tend to accept easily synchronistic phenomena. In this case, however, the Ego will interpret them magically, i.e., applying the principle of causality to an indiscriminated relationship of polarities.

Many Jungians and orientalists do not render the Ego much importance because they identify the Ego with a certain stage of development to be transcended, and fail to see its archetypal structure. The Individuation Process as described by Jung in the second half of life, and the search for Buddhahood, Nirvana, Zen or Tao, consist in transcending the Ego in the matriarchal and patriarchal dynamisms and, in the case of the oriental schools, very frequently in transcending also the Ego in the Anima-Animus dynamism, in order to attain Cosmic Consciousness. If we do not reason according to an archetypal-structural developmental theory of Consciousness, we tend to identify the Ego with one or more stages and treat it in general not as a structure *(Sein)*, but as a state *(Seiende)* to be transcended.

The intent to become a human being beyond the Ego is an inflation or an indiscrimination of the psychological phenomenology of what the concept of the Ego expresses. The Ego is inherent to the structural expression of the Central Archetype and therefore must change and be transcended according to each archetypal pattern of Consciousness, but cannot be transcended in its Egoness. In this sense, when

Buddhism preaches giving up all attachment and 'I' claims, and Christianity teaches loving one's neighbor as oneself, they are unconsciously urging believers to transcend the narcissism of the Ego inherent to the matriarchal and patriarchal patterns of development and attain the Ego of the Anima-Animus pattern where the 'I' and the Other relate in dialectical polarities. Not fully realizing the archetypal patterns of Ego transformation may lead us to affirm erroneously that the Ego structure is to be transcended in search of an Egoless state.

The Cosmic Cycle of Consciousness is directly coordinated by the Central Archetype. Like the other three cycles, it also starts in childhood and generally becomes dominant only late in life. Its pattern is to deal with wholeness directly beyond polarities. Hinduism, Jainism, Buddhism and Taoism frequently refer to the extinction of craving not only as going 'beyond the Ego', but also beyond all polarities. Archetypally this would mean not only going beyond the parental cycles, but also going beyond the Anima-Animus-Coniunctio Cycle. The phenomenology of this psychic state shows that it also has a pattern of Consciousness and of Ego. This pattern of Consciousness begins to be formed also through an archetypal cycle activated already in childhood. This cycle coordinates those experiences of totality with the most varied structuring symbols through which, ever since childhood, we experience the eternal and the infinite around us. These are summing up or summarizing experiences of the whole process which will eventually tend to become dominant. They form the fourth or Cosmic Cycle of the development of Ego and Consciousness. Again, due to identification of the Ego concept with the preceding states, the cosmic pattern of Consciousness has been repeatedly identified with an Egoless state. However, even though polarities are transcended, the Ego still exists here as the center of Consciousness. Yet, it is not an Ego which cares to recognize itself as different from the Other. The cosmic pattern of Consciousness has an Ego which is so open and intimate with the Central Archetype that most of its attention flows guided by the structuring symbol of an all-encompassing totality, regardless of how it expresses itself. Whatever name we choose, it is very important to realize that, in order to function in this state of Consciousness, the Psyche needs to function well in the other three or else intense indiscrimination of the Ego by the Central Archetype may occur.

## The Ego as Part of the Self

Three factors have contributed greatly to a current underrating of the Ego, which must be reassessed in Jungian Psychology.

The first factor is the ambiguous usage of the concept of the Self as synonymous with that of the Central Archetype referred to above. On the one hand, Jung clearly defined the Self as the sum total of conscious and unconscious processes[10], but on the other hand, he used the concept of the Self frequently as synonymous with the Central Archetype[11]. This has led Jungian analysts naturally to overvalue the archetypal aspect of the Self in detriment of its Ego aspect. The very denomination Ego-Self Axis chosen by Neumann, for instance, naturally tends to set the Ego as a complementary polarity to the Self and, therefore, logically excluded from it.

The second factor is the pitfall of the reductive usage of the evolutionistic concept, also already referred to, whose main victim in Psychology has been the Ego concept. As the Ego is, perhaps, the most intimate concept to the psychologist engaged in research, its changing nature is exposed more than that of any other psychic phenomenon. This has led many to overlook the fact that, like all other psychic phenomena which change like Proteus and, also like Proteus, have a divine, archetypal essence, the Ego, too, in spite of its perennial transformation, has an archetypal root which is none other than the Central Archetype itself. *Consciousness and the Ego are Structures.* I have not yet seen a school of developmental Psychology which evades the evolutionistic pitfall and considers carefully the structural aspect of the Ego. Psychoanalysis has fallen into this pitfall by imprisoning archetypal stages within libidinal stages which, once lived through, can only be reexperienced through the reducing concept of regression. Analytical Psychology has done likewise, situating the Process of Individuation mostly in the second half of life and Ego development as a problem of the first half of life. This attitude has contributed to separating Ego from Archetype during the developmental process. Even researchers who have conceived the archetypal origins of the Ego have not yet adequately recognized the archetypal patterns of the Ego throughout life.

The third factor is the notion that the Ego is not only linked to youth and immaturity (a notion which is already present in the second factor), but that the aim of psychic development is the extinction of the Ego and even of all Consciousness (Nirvana). This factor has been introduced into Psychology mainly from religious doctrines or philosophical theories. As shown above, this factor arises from the identification of the Ego with one of its archetypal patterns of development which then leads to the erroneous conclusion that, to attain the following pattern, instead of undergoing sacrifice and transformation, the Ego as such has to be transcended.

These three factors have to be made conscious and worked through if we are to evaluate correctly the function of the Ego structure in the Psyche, on which depends not only any archetypal theory of Ego, Persona, and Shadow formation, but also, consequently, the concept of the pathological Shadow, as well as the theoretical foundations of symbolic or archetypal psychopathology.

The Central Archetype may be expressed through many symbols of totality which do not necessarily express the actual global state of Consciousness and the Ego and which may even express compensatory factors situated opposite to the dominant direction of the Individual Self at that particular moment. Someone with an exhausted Ego, on the point of a psychological breakdown, may dream of a mandala, which expresses a compensatory reaction in order to maintain psychic balance. A patient with severe chronic schizophrenia and final dementia may have hallucinations with symbols of totality[24]. Children at an early age may begin to draw mandalas. At many instances during the long and complex psychological development of the personality, symbols of totality may appear in dreams, phantasies or visions showing the prospective nature of the process towards a goal. To consider these symbols of totality as symbols of the Self, which by definition encompasses the conscious and unconscious process of the total personality, creates an enormous confusion, not only to the whole symbolic developmental theory of the personality, but also to the importance of Ego development within the development of the total personality. All symbols of the Central Archetype obviously express potential characteristics of the Self, but this is very different from saying that they are already symbols of the Self at that particular moment in which they appear.

When we consider symbols of the Central Archetype always as symbols of the Self, we are liable to create inflation and alienation both for analysts and for analysands. I remember a training colleague who was very proud of himself because he frequently dreamt about the number four. Another began adopting an enlightened Persona with peculiar

[24] Perry, J. W. (1974). *The Far Side of Madness.* Englewood Cliffs, New Jersey, Prentice Hall, Inc.

attitudes, faces and tones of voice whenever he dreamt of a symbol of totality. They were trying to express the identity of the Central Archetype and Self, which they had learned was supposed to exist. Were these symbols not only of the Central Archetype but also of the Self, these colleagues would not have had to adopt an enlightened Persona. Their Ego would naturally have expressed it.

Symbols which express the Self appear during the development of the personality and bring into Consciousness the state of the whole personality at that particular moment. A woman who had lost her mother in childhood and was not allowed to live this loss because her family was taught not to show emotions, formed an intense pathological Shadow containing the symbol of the abandoned child. During analysis, as her defenses began to allow her to confront her Shadow, she began to dream of an immense deserted Earth inhabited by a lonely little girl.

Discriminating when symbols are the expression of the Central Archetype but not of the Self is often difficult. Under certain circumstances, a symbol of totality expresses apparently only the Central Archetype and not the Self, but in reality it also expresses the Self. Let us imagine the situation of a person with a very conflicted Ego who is about to give up his search for integrity because he feels threatened by a psychological breakdown. Watching a sunrise, he has a very moving experience, which stimulates him so much that he feels strong enough again to keep on. Given such a divided personality, the symbol of totality (the sunrise) apparently expressed only the Central Archetype and could not express his divided Self, but in reality that symbol of the Central Archetype had the power to unite the whole personality and, at the moment it was expressed, became also a symbol of the Self.

Symbols of totality which also express the Self, then, according to this theoretical perspective, must express the total conscious-unconscious situation and particularly the Ego-Central Archetype relationship. Therefore, it cannot be said that a symbol of totality expresses the Self if we do not know how Consciousness and the Ego relate to it. The progressive actualization of the Central Archetype into Consciousness and the Ego, which converges to quaternary and finally unitary Consciousness, marks the way of the Self towards the completion of the *opus individuationis*, or enlightenment. The state of Consciousness and the Ego is not only inseparable from this process, but also indispensable to estimate the various stages it goes through.

## Ego Formation, a Methodological Problem

Persona, Ego and Shadow are concepts which express the actualizing function of the Central Archetype. Persona and Shadow are collateral structures of Ego formation. The perspective from which we describe Ego formation affects fundamentally any psychological theory. Therefore, any description of Ego formation must be accompanied by a methodological position towards that which the Psyche is considered to be.

The methodological question which confronts us in Ego formation here is not where the Ego comes from, for in this respect our position is quite clear. The Ego develops through symbols coordinated by the Central Archetype, which is the central matrix of the unconscious process. The methodological question in Ego formation is what the unconscious process is and where its boundaries are. The traditional psychological tendency has been to situate the Psyche inside the body, particularly the head, and to consider the rest of the body and the world outside as non-psychic. This perspective originates from the identification of the Psyche with Consciousness and the Ego. We know from the study of Depth Psychology how limited this position is.

The greatest pitfall of this perspective is the psyche-matter dichotomy which, once entered methodologically, becomes a labyrinth, into which Depth Psychology followed Western scientific tradition and lost its way almost one century ago. The concept of projection applied to normal development was a great trap, a defense mechanism, which enchanted the Ego of the psychologist with the promise of the secret of discrimination, but, in reality, maintained it erred inside the labyrinth of 'objectivity' where hides the Minotaur, i. e., the monstrous dissociation of the Western Cultural Self into its subjective and objective polarities.

The Psyche is here considered a differentiation of the world and, therefore, inseparable from it in its unconscious roots. There are many types of energy in the world, psychic energy being here considered as one of them. This methodological position cannot yet be demonstrated because we still know very little about the physical properties of psychic energy and how this energy interrelates with the other types of energy and physical properties of the world around us. This hypothesis, however, seems the best one on the present frontier of modern Psychology so significantly enlarged by Jung's contributions to the knowledge of the nature of unconscious processes. To invalidate it today seems more difficult than to affirm it.

If we start from the premise that the unconscious Psyche and the world are theoretically inseparable and, therefore, that the human psychic differentiation from the world is a characteristic only of the Ego and Consciousness, then the usage of the concepts of projection and projective identification are unsuitable to explain Ego formation in symbolic developmental Psychology. Where there are still no boundaries, much less an inside and an outside, how can something be projected onto something else? Here lies the basic conceptual discrimination we want to propose in this paper in order to differentiate normal symbolic developmental Psychology from Symbolic Psychopathology. Jung partly differentiates these concepts when he differentiates unconscious identity or archaic identification from projection.[25]

Symbolic Psychology explains Ego formation through symbolic development. Every structuring symbol condenses conscious and unconscious psychic energy. Jung called this the constellation of a Symbol. When there is not yet an Ego, the child-primary environment[26] is the first symbolic constellation from which the Ego and the Other begin to deintegrate. It is most important to realize in symbolic development that the Ego deintegrates together with the Other and that the acquisition of the identity of the 'I' is the same process as, and is inseparable from, the acquisition of the identity of the Other. Not only the Ego, but also the Other, forms the complex which dynamically occupies the center of Consciousness. There cannot possibly exist Ego-consciousness without Consciousness of the Other, and vice versa. Each of the four archetypal patterns described above can be identified through a different pattern of relationship between the Ego and the Other. Theoretically, from this perspective, there exists no conscious activity which does not include the relationship of the Ego and the Other.

The structuring symbol organizes the personality and Consciousness by forming and enlarging at the same time the identity of the Ego and of the Other. Therefore, the structuring symbol contains the I-Thou reality in a very indiscriminated way which becomes increasingly discriminated as it organizes the personality and Consciousness. The structuring symbol contains a fusion of subjectivity and objectivity

[25] Jung, C. G. (1920). Psychological Types. Coll. wks. 6, definition of 'Projection', n. 48.
[26] Neumann, E. (1970). The Child. New York, G. P. Putnam's Sons, 1973.

which will be transformed into knowledge of the Other (objective knowledge) and of the Ego (subjective knowledge) through discrimination. The study of the structuring psychic process will bring symbolic knowledge, which includes subjective knowledge, objective knowledge and also knowledge of how this particular symbol is functioning inside the Self. Symbolic knowledge is, therefore, made of the meaning of symbols. Symbolic knowledge or symbolic science is a higher form of science than merely objective science, for it includes the knowledge of the subject and of the object. We must realize that objective knowledge, whether we are conscious of it or not, is brought about by the the Soul, by the Psyche, through its structuring symbols, i. e., by symbolic knowledge.

## Normal Symbolic Development and Defense Mechanisms

When the Ego is already partially formed, the constellation of any new structuring symbol in the developmental process brings to Consciousness a degree of indiscrimination proportional to the psychic energy contained in the symbol. This indiscrimination, designated by Janet as *abaissement du niveau mental,* stems from the introduction of this unconscious energy into Consciousness through the Symbol. Indiscrimination should not be identified with regression, a concept to be reserved either for a specific type of indiscrimination created by symbols present in the Pathological Shadow or by a defense mechanism expressed through infantile behavior. Indiscrimination is the first step in any creative transformation of the Ego and is followed normally by a new discrimination.

Regression conceived as a defense mechanism is a pathological phenomenon expressed through infantile behavior which hinders further discrimination of a symbol. Imagine, for instance, an adult analysand going through painful symbols of his childhood who begins to neglect his duties and systematically adopts a childish behavior to avoid further suffering from the confrontation of these symbols. His regression functions here as a defense mechanism and hinders the comprehension and further discrimination of these symbols. However, if we employ the concept of regression as a defense mechanism to describe the indiscrimination frequently produced by normal symbolic development, we either create an enormous ambiguity in normal and pathological perspectives, or we establish that every indiscrimination, i. e., all psychic transformation where Consciousness is deeply moved, is necessarily also a going backwards in the life process. Such a theoretical position does not favor the creative transformation of the personality and tends to identify maturity and progression with absence of indiscrimination, which may become a very reactionary attitude. Another person, for instance, can face painful symbols of his childhood and even become indiscriminated without adopting a childish behavior defensively, i. e., regressively.

Every new discrimination begins unilaterally either through the Ego or the Other and becomes complete only when both polarities acquire their full new identification in Consciousness. Frequently, this takes many years and even a lifetime. To become fully discriminated, any Ego-Other polarity must go through the discrimination of the four functions and the two attitudes of Consciousness; we know the difficulties of discriminating polarities through the least developed functions of each particular typology. Therefore Consciousness and the Ego-Central Archetype Axis are always occupied by a countless number of structuring Symbols in the most varied stages of discrimination.

The Other, anteceding the Ego in the field of Consciousness, has been called projection. Even when this Other is still mixed with aspects of parts of what shall become Ego, this is a stage of a symbolic development where the Ego-Other polarity is on its way towards further discrimination, and nothing has been projected onto this Other. Projection is a defense mechanism which can only act upon a Symbol that has been at least partially discriminated. Projection conceived as a defense mechanism functions against further discrimination and therefore cannot be used for normal developement without either becoming ambiguous or implying that normal development must, from its very outset, be restricted.

As the process goes forward, the Ego and the Other will separate more and more and discrimination will proceed towards completion. Let us examine, as an example, the symbol of professional ability as experienced by two brothers, who were not twins but who grew up very closely to one another. During many years, the elder admired the younger for his many attributes, including his manual skills. The elder, in turn, was admired and liked by the younger because of his poetical gifts. As they grew older, the elder began to draw and, in the beginning, felt somewhat awkward. Later on, he entered art school, and for many years felt that his younger brother would have been a better art student than he. Twice he had a dream in which his brother was a very good painter. He graduated and naturally developed into a good painter, while his brother became a very competent mechanical engineer. They remained close friends. This is an example of normal symbolic development and not of projection. Within the elder brother's Self, the younger had stood for a fusion of esthetic and mechanical manual skills. A further discrimination in development led the elder brother's Ego to discriminate and integrate this esthetic manual ability. The point to be made here is the difference between normal symbolic development and projection. In symbolic development there is no defense mechanism involved. In the case just referred to, even though part of the symbol of esthetic manual ability remained in the Shadow, it was gradually integrated. There is no reason for us to see this as projection.

In another case, we have a very different situation. Again, two brothers of approximately the same age, and both very intelligent: The younger distinguished himself in athletics and the elder in his studies. The younger was highly intelligent, but grew progressively weaker in his studies. One day, he developed an eye pain which prevented him from reading. Several medical examinations turned out negative. During analysis, he repeatedly dreamt of his brother in a distinguished intellectual position. Repressed envy and hate appeared in the relationship. In this case, we see symbolic development hindered by the appearance of defense mechanisms and severe resistance, which prevented the integration of the theoretical learning symbol blocked in the Shadow. This is a clear-cut example where the concept of projection as a defense mechanism can be justifiably used.

It seems theoretically plausible, then, to establish an etiological, as well as a functional difference between symbolic development without defense mechanisms in normal cases, and symbolic development with defense mechanisms in pathological cases. In normal symbolic development, structuring symbols can operate in the Shadow and be gradually integrated, while in pathological symbolic development, symbols which operate partially or completely in the Shadow become separated from the Ego by defense mechanisms which offer great resistance and block integration of the symbol. In such cases, we may speak of a pathological Shadow.

According to the discrimination between normal and pathological development just proposed, one important point which has brought indiscrimination and confusion between normal and pathological development is the fact that, in normal development, the symbol is discriminated asymmetrically. Sometimes the Ego pole appears first, and at other times, the Other precedes the Ego in Consciousness. As they first appear, each polarity is still incompletely discriminated and contains parts of the other one; as symbolic development proceeds, they will complete discrimination. Only in appearance does this indiscrimination resemble the pathological ambiguity of indiscriminated symbols circumscribed by defense mechanisms.

It seems to me that it was this asymmetrical process of discrimination in normal symbolic development, added to the inner-outer split or subject-object dissociation methodologically adopted as a natural psychic condition, which led to the idea that normal development began through a defense mechanism. Another very important factor which contributed greatly to this premise was Freud's concept of a Death Instinct, adopted fully by Melanie Klein. With such a fearful instinct confronting its Ego every time the child emptied its mother's breast, it was not difficult to agree with the idea that the weak emerging Ego desperately needed defense mechanisms in order to develop. Were these defense mechanisms conceived to express the child's needs or to 'prove' how bad human nature intrinsically is? If we question the existence of such a Death Instinct, however, and follow closely the process of symbolic development, we can perhaps accept the hypothesis that normal development does not need defense mechanisms. Indeed, we may even then admit that love and hate coexist in psychic life during normal development without needing either splits or defenses to ensure their structuring function. This does not mean that symbolic psychology denies the archetypal aspect of Death. On the contrary, for death is one of the most important symbols of the developmental process. The difference lies in the fact that death is here conceived of as a symbol which is constellated every time the Ego dies, in order to transform and renew itself, and not as an instinct which meaninglessly attacks the Ego and life in general merely for destructive purposes. Neither does this mean that Symbolic Psychology does not admit the possibility of psychopathological phenomena occurring together with defense mechanisms from the very beginning of Ego formation. What it does not admit is that these defense mechanisms necessarily take part in the normal process of Ego development.

According to this perspective, then, normal symbolic development naturally flows toward discriminations and new indiscriminations, whereas pathological development becomes fixed (although quite operative) and resists further discrimination with defense mechanisms.

This does not mean that normal development is painless. On the contrary, it means that pain and anxiety are normally compatible with Ego development and do not necessarily need defense mechanisms to avoid them. Psychoanalysis contributed further to this ambiguity when it described development through repetitive compulsion, another defense mechanism typical of a blocked symbol. Another strong argument against the hypothesis that symbols develop asymmetrically through defense mechanisms because of the anxiety and hardship of Ego development is the fact that all symbols develop asymmetrically whether they are agreeable or painful, loved or feared.

It remains to be explained why we find asymmetry in normal symbolic development. If a terribly frightening Death Instinct does not exist and if there is no defense mechanism hindering normal development, why is there asymmetry? Why do the Other and the Ego take turns at preceding one another during the discriminating process?

Let me first call attention to the fact that those who have used projection or projective identification to explain development have not only begun to do so through an improbable inner-outer split, but have also given priority to the inner appearing first through the outer. This does not seem valid because, according to my observation, Ego and Other alternate in this asymmetrical appearance. A child may primarily blame itself or the Other for its suffering. It is very difficult to foresee through which pole the Self will begin to discriminate a symbol. An alchemist who discovered a new property of a substance could begin discriminating this highly symbolical event either through concentrating attention on what the substance revealed or on how he himself felt about the discovery. The same will occur in psychopathology. Many will concentrate their symptoms on the Other and develop a paranoid dynamism, while many others will concentrate their symptoms on themselves and develop a manic-depressive dynamism. Likewise, it is difficult to foresee in the disturbances of discrimination of the primary relationship which patients will cling predominantly to the 'I' in detriment of the Other and form autism, and which will cling to the Other in detriment of the 'I' and form pathological symbiosis. The main thing here seems to be the fact that pathological symbiosis and autism are two complementary pathological forms of behavior which differ basically due to the antecedence of the 'I' or the Other in the process of discrimination. Once more, it is the presence of this asymmetry in the normal process of development which will allow us to understand the normal roots of pathological complementarity of the autism-pathological symbiosis polarity. In other words, it is upon this normal unilaterality present in development that defenses may act. In the cases of autism and pathological symbiosis, the defense mechanisms of dissociation and repression block the unilateral predominance of the Ego or the Other which was already present in normal development.

A Jungian analyst seeking an explanation for this unilaterality found in symbolic development cannot avoid associating it to the extravert and introvert attitude described by Jung. This association is very productive, because the extravert naturally tends to discriminate symbols beginning through the Other and the introvert through the Ego. However, I want to use here only one discovery of Jung's typological theory, namely, the fact that introverts express undeveloped extroversion but tend to develop it gradually, throughout life. As Jung showed, the same happens with all psychological types regarding their undeveloped functions. This fact demonstrates that not only the discrimination of symbols by Consciousness is asymmetrical, but that Consciousness itself, and with it the whole personality, develops unilaterally. As we saw above, first one part of the symbol, the Ego or the Other, develops and then the opposite part follows to complete discrimination. In the same way, first one function of Consciousness develops, and later on the opposite function will differentiate itself. The very quaternary structure of the Central Archetype develops unilaterally through the binary pattern of matriarchal dynamism and the ternary pattern of patriarchal dynamism to attain the quaternary pattern of Consciousness in the Anima-Animus-Coniunctio dynamism.

Traditionally, as mentioned above, this asymmetry has been attributed to projection. Many analysts work so extensively with this perspective, however, that they equate meaning with reintrojection. For them, the very terms interpretation and insight have become reduced to synonyms for the reintrojection of 'projected' symbols.

The task, then, is to recognize that Ego and Consciousness are structured by symbols unilaterally or asymetrically. As structuring symbols become discriminated, the Ego may sometimes appear before the Other in Consciousness, and at other times, the Other may precede the Ego. Whether the Ego or the Other appears first in Consciousness, however, they still present parts of one another which become further discriminated as the process goes on. The whole point, then, is to admit that all this occurs neither because there is some defense mechanism at work, nor because of a preexistent split, but because all psychic functions are polar and develop unilaterally. Asymmetry, therefore, is a normal psychic phenomenon. Pathology derives not from asymmetry itself but from blockage of further discrimination of a structuring symbol, which is already developing asymmetrically. It is this blockage which is operated by defense mechanisms and not the unilaterality and the discrimination themselves.

## The Normal Interrelationship of Ego, Persona and Shadow

The Persona and the Shadow are collateral structures for Ego development and play an indispensable and creative role in this development. The Persona and the Shadow acquired predominantly negative connotations because they were originally described by Jung from the perspective of the second half of life when the developmental process may become fully occupied with transcending the dominance of patriarchal and matriarchal dynamisms in order to establish the dominance of the Anima-Animus-Coniunctio dynamism. In this dynamism, the Ego-Persona and Ego-Shadow polarities, like all other psychic polarities, must be recognized and situated in a symmetrical, creative, dialectical relationship; if left asymmetrically hidden, disregarded and functioning autonomously, they can delay and even hinder the development of the personality. In the parental cycles, however, this is not so and the knowledge of how the Ego, Persona and Shadow are structured within them gives us a better idea of how useful and helpful they are to the development of the Ego. Another very negative connotation which contaminated the Shadow concept with much prejudice was its association with the religious concepts of sin and evil. This association, which is very productive in the dimension of the comparative sciences, contaminated the Shadow with the Christian concepts of sin and evil, distorted as they were by the Inquisition. This made it difficult for the dynamic interrelationship of Ego and Shadow to be approached and studied from a fresh start in Psychology.

The Persona is a psychic structure based on the gregariousness of our species in order to promote Ego and conscious development together with social adaptation. It becomes intensely and fundamentally active right from the primal relationship. As soon as the first Ego-Other discriminations become active, the notion that certain forms of behavior are socially acceptable, along with the notion that many useful discriminations have already been processed and are stored in traditional mores, become established as operative factors throughout life. The matriarchal Persona, with its pathways through which sensuous expression and pleasure (mainly bodily pleasure) may be obtained and enjoyed, is one of the most important channels of Ego discrimination in early infancy and remains so throughout life. In the matriarchal Persona lies one of the great drawbacks of Western Culture – to experience genuinely sensuous pleasure – in contrast to those cultures which benefit from a well developed matriarchal dynamism.

Persona, Ego and Shadow are formed and function dynamically, so closely intertwined that what happens to one invariably affects the other. The more limited the Persona, the more the Ego will lack traditional social paths to develop, the more the Ego will be left to its own devices when confronting new structuring symbols, and consequently, the more it will resort to Shadow formation during development. The disturbance of the matriarchal dynamism and severe limitation of the matriarchal Persona in Western Culture, due to the frequent cultural overdominance of the pathologically defensive patriarchal dynamism adopted by the Inquisition, lies at the root of many aspects of our exaggerated Collective Shadow formation.

The matriarchal Persona obeys first and foremost the fertility principle and is very naturally moulded within matriarchal binary dynamism. Precisely because it is formed through intense conscious-unconscious intimacy, however, it is even more inaccessible to conscious reasoning and change than the patriarchal Persona. The matriarchal Persona is shaped through experience and custom and only through experience and custom can it be modified.

It is very misleading to name the social conditions of personality development the 'principle of reality' and to equate this with objective reality because these social conditions are symbolic and therefore immensely variable. Theoretically, we can say that the Persona becomes active with the Ego because the Persona is formed by the social pathways placed at the disposal of Ego development. Although experienced personally and intimately in the primary relationship, these social pathways are culturally conditioned and express very personally tinged historical development. The fact that the Persona in the primary relationship and within the family might differ greatly from the cultural Persona will bring problems for the social adequacy of the Ego later in life. These Ego difficulties will reflect on the management of the Persona by the Ego throughout life. The assessment of the family Persona and of the primary-relationship Persona of an analysand is a necessary task in analysis and will help the analyst to understand many of the analysand's reactions and conflicts including those within the transference relationship. The analogy of the Persona formation with the Superego in Psychoanalysis is relatively useful but may be very misleading, because (among other things) the Superego is generally thought of as an "internalized institution" and the Persona is the structuring expression of the Ego-forming capacity of the Central Archetype in the social dimension.

The polarities of the patriarchal Persona being very strictly discriminated and set apart favors Ego development very unilaterally. This extraordinary unilateral development of the Ego in the patriarchal pattern is achieved at the cost of intense and systematic Shadow formation. There is nothing wrong with, or pathological about, this process. The patriarchal pattern, despite its rigid Persona and systematic Shadow formation parallel to Ego formation, is responsible for much of the individual and collective development of Consciousness. The patriarchal Persona not only favors systematic Shadow formation through its unilaterality but, for this very reason, is also adverse to Shadow confrontation. Whenever there occurs Shadow confrontation in the patriarchal pattern, the patriarchal Persona favors either its suppression or its substitution by another Shadow formation. If, for instance, any Shadow symbol of fear appears during indoctrination of courage to perform a certain task according to the patriarchal pattern, it may be dealt with by suppression or by substituting it by the fear of punishment or shameful discredit.

It is in the Anima-Animus-Coniunctio Cycle that Consciousness, through the acquisition of the quaternary pattern, will propitiate the Ego to interact in equal terms with all polarities, including Persona and Shadow. In the matriarchal and patriarchal cycles, the Persona may occasionally be used as a mask to strategically hide one's intimate reactions, but this is its secondary function. Its primary function is the growth of personality, of Consciousness and of the Ego through the acquisition of know-how in the social dimension. In the Anima-Animus-Coniunctio Cycle, the Ego learns primarily to wear the Persona as a mask, not only to hide itself when necessary (something the Ego already learns through the parental cycles), but also to confront the Other's Shadow and its own. Here, then, we have an important phenomenon in Symbolic Psychology. Whereas the Persona-Ego-Shadow interrelationship enhances Persona performance and Shadow formation in the archetypal parental cycles, it so favors Persona differentiation in the Anima-Animus-Coniunctio Cycle that it propitiates Ego exposure and confrontation both of its own Shadow and the Other's.

The Ego develops the capacity not only of using the Persona as a mask to hide itself consciously, but also of unmasking and exposing itself deeply whenever necessary. This approach to the Persona not only fails to further enhance Shadow formation, but actually diminishes significantly the Shadow already formed. Of course, the Shadow will continue forming, but its interaction with the Ego and the Persona will be very different and even opposite to the one experienced in the parental cycles. This is one more way in which we can verify the important transformation which the Ego undergoes together with Consciousness through each of the four archetypal patterns of personality development. Whereas in the first two, the Ego has to rely through the Persona on traditionally pre-established social patterns, and often form a Shadow which it seldom either can or may confront, in the third cycle, it acquires the capacity to choose between the social discrimination and its own, and to confront the Shadow, which it has helped to form.

In the Cosmic Cycle of personality development, polarities are transcended and Consciousness and the Ego express so thoroughly the quaternary pattern of the Central Archetype as a total unity that Persona and Shadow lose their polarity and therefore also their importance as structuring functions. The danger here lies in the Ego incapacity to express the unified quaternary pattern due to the failure to acquire the necessary preparatory differentiation in the other three cycles.

The Shadow is formed parallel to the Ego and the Persona as the structure that carries those structuring symbols only partially discriminated; for one reason or other, these symbols are not being further discriminated and, therefore, have not yet become Ego. Not only morally unacceptable symbols may be part of the Shadow, but all other types of symbols as well, including those intensely praised. Dynamically speaking, the Shadow is a para-egoic reservoir of structuring Symbols.

This definition of Shadow formation has an important corollary: the structuring symbols present in the Shadow are of the same creative nature as all symbols functioning in the Ego-Central Archetype Axis and differ from them only by the fact that they have not, for one reason or other, come to integrate Consciousness. It is this theoretical formulation of Shadow formation which allows us to understand quite clearly that what is present in the Shadow is missing in the Ego and, sooner or later, is bound to be confronted and integrated as a developmental necessity of the personality. This perspective, which is relatively simple from the standpoint of the structuring symbol, may become very difficult and frustrating when formulated only from the conscious standpoint, mainly if one tries *to define the Shadow* by pinpointing it either through its appearance or through the nature of its contents instead of *through its dynamic relationship to the Ego.*

The Shadow can be formed through various circumstances, which may include the nature of the structuring symbol, the disposition of Consciousness and the life situation. The nature of the structuring symbol may refer to quality or intensity. Sometimes one is allowed to experience hate, envy or despair, but only up to a certain intensity. Other emotions or ideas may not be allowed to be experienced at all. Some symbols come to make up the Shadow simply because we are not given the chance to experience them. For instance, an analysand raised in the city, who every other night dreamt about a man of his age who lived freely in a forest. Many symbols find their way into the Shadow because the attitude type or the conscious function needed to work them through are still undeveloped in the personality, as, for instance, a thinking type who used to dream about a friend whose hands were always cold, or a feeling type who dreamt frequently about someone who, although quite intelligent, absolutely refused to listen to anything explained through abstractions. Frequently, the Shadow is formed with symbols experienced with great suffering, or in situations of sickness or stress which do not allow sufficient psychic energy for the personality to work them through. The idea that the Shadow is formed mainly through structuring symbols which are morally unacceptable came into Psychology via puritanism and may be very misleading.

The Shadow, therefore, has to be considered dynamically as a parallel Ego structure containing symbols which have not yet been integrated into Consciousness. In this way, the Shadow is the analogy of the unconscious Ego parts of Psychoanalysis. In making the Ego the center of Consciousness, Jung had to create a concept which contained those symbols which the Ego had not been able to integrate, symbols which in a way pertained to the Ego, but remained unconscious.

Like the Ego and the Persona, the Shadow is also a structure which belongs to the behavior dimension of the Psyche and is active day and night. Stevenson's *Dr. Jekyll and Mr. Hyde* is a good example of Ego and Shadow behavior only if we see Dr. Jekyll's day life and Mr. Hyde's night life as symbolic of conscious and unconscious behavior and not as an existential separation of the behavior of Ego and Shadow. This behavior is so intertwined that many times during the day, Ego and Shadow act side by side in a surprisingly intimate way. This is due to the fact that Ego and Shadow are only partially strangers and opponents. There is a secret facet in the Ego-Shadow relationship where they are friends and have a pact through which they agree to put up with each other, to live and to act side by side. This is so even if the Ego spends part of its life and energy making up for inadequate situations and frequent painful consequences stemming from Shadow behavior. This surreptitious caring and making up for Shadow behavior on the part of the Ego is an important function developed in the parental cycles which prepares the Ego for direct Shadow confrontation in the Anima-Animus-Coniunctio Cycle.

The nature of the secret and paradoxical alliance between Ego and Shadow can only be understood through developmental psychology when we realize that the Ego, although normally incapable of seeing through Unconsciousness and observing the Shadow's behavior, participates not only as a witness, but also as an active accomplice in all Shadow formation. The pact between Ego and Shadow is signed and sanctioned at every new moment when the Shadow is formed. From then on, the Ego somehow knows that to confront the Shadow and ransom it from its unconscious state means to reexamine that contract and lose or sacrifice the advantages obtained by having signed it.

It is of the utmost importance to realize that Shadow formation is not something exclusive to the Ego and, like everything else the Ego does, it is archetypally patterned. The formation of the Shadow in the parental archetypal cycles is somehow accompanied by the Ego and patterned archetypally. Therefore, there is no reason to conceive of the action of defense mechanisms for normal Shadow formation, since archetypal patterning and relative Ego sanction suffice. By Ego sanction of Shadow formation, I do not mean that the Ego is conscious of what Shadow formation will imply for the whole functioning of the Ego-Central Archetype Axis. This is something which will happen only in the Anima-Animus-Coniunctio pattern, for there the Ego will relate meaningfully to the Other within totality. In so doing, the Ego will become fully aware of the consequences for the developmental process when it sanctions the passage of structuring symbols into the Shadow.

It is always on account of its limitations that the Ego sanctions Shadow formation. The inescapable fact is, that, be it on account of moral restriction, exhaustion, umbearable tension and suffering, lack of attention, intelligence, time and space, will power or dedication, or even due to cowardice and pure laziness, the Ego sanctions Shadow formation. The more we carefully consider the interaction of Ego and Shadow, the more we become conscious of how intimate and intertwined is their involvement.

By definition, the Ego is unconscious of the functioning of the Shadow. However, just as we have found out through developmental psychology that the Ego is not unconscious of Shadow formation, so we also must realize that the Ego is indirectly conscious of the Shadow's existence through its behavior. This is so because the Ego, as center of Consciousness, is responsible for the behavior of the personality, and when behavior appears in a way different from, or even contrary to, the Ego's intentions, the Ego becomes aware of the presence of a stranger and even of an opponent within the behavior-commanding unit. Naturally, this foreign presence can be covered up by excuses of various types, but it is nonetheless a fact which is difficult to deny over time. The problem is, that the Ego is consciously tolerant of this presence, for, although it has no knowledge of the Shadow's strategy, it conceded to the formation of the Shadow; at that moment, it gave up the discrimination of many of its structuring symbols and, in so doing, it also gave up the monopoly of behavior command. The Ego knows that the expression and discrimination of structuring symbols are part of its life contract with the Central Archetype because it is archetypally furnished with the inborn capacity for such knowledge. The awareness that it contributes to Shadow formation, that, to a certain extent, it allows Shadow behavior, and that it gives up the development of certain structuring symbols, fills the Ego with a sense of existential longing for completeness, guilt and inferiority feelings that will accompany it throughout the dynamics of the Anima-Animus-Coniunctio pattern.

From the structural developmental perspective, the Shadow is the Ego's younger bastard sibling, archetypally born to perform much of the dirty work of the family. From this perspective, then, the Shadow can be morally reproached as well as praised.

The relationship of the Ego with the Other in equal terms (equivalent to 'love thy neighbor as thyself' in Christianity, and 'give up all Ego claims' in Buddhism) acquired by Consciousness in the Anima-Animus-Coniunctio Cycle, allows the Ego to become aware of the true nature of its relationship with the Shadow, knowledge of which is quite discouraged in both parental dynamisms. To confront the Shadow is to cross the frontier of displeasure, madness, evil, sin and death for the sake of the developmental process. Matriarchal dynamism is ruled by the principle of pleasure and fertility and consequently does not favor Shadow confrontation. Patriarchal dynamism is oriented by planned behavior based on abstract dogmatic principles, which practically forbid any Ego-Shadow creative relationship ("But of the tree of knowledge of good and evil thou shalt not eat of it for in the day that thou eatest thereof thou shalt surely die", Gen. 11:17).

The Central Archetype provides a model for Ego development expressed by structuring symbols of the Hero Archetype which have a typical idealized expression in each of the four archetypal cycles. Every time Consciousness and the Ego become inflated or indiscriminated by a structuring symbol of importance coordinated by any archetypal pattern whatever, the Hero Archetype also becomes activated and enthuses the Ego-Central Archetype relationship through some heroic perspective which propitiates, stimulates, guides and patterns Ego performance. In a sense, all new Ego performance is heroic or 'sacred' because it expresses the fulfilment of the developmental matrix of the Central Archetype. This also occurs with structuring symbols functioning in the Shadow, in which case enthusiasm may appear with temptation or longing for an unknown experience, which frequently leads to creative work. *Mutatis mutandis,* creative work which deeply moves the Ego-Central Archetype Axis, quite often leads Consciousness towards structuring symbols functioning in the Shadow. This fact has frequently associated creative work and even curiosity with dangerous, revolutionary or sinful behavior. It explains Jung's empirical discovery that the first step of the Individuation Process is the encounter with the Shadow (the alchemist's *Nigredo*). I dare only to add that the encounter with the Anima only apparently follows that of the Shadow since, when seen developmentally, it is the constellated archetypal pattern of the Anima-Animus-Coniunctio Cycle which allows and enhances the creative encounter of Ego and Shadow. If we overlook this fact, we may not grasp the bisexuality of the Shadow and of the Anima Archetype and may feel tempted to describe a new archetype, such as the Animus in the male personality, to account for its masculine pole. This would not only reduce and mutilate the sexual bipolar nature of the Anima archetype, but would also obscure its dynamic nature as an archetypal structuring pattern of Consciousness in man which enhances the confrontation, on equal terms, of the Ego with the Other, be this woman or man, parent or child, society, creativity, Unconscious or even an image of the Central Archetype itself. The same, of course, can be said of the Animus in relationship to the woman's Psyche. The fact that the Anima Archetype is frequently expressed by structuring symbols with images of women and the Animus with images of men does not invalidate their being basically archetypes of equal relationship between the Ego and the Other.

It is Shadow formation which shows the Ego again and again that, although often heroic and successful, it is not the Hero Archetype. The great death and rebirth experiences which accompany intense Ego transformation are coordinated, side by side, with the dominant archetype, also by the Hero Archetype. Were the Ego not counterbalanced by some other psychic function, it would risk becoming too intensely possessed by the Hero Archetype and of leading the personality literally into death. Therefore, not only can Shadow awareness at times be the best way to fight uncontrolled inflation, but Shadow formation is the inborn archetypal way of regulating the danger of exaggerated indiscrimination by the Hero Archetype. The awareness of the dynamics of Shadow formation and functioning acquired in the Anima-Animus-Coniunctio Cycle is essential for the Ego to realize its limitations in order to avoid being possessed when dealing with the indiscrimination naturally produced by structuring symbols. This knowledge is of inestimable value for the Ego-Other relationship, especially the Ego-Shadow creative relationship.

If the Ego is conscious of Shadow formation and of many consequences of Shadow behavior, we may conclude that the Ego is only relatively unconscious of the Shadow. Through this awareness, the Ego participates indirectly in the Ego-Central Archetype Axis, an inborn capacity to deal with the Shadow and regulate its extension and intensity. Beyond a certain point, the Ego-Central Archetype Axis naturally favors Ego-Shadow confrontation, spontaneously sacrifices the advantages of having formed the Shadow, and automatically channels the Shadow's structuring symbols towards Consciousness. In these circumstances, the Ego-Central Archetype Axis completes the Yang-Yin mandala of Ego-Shadow interrelationship. Yang, active and penetrating when the Ego helps to push symbols into Shadow formation, Yin, accepting and being penetrated when the Ego allows these symbols back to undergo further transformation through them. This normal mandala of Ego-Shadow interaction is regulated both by Ego and Shadow behavior and, underneath and around them, by the structuring and compensatory functions of the Central Archetype.

The conscious-unconscious global structure of the Individual and of the Cultural Self remains relatively balanced during their permanent creative developmental activity. Structuring symbols, which become discriminated, expand Ego and Consciousness and express the end-product of the Central Archetype into existence. As the Central Archetype becomes more and more conscious, the symbol of the *quaternio* (one of the main structuring symbols of the human mind, as Jung discovered) becomes structured into Consciousness and the Ego-Other relationship attains the quaternary pattern of otherness. Consciousness is an incomplete existential mandala with the Ego-Other polarity at its center. Shadow formation completes the mandala of Consciousness with unconsciousness through incompletely discriminated symbols and this produces the tension inherent in the mandala of the Ego-Shadow relationship. Shadow formation and behavior, although satisfactory on the one hand, because Ego is eased in its discriminatory work and because Shadow symbols, although indiscriminated, take active part in behavior, on the other hand are quite unsatisfactory, because they create a tension in the overall coherence of Consciousness. This tension occurs because of the totality-enhancing structuring function of the Central Archetype over Consciousness. It is this pressure striving for totality and coherence that urges the Ego to open itself up to the Shadow, mainly in the Anima-Animus Coniunctio Cycle, in order to reduce the Shadow's structuring symbols in number and intensity and to expand the power of the Ego and the coherence of Consciousness. In the Parental Cycles, this same function is carried out by exaggerating Shadow behavior in such a way that Ego-Shadow confrontation is forced indirectly through behavior, and becomes unavoidable. The Persona is susceptible both to direct and indirect Shadow confrontation and functions to accomodate the Ego-Shadow tensions creatively.

This is the normal cycle of Persona-Ego-Shadow articulation coordinated by the Central Archetype. One of the main sources of psychopathology is the blockage of this dynamic Persona-Ego-Shadow-Central Archetype interaction through defense mechanisms. To define the Shadow functioning under such circumstances, I suggest the designation of pathological Shadow. In so doing, my intention is to construct a theory of psychopathology based on the developmental approach as seen from both the archetypal and conscious perspectives of the structuring symbol.

Shadow behavior is not integrated into the coherent conscious world of discriminations and naturally creates undesired conflicts with other people and with the Ego's own devices. Normally this tension can be used for Shadow structuring symbols to come into Consciousness and be worked through. When there is special Ego dedication, this task may be greatly enhanced. Not so, however, in the case of the pathological Shadow, because the defenses which surround this Shadow were built especially to prevent the natural and spontaneous Ego-Shadow interaction.

## The Concept of the Pathological Shadow and Defense Mechanisms

These concepts and the difficulties which surround their formulation can only come into focus when seen from the historical and cultural perspective. It seems to me that the Western Cultural Self formed a huge dissociated Shadow during the three-century-long conflict between, on the one hand, the immense creativity that followed the Renaissance and gave birth to modern science and modern nations, and, on the other hand, the equally intense reactive repression from the Inquisition, which controlled the birth of modern Western Collective Consciounsness and oriented its 'education'. This pathological dissociation spread throughout all cultural dimensions of the wounded Western Cultural Self and one of its main expressions became the subjective-objective dissociation. Around this dissociation numerous defense mechanisms were formed, among which we find the nineteenth century materalistic ideologies (Positivism, Dialectical Materialism, Scientific Materialism, Agnosticism, etc.), as well as their spiritual counterparts. At the core of these ideologies lives a concept of objectivity according to which knowledge and truth can be arrived at only through rational logical thinking, without any subjective irrational involvement whatsoever. In this materialistic philosophy of Science, unconscious symbols which are not logically and rationally clear have no value in the search for truth.

My experience of the opposite made it clear to me that materialistic philosophy is imbedded in a huge rationalization, i. e., a defense mechanism to hide and protect this cultural pathological dissociation. In trying to demonstrate this diagnosis, however, I discovered this dissociation to be even more serious than it seemed. First, because it does not have the appearance of a dissociation but, on the contrary, presents itself pretensiously as a straight golden path towards truth. Second, because when we try to demonstrate it, we have as yet no scientific cultural psychopathological body of concepts to verify our diagnosis. Third, because the historical conditions in which for centuries the Inquisition persecuted, tortured and handed over to death thousands of the most intelligent, courageous and creative people of Western Culture no longer exist as such today. Just as, before Freud's time in personal Psychology, we still cannot accept in Anthropology and History that a culture may pathologically experience symbols today due to sufferings it went through many many centuries ago. In this respect, most scientists still truly believe that this materialistic philosophy originated in science and, therefore, is as trustwortly as the scientific method. They fail to see that the materialistic Philosophy, being from its very birth in the eighteenth century the expression of the subjective-objective dissociation of Western Humanism, defensively evades precisely the study of the subject-object relationship by the scientific method.

The fourth reason which makes our task even more difficult is that, when we try to apply the concept of defense mechanisms discovered by Freud in individual clinical Psychology to make our diagnosis of cultural dissociation, we find out that this very concept has already been distorted from birth. Indeed, it stuns us to realize that such a promising diagnostic instrument created in personal Psychology was contaminated upon discovery by the same cultural dissociation which we now want to diagnose. The moment the concept of defense mechanism was used ambiguously to describe pathological and normal individual development, we invalidated the certainty of making a diagnosis of pathology when we find defense mechanisms in the cultural Self.

It is like an accomplice of a murderer who surreptitiously stains innocent people with blood so that he cannot be accused if blood is discovered on his own clothes. Not feeling sufficiently safe, however, this person may convince public opinion that everybody is 'naturally' willing to die so that, when the corpse of his crime is discovered, the police will have much more difficulty in accusing him. Something like this happened when Psychoanalysis, after describing defense mechanisms ambiguously in normal and pathological development, went on to 'discover' a Death Instinct. I am sure that many people, once equipped with such a concept, will find it quite normal if one day, due to this dissociation, we psychotically embark on an atomic war. This severe pathological dissociation and its defense mechanisms, mainly of repression, projection and rationalization, seem already to be paving the way for the Western pathological cultural Shadow to act once more through war, in which case the main structuring symbol acted could be said to be that of the anti-Christ. (The structuring symbol of Christ dissociated into the Western pathological Shadow.)

Many of us analysts will readily admit that the personal neurotic Shadow is quite able to act so surreptitiously. How many of us, however, are ready to admit that a Cultural Shadow can also operate like this? Shall we ever concede that the Western cultural Shadow did exactly this when it contaminated with pathological concepts the scientific theory of normal personality development, the very instrument which it knew could identify its pathology? In order to admit this, the Social Sciences have first to recognize the unavoidable mixture of subjective and objective components in structuring symbols, which can only become discriminated during the process of formation of Individual and Collective Consciousness. Only after admitting this will they be able to see how much Western Humanism is so deeply imbedded in a dissociation that even the creativity of its geniuses may not escape contamination by the defenses of its pathological Shadow (Symbolic contamination of Anima with Shadow symbols). This can only happen, however, when symbolic Science is seen to include subjective and objective Science, i. e., when the structuring symbol is recognized as a necessary psychological vehicle for the acquisition of objective knowledge. All this insight resists coming to Consciousness due to the very defense mechanisms formed for centuries around this dissociation which are now being daily expressed technically through the worldwide dissociating barrier of atomic missiles.

Due to these circumstances, whenever we try to get at the pathology of our Cultural Self, we enter a labyrinth, and after great effort, we only end up where we started, incapable of making a diagnosis, much less beginning a treatment. We shall remain in this hopeless situation until we realize how much our therapeutic instruments, which in this case are our psychological concepts, have been, from their very start, contaminated by our cultural disease, and how much, in order to diagnose this disease and begin its treatment, we must first disinfect our tools; we must, first of all, discriminate between our normal psychological concepts and their pathological contaminations, and vice versa.

In the preceding pages, I hope to have prepared this decontamination by formulating the normal interrelationship of Persona, Ego and

Shadow within the actualizing function of the Central Archetype through the structuring symbols of the Ego-Central Archetype Axis without the use of defense mechanisms. I hope, further, to have shown that all psychic functions develop unilaterally and that the Psyche normally makes up for this asymmetry through continuing development, likewise without the employment of defense mechanisms. Finally, I hope to have shown that the Persona, Ego and Shadow interact dynamically in normal development coordinated by the Ego-Central Archetype Axis, and that they participate jointly in Shadow formation, Shadow behavior and Shadow integration as a mandala-like system at the service of conscious development, once again without defense mechanisms being needed to explain it. This understanding of the normal dynamics of Shadow formation and functioning is basic to the understanding of the pathological functioning of the Shadow.

In order to complete the disinfection of our conceptual microscope, which will allow us to diagnose our Cultural dissociation and consciously begin the search for its proper treatment, we need to dwell on the formation and functioning of defense mechanisms. This we can do, I believe, through the concept of the pathological Shadow, which designates a determined way for the Shadow to function inseparably from the presence of defense mechanisms, and which is the most basic and frequent precondition of psychopathology.

The pathological Shadow interrupts the mandala cycle of normal Shadow formation and reintegration through the normal Persona-Ego-Shadow interaction described above, and fixates Shadow behavior through the repetitive-compulsive dynamism first described by Freud, which here may be called a defense mechanism of the Ego-Central Archetype Axis. This psychodynamic explains the splitting of the personality found in neurosis and extensively referred to in many psychological writings. This split has been confused ambiguously with normal asymmetrical development, despite being very different from it. Whereas normal asymmetrical development leads to psychic unilaterality to be completed through development, the split pathological Shadow opposes further reintegration through defense mechanisms which block, resist, sabotage and use many other strategic devices specifically directed to prevent the re-entrance of Shadow symbols into Ego formation.

The pathological Shadow, when pressed by the Ego-Central Archetype Axis for Ego confrontation, reacts quite differently from the normal Shadow. When pressed by the Self dynamics for confrontation, the normal Shadow may present resistance, but this resistance occurs within the flow of Shadow reintegration, which is bound to occur in due time. In the case of the pathological Shadow, however, resistance is at the service of some defense mechanism which increases the split in the personality and may intensify dangerously neurotic or psychotic symptomatology already present. The resistance of the normal Shadow after some pressure may even be taken up also by the Ego and the Persona and eventually become a reaction of the whole personality. In general, this is not so with the pathological Shadow, whose resistance, when pressed, may be completely antagonized by Ego and Persona and dangerously increase the existing split. Whereas the normal Shadow's resistance may be confronted directly by will power as a moral necessity, the pathological Shadow, when directly confronted, may increase defensive behavior and lead to a psychological break-down. As is well known, confrontation of the pathological Shadow requires a working through of its defense mechanisms, which will bring a significant change of personality before Shadow confrontation can take place. Many psychic crises, which, in analysis, present significant improvement, frequently accompanied by significant growth of the personality, may be considered as encouraging 'cures' of psychotherapy, whereas, in reality, they are cases in which the normal Shadow is quite predominant over the pathological Shadow.

Defense mechanisms are created by the Ego-Central Archetype Axis when the normal Shadow is split and becomes pathological, i. e., when the cycle of Shadow reintegration is blocked and reintegration permanently impeded. These structuring symbols are prevented from overcharging the Ego by defense mechanisms, but, at the same time, are allowed to maintain their function (although indiscriminated) within the developmental process. Pathology, in this case, is a device to maintain certain structuring symbols functioning permanently in the Shadow. The causes of pathological Shadow formation are most variable, for they may be found either in the nature and intensity of the structuring symbol, or in the state and phase of Ego development, or in Ego-Symbol interaction, as well as in many other psychic conditions. The formation and existence of the pathological Shadow is a frequent occurrence and we may say that a certain part of everyone's Shadow functions according to this pathological dynamism.

The gravity of the pathological Shadow depends not only upon its extension and intensity, but also upon its state of discrimination. As the normal Shadow contains structuring symbols in all stages of discrimination, its blockage paralyzes structuring symbols in their present state of discrimination. The various defense mechanisms which maintain the Shadow blocked also maintain the behavior of these structuring symbols fixated in this state of discrimination. The more archaic the state of discrimination of a symbol, the greater will be the difficulty to work through the pathological Shadow. Defenses such as projection, rationalization, negation and repression, for instance, deal with symbols already somewhat discriminated, whereas pathological symbiosis and autism deal with symbols with much less discrimination. Of course, the most difficult cases are those where the pathological Shadow not only presents undiscriminated symbols, but is itself so undiscriminated from the Ego that we have a pathology of identity, as when Ego and Shadow are involved together in character disorders.

Defense mechanisms are archetypally patterned and therefore bear many characteristics of the patterns of the archetypal cycles of personality development in which they occur. The projection, repression, dramatization and negation found in hysteria, for instance, present the same dynamism as the great Mother archetypal pattern of Consciousness, whereas the repression and projection of obsessive neurosis present the same dynamism found in the patriarchal pattern of Consciousness.

Defense mechanisms show the defensive compulsive characteristic necessary to maintain the pathological Shadow blocked, yet are quite creative in their defensive nature. Every psychotherapist knows how much energy he spends daily in order to work through a certain defensive pattern and the countless substitutes for every worn-out defensive procedure. In this sense, the secondary gains of neurosis described by Freud function also in many cases as the further perfecting of defenses which creatively disguise, through adaptation, the pathological Shadow functioning underneath.

Working through the defenses of the pathological Shadow requires, first and foremost, knowledge of the symbolic development of the personality. Only the meaningful working through of the structuring symbols present in the pathological Shadow, and the careful consideration of the dynamic difficulties of their blockage within the defensive transference, will allow defense mechanisms to give way for these symbols to be further discriminated. The pathological Shadow can, therefore, only become part of the normal process when worked through side by side psychotherapeutically with the normal creative process; otherwise, the defenses of the pathological Shadow and its behavior may become deeply altered, liberating the structuring symbols of the pathological Shadow into the normal developmental process.

The pathological Shadow takes part in behavior together with defense mechanisms; we know how much defensive behavior is part of every neurosis. Due to encirclement by defense mechanisms, the pathological Shadow only rarely transforms itself through behavior, unlike the normal Shadow, which transforms itself into Ego through behavior as part of the Ego-Shadow interrelationship. In some cases of extraordinarily creative and courageous people, I have seen the transformation of the pathological Shadow by exposure of its defenses in everyday life. To do so, these people must be creative enough to sacrifice their Persona in a productive way and not run the risk of self-destructive behavior through an acute reintensification of the defense mechanisms so exposed. These cases show us the great danger of forcing a confrontation with the pathological Shadow without a careful working through of its defense mechanisms within a psychotherapeutic relationship.

The pathological Shadow participates in behavior and in personal relationships while remaining blocked to further discrimination in Consciousness, yet stays quite engaged in life through the creative action of defense mechanisms. Unconscious processes have no defined boundaries with the world around us and the pathological Shadow participates actively in all unconscious processes. The pathological Shadow, just as the normal Shadow, remains a para-Egoic reservoir of living symbols which is constantly active, the only difference from the normal Shadow being that its symbols are prevented by defense mechanisms from re-entering Consciousness for further discrimination. The more intimate a relationship, the more interpersonal unconscious processes intermingle. Intimate relationships, such as the family, are the ideal circumstances for detecting and differentiating normal and pathological Shadow behavior, not to mention, of course, the psychotherapeutic relationship.

In conclusion, I would like to point out that, in spite of the theoretical importance of the concept of the pathological Shadow and its association with defense mechanisms, in order for this discrimination to be throughly understood, it needs the initiation of the consulting room. The analyst who is himself blocked within defensive techniques will have difficulty in making this discrimination, as will also the analyst who believes in creativity, but knows little about psychopathology.

This discrimination between the normal and the pathological Shadow can best be made by analysts who can differentiate the creative transference from the defensive transference, and who can work with these two transferences side by side. These analysts can endorse the expression and psychological development of their patients through expressive techniques within a creative therapeutic relationship and, at the same time, can consider and work through the presence and action of defense mechanisms and their blocking effect.[27]

[27] Byington, C. (1980). "Symbolic Psychotherapy, a Post-Patriarchal Pattern in Psychotherapy. An interpretation of the Historical Development of Western Psychotherapy through a Mythological Theory of History". In Money, Food, Drink and Fashion and Analytic Training. The Proceedings of the Eighth International Congress for Analytical Psychology. Fellbach-Oeffingen, Ed. John Beebe, Verlag Adolf Bonz, pgs. 441–472.

# The Symbolic Life of Man

Donald F. Sandner (San Francisco)

## Part I

We will start with the assumption, amply demonstrated in the work of Jung and his associates, that symbols are the fundamental units of man's psychic life. They channel psychic energy from one place in the psyche to another, they store or divert it, and they transform it. Since energy, by means of its qualities, creates feeling and value, and since it is by means of symbols that energy is evoked and governed, then only by means of symbols can we create meaning. Symbols operate in elaborate networks or systems of interlocking units (such as the Navaho curing ceremonies). Such a network taken as a whole may be called a *symbos*. These systems give and receive meaning to and from its parts. They are organs of the psyche, and like organs of the body – the liver, the heart, the spleen, etc. – each has a specialized function.

We shall examine two of the most important of these functions, and by focusing on their operation in tribal cultures, reflect back on them in contemporary culture.

The first of these symbolic functions is to imbue meaning to one's position in space and time. Symbols create a psychic envelope in which man may live. From the center, space extends outward and moves on an axis through time. This raw fact is thoroughly embellished by symbols until one is oriented by the four directions, each of which is full of mythical association, a member of a particular society living at the center of the universe, restricted by outer limits which are symbolically determined and moving through several interlocking cycles of birth, life and death – the human element of time.

The function of the mandala is the construction and projection of a psychic world in which the individual can feel familiar, safe, and comfortable. Eliade said of this function: "The mandala is primarily an *imago mundi*; it represents the cosmos in miniature and, at the same time, the pantheon. Its construction is equivalent to a magical re-creation of the world."[1] There are two levels to this re-creation: the greater or macrocosmic mandala and the lesser or microcosmic one. The macrocosmic mandala is the symbolized geography of the ancient tribal land interwoven with the annual round of the seasons and the stages of human life. It puts all these into relation with one another; they are the physical facts of life which must be tamed and made livable. The second level of symbolism found in sand paintings, schematic drawings and personal ideograms, mirrors this world order in microcosm. Everything is contained, ordered and harmonized by myth and ritual, and life goes on. Let me give some specific examples.

It may come as something of a surprise to you, as it did to me, to find that the macrocosm of every culture does not orient itself to north, east, south and west, as we do. In Bali, for instance, position in space is determined by the direction toward the central mountain, away from it, and then to the right and left of this axis. The resulting mandala, given meaning on several inter-relating levels, is called the *nawa sangga*, or Rose of the Winds.

In this cultural mandala, the guardians of the cardinal points and their ruler at the center symbolize the orderly Balinese universe. It is the lotus with eight blossoms and a center. Toward the central mountain is *Kadja*, symbolized by the patron god, *Wisnu*, the color black and the holy syllable *Hang*; away from the central mountain is *Klod*, symbolized by *Brahma*, the color red and the syllable *Bang*. To the right is *Kangin*, symbolized by *Iswara*, the color white and the syllable *Sang*. To the left, *Kauh*, the god *Mahadewa*, the color yellow and the syllable *Tang*. The center, *Puseh*, is represented by *Siwa*, many colors and the sacred syllable *Ing-Yang*. The syllables are part of special mantras that are repeated in rhythmic sequences and produce the ecstasy in which the Balinese priests commune with god. There are many associations to this system, and a symbolic explanation of the Rose of the Winds would go on indefinitely. The center corresponds with the central mountain of Bali, *Gunung Agung*, the 'navel of the world', and along with other mountains (*Mt. Batur, Batukah* and the *Tafelhoeck)*, the macrocosmic mandala is formed. The symbolism of the Rose of the Winds refers not only to the general geography of the island, but to the orien-

[1] M. Eliade, *Myth and Reality* (New York and Evanston, Ill.: Harper and Row, Harper Torchbooks, 1968), p. 25.

tation of every village, every household and even the body of every person. In addition to this structure, a Balinese religious book, *The Catur Yoga*, describes vertical layers which enclose and complete the picture. The lowest layer is the turtle, *Badawang*, created by the great serpent *Antaboga*. Above the turtle are coiled two primordial serpents and then the Black Stone. Beneath the stone there is no sun, no moon, nor any light, and this underworld is ruled by the god, *Kala*. Above that is the earth on which flows a layer of water, then a layer of mud which dries to make fields and mountains. Next, above, is the floating sky ruled by *Semara*, god of love. Then the blue sky of the sun god, *Surya*, and still higher, the perfumed sky where live the *Awan* snakes, seen as falling stars. Above that is *Swarga*, the flaming home of the ancestors, and finally, above all, the abode of the divine guardians. There is a connection here to the life cycle. When a person dies, his soul ascends to *Swarga* and becomes an ancestor. There the soul awaits rebirth and keeps watch over the people of Bali.

Balinese time is also divided into cyclical systems of concurrent 2, 3, 4, 5, 6, 7, 8, 9, and 10 day weeks of which 3, 5, 6, and 7 are the most important. Auspicious days occur when these cycles intersect. The social system itself is layered into castes. The whole system is greatly overdetermined. Within this strict structure of space, time and social order, the people are comfortable and dreamy. This exceedingly safe world order allows the trance states to which the Balinese are exceptionally predisposed.

In another culture, the American Indians have developed both the macrocosmic and microcosmic mandalas to a high degree. Black Elk has described the macrocosmic mandala as it looked to the Oglala Sioux:

> Everything the Power of the World does is done in a circle. The sky is round, and I have heard that the earth is round like a ball, and so are all the stars. The wind, in its greatest power, whirls. Birds make their nests in circles, for theirs is the same religion as ours. The sun comes forth and goes down in a circle. The moon does the same, and both are round. Even the seasons form a great circle in their changing, and always come back to where they were. The life of man is a circle from childhood to childhood, and so it is in everything where power moves. Our tepees were round like the nests of birds, and these were always set in a circle, the nation's hoop, a nest of many nests, where the Great Spirit meant for us to hatch our children.[2]

[2] Black Elk, *Black Elk Speaks*, transcribed by J. Niehardt (Lincoln: University of Nebraska Press, 1961), pp. 198–200.

The Navaho also see their ancient land, the *Dineh,* as a gigantic mandala. The main features are the sacred mountains, which delineate the borders in the four directions and have a substantial geographical reality. For instance, *Doko'o'slid* is the Shining-on-Top Mountain of the west, always identified with Mount Humphreys in the San Francisco Peaks near Flagstaff, Arizona. It is represented by the color yellow, the color of wisdom, holiness and spiritual essence. It is covered by yellow evening light and fastened to the earth by a sunbeam. On its peak are the jewel symbols of abalone; the yellow warbler is its bird and the yellow corn its plant. On it live White Corn Boy and Yellow Corn Girl, Evening Light Boy and Abalone Girl. It is known for dark clouds, heavy rain (called male rain), yellow corn and wild animals. Its deity is named 'Calling God'. The inner form is described as a Beautiful One dressed in radiant abalone. This cluster of symbolism of the western mountain is repeated for each of the directions and for several other symbolically significant mountains in Navaho country.

The geographic mandala and the turning seasons of the year are part of the great round, which is in constant rhythmic movement. In his version of the creation myth, the Navaho's greatest medicine man, Hosteen Klah, said:

> They made the Sun of fire with a rainbow around it, and put the Turquoise Man into it as its spirit. They put the Fall and Winter in the West and North, and the Spring and Summer in the South and East... Then all the spirits went to the places where they belonged, and they raised the Sun and Moon, Stars and Winds. The Fire God placed the North Star, and the other Gods placed their constellations, the women placing the Milky Way and other stars... They put the forty-eight cyclones under the edges of the world in the four directions to hold it up, and sent other winds to hold up the sky and stars. (The high god)... motioned to all creation and it came to life and moved at different speeds.[3]

This mythical drama of the Navaho is enacted in a smaller but more intense form in the microcosm of the stand paintings. These are sacred pictures made of naturally colored sands on the earth floor of the ceremonial hogans. When completed, the medicine man evokes healing power and channels it into the painting. The Navaho name for sand painting means, 'where the gods come and go'. The patient then sits on some part of this altar, and with his hands, the medicine man transfers

[3] Hosteen Klah, *Navaho Creation Myth* (Santa Fe, N. M.: Museum of Navaho Ceremonial Art, 1942).

power from the painting to various parts of the patient's body. Prayers and songs accompany the ritual. A good example is a sand painting from the Male Shooting Chant, which shows the Holy Family in relation to the heavenly bodies and the four directions. The holy people are arranged in mandalic form. Holy Man is in the east, touching with his powerful bow a basket in which rests the blue Sun. The Sun in Navaho mythology is seen as blue because of the heat and radiance associated with turquoise. Holy Woman at the west touches the White Moon. Holy Boy at the south touches Black Wind and Holy Girl at the north touches Yellow Wind. Here the male and female deities are in perfect balance, and this sand painting presents one of the intuitive concepts that characterize Navaho genius. Here the polar relationship is not only between the Great Mother and the Great Father, but also includes the Holy Son and the Holy Daughter. In the four directions are expressed the relationship between father and son, father and daughter, and also mother and daughter and mother and son. In our civilization, we have explored one of these dimensions, father and son (the Father God and Christ). This has taken us two thousand years; we still have the other three relationship possibilities remaining. Already in this painting, the great heavenly bodies have been harnassed by man in whirling feathered baskets and the mandala is in motion.

This motion is shown even more clearly in a sand painting from the Night Chant which shows a mandalic cross of four giant logs in the sacred lake. On each of the logs sits a pair of deities, and the whole giant swastika-like figure is being rotated by the great Navaho gods: Talking God, the tutelary diety for the Navaho heroes; Calling God, the deity of domestic life and fertility; and two humpbacked gods reminiscent of the little humpbacked trickster who roams the Southwest Indian world with his flute, his phallus and his hump full of all the seeds that mean food and sustenance to the people. The Rainbow Guardian surrounds the painting with the opening to the east. Here the clockwise motion shows the change from stability and orientation – the first function of the mandala – to the second function, which is to engender movement, change and transformation.

Before we move on, let us consider our own macrocosmic mandala, the earth. Black Elk says: "I have heard the earth is round as a ball." This could be carried further. Not only is it round, it turns around on its axis, clouds swirl in great arcs, and sea currents circle the oceans. Nor does the circling end there. The sun itself revolves in a great galactic wheel, and the stars wheel and turn in vast space. Black Elk says: "And so it is in everything where power moves… a nest of many nests, where the Great Spirit meant for us to hatch our children."

Upon this whirling globe we have applied the myths of science. The myth, for instance, that each revolution is divided into twenty-four parts; that the globe itself has equators and meridians, divided into longitudes and latitudes; that its curvature is measured in miles; that the days and months and years are named and numbered. Thus, like the Mayans, we find repose in a calendared and numbered mythic envelope built on a shifting, sliding and always dangerous cosmos.

In order for change and transformation to occur in this cosmos, one mandala must deteriorate and collapse so that another may arise. Mythologically, this is represented as death and rebirth. Psychologically, it means loss of conscious control, weakening or temporary collapse of the ego, and submission to a new influx of raw symbolic stuff from another place, the deep unconscious. This is felt to be a great sacrifice, a dying to one's old self, a wrenching farewell to a familiar and cherished path. The symbolic process of death and rebirth is found wherever there is a life crisis necessitating rites of transformation, rechanneling psychic energy from old worn-out patterns to more functional new ones. Healing rites are one form of these transformations, rites of passage, another. Among the latter are the familiar initiation ceremonies of tribal cultures, with their elaborate ordeals and rituals designed to bring adolescents into full tribal membership. This also includes initiations into special cults, mystery religions, and secret societies. Even the symbols associated with burial customs depict death as a preparation for rebirth.

The structure of the psyche itself, as it is understood in Jungian psychology, demonstrates the pattern of death and rebirth. First, there is a state of wholeness, a condition of the early infant psyche which may be thought of as the primary unconscious Self. This undergoes a process of 'deintegration' (to use Michael Fordham's term) into discrete psychic units or complexes. They may enter into either the formation of ego identity or outward projections as part of the complicated mechanism of object relations. The conflicts that occur then awaken the ego to greater consciousness, striving toward the goal of reintegration. The primary Self undergoes a kind of death. It is torn asunder and reconstructed, or mythologically reborn, at the expense of great suffering and work on the part of the conscious ego. This work takes a whole lifetime.

In adult life, the frequent need for healing ceremonies occurs during mental or physical breakdown or illness. Such unfortunate interruptions of normal life signal an exhaustion of the old way and an urgent need for processes to speed the re-formation of the new one. Healing has always occupied a high place in man's symbolic life because it stimulates change and renewal.

I am indebted to Rosemary Gordon[4] for reasserting the distinction between curing and healing. Thus far in my work, I have used these terms interchangeably, but there is a useful differentiation. In the standard dictionary, 'to cure' means 'to take care of' and also 'successful medical treatment'. On the other hand, 'to heal' means basically 'to make whole' and is an ancient word in the English language, closely related to the word 'holy' – the sacred.

In this paper, I use the term 'curing' to refer to objective, rational, scientifically based therapy. By the term 'healing', I mean symbolic therapy, such as used in tribal cultures, usually based on the older forms of myth and ritual, or the newer forms of dreams and visions. There is overlap between the two.

Scientific curing makes use of empirical facts and builds a base of sound anatomical, physiological, and pharmacological knowledge. It focuses on specific organs, rarely on the body as a whole, and is based on tested and verified procedures. It has in its repertoire a wide spectrum of highly skilled techniques ranging from surgical operations and complex biochemical laboratory determinations, to internal and external medication of experimentally proven worth. Its practitioners are trained in highly technical medical schools with a large faculty of specialized teachers.

Because the biology of man is roughly alike throughout the species, scientific medicine is genuinely cross-cultural. It will work as well, within limits, on a Navaho Indian as on an American office worker. When the appendix is inflamed, an appendectomy is the best procedure, no matter to what culture the patient belongs. Penicillin and related antibiotics combat infection wherever they are judiciously administered. The patient is expected to follow the doctor's directions passively, to be grateful for the abatement of symptoms which frequently follows, and to pay a substantial fee. The drawback of this kind of therapy is that it ignores the patient's humanity and neglects the

[4] R. Gordon, "Reflections on Curing and Healing", *Journal of Analytical Psychology*, vol. 24, no. 3 (July 1979).

effect of cultural symbols on the mind and body. It may restore the specific organ (and grateful we are for that), but it does not give meaning to the occurrence of illness in the patient's life and it does not satisfy the patient in his search for the meaning of his disease and its significance to his whole being. That can only be achieved through symbols.

Therefore, every culture has some form of symbolic healing which does not rely on detailed scientific knowledge of bodily organs. It relies for its effect on identification of the patient with supernatural or intrapsychic power through the mediation of the symbol. All phases of treatment – nosology, etiology, diagnosis, therapy and prognosis – are based on symbolic identification. The cause of disease and its treatment are connected to the greater mythological whole, and are seen against the background of man's soul. The 'doctor' is the shaman or medicine man or priest who has undergone an initiatory apprenticeship, sometimes with only one teacher, in the beliefs and rituals of his culture. The patient must also share in these beliefs, or the healing won't work. One Navaho medicine man said to me: "If the patient really has confidence in me, then he gets cured. If he has no confidence, then that is his problem. If a person gets bitten by a snake, for example, certain prayers and songs can be used. But if the patient doesn't have enough confidence, then the cure won't work." This healing also depends on the consensus of the community as a cultural unit to give validity to its symbols. If skepticism and conflict with other systems caused the symbols to fall into disrepute, then the core of the healing system would collapse.

The drawback is that symbolic healing often ignores the patient as a biological organism, and fails to observe the simplest rules of bodily care and hygiene. Gladys Reichard once described how an elderly Navaho woman was subjected to the prolonged exertion and chilling exposure of a rigorous chant ceremony lasting several days, in spite of the fact that she was suffering from severe pneumonia.

The two systems can work together. There is nothing inherently antagonistic in their operations as long as they stay within their sphere of effectiveness.

Even though symbolic healing is not scientific, it is more than vague and exotic fantasies jumbled together. It has a definite structure and there are certain stages through which it proceeds, though these are neither strictly chronological nor mutually exclusive.

The purpose of these stages is to enhance the reality of the symbols used and the meaning they carry. The stages in the process I am describing are as follows: purification of the participants, evocation or reification of the symbol, identification of the patient and the medicine man with the symbol and its meaning, inner transformation, and final release. I will illustrate these using the Blessing Way ritual of the Navaho. Blessing Way is the original prototype for the entire Navaho chant system. It is short by comparison, only two nights and one day; it is filled with holiness and contains no evil, and it is used for a variety of everyday purposes, all of which need the support of the symbolic power which it carries. It is used to invoke good luck, good health, and blessing, to install a chief or head man, to obviate the bad effects of mistakes in ceremonials, to dispel fear from bad dreams, for protection of flocks and herds, to cure insanity, or to consecrate ceremonial paraphernalia.

The Blessing Way chant always takes place in a ceremonial hogan. It is constructed of a framework of logs overlaid with earth. The door always faces the east and the rising sun. The construction of the hogan mirrors the structure of the Navaho universe, and its center is the center of that universe.

At the beginning of the chant, the medicine man blesses the four cardinal supports of the hogan with pollen, the most sacred symbol of the Navaho mythology, signifying the essence of power and goodness. Washington Matthews said: "Pollen is the emblem of peace, of happiness, of prosperity, and it is supposed to bring these blessings... When in prayer the devotee says 'May the trail be in pollen', he pleads for a happy and peaceful life."[5] The purifying pollen is put first on the supporting pole to the east which is dedicated to Earth Woman, then on the pole to the south dedicated to Mountain Woman, the pole to the west dedicated to Water Woman, and the pole to the north dedicated to Corn Woman. Thus the hogan is purified.

Now comes the purification of the patient. A small mound marked with a white cross is made from soil brought in from the corn fields. The white cross is the simplest form of the microcosmic mandala, placing the patient at the very center of the directional powers. Then a ceremonial basket filled with yucca suds is placed on the mound, and the medicine man washes the patient.

In the original myth of Blessing Way, two children were carried to the home of the earth goddess, Changing Woman. They were picked up in a corn field and, before entering her home, were subjected to a purifying bath because of the human smell that clung to them. The patient

[5] W. Matthews, "Navaho Legends", *Memoirs of the American Folklore Society,* vol. 5 (1897), p. 299.

is purified in the same way as the children, first with the yucca suds, and then with corn meal. The suds and the corn meal are always applied from the feet upward to the head. In this way, the patient is identified with the corn deities and with the two children, who were abducted and taught by Changing Woman. All during the ceremonial baths, the medicine man sings songs linking the patient with the inner forms of corn and pollen. Leaving the corn meal in place, the patient dresses and leaves.

Even though the emphasis in the preceding ritual is on purification, evoking of the deities through the bathing songs, and identification of the patient with the two children who visited Changing Woman has already begun. Further evocation of the desired supernatural power proceeds with the laying out of the medicine bundle and with the songs and prayers which occupy much of the next day and night. The most important item in the medicine kit is the mountain-soil bundle, which contains bits of soil from the four sacred mountains that mark the boundaries of the Navaho land. It is the only piece of religious property absolutely necessary for the performance of Blessing Way. Each portion of the sacred soil is supposed to be wrapped separately, and the whole is wrapped in an unwounded buckskin with a white shell bead on the outside to mark the position of the east bundle. Once the bundle has been closed, it is not disturbed; it is guarded carefully as an heirloom of the singer and his family or clan. The medicine bundle may also contain flint crystals, bags of pollen with an organite stone to keep the pollen 'alive', pieces of wood from lightning-struck trees, or talking prayer sticks. The patient holds the mountain-soil bundle and the talking prayer sticks while important prayers are recited.

The songs continue through the entire night. The images of the gods are built up detail by detail in slow and painstaking repetition. The patient is closely and repeatedly linked with the inner forms of Earth, Changing Woman, Corn, Talking God, and other deities. The beauty and power of each sacred personage is patiently explored, and the emotional effect is repeatedly emphasized by expressions of surprise and delight. The songs, myths, rites and prayers are fused together intimately and intensively. This induces the great inner concentration necessary to unite the patient physically with those archetypal powers that can give release from pain and sorrow, bestow strength and vitality, and point the way to a long and rewarding experience of life.

At the first hint of dawn, the patient goes outside the hogan, faces east, and breathes in the dawn four times.

The main business of the chants – identification of the patient with the gods and the use of their sacred power for a healing transformation – is performed most intensively in the ritual of the sand painting and the prayers. In a nine-day chant, the first four days and nights are devoted to purification and evocation. Exorcistic rites are performed; sweat baths and emetic medicines are taken by the patient. The prayer sticks and other ritual offerings are made; songs and prayers evoking the gods are performed. Thus by the fourth day, the area of the chant in and around the sacred hogan has been emptied of negative influences and refreshed. The vigorous new power has begun to enter, and it is time to make the sand paintings proper to the chant being used and the condition of the patient.

While the painting is being made, the medicine man and his assistants may joke and relax, but when the painting is finally done, the mood changes. The medicine man begins the prayers that bring the power of the gods into the sacred figures. At a certain point, the patient is brought in to see the sand painting for the first time. Then the ritual transfer of power takes place.

This is the part of the ceremony that is most crucial. The medicine man and the patient are identified with the sacred power through the symbolic medium of the sand painting. As a result, the transformation indicated in this prayer from the Night Chant is expected to occur.

> Happily I recover.
> Happily my interior becomes cool.
> Happily my eyes regain their power.
> Happily my head becomes cool.
> Happily my limbs regain their power.
> Happily I hear again.
> Happily for me the spell is taken off.
> Happily I may walk.
> Impervious to pain, may I walk.
> With lively feelings, I walk.[6]

The prayer also describes the coming of the power:

> Above it thunders,
> His thoughts are directed to you,
> He rises toward you.
> Now to your house,
> He approaches for you.

6 W. Matthews, "The Night Chant: A Navaho Ceremony", *Memoirs of the American Museum of Natural History*, vol. 6 (1902), p. 144.

He arrives for you.
He comes to the door,
He enters for you.
Behind the fireplace
He eats his special dish.
"Your body is strong,
Your body is holy now" he says.[7]

After the ceremony, there is a period of time, four nights for the larger chants, during which the power is released and ebbs away. There are certain restrictions on the patient at this time. He must keep to himself, he must not sleep until sunset and he must not eat certain foods. Then the power is gone and the ceremonial cycle is complete: purification, evocation, identification, transformation, and release.

The process of breakdown and renewal is, in my opinion, characteristic of symbolic healing and may be the basic archetype which appears from culture to culture in many guises and variations. It has three aspects which are especially important. The first is the return to the origins, the second is the recognition and management of evil, and the third is the core myth of death and rebirth. All these refer to the same process, but they emphasize different points of view.

The first one, return to the origins, refers to the psychological dynamic of regression. It implies a return, not only to childhood and infancy, but to the beginnings of consciousness, which is symbolized in myth as the time of creation. The significance of this symbol has been spelled out by Mircea Eliade as follows:

> As the exemplary model for all 'creation', the cosmogonic myth can help the patient to make a 'new beginning' of his life. The *return to origins* gives the hope of rebirth... The medical rituals we have been examining aim at a return to origins. We get the impression that for archaic societies life cannot be *repaired,* it can only be *re-created* by a return to the sources. And the 'source of sources' is the prodigious outpouring of energy, life, and fecundity that occurred at the Creation of the World.[8]

All the Navaho chants have myths which recount how the chant hero or heroine dared to leave familiar country and visit the 'other land', the upper or lower worlds, where they underwent ordeals and

[7] Ibid, p. 153.

[8] M. Eliade, *Rites and Symbols of Initiation* (New York: Harper and Row, Harper Torchbooks, 1958), p. 30.

endured suffering; sometimes they were totally disintegrated and then restored by the forces of nature. They were finally successful in acquiring the secrets of the chant itself for the use of the Navaho people. Thus chant myths are all origin myths. The Navaho patient relives these myths and adventures symbolically in the prayers, songs and rituals of the chants, many of which commemorate and re-enact some part of the hero's adventure. On the last night of every chant, songs of this type are sung all night long with many repetitions. Consciousness is dimmed and the ego is brought into intimate contact with the cultural archetypal forms of the Navaho, strong symbols from the collective unconscious.

Some of this process is shown in sand paintings. There is a sand painting which commemorates the emergence of man from the four underworlds. The black central circle is the place of emergence from which the gods, early man, and animals entered this world from the third world beneath it. The oval shapes radiating from the center in the shape of a flower symbolize the four worlds beneath the present one, each represented by a color: black, blue, yellow and white. The seven-jointed big reed extending from the yellow world is the escape route the Navaho ancestors took to escape the primeval flood, represented by the large blue square bordered by a rainbow. The black figure with the blue mask is the Sun and near his feet is Badger, whose feet became black when he emerged. The white figure is the Moon, and nearby is Coyote. The four oval shapes outside the blue square are the four holy mountains which border the Navaho homeland, and the turquoise and white squares are the homes of Changing Woman and her sister, White Shell Woman.

Navaho man came from the wombs of nature, and it is to the powers of nature he turns for healing. All the parts of his body were made from nature, which is in a way congruent with our scientific ideas, but very different in symbolic impact, as this brief part of the origin myth demonstrates:

> They made his feet and his toe nails and his ankles of the soil of the Earth, his legs of lightning, his knees of white shell and his body of white corn and yellow corn. His heart was of obsidian and his breath was the white wind... They took all the flesh of all the different animals to make his body, and also all kinds of flower pollen. They made him of all kinds of water: rains, springs, lakes, rivers, and the sky and the female rain, and they made his arms of the rainbow. His hair was made of darkness, his skull of

the sun… and the name of this new kind of human being was Created-From-Everything.[9]

## Part II

The recognition and management of evil, the second aspect of symbolic healing, is vividly illustrated in Balinese ritual. In Bali, the collective unconscious is never far away. Many persons are able to go into trance with great ease, and remain there as long as desired. No prolonged dancing, praying or trance-inducing drugs are necessary. Even the local shamans or *balyans* are taught through the collective unconscious itself; they usually do not go through an extensive apprenticeship with an older shaman. One day they are simply entered and possessed by a god or ancestor who, from that time on, will help them practice and tell them what to do. Particularly in Bali, the demarcation between the recently dead, the more distant ancestors and the gods is an indistinct one, and one shades off into the other.

When the *balyan* (very often a woman) is consulted by a patient for problems ranging from illness, poor business and family troubles to unexpected misfortunes or withchcraft, she goes into trance and, through her contacts in the inner world, she calls forth an ancestor or recently deceased family member of the patient. This personage tells her what the patient should do to correct his problem. Sometimes this is one of the innumerable ritual obligations that are so frequently required in Bali. At other times, it is something quite specific and personal pertaining to the family relationships. In any case, the *balyan* herself takes no responsibility for the answer. It is simply given to her in trance and she transmits it to the patient. This follows the pattern of ego regression and descent into the unconscious, although to call it 'death and rebirth' seems to overstate the case. It is more like a quiet slipping aside of the ego allowing the unconscious boldly and dramatically to take control. The ego still maintains overall direction, and can begin and terminate the process more or less at will. This is not so true of the trance dancers in the communal exorcistic rituals. Often they must be subdued by others and brought back to normal consciousness by the priest using holy water.

9 Hosteen Klah, *Navaho Creation Myth* (Santa Fe, N. M.: Museum of Navaho Ceremonial Art, 1942), p. 102.

One of the Balinese healers I studied is Ni Wayan Rendo of Abienkapas near Denpasar. She is in her forties, and has been a *balyan tetakson* (a shaman who operates through trance) for about fourteen years. Before that, she was a peanut vendor, but made a poor living because she did not tend to business. Then one day, while she was in the temple, she was entered and possessed by a god who became her psychic mentor. She was told to become a practicing healer, and she complied. In Bali, that is both a great honor and an exhausting burden, because she must see all those who come, and take only what they voluntarily offer without demanding more.

When she sees a patient, she has certain signals, feeling suddenly hot or cold inside. Then her inner mentor becomes active and, while she is in trance, the mentor contacts an ancestor, often a recently deceased family member of the patient. She says:

> It is like a shadow. I can contact it easily if someone wants to know something. The patient must make a little offering and ask the ancestor to come to me. Sometimes there is something wrong, and they can't come to me. Then I can't help them.

On the auspicious days when she can practice, she has many patients who come from all parts of the island to consult her. She sits on a *balé*, a wooden platform on which are offerings of food, rice, small coins, holy-water, incense and other things. The patients sit around her and in an adjoining room on wooden benches waiting their turn to move forward to the bench just in front of her. For each one, she goes easily and quickly into a trance, using only incense, some betel nut, prayer, and holy water.

Ordinarily she is a modest, soft-spoken woman, but in the trance state she becomes different. She takes on a tone of authority, laughs, scolds patients for their neglect of ritual duties, consoles them, and generally conducts a most emotional interview.

She told one young Balinese man, for instance, that she was talking to the soul of his mother, who had been dead only a few months. She admonished him for neglecting a shrine in his family compound. She also told him that he was too often angry and cruel to his father, from whom he was estranged; she urged him to purify himself of evil and make amends to his father. She said:

> Purify your body for all your family, and also for your father. You feel much sadness. That is caused by your forgetfulness of the holy soul (in the family shrine). You were right to come here quickly or else the trouble will get bigger.

She also saw a young couple whose child had recently died. She told them that the child had died because of the bad feelings (envy) of a niece who lived nearby. There was some hint that witchcraft was involved. She advised them to move away and take up their life elsewhere, where they would not be in contact with this malicious relative.

In another case, a middle-aged man was sadly grieving for his wife who had recently died. In this case, she spoke to the soul of the wife and advised that he perform several more ceremonial procedures that could help the dead woman to make her path easier. The fact that he could actively still do something to help his wife seemed to comfort him.

The Balinese world is held in balance by two opposing forces: a right-handed force which is benign and favorable to man, and a left-handed force which is malicious and evil. The latter brings sickness and death, and is influenced by black magic. When too much black magic is concentrated in a village, a purification ceremony is necessary to correct the balance. Such is the mystical, symbolic drama of the two protagonists, the *Barong* and *Rangda*.

During this ceremony, many of the participants from the village enter into deep trance to enact their roles. Here the management of evil, our second aspect of archetypal healing, is emphasized. But the return to the original historical battle, which occurred centuries ago, in which the witch was neutralized, is here repeated in dramatic form – a return to the origin. The aspect of ego death and renewal is embodied in the entire drama.

Often the play itself is embedded in a story borrowed from the Indian epic, *The Mahabharata*, but the essence of the drama, the struggle between the two cosmic forces, always remains the same. The village is being threatened by the evil witch, *Rangda*, and the framework for the action is set.

Then the *Barong* enters, ready to defend the village. The *Barong*, a mystical creature with a long swayback and curved tail, represents the protector of mankind, the glory of the high sun, and the favorable spirits associated with the right-handed force and white magic. He is danced by two men who form the forelegs and the hind legs. His mask has several variations. It may be that of a wild boar, a tiger, a lion or an elephant, but the most frequent mask represented is that of 'The Sovereign Lord of the Forest', a mythical beast.

The *Barong* does a lively dance to the music of the *gamelan* orchestra, giving the appearance of a large appealing puppy. He prances and whirls, puts his head on his paws, and wags his long curved tail. His dance is ended by the appearance of *Rangda* riding on the shoulders of her accomplices. She has a flaming tongue lolling out of her mouth, and wears a necklace of entrails. She stalks the *Barong,* cursing and howling. At the same time, she waves her magic white cloth, the source of her evil magic.

The two protagonists clash in a deadly struggle upon which the fate of the village depends. When the *Barong* is nearly overcome by *Rangda,* he summons the men of the village to his aid. In a trance, they rush out to attack the witch with reckless violence. Waving her magic white cloth, the witch turns the fury of the *Barong's* men back onto themselves and they turn their long curving daggers against their own breasts. The men would surely die except that, at the last moment, the *Barong* is able to invoke a powerful charm which prevents the blades from entering their bodies. Then the drama ends with the *kris* dancers in trance, apparently striving to drive the *kris* into their chests, but forever unable to do so. The *Barong* has cast a protective sheath about their bodies so that the skin is not even punctured. If the trance is deep, the men have to be forcibly prevented from exhausting themselves. They are dragged over to the priest (or *pemangku*), and restored. He sprinkles them with holy water that has been dipped in the beard of the *Barong,* which is his most sacred part and made of human hair.

Thus the drama ends once more in a stand-off. Neither the *Barong* nor the witch, *Rangda,* can prevail. It is with an uneasy balance such as this that the village will have to live.

Another communal effort to manipulate and control evil is the famous *Sanghyang Jalan.* This is a characteristic shamanic performance, representing the shaman's ability to control fire, and also the evil forces threatening the village. The men build a large fire of coconut husks. The trance dancer enters and rides his hobby horse around the temple courtyard. The hobby horse is a symbol of the shaman's magic steed. The dancer has previously been entranced by the priest, and now he embodies a divine presence and is respected by the villagers. All of a sudden, he rides directly into the roaring fire, and does so again and again until it is extinguished. There are always guardians standing by and, after he runs free of the fire and continues prancing about in an agitated manner, they run out and gently subdue him, bringing him over to the priest, who awakens him out of his trance with holy water.

His feet are unharmed by the experience, and he has demonstrated again the power of trance to protect himself and the village from evil influence.

My third example of symbolic healing is more direct and primitive. Among the indians of the Amazon Basin and the coastal areas of Colombia, Peru and Ecuador, symbolic healing is effected by means of visionary plants. One of the most important of these is *yaǵe*, or *ayahuasca,* which means 'Vine of the Soul'. The main active ingredients of this plant are the alkaloids harmine and harmaline, also found in modern psychiatric drugs. The use of *yaǵe* requires a minimum of ritual ceremony because the effects themselves are so real that other forms of lowering ego awareness are unnecessary. In Amazonian tribes where *yaǵe* is used, many persons may become shamans, and the visionary state of consciousness is available to anyone who participates.

Preparations for the ceremony are described for a small tribe of Indians in southeastern Peru (the Cashinahua) by Kensinger.[10] They go to the jungle and without ritual gather some of the sacred vine. They take it home and cut it into six- to eight-inch sections, which are then pounded and boiled in a cooking pot. It is boiled for about an hour and then ladled off. During the ceremony, the men sit around the hearth and each man, after chanting an invocation asking the brew to show him many things, drinks a pint of the black brew.

Usually the experience is shared by a group, and often the members are in close physical contact. Soon there is extreme nausea, vomiting, and sometimes diarrhea. Then comes the visionary state. The soul seems to leave the body and enter into another world. Snakes or jaguars are common visitors. The person may fly like a bird and visit ancestors or the world beyond. Mythical figures may appear and speak. One participant of the Cashinahua tribe describes his experience in these words:

> Soon I began to shake all over. The earth shook. The wind blew and the trees swayed... Snakes, large brightly colored snakes were crawling on the ground. They began to crawl all over me. One large female snake tried to swallow me, but since I was chanting she couldn't succeed... The world was transformed. Everything became bright. I moved very fast. Not my body but my eye spirit... I came down the trail to a village. There was much noise, the sound of peiple laughing... Everybody was laughing.

10) K. Kensinger, "Banisteriopsis Usage Among the Peruvian Cashinahua", in *Hallucinogens and Shamanism,* M. Harner, editor (New York: Oxford University Press, 1973).

> Many of the woman were pregnant. I was happy. I knew we would be well and have plenty to eat.[11]

All the symbolic aspects of the healing archetype are brought out vividly here. In a recent trip by bus, across the Andes, by boat into the western Amazon basin (which is part of Ecuador's Oriente Province), I was able to experience this first hand. We followed the Rio Napa, which comes down from the mountains and proceeds eastward toward the settlement of Coca about fifty miles away. From there, we went to the jungle plantation of a Quijos Indian shaman named Domingo Mamallacta. His house was raised on poles, surrounded by jungle gardens containing pineapple, red peppers, bananas, lemon trees and wild avocados.

Domingo was a gentle, sweet person who looked younger than his fifty years, and did not hesitate to welcome us with a great show of hospitality. After a light supper, the *ayahuasca* vine was produced and treated in the manner described above with very little accompanying ritual. In the early evening, we all took a half cup of the black, bitter brew. The effect was the worst I have ever experienced. It tasted like bile, and had to be drunk all at once, or not at all. Then, after about twenty minutes, the awful heaving of the stomach began, accompanied by waves of nausea. Since we hadn't eaten much, not much came up, but the feeling was one of acute illness. The Indians also experienced this effect, but not nearly as much as we did. They thought our discomfort was extremely funny. When the acute misery was at its height, there was a sudden detachment of the mind from the body, and one could see as at a distance one's bodily discomfort, but it no longer registered as such and seemed of no consequence. The main sensation was of floating in a kind of dreaming ectasy. After we had all calmed down, Domingo began his purifying ceremony in complete darkness. One by one, we were seated before him, while he sang softly, blew tobacco smoke over our bodies, and began gently to shake a bunch of leaves against our faces. Then he began the sucking therapy, starting with the top of my head, and then each finger. This was accompanied by a loud retching sound and a dramatic enactment of spitting something into a small bowl.

In my experience, the singing and shaking of the leaves over my body had an eerie feeling. Enhanced by the effects of the drug, it produced a state of profound excitement. The sucking felt like a vacuum cleaner

[11] Ibid, pp. 9–10.

was pulling at the top of my head and then from each finger down into my chest and abdomen. There was the most real feeling that some noxious substance was being drawn up by strong suction and then expelled through the head and fingers. Afterward, the feeling that my body had indeed been cleansed and purified persisted for about a month.

This was repeated for everyone present, including the visiting Indians and members of the healer's family. If there was something specifically wrong with someone, the sucking was also done on the part of the body that was ailing. The rest of the night was spent in trance with the shaman continuing to sing. I experienced a succession of visionary images, as did others, but the most persistent one was of a large bird – who either was me, or held me on its back. It was hovering over a wide jungle area that led to a low range of mountains, not as high or rough as the Andes. The bird was trying to soar through a far off gap in the mountains. Either because of the unfamiliar jungle environment, or the general haste of the whole proceedings, I did not permit this to continue and the bird got only a little way above the jungle, but not over the mountain. More *ayahuasca* and a strong concoction of native tobacco juice were offered at intervals during the night, as well as *trago*, a heavily alcoholic drink, but I could not bring myself to go any further on this occasion.

The impression exists for me that I actually felt the symbolic reality of the lowering of ego control, the nearness and vividness of the collective unconscious, and the profound feeling of purification through sucking. Sucking is one of the oldest known forms of medical treatment and has been used in all parts of the world, probably since paleolithic times. More people have been treated by this method than any other. It has always been something of a puzzle to me that the power of such simple suggestion could be so strong and enduring. But after this experience in the Amazon with the symbol-enhancing effect of the drug, I no longer felt puzzled. It seemed plain to me that the symbolic effect of sucking was real and physical, and had actually done what it was supposed to do, cleansed the body. I also had no doubt that if I had continued farther into the vision, I would have entered a very real inner world, and experienced contact with deep layers of the unconscious.

Now we have looked briefly at symbolic healing methods in three very different cultures. Though it is not difficult to see the healing archetype in each of the cultures, the mode of expression is very different in each. To round out our survey, we will compare with these three a final fourth culture, our own. In order to compare symbolic healing in such vastly different cultures, it is necessary to keep in mind the relationship between the doctor, medicine man or shaman, the symbolic system, and the patient. Then one can see three differing modes of symbolic healing pertaining to the cultures we have discussed.

The first is the mode of the shaman. He enacts the symbolism in his own person through periods of ecstatic trance. He alone is the carrier and focus of symbolic power; the patient is only a passive participant who goes along with him. This is most characteristic of the Balinese healers as I have described them. They go into trance, contact the ancestors or gods, and they tell the patient what to do. The patient is a passive receiver.

The mode of the medicine man is characteristic of the Navaho. The Navaho medicine man does not act out the symbolism in his own person. He remains impassive and reserved, and the main focus of symbolic action is presented to the patient through the songs, prayers, and sand paintings. The medicine man draws upon a vast body of traditional symbolism, but he does not live it out. The mythic hero is the protagonist of the chant, and this journey occurs in the myth.

The third mode of symbolic healing is found in modern psychotherapy. In this mode, the doctor is comparatively passive. There are no ecstatic journeys, and no dancing, singing, sand painting, or any of the other culturally prescribed activities of the first two modes. There is no large traditional body of symbolism for the doctor to draw upon for the benefit of the patient. The main focus of symbolic action is from the patient himself. He must produce the symbols from his own dreams, fantasies and personal visions. The doctor's role is a catalytic one, mostly limited to reflection, interpretation and encouragement. He listens to the patient, encourages him to explore his inner life, and through interpretation gives him a perspective in which to work.

Most of the medical therapy in our society is curing, in the sense that Rosemary Gordon has defined it. This includes holistic healing, which means treating the mind and the body, but still separately. Symbolic healing treats the whole, not by many different techniques, but by constellating a symbol of wholeness. Symbolic healing is not much concerned with symptoms or clinical diagnosis. The troubles may be physical or mental illness, or misfortune. Therapy tries to remedy these situations by means of a symbol wrested from the deeper psyche. Healing comes from 'the god within'.

The stages I have delineated for tribal culture have direct relevance to the psychotherapeutic situation. The *purification* is the isolation of the patient and therapist in the *temenos* of the consulting room. The *evocation* is the preliminary discussion of how the work will be done; the *identification* and *transformation* come through the transference and the patient's dreams, fantasies and visions. Release is the resolution of these bonds and the termination of the psychotherapeutic process.

The archetypal aspects or principles are also fully present in modern healing. The first is the *return to the origin* or source. For the modern patient, this means a return to the origin of his life. Almost all forms of psychotherapy look backward to the patient's childhood to examine the familial and cultural influences on his illness. Sometimes this extends back to birth, the 'place of emergence' for modern psychology, and the very earliest mothering experiences. What the Navaho medicine man does with myths, prayers, and sand paintings, returning his patients to the mythic origin of his people; what the Balinese healers do with their trance sessions, putting the patient in touch with his ancestors; and what the Amazon Indians do with visionary drugs, returning the patient to the deepest 'other world' of the unconscious; we do with memories, dreams, and fantasies. In psychotherapy, we return the patient, by means of regression, to the beginning of his life, and to the original shaping of his energy.

The second archetypal principle or aspect is the management of 'evil', what we refer to as 'shadow work'. In tribal healing, this is often done by symbolizing evil as a small object or spirit that intrudes into the patient's body, and must be dramatically removed. When the symbol is removed, the evil goes with it. Often the object is thought to have been placed there by a witch so that the cure takes the form of a struggle between the medicine man and the witch, hopefully ending with the destruction of the witch. In the Navaho evil-chasing chants, for instance, the evil is brushed, blown, cut, frightened or prayed away.

In modern psychotherapy, the therapist and the patient must also confront whatever is 'evil' for that particular patient. The content of that evil, the actual analytic work with the shadow, is not as important as the process of dealing with that evil.

The content of the 'evil' will vary from culture to culture, and will be in accord with the patient's and therapist's cultural expectations. Together they call it forth and deal with it. There is probably always a time in intense analytic work when the therapist actually takes on the projection of the patient's evil, before it can be even partially integrated. There will be a residue that must be neutralized or 'exorcized', put out of the way, before the final aspect of symbolic healing is activated.

The third basic aspect of symbolic healing is the theme of death and rebirth, breakdown and renewal. In the Navaho system of healing, it is found in the myths of the hero's journey, and experienced by the patient and the medicine man in the solemn recitation of the prayer litanies and all-night song sequences. In the Balinese culture, it is found in the easy relinquishment of consciousness, the slipping into trance permitting close contact with the gods and the ancestors. In the Amazon, it is found in the suppression of the ego by the visionary drugs, and the crossing of the boundary for direct experience of the unconscious. This symbolic theme is found whenever there is an initiatory experience, whenever a psychic threshold is reached and crossed. This is often shown in the underlying thematic structure of patients' dreams, fantasies, and visions. The symbolic mode of death is experienced, leading to a breakdown in the equilibrium of the ego. This tends to evoke an upsurge of archetypal material with the possibility of a resurgence of life in a new form.

These principles have served the main healing function for the entire human race for a period of time that can only be measured in millenia. They are archetypal forms and as such function outside the sphere of conscious intent, giving rise in every age to new intuitive adaptations to an everchanging cultural environment.

It is in service to this archetype and its modern expression that we as healers find our vocation. Our kinship goes back much farther than the development of dynamic psychotherapy, farther even than the earliest appearance of scientific medicine. It goes back to the shamans and the medicine men of the most ancient times. Our tools and techniques have greatly improved, but our archetypal foundation is the same.

# First Review of the Congress

Aldo Carotenuto (Rome)

We might begin by asking ourselves the question as to what it means to resume a congress of analytical psychologists for whom their personal and, above all, individual characteristic remains the one feature that cannot be disregarded. Any congress certainly presupposes an original subject matter. Furthermore, it implies thinking about the meaning of one's own work, and, in our case, the reason why we deal with the psyche as we experience it each day through our own consciousness and through the suffering of our patients. Yet there is a difficulty which – I must stress – is not found in other congresses where the aim is a deepening of things which are already being dealt with at work. In our case, on the other hand, we have not merely to discover deeper truths, but we are compelled, in one way or another, to pay tribute to a man who preceded us in our field of research. Now, if we acknowledge that this man enjoyed a degree of foresight defying time, we are led to draw the conclusion that our congresses amount to nothing more than an attempt at furthering his line of thought in order to try and grasp a realm of meaning which escapes us due to our position in the present. But I do not believe that we should give up thinking about new things, new experiences, new ways of doing our work. I should also like to add that Jung, too, just like any original thinker, did not want imitators, but rather people who are able to cope with the new problems with which life constantly presents us.

Indeed, the topic of the Jerusalem Congress – at least this is the intention of its organisers – has deliberately brought together various analysts who have felt the influence of the Jungian school of thought. The subject of discussion reminds me strangely of one that, in one way or another, was always present in Nietzsche's intellectual development, namely the conflict between Apollo and Dionysus. For the purposes of our discussion, Apollo may be considered as the 'clinician' with a preference for form and expressive clarity, while Dionysus, thanks to his continual changes and transformations, cannot but allude to the 'symbolic'. Thus our subject covers the symbolic and the clinical. Should we be discussing synthesis or rather contrast? I think that we can answer this question only if the problem is made extremely clear. I believe that the symbolic preceded the real in the history of mankind. Indeed, the real presupposes a knowledge that we probably only began to acquire at the beginning of the time of Galileo. We are indebted to Galileo for the well-known statement that, if we wish to get to know nature, we must ask the right questions. But what exactly was nature prior to Galileo? It tended to express man's desires, it was full of his projections, it consisted, as it were, of man's own psyche that moulded matter according to his fears and hopes. When knowledge based on facts, and not on desire, came into being, it radically changed the dimension of human life, above all concerning the expectations that such knowledge gave each one of us: a transition from a mysterious and totally allusive world to one that is steadily being brought under our control. This need, quite rightly, is a perfectly legitimate one, but there are parts of our lives with which we remain dissatisfied. Let us concentrate on this statement by Jung:

> The more the critical reason dominates, the more impoverished life becomes; but the more of the unconscious and the more of the myth we are capable of making conscious, the more of life we integrate. Overvalued reason has this in common with political absolutism: under its dominion the individual is pauperized.[1]

What did Jung mean by these words? Something very simple. He certainly did not mean a return to the shadows and the realm of the incomprehensible as such, but he was referring, above all, to the necessity for man, safe in his tower of reason, to continually attempt to grapple with what is new and incomprehensible in order to direct his footsteps towards the deeper truths of his life. This implies a continuous journey to a centre which, once reached, leads to other centres to be investigated. This is all considered from a new point of view, if we bear in mind another statement by Jung:

> In the final analysis the decisive factor is always consciousness, which can understand the manifestations of the unconscious and take up a position toward them.[2]

[1] Jaffé, A. (ed.), *Memories, Dreams, Reflections*, by C. G. Jung (New York: Vintage Books, 1961), p. 302.

[2] ibidem, p. 187.

These considerations bring us back once again to our subject. As early as 1981, Giuseppe Maffei wrote that the symbolic/clinical binominal underlines a real differentiation existing within the Jungian School. In fact, the explanation for the choice of subject was formulated as follows:

> This subject has been chosen since it is likely to underline the differences in attitudes that have neither been considered nor evaluated by the various Jungian societies, even if they all probably adopt the symbolic approach as well as the clinical one.[3]

I am not in complete agreement with the word, 'probably', because the use of the *clinical* and of the *symbolic* does not concern so much an awareness of what one should nor should not do, nor is it something that, in my opinion, is taught and learned, but its use is derived from a vision of the world that guides each individual therapist. In other words, the clinical and the symbolic are not linked to a knowledge, but to a structure of man. Let us try to understand why this is so. We need not waste time on the existence of psychological types, nor is it of any interest in this paper to dwell on the nature-nurture dilemma. However, it is still true that the important Platonic-Aristotelian dichotomy lies at the base of our psychic life. I could give innumerable examples to show this clear distinction among men. In recent years, physiologists of the brain have localised evocative language in the right hemisphere of the brain while placing rational processes in the left hemisphere. Now, I believe that the predominance of one typology over another not only leads to a preference of one psychological intervention over another which is judged less suitable, but, in the same area of reference, which might be that of Jungian psychology, a different typology shows diverse kinds of behaviour. Moreover, Maffei, while commenting on several researches from the last congress of analytic psychology, notes that they were either clinical or symbolic, in absolute contrast with the significant Jungian discovery indicating that clinical and symbolic are inseparable. In fact, Jung "went beyond this dichotomy and he united it (in a manner which is still not fully understood by those who do not know his works deeply) in order to formulate his fundamental concepts of personal equation and transcendent function… The problem is a serious one, including as it does the moral duty to promote the continuation of a procedure which all Jungians consider to be essential. This procedure differs from the points of view

[3] Maffei Giuseppe, "Nota Editoriale", *Rivista di Psicologia Analitica*, n. 24/82, p. 3.

that are popular today and it is difficult to keep alive, but we must, nonetheless, feel a great responsibility to do so".[4]

In my opinion, our colleague Louis Zinkin has dealt with the theme of the clinical and symbolic along these lines. I agree with his contention that no pyschologist can totally abandon the medical model, especially if we reach an agreement as to the meaning of this term. The medical model has its origins in the experimental one deriving from Galileo's thought, and whether we like it or not, we are all compelled to adopt it. Zinkin quite correctly points out that it is difficult to choose between a clinical and symbolic approach insofar as they are indissoluble. Maybe the real problem does not lie in their being inseparable, but in the importance that each of us, according to his own psychological type, attributes to one of the two. However, things get far more complicated, in my mind, when the problem of a model is coupled with the one of a science. I have honestly to admit that, in effect, one never manages to tackle the problem sufficiently well because a science is always brought into question rather than *a scientific method.* Logically speaking, a scientific method is really all that exists. Moreover, this method is more or less the one invented by Galileo. Science, in abstract, does not exist, but rather a series of facts linked together by a number of connecters. To these disciplines, we can give the names of physics, chemistry, astrology, botany and literature; it is a scientific method, however, that gives them the dignity of a science. Today, scientists the world over are only in agreement concerning a method; they all speak the same language, into which it is necessary to translate all the other languages that are represented by each individual discipline. It has been noted that several disciplines can be translated very well; or, leaving aside the metaphor, it might be said that the scientific method is highly suitable for certain disciplines. In other words, by using a scientific method, one can control the theories joining together several propositions of a discipline. I think that it is easy to understand why a discipline, about which it is difficult or even impossible to adopt a scientific method, is not necessarily false. It might not be formulated in such a way as to lend itself to be studied by the method, but nonetheless its conclusions might be perfectly exact. Yet, in this case, as Zinkin quite rightly points out, a model might, or might not, be useful or, in our specific case, the symbolic model and the clinical one could in the future form the basis of a theory or of a praxis linked together consequentially.

[4] Maffei Giuseppe, "Nota Editoriale", *Rivista di Psicologia Analitica,* n. 24/82, p. 2.

Moreover, it should not be forgotten that an exclusively clinical approach can only lead to reductionism which, even if useful with respect to the natural sciences, has been shown to be somewhat worthless in the field of those sciences dealing with man and his significance. Yet, it should be remembered that most psychology and contemporary clinical psychiatry tends to lean towards the clinical: one attempts to study the facts as they are, to deduce concepts of normality and deviance as well as establishing a therapeutic praxis aimed at well-being. So one overlooks in this way the positive worth of conflicts and suffering. It follows that psychology and psychiatry finish up by being the slaves of adaptation and ideology. However, they do have a positive side in so far as they are open to what is real and new. The clinician must also deal with new elements, according to his own ideology, and not react by refusing them since they are in conflict with his own conception of the world. He should treat the new as something to be understood and which could in the end modify his own conception. Maybe we never pay due attention to the school of clinical medical diagnosis where any diagnostical preconception always runs the risk of being belied by reality. With such an approach one continually has to pay heed to anything new that might appear in the course of a clinical case. Even if Freud was deeply influenced by clinical elements, he was not afraid to modify his own theoretical conception, on several occasions, according to clinical needs.[5]

Of course, not only the symbolic tends to attribute meaning to the symptom and to create, as it were, a new truth concerning the meaning of suffering, but the clinical also adds its own significance, even if this is connected, at least apparently, with the past. Moreover, it is for this reason that our colleague Mario Trevi suggests a psychodynamic terminology to:

> contrast the Freudian symbol with the Jungian one insomuch as the first might be defined as a *sinizetic* symbol (from *synizanein*, meaning to return to a previous state) and the second, on the other hand, might be called *metapoietic* (from *metapoiein*, to transform).
> In reality Jung never denied either the existence or the enormous heuristic value of the *sinizetic* symbol; according to him, the "sign" (or symptom) largely derives from an individual's imaginative life, both in his dreams and his day-dreaming, even if the psychologist's task should be above all to

5) Zinkin, Louis, see his contribution to this volume, pp. 99ff.

grasp, from the inevitable myriad of signs, the true symbol, in other words, the authentic driving force behind the individual's psychic life.[6]

But, as Trevi correctly continues, Jung only stressed the distinction and does not appear to have attempted a search for a dialectical link between symptom and symbol.

Now, I believe that the present congress has posed itself this very task. What is the real relationship between the symbolic and clinical? Few researchers have attempted to deal with this problem. To a certain extent, Kenneth Newman tries to answer the question in his stimulating essay about plastic, defined as a man-made substance which is in contrast with those elements found in nature. After proposing a typology of psychotherapies that are distinguishable according to their movement upwards, downwards, to the left or to the right, the author puts forward the hypothesis that the clinical approach and the symbolic one are part of the downward category, since both of them have a meaning that was drawn from the internal and external world. In fact, even if they are different with respect to their content and interpretative style, both methods derive from a 'plastic imagination', at the service of the true spirit animating our psychology. Moreover, it is in this way that a dialectical link can be discovered between the clinical and the symbolic insomuch as energy generated by the clinical allows the symbolic to unravel itself. In this respect, I believe that the contributions by Wilke and Zielen, thanks to their description of several cases, underline once more how important it is to integrate the clinical and the symbolic approaches. It is obvious, however, that a symbolic approach is indispensable when faced with deep psychic troubles. We are indebted to Jung, moreover, as he was the first to treat psychoses using psychodynamic procedures. His experience in this field made him understand how "certain complexes (…) belonging to a patient prove destructive because he is not able to assimilate or integrate them."[7]

By showing to such patients, as Jung did, the universal nature of their archetypal representations so that they might integrate them, means in other words, formulating one of the most essential elements in the psychotherapy of schizophrenia, namely the message that anything disguised by a symbol, and which in this disguise grows destructive, can

6 Trevi Mario, "Il simbolo trasformatore", in Moreno, Mario, ed., *La dimensione simbolica,* Marsilio Editore, Padova 1973, p. 13.

7 Benedetti, G., "Jung e la schizofrenia", in: *Rivista di Psicologia Analitica,* N. 2, 1973, p. 411.

on the other hand, if correctly understood and represented, constitute the major component in an individual's constructive development."[8]

It is known, moreover, that, during the period between 1912 and 1916, Jung willingly set out to explore the images in the world of the unconscious. This experience might not be fully understood if one fails to read the account given by Jung himself, in which he points to an enormous difference between an anticipated psychosis and a real one. An anticipated psychosis always takes place under the influence of the ego, and even if the degree of involvement might make it appear like a real psychosis, the individual in this case is able to integrate the imaginary material, whilst the sick person remains a victim, who, once sucked in again, remains unable to accomplish any sort of integrative process. And this is why Gullotta very rightly discusses the difficulty that the therapist finds in the relationship with his schizophrenic patient. In fact, in order to achieve positive results with patients, the therapist must be able – or one might even say he should have the courage – to carry out a desymbolising activity during which he detaches himself from the consciousness of the ego so as to draw nearer to his patient on a deeper level, where there is only a universe of primordial symbols. Later on, it is necessary to reorganise the symbols. In other words, it is a matter of a process activated in the psyche of the schizophrenic by the therapist's presence, thereby allowing the patient's ego to adopt the ordinary symbolic function.

But now let us return to several initial suggestions. The subject of originality and the clinical/symbolic dichotomy. A friend pointed out to me that, in the Olympic Games long ago, the athletes' victories were always outright and indisputable. In more recent times, given the steadily more sophisticated techniques, Olympic medalists have had to make do with split-second victories. We are in a similarly unhappy plight; it is becoming very difficult to succeed in saying something new unless one invades investigative fields for which a new interpretive model would be necessary. At this point, the very serious problem concerning orthodoxy and creativity arises. Sometimes I wonder if it is not actually the case of a pseudo-problem. For a theory to be valid, it must be capable of stimulating continual development, and in general, any attempts to crystallize it are condemned to failure. The psychological constructions which seek to provide a complete vision of human motivations do not escape the risk of being turned into visions of the world.

[8] ibid.

This situation hides the danger of the orthodoxy which Jung struggled against for so long, giving him his reputation as a rebel. I think that the crux of the matter is the following: we must fight the temptation of becoming guardians of something which does indeed need absolute freedom. Thought does not need bounds since it stretches over the universe itself. In this dimension, there is room for any amount of originality, even if insignificant, that might be grafted upon the territory which others have made ready for us. With respect to the topic of the congress, it seems to me to refer to two ways of psychological intervention. Yet, as I listened to the papers, I had the impression that many speakers did not tackle the problem (this is a very strange matter that should give us food for thought). Others have agreed upon the necessity of not dividing the two approaches and so I asked myself: Why choose a subject that is not controversial? Where there are no differences of opinion, we should at least try to create some. But with this question, I think I have come round full circle to the initial problem mentioned at the outset. I do not believe it is a matter of methodological choice, but rather of a typological attitude, implying a rather different view of the problem. Some of us know how to cope with the clinical approach, while others feel more at ease with symbolic language. An integration of the two is certainly necessary, but the recognition of one's own prevailing attitude during therapy is a *sine qua non* condition.

# Second Review of the Congress

Luigi Zoja (Milan)

I have been asked to formulate my comments, conclusions and hopes in connection with the Jerusalem Congress: I shall express my feelings about the congress as a whole, but for practical reasons, I shall basically be commenting on the nine major morning papers.

Our theme was: *The differing uses of symbolic and clinical approaches in practice and theory.*

We can interpret this in two different ways: one can understand it in a wider sense and stress *uses of symbolic and clinical approaches in practice and theory.*

We would, in this case, have a large theme, encompassing most of our various interests.

Or one can stress *differing uses* – which I understand to be stronger than *different,* in that it implies a contraposition.

By interpreting it in this narrower sense, we shall have a much more specific theme, focusing on a controversial issue.

We may assume that the latter corresponds to a provocative intention of the Organizing Committee. Incidentally, one could observe that such intention survives in the German title (*unterschiedliche* as opposed to *verschiedene*), becomes less noticeable in the French (*différents* as opposed to *divers*) and totally disappears in the Italian *(diversi),* thereby following, not by chance, the range of importance of our four languages.

This is not at all meant to be a criticism of the Organizing Committee, which has been more than fair towards the Italian group. It is simply the ascertainment that the possibility of understanding major languages is important but insufficient. In order to take part in the debate – actively and without hesitation – one should think directly in English.

Of the nine morning papers, only three are focused on the contraposition between symbolic and clinical: those of Dr. Wilke, Dr. Ziegler and Dr. Zinkin. This proportion reappears in other parts of the agenda.

Even considering the possibility that some speakers might have been misled by the somehow different – better: differing – titles according to language, the proportion remains low. The majority understood the theme in its wider meaning: thereby the majority implicitly showed what they preferred.

We could ask ourselves whether it is psychologically sensible to foster controversy and polemics among people who, realistically, consider a congress also as a vacation and are, therefore, not quite in a fighting mood. And we could ask ourselves whether it makes sense to chose a rather specific theme, implying common debate, for people who happen to consider individuation a basic guideline.

Last, but not least, I felt that, unlike the previous congresses, this one has also a *latent* theme, connected with Jerusalem and Jewishness. This latent theme constellated stronger affect than the official one, as shown for example in a non-official meeting Saturday night. Returning to the morning papers, I shall now apologize to the above mentioned majority of speakers and comment briefly on the responses to our provocative title.

"If we really had this choice, which of us would not choose the symbolic?", asks Dr. Zinkin.

His comment synthesizes much of the debate and is so clear, straight and, simply, pertinent.

In fact, on a purely conceptual level, these two terms strike us as being already imbued with value judgements and, therefore, leaving us no choice.

Many etymological dictionaries, in deriving the term *clinical*, confine themselves to *κλινη (klíne)*, the bed in Greek. Yet both klíne and *κλινικη (kliniké*, medical art) derive in their turn from the verb *κλινω (klino), to bend.** The implications of this term are not just to assist the patient in bed and not only to bend the sickness, but *to bend nature*: innumerable terms derived from *klino* indeed indicate the usage of instruments or techniques. Therefore, it could suggest an early Freudian attitude, its positivism and its ego-centered psychology. It is

* P. Chautraine: *Dictionnaire étymologique de la langue grecque*, Paris, Ed. Klincksieck, 1968, pp. 543–544.

not by chance that the Greek *klíno* is the translation of the Latin *flectere*, from which Freud chose the motto: *Flectere si negueo Superos, Acheronta movebo** (If I cannot bend the Gods above, I'll devote myself to those under the earth).

For the Jungian-trained analyst, it is, on the contrary, quite normal to associate positive implications with the symbol. Jungian psychology does not aim at the absolute prevailing of the ego, but at the Self: 'symbol' (from *σγνβαλλω syn-ballo*, to throw together) of the totality of conscious and unconscious. Again not by chance, the etymological opposite of *syn-ballo* is *dia-ballo*, hence *diabolus*, the devil, the archetypal negative polarity.

There is no free choice between symbolic and clinical because they are from the beginning endowed with definite value (at least for the Jungian analyst). The real alternative is: are we obliged to contemplate the symbolic approach as corresponding to the structure of our work and the clinical to an overstructure, maybe fortuitous? Or can and must they complement each other?

Dr. Ziegler speaks of an *Unvereinbarkeit*, the impossibility of reconciling "unit of the disease and image of ailing". He does so both for qualitative reasons – their structural difference – and quantitative ones – the massive repression exerted by official medicine on our imaginative faculties.

Dr. Zinkin, points to a possible 'supramodel' in which the two terms could be reconciled. A complementarity is proposed also by Dr. Wilke, in that symbolic is seen as rather psychological and clinical as rather concrete.

Should we conclude, with the majority, that clinical and symbolic have the same right to citizenship in analytical psychology?

In daily practice, yes – and, not by chance, both papers supporting this point of view make many references to practice. But this congress also seems to aim at theoretical questions involving the identity of our discipline. In this sense, the answer is not easy, partly because Jungian psychology has a rather loose theoretical framework and tends to answer more through images, symbols and analogous stimulations than in a typically Aristotelian logical manner.

Along with this tradition, one could question the syncretic suggestion of Drs. Wilke and Zinkin. One could ask whether their pro-

* Virgil, *Aeneid*, VII, 312.

posed synthesis of the two approaches, or models, isn't also an attempt to *sym-bolize* the analytic attitude as a whole. *Syn*cretic, *sym*bolic, etc., are, not by chance, analogous. Besides, the concept of 'supramodel', where 'the opposites can be reconciled' is based on a corresponding 'symbolic model'.

One could say to Dr. Zinkin: Your defense of the medical model is convincing, even necessary in order to break a latent conformity. Yet, you suggest that the analysts "should be able to switch models".

Some of us could comment that you are then following the individuation-model, which would then include the medical model, but not vice-versa.

And others might remark that the term 'medical' is here misleading: are you proceeding along the methodological lines of a truly medical perspective and within the framework of the natural sciences *(Naturwissenschaft)?* Or do you see 'medical' as the manifestation of some sort of depth psychological structure? In this case, if the medical model is an unconscious pattern leaving a psychological imprint, it then corresponds to an archetypal idea; and the related ideas, such as medical doctor, treatment, etc., would be *metaphors*. Again, the medical would be included in the symbolic, but not vice versa. I think these distinctions are difficult to trace and may become too theoretical: but they are not irrelevant.

Turning to Dr. Wilke, one could feel misled by a lack of univocal key terms or definitions – let alone translations – which harass analytical psychology.

While one could observe that a symbolic experience is often even more concrete than a clinical one, and an image more real than a person in the flesh, another might object to his attributing to the symbolic *Sinn* (wider meaning), *Be-deutung* (narrow meaning), *Finalität* (finality).

*Sinn* and *Finalität* do belong to the symbol; yet *Bedeutung* refers to the sign, therefore to the symptom, therefore to the clinical. Or at least to the Freudian approach, whose declared intention is precisely *Deutung*, interpretation.

The other attribute of the symbol mentioned by Dr. Wilke is the existence of something hidden *(Verborgenes)*. It seems a good point in order to sum up a specific impression of the congress.

We Jungians do not primarily look, with detective flair, for hidden objects. In our congresses and works we care more about the *syn*thesis – if not always about *sym*bols – than about analysis. And more about hermeneutics than about interpretations, etc. Our psychology has not refined 'suspicion' as its main instrument. It has not followed the 'negative path' of Freud, a criticism anticipated by Jaspers,* expanded upon by Paul Ricoeur** and recently entrusted to the mass media by speeches of Pope Wojtyla.

We – on the contrary – are – or appear to be – more constructive. In our work the sense – reached or touched upon – prevails over the unmasked falseness.

I wonder whether a conclusion of the congress could be to ask ourselves if the denomination *analytical* psychology still sounds the best to us. And we could suggest this as a possible theme for a future congress.

For the time being, let me close in another way. Let me imagine that I have been asked to analyze the congress proceedings as if they were a whole patient. I would feel that he is not a bad patient and, without giving him a specific diagnosis or suggestion, encourage him, by means of a warm, accepting attitude, to be himself with less hesitations.

Indeed, seeing him suffering in his ambivalence between clinical and symbolic, I would feel that a complex is constellated in him. Of course, neither can I, by definition, identify a complex clearly, nor can I tell the patient about it too directly.

But, among us, I think we could agree that a major component of this complex has to do with being *scientific* – The contrast between symbolic and clinical is indeed relative. It is not difficult to imagine Dr. Ziegler using images of ailment for the sake of traditional healing. Nor it is difficult to imagine Dr. Zinkin locating his medical model in a context of metaphors and symbolic operations.

It is, on the contrary, very difficult to speak of 'clinical' without evoking at least some unconscious associations with the natural sciences and their values. This is, I believe, another aspect of their *superbia*, as pointed out by Dr. Ziegler. Because of this, the riddle proposed by the congress theme is unsolvable. It is analogous to the basic rules we were taught at school, according to which certain operations require homogeneous categories.

In this sense, confronting clinical and symbolic is impossible, like confronting time with animals or subtracting cows from eggs.

* K. Jaspers: *Allgemeine Psychopathologie*, Berlin, Springer 1959, 2nd part, end of first chapter (It. ed. Roma, Pensiero Scientifico, 1965, pp. 388ff.).

** P. Ricoeur: *De l'interprétation. Essai sur Freud*, Paris, Seuil, 1965, first book, 2nd chapt. (It. ed. Milano, Saggiatore, 1966, pp. 46ff.).

Of course, the whole operation would be a lot casier if we were to declare that we use expressions like 'clinical' in a sense which is extraneous to natural science and refers, on the contrary, to some archetypal or depth psychological reality.

But this is precisely what we tend not to do: in spite of Jung's paradoxical forecast that psychology will have to "cancel itself out as a science" in order to "reach its scientific goal".* Being on the common ground between science and a self-contained therapeutic discipline, we often use some concepts in a way contradictory both to our colleagues and to our own use of these concepts.

The arrogance, the *superbia*, of Western natural science is so great that it has narrowed down the meaning of the whole faculty of knowing about things (*scire*; compare also the German *wissen*) to its very specific way of knowing (science; *Wissenschaft*): a way of knowing which neglects the existential sense, the depth psychological sense, the moral sense.

We know that our healing is usually more an ethical or cultural restoration than a scientific operation, yet we usually avoid insisting on the latter: as if a lack of science might prove to be a lack of knowledge altogether.

In many of us, this fear must touch some Cinderella syndrome. Some fear that if we lose our vague link with science – from which our studies emanate through Freud's early interest in natural science – we will forever be orphans.

In this sense, we act 'as if'. As if we were still expecting some missing link with science. As if depth psychology had no ultimate ground of its own, as if it were doomed to depend upon an external justification.

Let me try to use an image for this. Most of our banknotes specify, in different languages, that a Central Bank promises to pay X amount to the bearer of the note. The latter is only a piece of paper, but you can act 'as if' it had a certain value. Theoretically, the Central Banks should dispose of a corresponding amount of gold; in practice, they only keep reliable foreign currency, namely dollars. These, in their turn, were the only ones exchangeable for gold.

One day, a signature (of President Nixon, if I am not mistaken) suppressed this possibility. The promises of the Central Banks were no longer exchangeable with anything concrete, but only with other promises.

* C. G. Jung, CW VIII, § 429.

Theoretically, the world economy could have collapsed; but it carried on. The ultimate value of money – even of gold – corresponds to our trust, to what we project into it. Endowed with such trust, banknotes had become more a symbol than a sign.

Now, of course, I am not seriously suggesting that a discipline like ours should intentionally deny every link with science in order to verify if it can survive in such an orphan state.

But for future congresses one could envisage such themes as: 'Is analytical psychology a science?', or 'How does it contribute to other sciences, if it is not one of them?'

Yet, these themes might seem too abstract or too radical to many of us. In fact, they sound so even to me: and, once again, you are not bound to take my proposition seriously.

# We are such Stuff that Dreams are made of

Adolf Guggenbühl-Craig (Zürich)

My term as President of the I.A.A.P. has come to an end, as has my membership on the Executive Committee, of which I have been a member for more than twenty years. The political activity has made me as aware of the different layers of my soul as any personal analysis did. It was very pleasant to meet so many people, people I like, and what matters even more, people I dislike. I reflected upon my experiences within the I.A.A.P. as I did upon my dreams: every figure, likeable or unlikeable, I considered a part of myself.

I approached the politics of the I.A.A.P. not only from a 'clinical', but also from a symbolic point of view.

In the following, I will consider one or two matters which came up during my term as president and which will certainly appear again. I look at them within the framework of the theme of this congress.

Licensing is such an issue. Many States in this world allow psychotherapists and analysts to practise only under certain conditions, with specified degrees, with a training which is precisely prescribed. The idea of what an analyst or psychotherapist should be, what kind of training he should undergo, varies from state to state and differs from what we imagine. We, as Jungians, are, for instance, convinced that personal analysis is the basis of every good training. We are convinced that it is in the personal analysis that we meet the psyche and learn to understand it. But this idea is not shared by many legislators. There are even some who say that to demand personal analysis is to be against freedom of religion. It makes a 'religious belief', a *Weltanschauung*, a condition of practising.

Other legislators demand a clinical training which is longer and more intensive than what we require.

It is unlikely that the ideas of a state legislator would coincide with those of most Jungians, who are a minority even among psychotherapists and analysts.

The problem of licensing touches our emotions and it is strange to see how readily and uncomplainingly we obey the state and comply with its requirements. Some of us would even prefer that our membership be restricted to state-licensed psychotherapists and analysts only. We, the experts of the psyche, hand over the right to judge what is good and what is bad training to political bodies. We, who are Jungians firmly believing in our vision of the psyche, without a murmur join people who are not interested in this vision, and who have completely different ideas.

Why is this so? It cannot be only for economic reasons, nor out of greed, for people who are economically greedy do not become analysts in the first place; and it cannot be out of fear of the society and the state, because cowardly people do not become Jungians.

I do not think either that it is simply for practical reasons. Why could every group not have two types of Jungian members – both qualified by our standards, yet one state-licensed and the other not? Those belonging to the latter group could practise only in a very limited way, but by having them as members, we would show that we accept them.

How can this need to adapt be explained?

This issue cannot be approached only in a practical, rational or clinical way. It is a symbolic issue. Strange as it may seem, I think symbols of individuation are mixed up with it.

We Jungians look at the soul in a very particular way. It is not only that we have different methods – in the sense of, 'I use the Jungian method'; we understand psyche differently from most other schools. It could easily happen, therefore, that we become sectarian; that, in the eyes of the collective, we are regarded as freakish – freakishness being the other side of individuation. Not being licensed ourselves, or having colleagues who are not licensed, is the symbol of our isolation – or individuation. We symbolically demonise the licensing issue – because the freakish side of individuation has something frightening. We want to be respectable, taken seriously by our academic and medical colleagues.

"But you foster illegal practice" was often thrown at me when I tried to resist smooth adjustment to licensing laws, when it was a question of defending our attitude to training.

It is quite clear that the issue of licensing cannot be looked at only from a *clinical* point of view. It has to be understood *symbolically*: do we personally and professionaly lie partially outside the academic and medical collective? Not to be licensed, to have non-licensed colleagues, becomes a symbol of our freakishness.

Now, on the subject of *training*, it is interesting to note how afraid we are that some groups, particularly new groups, may not be training properly. I have even heard the startling suggestion that every group should be checked every ten years, in order to find out whether or not they are still training seriously.

The discussion on whether one should have 300, 350, 400, etc., hours of personal analysis can go on endlessly. We could make 'studies', compare results, etc., etc.

Yet I do not think the clinical approach can decide the issue. It has to be approached symbolically, too. Training is a ritual, an initiation rite; a ritual for the initiation of the psyche. It can never be taken too seriously. It is correct to talk endlessly of whether we should have 300, 350 or 400 hours of analysis. All of these discussions show symbolically that we take the soul seriously. Rituals have to be precise. The mass has to have a certain form, must be read correctly. The sacraments have to be right – the symbols – but you cannot clinically test whether the proper mass or the incorrect mass has a larger or smaller effect.

To be very concrete: maybe it would be as important to discuss the symbolic meaning of numbers *per se* when we discuss the minimum number of hours. Is the number 300 a more adequate symbol, for instance, than 400 for what we want to achieve?

The questions of whether one should acquire personal analysis through two persons, whether two male analysts or two female analysts would do, or whether the two analysts should be a man and a woman, etc. – all of these questions can lead to heated discussions too.

The requirement of being analysed by a man and a woman is a beautiful symbol; we should face the feminine *and* the masculine. But we know that every analyst can work with his/her masculine or feminine side, regardless of whether he/she is a man or a woman. *Clinically* the requirements of a masculine and feminine analyst are very dubious. As a *symbol*, these requirements are very important.

Another issue which can dominate our discussions is the phenomenon of the splitting of old societies and the appearance of new groups.

In every society, there are different groupings with entirely different ideas, fundamentally in opposition as to the way they understand

Jungian psychology. From a purely rational clinical point of view, one could say: "Why don't they just split up and form two societies?"

What about new societies? All over the world, new groups want to form; very often, nothing results from these well-meant attempts, but often new groups apply for membership in the International Society. Usually, however, these new groups are not welcomed with open arms. "Why do these newly-hatched chickens not stay with the mother hen a bit longer?", is a question often asked on such occasions. Or again: "They are not quite mature yet" – although their average age may be around forty-five.

We usually deal with the 'splitting' and the new society issue very conscientiously. We are interested in the theoretical differences of the splitting groups; we might even observe that power problems play a big role in the splits. We further examine the constitutions and the members of new societies with great care.

This is the clinical approach to the problem of new societies and of splitting. But I think the symbolic approach comes closer to understanding our reactions.

I sometimes wonder if the archetype of the chosen few, in the sense of 'many are called, but few are chosen', is at work here. The archetype of those who sit beside the Lord in Heaven, in the company of saints.

I remember well how, at one of our first congresses, spouses who were not analysts themselves were not supposed to attend the lectures, even when their husbands or wives were lecturing.

An archetype is neither good nor bad, but it is very powerful and dictates our behaviour.

The archetype of the chosen few is not recognized today, but it plays a big role in all our battles concerning new societies and the splitting up of groups nevertheless.

A clinical approach neglects the archetypal – symbolic – nature of these problems. The splitting is very painful for people dominated by the archetype of the chosen few. It is the story of Lucifer, of the fallen angel who becomes the devil, who was very close to God and is now His enemy. One of the select few falls. It is frightening to realize that even the select may harbour a few destined to fall into Hell.

Furthermore: The chosen few have to stay the chosen few. They must remain special, different from all others, and restricted in numbers.

That is why every newcomer is a potential threat. The boat is full. In the end, we may not be able to distinguish who is the elect, and who not.

The chosen saints symbolize the part of our psyche which is close to God, to the self.

I think we, as Jungian analysts, should have a slightly different approach to our internal and external political problems. We should approach these clinically, practically and rationally. But we should approach them symbolically, too. I think even a delegates meeting, for instance, should, on the one hand, be regarded as a democratic process for figuring out what we want and how we wish to shape our society and societies. But, on the other hand, it should be looked upon as a dream, where all the actors have symbolic significance, each representing a part of our psyche.

Conflicts become insolvable when we discuss them with clinical methods, not noticing that, in reality, symbols are at stake. Then we argue clinically and feel – so to speak – symbolically. We behave rather like a warrior in the Middle Ages who gives his life to save the banner of his king and argues that he must do so because the cloth of the banner is very expensive. Those against dying for the banner would ask, "Is it worth sacrificing a life for this piece of cloth when it costs only ten pounds?" The other party would reply, "No, the cloth is much more expensive, it costs twenty thousand pounds!", and the discussions would become heated and quite beside the point.

It would be fascinating if the Jungian societies would develop a political style all of their own, a unique style expressing the fact that many of our issues are about symbols and not about clinical 'realities'.

Sometimes one has a bad dream, one tries desperately to wake up, and is glad when one succeeds. I wish the reverse for the politics of the I.A.A.P.: That we suddenly discover it was and is a dream, and that we try to understand it as such.

**Meetings with Jung** is the first publication of personal diary entries made by British psychiatrist E. A. Bennet during his frequent visits in the household of Swiss analyst C. G. Jung during the last years of Jung's life, 1946–1961. The notes are at once deep, lively, serious and entertaining; an ideal introduction to Jung for the casual beginner, a warm and intimate addition to more scholarly works for advanced students of Jung.

ISBN 3-85630-501-7

## German Language Editions from Daimon Verlag:

**Träume** – Volume I of the selected writings of Marie-Louise von Franz – has now appeared in a hard-bound German-language edition of 230 pages. In addition to introductory chapters on the significance of dreams and some means of interpretation, it contains essays discussing the dreams of such historical figures as Socrates, Descartes and Hannibal, and the effects of these dreams on their lives.

ISBN 3-85630-023-6

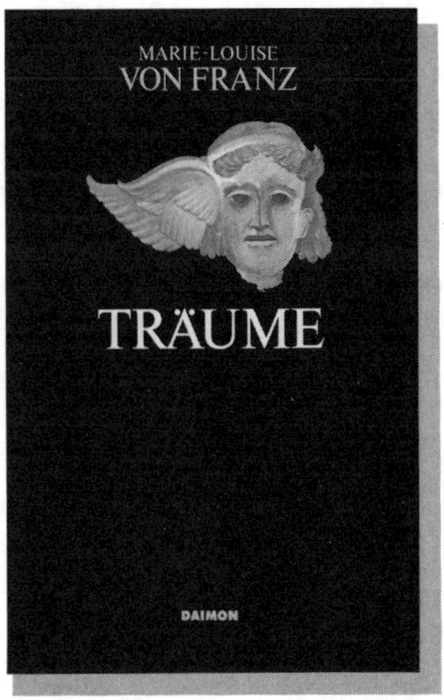